Dynamic Worlds

APPLIED LOGIC SERIES

VOLUME 12

Managing Editor

Dov M. Gabbay, *Department of Computer Science, King's College, London, U.K.*

Co-Editor

Jon Barwise, *Department of Philosophy, Indiana University, Bloomington, IN, U.S.A.*

Editorial Assistant

Jane Spurr, *Department of Computer Science, King's College, London, U.K.*

SCOPE OF THE SERIES
Logic is applied in an increasingly wide variety of disciplines, from the traditional subjects of philosophy and mathematics to the more recent disciplines of cognitive science, computer science, artificial intelligence, and linguistics, leading to new vigor in this ancient subject. Kluwer, through its Applied Logic Series, seeks to provide a home for outstanding books and research monographs in applied logic, and in doing so demonstrates the underlying unity and applicability of logic.

The titles published in this series are listed at the end of this volume.

Dynamic Worlds

From the Frame Problem to Knowledge Management

edited by

REMO PARESCHI
Xerox Research Centre Europe,
Meylan, France

and

BERTRAM FRONHÖFER
Technische Universität München
Germany

KLUWER ACADEMIC PUBLISHERS
DORDRECHT / BOSTON / LONDON

A C.I.P. Catalogue record for this book is available from the Library of Congress.

ISBN 978-90-481-5159-2

Published by Kluwer Academic Publishers,
P.O. Box 17, 3300 AA Dordrecht, The Netherlands.

Sold and distributed in North, Central and South America
by Kluwer Academic Publishers,
101 Philip Drive, Norwell, MA 02061, U.S.A.

In all other countries, sold and distributed
by Kluwer Academic Publishers,
P.O. Box 322, 3300 AH Dordrecht, The Netherlands.

Logo design by L. Rivlin

Printed on acid-free paper

EDITORIAL PREFACE

This volume deals with actions change and updates. This area is more than central in non-classical logic. Given the way applied logic is developing at the moment, it is likely that these subjects become dominant in the area. It is clear that in real applications, reasoning is intermingled with actions. Since reasoning is non-monotonic, additional information can knock down assumptions and invalidate conclusions. Additional data can therefore destroy the basis of preconditions of actions.

In modelling real reasoning/action situations we need to address a typical proof-action-proof-action cycle which goes as follows:

To prevent action b from happening, try and destroy its preconditions. To achieve that, try and (non-monotonically) derive the preconditions of action a and its post conditions will revise the (non-monotonic) database and from the revised version the preconditions of b are no longer derivable. Thus non-monotonic proof theory, actions, time and revision all get mingled together!

We welcome this volume to our series.

D. M. Gabbay

CONTENTS

CONTENTS

PREFACE

Reasoning or drawing conclusions is an integral part of many software systems in important fields like data bases, logic programming, robotics, knowledge engineering, human/computer interfaces, programming environments, etc. In reality any such system has to cope with a changing world and its dynamics. Hence it is of high importance that reasoning must account for coping with change in order to be truly useful in practice. The book comprises several contributions to current ways of approaching this problem.

In the paper by *Narciso Martí-Oliet* and *José Meseguer* rewriting logic is proposed as a logic of concurrent action and change that solves the frame problem and that subsumes and unifies a number of previous logics of change, including linear logic and Horn logic with equality. Rewriting logic can represent action and change with great flexibility and generality. This flexibility is illustrated by many examples, including examples that show how concurrent object-oriented systems are naturally represented. In addition, rewriting logic has a simple formalism, with only a few rules of deduction: It supports user-definable logical connectives, which can be chosen to fit the problem at hand, it is intrinsically concurrent and it is realizable in a wide spectrum logical language (Maude and its MaudeLog extension) supporting executable specification and programming.

The paper by *Michael Wollowski* and *Eric Hammer* presents a diagrammatic representational system that is designed to deal with the inferential complexities of a particular dynamic world, that of planning in a blocks world. It gives a rigorous syntax for the diagrams and a situation theoretic semantics modelling the domain in question. It also presents a sound and complete set of rules of inference for proving whether or not there is a plan that leads to some desired final state, given some initial state and various constraints about the world and possible transformations. The diagrams incorporate some of the constraints holding in the domain, thereby alleviating inferential complexity. By making some modifications to the system, one may even further speedup inferential tasks. Finally, some theoretical problems surrounding the use and application of formal systems of diagrams in artificial intelligence are discussed and these problems are compared to those of language oriented systems.

In the paper by *Chitta Baral*, *Michael Gelfond* and *Richard Watson* an extension $\mathcal{L}_2$ of the action description language $\mathcal{L}_1$ is proposed. It allows to express both actual and hypothetical situations, concurrent execution of actions, observations of the truth values of fluents in these situations (as opposed to hypothetical values of fluents expressible in the earlier languages $\mathcal{A}$

and $\mathcal{A}_C$), observations of actual occurrences of (possibly non-deterministic combination of) actions. The corresponding entailment relation formalizes various types of common-sense reasoning about actions and their effects not modeled by the previous approaches. Finally a translation of domain descriptions in $\mathcal{L}_2$ to disjunctive logic programs is given.

The paper by *Dov M. Gabbay* proposes a refined approach to belief revision which is called Compromise Revision. Suppose we want to add a consistent well-formed formula C to a consistent database $\mathbb{K}$ and suppose it cannot be accepted because $\mathbb{K} \cup \{C\}$ is not consistent. In this case it is proposed that we do not necessarily either reject C or revise $\mathbb{K}$, but to 'compromise' instead, whereby some of the consequences of C are put into $\mathbb{K}$ (though not C itself) and thus a consistent 'compromise theory' $\mathbb{K} + C$ is obtained. In addition, a compromise revision framework for arbitrary logics (not necessarily classical logic) and for Labelled Deductive Systems is discussed.

The paper by *Fátima C. C. Dargam* presents a specific compromise-based model to knowledge base revision. A model for reconciling logically conflicting inputs into knowledge bases is proposed, by choosing some of their consequences. The database is updated with as many consistent consequences of the inputs as possible, while rejecting the inputs. Should a revision apply, as many as possible of the consistent consequences of the retracted sentences are kept as a compromise. Non-relevant consequences, such as unwanted disjunctions involving all the sentences of the language, are avoided. This approach provides an application-specific mechanism for knowledge base revision. It caters for those applications where compromise solutions make practical sense.

The paper by *Jinxin Lin* and *Alberto O. Mendelzon* deals with resolving conflicts among a group of agents. A common practice is to let the majority decide. This principle is formalized and appled to the problem of merging the knowledge of multiple agents. Logical properties that all knowledge merging operators should satisfy are postulated and a model-theoretic characterization of all merging operators that satisfy the postulates is given. It turns out that the operators that satisfy the postulates are precisely those that induce a certain kind of partial pre-order over the set of possible worlds such that the models of the merged knowledge base are the possible worlds that are 'minimal' with respect to the pre-order. Several previous approaches are reviewed and analysed in light of the proposed postulates. Next a particular method for knowledge merging, *CMerge*, is presented which satisfies all the postulates. It is shown by example that *CMerge* appears to resolve conflicts among knowledge bases in a plausible way. Finally, it is shown that *CMerge* can be implemented by an efficient syntactical transformation from the set of knowledge bases to be merged.

The paper by *Elisa Bertino*, *Giovanna Guerrini* and *Luca Rusca* deal with evolution in object-oriented databases. In this area two different forms of evolution can be distinguished, evolution of schema and evolution of instances. The paper focuses on the latter in the context of the Chimera object-oriented deductive data model. In particular, problems related to object migration, dynamic object classification and multiple class direct membership are discussed.

The paper by *Ulrich Reimer, Andreas Margelisch* and *Bernd Novotny* presents EULE2, a knowledge-based decision support system for office tasks. After motivating the need for such a system, the paper sketches its functionality and discusses the three main knowledge sources it makes use of: terminological knowledge, knowledge about actions, and knowledge about federal law and company regulations. The terminological knowledge provides all the concepts relevant in the domain of discourse, and allows to introduce instances of those concepts. Knowledge about actions serves two purposes: to determine what changes have to be made when executing an action, and to decide what actions can or cannot be performed at a certain point in an office task. A representation formalism that satisfies both, quite heterogeneous requirements is described in detail. Knowledge about federal law and company regulations is needed to ensure that all office tasks are properly executed — this is the main functionality offered by EULE2. Subsequently, the paper deals with how to properly integrate knowledge about law and regulations with the knowledge about actions. For this purpose a hybrid integration approach is proposed that keeps the representation of both kinds of knowledge independent from each other but ensures that the reasoning takes all relevant pieces of knowledge into account. It is argued that the resulting, hybrid integration approach drastically increases maintainability and reusability of knowledge bases as compared to former approaches.

Remo Pareschi

Bertram Fronhöfer

NARCISO MARTÍ-OLIET AND JOSÉ MESEGUER

ACTION AND CHANGE IN REWRITING LOGIC

1 INTRODUCTION

After making precise what we mean and do not mean by "the frame problem" and discussing some recent approaches, we summarize the main features of the solution offered by rewriting logic.

1.1 What the frame problem (in our sense) is

Since the frame problem has been the subject of much controversy and unfortunately means different things to different people, any paper touching upon the subject runs the risk of unintentionally increasing confusion. The best way out of this danger is to state in plain English right at the beginning what we mean by "the frame problem." In this way, any objection to our arguments that is based on a different meaning of the words can then be dismissed as a failure to understand the terms of the discussion.

In our sense, the frame problem [41, 27, 30] consists in formalizing the assumption that facts about a situation are preserved by an action unless the action explicitly says that a certain fact becomes true or false. In the words of Patrick Hayes [27, p. 125],

> "There should be some economical and principled way of succintly saying what changes an action makes, without having to explicitly list all the things it doesn't change as well [...]. *That is the frame problem.*"

In our view, the heart of the frame problem is the essential inadequacy of standard logics for dealing with action and change. The term "standard" is used here in a fairly wide sense that includes not only first-order logic, but also higher-order logics and constructive type theories with the exception of linear logic [19]. The reasons for this inadequacy are fundamental, and have to do with the essentially Platonic nature of standard logics. Because those logics were developed as tools in the foundations of mathematics and were therefore designed to reason about unchanging entities such as numbers or geometric figures, it should come as no surprise that they deal very poorly with action and change.

1.2 What the frame problem (in our sense) is not

In some very wide sense of the term "frame problem," by insisting on a perfectly accurate modelling or simulation of systems in the real world, the

1

R. Pareschi and B. Fronhöfer (eds.), Dynamic Worlds, 1–53.

frame problem may be insoluble in the sense that any formalism whatsoever
will always simplify and abstract reality. But of course at that level we are
all more or less in the same boat. In this respect, Patrick Hayes says in [27,
p. 131]

> "Several papers use the term "frame problem" to refer to sev-
> eral different, usually more vaguely defined, problems. In sev-
> eral cases this seems to be something like the problem of getting
> a machine to reason sensibly about the world, what might be
> called the Generalised AI Problem, or GAIP. Sometimes it seems
> to be something like the general representation problem, some-
> times the general control, or theorem-proving, problem. Now,
> the trouble with all these discussions is that none of these "prob-
> lems" is really a problem in a technical sense. There will never
> be a solution to any of these "problems" because they aren't
> well-defined enough to have a solution. They are in the same cat-
> egory as the general bridge-lengthening problem (which is how
> to build longer bridges) or the problem of making better plas-
> tics or the problem of improving international relations. These
> aren't problems—they are areas of study. Of course we won't
> suddenly discover the answer to the GAIP, and to criticize the
> field because it hasn't solved it is simply to misunderstand the
> nature of research."

In the AI literature, the frame problem usually appears associated with
other problems, like the prediction problem ("Sometimes a prediction does
not come true; a certain sequence of operations has been calculated to solve
a certain problem, but when the plan is executed it somehow fails to accomplish its goal." [30, p. 9]) or the qualification problem ("A complete
representation of all conditions that must be satisfied to guarantee a successful performance of an action puts an unreasonable, maybe unlimited,
amount of qualifications on the laws defining the action." [30, p. 13]), mainly
because all of them have been approached by means of nonmonotonic logic
[42, 43]. From our point of view, some of these problems are due to the
idealization and simplification inherent in the modelling of the real world,
and we do not try to solve them in any way.

In particular, the kinds of changes that we will model in rewriting logic
will be discrete changes that happen in atomic steps, but that can happen
concurrently. This of course seems reasonable for systems modelled or simulated by digital computers and—given the close connections between logical
systems and models of digital computation—is also the level of abstraction
that one would expect to be at using a logical formalization. Real time
issues can in fact be handled quite effectively by such systems, but only in
a digitized, discrete, approximation to continuous time.

1.3 The current state of the frame problem

In fact, the frame problem has remained remarkably resilient to attacks using standard logics, which have proved unsuccessful at solving it. In a recent survey of logic in artificial intelligence [56, p. 50], Nilsson states:

> "Although the frame problem has been extensively studied, it remains a formidable conceptual obstacle to the development of systems that must act in a changing world. This obstacle is faced by all such systems—even those whose knowledge about the world is represented in procedures. The designer of any intelligent machine must make assumptions (at least implicit ones) about how the world changes in response to the actions of the machine if the machine is to function effectively."

Moreover, in a very telling passage of his "second naive physics manifesto," Patrick Hayes [26, p. 479] makes explicit the futility of trying to deal with *concurrent* action and change using standard approaches:

> "The now classical approach to describing time and change, invented first by J. McCarthy (1957), uses the idea of a state or situation (or: world-state, time instant, temporally possible world,...). This is a snapshot of the whole universe at a given moment. Actions and events are then functions from state to state. This framework [... is very widely used...] but a slightly broader view condemns it.

> Consider the following example (which Rod Burstall showed me many years ago, but I decided to put off until later). Two people agree to meet again in a week. Then they part, and one goes to London, while the other flies to San Francisco. They both lead eventful weeks, each independently of the other, and duly meet as arranged. In order to describe this using world-states, we have to say what each of them is at just before and just after each noteworthy event involving the other, for each world-state encompasses them both, being a state of the whole world. But this is clearly silly."

This unfortunate state of affairs has persisted for too long due, in our view, to the common mistake of identifying "logic" with standard logics (preeminently first-order logic), or at least with appropriate extensions of such logics to be developed in the future ("what else could it be?"). However, when logics are considered at a more fundamental level as rigorous ways of reasoning correctly about some aspects of reality, there is no reason why the objects involved in the reasoning cannot change; indeed, the relevant reasoning may precisely deal with such change. Such a broadening of the point of view can then suggest that the inadequacies are not inadequacies of logic *per se*, but only of the standard logics that have traditionally been used.

Indeed, in the past few years there have been important new contributions in the area of logics of change. Those contributions have been reported in several workshops on this topic and in other publications and have exhibited important advances in eliminating the frame problem. In particular, a variety of approaches, such as for example those of [2, 3, 8, 23, 24, 29, 39, 40, 59], have proposed different logics of change and have shown the adequacy of those logics by means of concrete examples. A commonly emerging theme is that of "resource-conscious logics," a notion that can be traced back to linear logic [19], on which some of these approaches are based [2, 3, 39, 40]; others are based on Horn logic with equality [10, 23, 24, 29].

At present, two important topics, among others, that can benefit from further research are:

1. Understanding how the different logics of change that have so far been proposed can be related to each other in order to gain a better overall view of the field; and

2. Extending the representational capabilities of logics of change so that the class of systems that can be represented is as wide as possible, and their representation is as natural and direct as possible.

The second topic is particularly important for the success of this promising research direction. As Reichwein, Fiadeiro, and Maibaum [57] point out:

"It is not enough to have a convenient formalism in which to represent action and change: the representation has to reflect the structure of the represented system."

1.4   In what sense rewriting logic solves the frame problem

The present work proposes *rewriting logic* as a logic of concurrent action and change and presents detailed justification for the claim made in [45] that rewriting logic avoids the frame problem. The two topics mentioned above are addressed. Indeed, we show that rewriting logic subsumes a number of previous logics of change and provides a unified logical framework in which such logics can be compared. We also give many examples illustrating the wide representational capabilities of rewriting logic as a logic of change, capabilities that surpass those exhibited so far by other approaches.

The most general way to see why the frame problem is avoided is to consider the four rules of deduction of rewriting logic (see Section 2.2), specially the rules of *Congruence* and *Replacement*. Repeated application of the *Congruence* rule expresses that the change can take place in any context[1], and the *Replacement* rule even allows the contexts of the changes to be nested within each other. Therefore, the bookkeeping of context in the change is implicit and automatic in rewriting logic. In addition, the rules of *Congruence* and *Replacement*, by allowing several local rewrites to be incorporated within a single deduction step, make clear the intrinsically *concurrent* nature of the solution provided by rewriting logic.

It is in the sense of providing a logic of *execution*, or of *simulation* (i.e., of *action*), that rewriting logic solves the problem. The main difference—besides its generality—with *ad hoc* or procedural approaches is that rewriting logic places change on a logical basis rather than on an operational one, like for example in STRIPS [17]. Therefore, the solution is *declarative*, and provides an answer (at a certain level) to the question of how the frame problem should be solved in *logical* terms. By "at a certain level" we mean that even in logical terms our solution does not address everything. Specifically, it only covers limited aspects of what might be called the *specificational* side. Indeed, at the level of specification, as distinct from the level of execution, two types of logical formalisms can be used. On the one hand, one can use a logic of execution where the deduction directly corresponds to the change (as ours). On the other hand, more abstract descriptions may also be useful, and one may then want to use a nonexecutable logic to talk more indirectly about such changes (for example, to express certain safety properties that are invariant in all changes, etc.); this is a very important aspect in which we are also working, but no attempt will be made to cover nonexecutable specifications in this paper.

We illustrate the flexibility and generality of rewriting logic to represent action and change by many examples, including examples that show how concurrent object-oriented systems are naturally represented. The discussion of how an object-oriented point of view is supported by rewriting logic is not an essential point in our argument; its primary purpose is to further illustrate the flexibility that, from the point of view of representing knowledge, is available in rewriting logic. However, an object-oriented approach seems quite natural for many problems involving change in the world. Given that an object-oriented modelling of objects changing concurrently in the real world is often very natural, being able to express such modelling formally within rewriting logic gives further evidence that it is very well suited, from the knowledge representation point of view, to express action and change. Two even more particular points are made in the section on object-orientedness, namely:

1. That some conventions about rules can make even simpler the statement of changes, and

---

[1]Unless the rule expressing the change is *conditional* (see footnote 2), in which case the condition in question must be satisfied.

2. That inheritance, which is very natural for many examples, is also supported by the logic

In summary, the absence of frame axioms is inherent to rewriting logic in general, whereas the support for object-orientedness gives further evidence that the approach is natural and flexible from a knowledge representation point of view.

We can summarize the main advantages of rewriting logic as a logic of change as follows:

- It *has a simple formalism*, with only a few rules of deduction that are easy to understand and justify;

- It *is very flexible and expressive*, capable of representing change in systems with widely different structure;

- It *allows user-definable logical connectives*, with complete freedom to choose the connectives and structural properties appropriate for each problem.

- It *is intrinsically concurrent*, representing concurrent change and supporting reasoning about such change;

- It *supports modelling of concurrent object-oriented systems* in a particularly simple and direct way;

- It *has initial models* that support a "no junk, no confusion" version of the closed world assumption.

- It *provides a concurrent planning language via proof terms*, which can be identified with concurrent processes as in [15];

- It *solves the frame problem*, including residual difficulties in dealing with properties that must remain unchanged appearing in other otherwise successful approaches;

- It *subsumes and unifies a variety of logical formalisms* previously proposed as logics of change, including linear logic and Horn logic with equality, within a single logical framework;

- It *is realizable in a wide spectrum logical language* (Maude and its MaudeLog extension) supporting executable specification and programming, and having powerful modularity, inheritance, and parameterization mechanisms.

1.5 About the rest of this paper

The paper is structured as follows. Section 2 explains rewriting logic, including its syntax, its rules of deduction, and its model theory, and briefly introduces the Maude and MaudeLog languages that are used in examples throughout the paper. Section 3 presents a sequence of increasingly more challenging planning examples showing how a number of formalisms proposed by other researchers to solve those examples are easily expressed in rewriting logic. Since the examples discussed in Section 3 correspond to theories in adequate fragments of linear logic or of Horn logic with equality, a more systematic way of understanding how, and why, rewriting logic subsumes all these examples is to show, as we do in Section 4, adequate maps from linear logic and from Horn logic with equality into rewriting logic that allow theories in first-order linear logic and in Horn logic with equality to be faithfully represented in rewriting logic. Section 5 shows how concurrent object-oriented systems are naturally represented in rewriting logic. Section 6 shows how rewriting logic provides a fully satisfactory solution to the frame problem, including residual aspects of the problem that are often hard to deal with. The paper ends with some concluding remarks.

2 REWRITING LOGIC AND MAUDE

This section gives the rules of deduction of rewriting logic as well as its semantics, and explains its computational meaning. The Maude and Maude-Log languages, based on rewriting logic, are also briefly discussed.

2.1 Basic universal algebra

For the sake of simplifying the exposition, we treat the *unsorted* case; the many-sorted and order-sorted cases can be given a similar treatment. Therefore, a set Σ of function symbols is a ranked alphabet $\Sigma = \{\Sigma_n \mid n \in \mathbb{N}\}$. A Σ-algebra is then a set A together with an assignment of a function $f_A : A^n \longrightarrow A$ for each $f \in \Sigma_n$ with $n \in \mathbb{N}$. We denote by T_Σ the Σ-algebra of ground Σ-terms, and by $T_\Sigma(X)$ the Σ-algebra of Σ-terms with variables in a set X. Similarly, given a set E of Σ-equations, $T_{\Sigma,E}$ denotes the Σ-algebra of equivalence classes of ground Σ-terms modulo provable equality using the equations E, which is denoted $\equiv_E$; in the same way, $T_{\Sigma,E}(X)$ denotes the Σ-algebra of equivalence classes of Σ-terms with variables in X modulo $\equiv_E$. Let $[t]_E$ or just $[t]$ denote the E-equivalence class of t.

Given a term $t \in T_\Sigma(\{x_1, \ldots, x_n\})$, and terms $u_1, \ldots, u_n$, we denote by $t(u_1/x_1, \ldots, u_n/x_n)$ the term obtained from t by *simultaneously substituting* u_i for x_i, $i = 1, \ldots, n$. To simplify notation, we denote a sequence of objects

$a_1, \ldots, a_n$ by $\bar{a}$. With this notation, $t(u_1/x_1, \ldots, u_n/x_n)$ can be abbreviated to $t(\bar{u}/\bar{x})$.

2.2   The rules of rewriting logic

A *signature* in rewriting logic is a pair (Σ, E) with Σ a ranked alphabet of function symbols and E a set of Σ-equations. Rewriting will operate on equivalence classes of terms modulo the set of equations E. In this way, we free rewriting from the syntactic constraints of a term representation and gain a much greater flexibility in deciding what counts as a *data structure*; for example, string rewriting is obtained by imposing an associativity axiom, and multiset rewriting by imposing associativity and commutativity. Of course, standard term rewriting is obtained as the particular case in which the set E of equations is empty.

Given a signature (Σ, E), *sentences* of the logic are sequents of the form $[t]_E \longrightarrow [t']_E$ with t, t' Σ-terms, where t and t' may possibly involve some variables from the countably infinite set $X = \{x_1, \ldots, x_n, \ldots\}$. A *theory* in this logic, called a rewrite theory, is a slight generalization of the usual notion of theory—which is typically defined as a pair consisting of a signature and a set of sentences for it—in that, in addition, we allow rules to be labelled. This is very natural for many applications, and customary for automata—viewed as labelled transition systems—and for Petri nets, which are both particular instances of our definition.

DEFINITION 1. A *rewrite theory* $\mathcal{R}$ is a 4-tuple $\mathcal{R} = (\Sigma, E, L, R)$ where Σ is a ranked alphabet of function symbols, E is a set of Σ-equations, L is a set of *labels*, and R is a set of pairs $R \subseteq L \times T_{\Sigma,E}(X)^2$ whose first component is a label and whose second component is a pair of E-equivalence classes of terms, with $X = \{x_1, \ldots, x_n, \ldots\}$ a countably infinite set of variables. Elements of R are called *rewrite rules*[2]. We understand a rule $(r, ([t], [t']))$ as a labelled sequent and use for it the notation $r : [t] \longrightarrow [t']$. To indicate that $\{x_1, \ldots, x_n\}$ is the set of variables occurring in either t or t', we write $r : [t(x_1, \ldots, x_n)] \longrightarrow [t'(x_1, \ldots, x_n)]$, or in abbreviated notation $r : [t(\bar{x})] \longrightarrow [t'(\bar{x})]$.

Given a rewrite theory $\mathcal{R}$, we say that $\mathcal{R}$ *entails* a sequent $[t] \longrightarrow [t']$ and write $\mathcal{R} \vdash [t] \longrightarrow [t']$ if and only if $[t] \longrightarrow [t']$ can be obtained by finite application of the following *rules of deduction*:

---

[2] To simplify the exposition the rules of the logic are given for the case of *unconditional* rewrite rules. However, all the ideas and results presented here have been extended to conditional rules in [46] with very general rules of the form

$$r : [t] \longrightarrow [t'] \quad if \quad [u_1] \longrightarrow [v_1] \wedge \ldots \wedge [u_k] \longrightarrow [v_k].$$

This of course increases considerably the expressive power of rewrite theories, as illustrated by several of the examples presented in this paper.

1. **Reflexivity.** For each $[t] \in T_{\Sigma,E}(X)$, $\dfrac{}{[t] \longrightarrow [t]}$.

2. **Congruence.** For each $f \in \Sigma_n$, $n \in \mathbb{N}$,

$$\frac{[t_1] \longrightarrow [t'_1] \quad \ldots \quad [t_n] \longrightarrow [t'_n]}{[f(t_1,\ldots,t_n)] \longrightarrow [f(t'_1,\ldots,t'_n)]}.$$

3. **Replacement.** For each rewrite rule
$r : [t(x_1,\ldots,x_n)] \longrightarrow [t'(x_1,\ldots,x_n)]$ in R,

$$\frac{[w_1] \longrightarrow [w'_1] \quad \ldots \quad [w_n] \longrightarrow [w'_n]}{[t(\overline{w}/\overline{x})] \longrightarrow [t'(\overline{w'}/\overline{x})]}.$$

4. **Transitivity.** $\dfrac{[t_1] \longrightarrow [t_2] \quad [t_2] \longrightarrow [t_3]}{[t_1] \longrightarrow [t_3]}$.

Equational logic (modulo a set of axioms E) is obtained from rewriting logic by adding the following rule:

5. **Symmetry.** $\dfrac{[t_1] \longrightarrow [t_2]}{[t_2] \longrightarrow [t_1]}$.

With this new rule, sequents derivable in equational logic are *bidirectional*; therefore, in this case we can adopt the notation $[t] \leftrightarrow [t']$ throughout and call such bidirectional sequents *equations*.

Note that there are equivalent presentations using different rules; in particular, our presentation is not minimal in the number of rules. The main reason for this choice of rules of deduction is that they correspond to the algebraic structure on the models of rewriting logic sketched in Section 2.5 below.

A nice consequence of having defined rewriting logic is that concurrent rewriting, rather than emerging as an operational notion, actually coincides with deduction in such a logic.

DEFINITION 2. Given a rewrite theory $\mathcal{R} = (\Sigma, E, L, R)$, a (Σ, E)-sequent $[t] \longrightarrow [t']$ is called a *concurrent $\mathcal{R}$-rewrite* (or just a *rewrite*) if and only if it can be derived from $\mathcal{R}$ by finite application of the rules 1–4.

2.3   Example: Petri nets

Petri nets [58] provide a simple, yet rich enough, example of systems exhibiting concurrent change. Therefore, the problem of representing in logical terms the concurrent change of a Petri net system provides an interesting first illustration of how rewriting logic formalizes such change. In addition, since the state of a Petri net can be viewed as a conjunction of elementary resources, Petri net reachability provides a simple example of conjunctive planning, and exhibits some of the essential characteristics of the more general planning problems to be discussed in Section 3.

Usually, a Petri net is presented as a set of places, a disjoint set of transitions and a relation of causality between them that associates to each transition the set of resources consumed as well as produced by its firing. Meseguer and Montanari recast this idea in an algebraic framework in [52]. From this point of view, resources are represented as multisets of places, and therefore we have a binary operation (multiset union, denoted $\otimes$ here) that is associative, commutative, and has the empty multiset as an identity[3] but is not idempotent. Then, a Petri net is viewed as a graph whose arcs are the transitions and whose nodes are multisets over the set of places, usually called *markings*.

The following Petri net represents a machine to buy cakes and apples; a cake costs a dollar and an apple three quarters. Due to an unfortunate design, the machine only accepts dollars, and it returns a quarter when the user buys an apple; to alleviate in part this problem, the machine can change four quarters into a dollar.

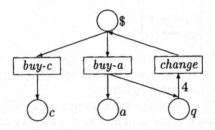

As a graph, this net has the following arcs:

$$buy\text{-}c: \quad \$ \longrightarrow c$$
$$buy\text{-}a: \quad \$ \longrightarrow a \otimes q$$
$$change: \quad q \otimes q \otimes q \otimes q \longrightarrow \$$$

The expression of this Petri net in rewriting logic is now obvious. We can view each of the labelled arcs of the Petri net as a rewrite rule in a rewrite theory having a binary *associative, commutative* operator $\otimes$ (multiset union) with *identity* 1 so that rewriting happens modulo ACI, that is, is multiset rewriting. Adopting an order-sorted [21] version of rewriting logic, we can gather together the "places" $\$, q, a, c$ into a type Place and view the states of the net, usually called *markings*, as elements of a supertype Marking containing Place and endowed with a multiset union operator. Using the syntax of the Maude language, the rewrite theory corresponding to the above Petri net can then be expressed as follows:

---

[3]From now on the associativity, commutativity, and identity axioms are denoted by the acronym ACI.

```
mod PETRI-NET is
  sorts Place Marking .
  subsort Place < Marking .
  op 1 : -> Marking .
  op _⊗_ : Marking Marking -> Marking [assoc comm id: 1] .
  ops $ q a c : -> Place .

  rl buy-c : $ => c .
  rl buy-a : $ => a ⊗ q .
  rl change : q ⊗ q ⊗ q ⊗ q => $ .
endm
```

A Maude module contains sort and subsort declarations introduced by the keywords sort(s) and subsort(s) stating the different sorts of data manipulated by the module and how those sorts are related. Each of the operators declared in the module, as well as the sorts of their arguments and the sort of their result, is introduced using the keyword op. The syntax is user-definable, and permits specifying function symbols in prefix, infix ($\_\otimes\_$, for example) or any "mixfix" combination as well as standard parenthesized notation.

A Petri net provides a very simple setup in which to deal with conjunctive planning problems. For example, assuming a user of the above machine that has five quarters in his pocket,

1. Can such a user get a cake *and* have some change left?

2. Can such a user get an apple *and* have some change left?

Rewriting logic provides a logical calculus to answer questions of this kind, that is, to make sound and complete deductions about the changes possible in a system.

Convention. In rewriting logic we deal with equivalence classes $[t]_E$ modulo the structural axioms E of the given theory. However, from now on, we usually drop such square brackets, with the implicit convention that a term t denotes the equivalence class $[t]_E$ for the appropriate set of equations E.

Consider our user with five quarters in his pocket. He can indeed buy a cake and be left with one quarter, as shown by the following PETRI-NET-rewrite (proof in rewriting logic).

$$q \otimes q \otimes q \otimes q \otimes q$$
$\longrightarrow$ *Cong* [*Repl* [change] , *Refl*]
$$\$ \otimes q$$
$\longrightarrow$ *Cong* [*Repl* [buy-c] , *Refl*]
$$c \otimes q$$

Hopefully, the notation is evident. For example, this proof would be displayed in tree form as follows (where the expression $q \otimes q \otimes q \otimes q$ has been abbreviated to q^4 in order to save space):

$$\cfrac{\cfrac{\overline{q^4 \longrightarrow \$}\,Repl \qquad \overline{q \longrightarrow q}\,\substack{Refl \\ Cong}}{q^4 \otimes q \longrightarrow \$ \otimes q} \qquad \cfrac{\overline{\$ \longrightarrow c}\,Repl \qquad \overline{q \longrightarrow q}\,\substack{Refl \\ Cong}}{\$ \otimes q \longrightarrow c \otimes q}}{q^4 \otimes q \longrightarrow c \otimes q}\,Tran$$

Similarly, the user can also buy an apple and be left with two quarters, applying now *Transitivity, Congruence, Reflexivity*, and *Replacement* with the rewrite rules change and buy-a:

$$q \otimes q \otimes q \otimes q \otimes q \longrightarrow \$ \otimes q \longrightarrow a \otimes q \otimes q.$$

The sense in which rewriting logic provides a sound and complete logical calculus to answer questions about what states can be reached in a Petri net is made precise by the following

THEOREM 3. *[46] Let N be a Petri net with set of places S and set of transitions T, let $N^\sharp$ be the rewrite theory representing such a net as explained above, and let M, M' be markings on S. Then, the marking M' is reachable from M in the net N if and only if the rewrite $[M] \longrightarrow [M']$ is a provable consequence of the theory $N^\sharp$ using the rules of deduction of rewriting logic.*

As we have already seen in the above planning examples, the multiset union operator $\otimes$ can be viewed as a form or resource-conscious non-idempotent conjunction. For example, the state $a \otimes q \otimes q$ corresponds to having an apple *and* a quarter *and* a quarter, which is a strictly better situation than having an apple *and* a quarter (non-idempotence of $\otimes$). Several researchers realized independently that this ACI operation on multisets corresponds to the conjunctive connective $\otimes$ (*tensor*) in linear logic [4, 9, 25, 35, 36]. This complementary point of view sees a net as a theory in this fragment of linear logic. Then, it is possible to establish a precise connection between reachability in Petri nets and provability in tensor logic.

For example, in order to get the tensor theory corresponding to our Petri net above, it is enough to change the arrows in the graph presentation into turnstiles, getting the following axioms:

$$buy\text{-}c: \quad \$ \vdash c$$
$$buy\text{-}a: \quad \$ \vdash a \otimes q$$
$$change: \quad q \otimes q \otimes q \otimes q \vdash \$$$

Note that there are no variables involved in the rules (where the rules now are viewed as axioms in tensor logic), i.e., all the terms involved are ground. Therefore, in this case, the *Replacement* rule of rewriting logic does not require any arguments, and the rules of rewriting logic reduce to the rules of tensor logic, the fragment of propositional linear logic consisting only of the connective $\otimes$ and its neutral element 1 (see [46, Sections 5.3.1–2]). Therefore, the following triple equivalence (including the previous equivalence in Theorem 3) is immediate:

THEOREM 4. *[35, 46] Let N be a Petri net with set of places S and set of transitions T, and M, M' be markings on S. Then, the marking M' is reachable from M if and only if the sequent $M \vdash M'$ is provable in tensor logic from the axioms corresponding to T, if and only if there is an $N^{\natural}$-rewrite $[M] \longrightarrow [M']$ (where $N^{\natural}$ denotes the corresponding rewrite theory).*

2.4 The meaning of rewriting logic

A logic worth its salt should be understood as a method of correct reasoning about some class of entities, not as an empty formal game. For equational logic, the entities in question are sets, functions between them, and the relation of identity between elements. For rewriting logic, the entities in question are *concurrent systems* having *states*, and evolving by means of *transitions*. The signature of a rewrite theory describes a particular structure for the states of a system—e.g., multiset, binary tree, etc.—so that its states can be distributed according to such a structure. For example, the states of a Petri net have as we have seen a multiset structure given by an ACI multiset union operator $\otimes$. The rewrite rules in the theory describe which elementary local transitions are possible in the distributed state by concurrent local transformations. What the rules of rewriting logic allow us to reason correctly about is which general concurrent transitions are possible in a system satisfying such a description. Clearly, concurrent systems should be the *models* giving a semantic interpretation to rewriting logic, in the same way that algebras are the models giving a semantic interpretation to equational logic. A precise account of the model theory of rewriting logic, giving rise to an initial model semantics for Maude modules and fully consistent with the above system-oriented interpretation, is given in [46], and summarized in Section 2.5 below.

Therefore, in rewriting logic a sequent $[t] \longrightarrow [t']$ should not be read as "$[t]$ *equals* $[t']$," but as "$[t]$ *becomes* $[t']$." Clearly, rewriting logic is a logic of *becoming* or *change*, not a logic of equality in a static Platonic sense. The apparently innocent step of adding the symmetry rule is in fact a very strong restriction, namely assuming that all change is reversible, thus bringing us into a timeless Platonic realm in which "before" and "after" have been identified.

A related observation is that $[t]$ should not be understood as a *term* in the usual first-order logic sense, but as a *proposition* or *formula*—built up using the *propositional connectives* in Σ—that asserts being in a certain *state* having a certain *structure*. For example, in the Petri net of Section 2.3, the term a $\otimes$ q $\otimes$ q asserted the proposition of being in a state consisting of an apple *and* a quarter *and* a quarter. However, unlike most other logics, the logical connectives Σ and their structural properties E are entirely *user-definable*. This provides great flexibility for considering many different state structures and makes rewriting logic very general in its capacity to deal with many different types of concurrent systems. This generality is discussed at length in [46] (see also [37] and Section 5.1 below).

The Petri net example in Section 2.3 illustrated another general point: the state of a system is distributed precisely because it can be decomposed into smaller fragments that are combined together by algebraic operations in the signature Σ, operations that from a logical point of view can be regarded as logical connectives. For example, the state $ $ \otimes $ $, by being distributed into two separated copies of $, allows the concurrent buying of a cake and an apple (plus getting one quarter back) in the Petri net of Section 2.3.

In summary, the rules of rewriting logic are rules to reason about *change in a concurrent system*. They allow us to draw valid conclusions about the evolution of the system from certain basic types of change known to be possible thanks to the rules R. Our present discussion is summarized as follows:

$$
\begin{array}{ccccc}
\textit{State} & \longleftrightarrow & \textit{Term} & \longleftrightarrow & \textit{Proposition} \\
\textit{Transition} & \longleftrightarrow & \textit{Rewriting} & \longleftrightarrow & \textit{Deduction} \\
\textit{Distributed} & \longleftrightarrow & \textit{Algebraic} & \longleftrightarrow & \textit{Propositional} \\
\textit{structure} & & \textit{structure} & & \textit{structure}
\end{array}
$$

2.5   The models of rewriting logic

This section makes mathematically precise the idea put forward in Section 2.4 that the models of rewriting logic theories are concurrent systems.

We first sketch the construction of initial and free models for a rewrite theory $\mathcal{R} = (\Sigma, E, L, R)$. Such models capture nicely the intuitive idea of a "rewrite system" in the sense that they are systems whose states are E-equivalence classes of terms, and whose transitions are concurrent rewritings using the rules in R. In particular, the initial model of a rewrite theory $\mathcal{R}$ provides a "no junk, no confusion" type of *closed world assumption* in which the only states in the system are those describable in the language of $\mathcal{R}$, the only transitions possible in the system are those logically provable from $\mathcal{R}$, and no states or transitions are identified unless they are equal in all models.

By adopting a logical instead of a computational perspective, we can alternatively view initial and free models as "logical systems" in which formulas are validly rewritten to other formulas by concurrent rewritings which correspond to proofs for the logic in question. Such models have a natural *category* structure [34], with states (or formulas) as objects, transitions (or proofs) as morphisms, and sequential composition as morphism composition, and in them dynamic behavior exactly corresponds to deduction.

Given a rewrite theory $\mathcal{R} = (\Sigma, E, L, R)$, the model that we are seeking is a category $\mathcal{T}_{\mathcal{R}}(X)$ whose objects are equivalence classes of terms $[t] \in T_{\Sigma,E}(X)$ and whose morphisms are equivalence classes of "proof terms" representing proofs in rewriting deduction, i.e., concurrent $\mathcal{R}$-rewrites. The rules for generating such proof terms, with the specification of their respective domain and codomain, are given below; they just "decorate" with proof terms the rules 1-4 of rewriting logic. Note that we always use "diagrammatic" notation for morphism composition, i.e., $\alpha; \beta$ always means the composition of α *followed by* β.

1. **Identities.** For each $[t] \in T_{\Sigma,E}(X)$, $\quad \overline{[t] : [t] \longrightarrow [t]}$.

2. **Σ-structure.** For each $f \in \Sigma_n$, $n \in \mathbb{N}$,

$$\frac{\alpha_1 : [t_1] \longrightarrow [t'_1] \quad \ldots \quad \alpha_n : [t_n] \longrightarrow [t'_n]}{f(\alpha_1, \ldots, \alpha_n) : [f(t_1, \ldots, t_n)] \longrightarrow [f(t'_1, \ldots, t'_n)]}.$$

3. **Replacement.** For each rewrite rule $r : [t(\overline{x}^n)] \longrightarrow [t'(\overline{x}^n)]$ in R,

$$\frac{\alpha_1 : [w_1] \longrightarrow [w'_1] \quad \ldots \quad \alpha_n : [w_n] \longrightarrow [w'_n]}{r(\alpha_1, \ldots, \alpha_n) : [t(\overline{w}/\overline{x})] \longrightarrow [t'(\overline{w'}/\overline{x})]}.$$

4. **Composition.** $\quad \dfrac{\alpha : [t_1] \longrightarrow [t_2] \quad \beta : [t_2] \longrightarrow [t_3]}{\alpha; \beta : [t_1] \longrightarrow [t_3]}$.

Each of the above rules of generation defines a different operation taking certain proof terms as arguments and returning a resulting proof term. In other words, proof terms form an algebraic structure $\mathcal{P}_{\mathcal{R}}(X)$ consisting of a graph with nodes $T_{\Sigma,E}(X)$, with identity arrows, and with operations f (for each $f \in \Sigma$), r (for each rewrite rule), and $\_;\_$ (for composing arrows). Our desired model $\mathcal{T}_{\mathcal{R}}(X)$ is the quotient of $\mathcal{P}_{\mathcal{R}}(X)$ modulo the following equations[4]:

1. **Category.**

   (a) *Associativity.* For all α, β, γ, $\quad (\alpha; \beta); \gamma = \alpha; (\beta; \gamma)$.

   (b) *Identities.* For each $\alpha : [t] \longrightarrow [t']$, $\quad \alpha; [t'] = \alpha$ and $[t]; \alpha = \alpha$.

2. **Functoriality of the Σ-algebraic structure.** For each $f \in \Sigma_n$,

---

[4]In the expressions appearing in the equations, when compositions of morphisms are involved, we always implicitly assume that the corresponding domains and codomains match.

(a) *Preservation of composition.* For all $\alpha_1, \ldots, \alpha_n, \beta_1, \ldots, \beta_n$,

$$f(\alpha_1; \beta_1, \ldots, \alpha_n; \beta_n) = f(\alpha_1, \ldots, \alpha_n); f(\beta_1, \ldots, \beta_n).$$

(b) *Preservation of identities.* $f([t_1], \ldots, [t_n]) = [f(t_1, \ldots, t_n)].$

3. **Axioms in** E. For $t(x_1, \ldots, x_n) = t'(x_1, \ldots, x_n)$ an axiom in E, for all $\alpha_1, \ldots, \alpha_n$,

$$t(\alpha_1, \ldots, \alpha_n) = t'(\alpha_1, \ldots, \alpha_n).$$

4. **Exchange.** For each $r : [t(x_1, \ldots, x_n)] \longrightarrow [t'(x_1, \ldots, x_n)]$ in R,

$$\frac{\alpha_1 : [w_1] \longrightarrow [w_1'] \quad \ldots \quad \alpha_n : [w_n] \longrightarrow [w_n']}{r(\overline{\alpha}) = r([\overline{w}]); t'(\overline{\alpha}) = t(\overline{\alpha}); r([\overline{w'}])}$$

Note that the set X of variables is actually a parameter of these constructions, and we need not assume X to be fixed and countable. In particular, for $X = \emptyset$, we adopt the notation $\mathcal{T}_R$. The equations in 1 make $\mathcal{T}_R(X)$ a category, the equations in 2 make each $f \in \Sigma$ a functor, and 3 forces the axioms E. The exchange law states that any rewriting of the form $r(\overline{\alpha})$—which represents the *simultaneous* rewriting of the term at the top using rule r *and* "below," i.e., in the subterms matched by the variables, using the rewrites $\overline{\alpha}$—is equivalent to the sequential composition $r([\overline{w}]); t'(\overline{\alpha})$, corresponding to first rewriting on top with r and then below on the subterms matched by the variables with $\overline{\alpha}$, and is also equivalent to the sequential composition $t(\overline{\alpha}); r([\overline{w'}])$ corresponding to first rewriting below with $\overline{\alpha}$ and then on top with r. Therefore, the exchange law states that rewriting at the top by means of rule r and rewriting "below" using $\overline{\alpha}$ are processes that are independent of each other and can be done either simultaneously or in any order. Since $[t(x_1, \ldots, x_n)]$ and $[t'(x_1, \ldots, x_n)]$ can be regarded as functors $\mathcal{T}_R(X)^n \longrightarrow \mathcal{T}_R(X)$, from the mathematical point of view the exchange law just asserts that r is a *natural transformation*.

LEMMA 5. *[46] For each rewrite rule* $r : [t(x_1, \ldots, x_n)] \longrightarrow [t'(x_1, \ldots, x_n)]$ *in R, the family of morphisms*

$$\{r([\overline{w}]) : [t(\overline{w}/\overline{x})] \longrightarrow [t'(\overline{w}/\overline{x})] \mid [\overline{w}] \in T_{\Sigma, E}(X)^n\}$$

is a natural transformation $r : [t(x_1, \ldots, x_n)] \Rightarrow [t'(x_1, \ldots, x_n)]$ *between the functors* $[t(x_1, \ldots, x_n)], [t'(x_1, \ldots, x_n)] : \mathcal{T}_R(X)^n \longrightarrow \mathcal{T}_R(X)$.

The category $\mathcal{T}_R(X)$ is just one among many *models* that can be assigned to the rewrite theory $\mathcal{R}$. The general notion of model, called an *$\mathcal{R}$-system*, is defined as follows:

DEFINITION 6. Given a rewrite theory $\mathcal{R} = (\Sigma, E, L, R)$, an *$\mathcal{R}$-system* $\mathcal{S}$ is a category $\mathcal{S}$ together with:

- A (Σ, E)-algebra structure given by a family of functors

$$\{f_{\mathcal{S}} : \mathcal{S}^n \longrightarrow \mathcal{S} \mid f \in \Sigma_n, n \in \mathbb{N}\}$$

  satisfying the equations E, i.e., for any $t(x_1, \ldots, x_n) = t'(x_1, \ldots, x_n)$ in E we have an identity of functors $t_{\mathcal{S}} = t'_{\mathcal{S}}$, where the functor $t_{\mathcal{S}}$ is defined inductively from the functors $f_{\mathcal{S}}$ in the obvious way.

- For each rewrite rule $r : [t(\overline{x})] \longrightarrow [t'(\overline{x})]$ in R a natural transformation $r_{\mathcal{S}} : t_{\mathcal{S}} \Rightarrow t'_{\mathcal{S}}$.

An $\mathcal{R}$-homomorphism $F : \mathcal{S} \longrightarrow \mathcal{S}'$ between two $\mathcal{R}$-systems is a functor $F : \mathcal{S} \longrightarrow \mathcal{S}'$ such that it is a Σ-algebra homomorphism—i.e., $f_{\mathcal{S}} * F = F^n * f_{\mathcal{S}'}$, for each f in Σ_n, $n \in \mathbb{N}$—and such that "F preserves R," i.e., for each rewrite rule $r : [t(\overline{x})] \longrightarrow [t'(\overline{x})]$ in R we have the identity of natural transformations[5] $r_{\mathcal{S}} * F = F^n * r_{\mathcal{S}'}$, where n is the number of variables appearing in the rule. This defines a category $\mathcal{R}$-**Sys** in the obvious way.

The above definition captures formally the idea that the models of a rewrite theory *are systems*. By a "system" we mean a machine-like entity that can be in a variety of *states*, and that can change its state by performing certain *transitions*. Such transitions are transitive, and it is natural and convenient to view states as "idle" transitions that do not change the state. In other words, a system can be naturally regarded as a *category*, whose objects are the states of the system and whose morphisms are the system's transitions.

For *sequential* systems such as labelled transition systems this is in a sense the end of the story; such systems exhibit *nondeterminism*, but do not have the required algebraic structure in their states and transitions to exhibit true concurrency. Indeed, what makes a system *concurrent* is precisely the existence of an additional *algebraic structure* [46]. First, the states themselves are distributed according to such a structure; for example, for Petri nets the distribution takes the form of a multiset. Second, concurrent transitions are themselves distributed according to the same algebraic structure; this is what the notion of $\mathcal{R}$-system captures, and is for example manifested in the concurrent firing of Petri nets, the evolution of concurrent object-oriented systems [48] and, more generally, in any type of concurrent rewriting.

The expressive power of rewrite theories to specify concurrent transition systems is greatly increased by the possibility of having not only transitions, but also *parameterized transitions*, i.e., *procedures*. This is what rewrite rules (with variables) provide. The family of states to which the

---

[5]Note that we use diagrammatic order for the *horizontal*, $\alpha * \beta$, and *vertical*, $\gamma; \delta$, composition of natural transformations [34].

procedure applies is given by those states where a component of the (distributed) state is a substitution instance of the lefthand side of the rule in question. The rewrite rule is then a *procedure* which transforms the state *locally*, by replacing such a substitution instance by the corresponding substitution instance of the righthand side. The fact that this can take place concurrently with other transitions "below" is precisely what the concept of a *natural transformation* formalizes. The following table summarizes our present discussion:

System	⟷	*Category*
State	⟷	*Object*
Transition	⟷	*Morphism*
Procedure	⟷	*Natural transformation*
Distributed structure	⟷	*Algebraic structure*

A detailed proof of the following theorem on the existence of initial and free $\mathcal{R}$-systems for the more general case of conditional rewrite theories is given in [46], where the soundness and completeness of rewriting logic for $\mathcal{R}$-system models is also proved.

THEOREM 7. *The $\mathcal{R}$-system $\mathcal{T}_\mathcal{R}$ is an initial object in the category $\mathcal{R}$-Sys. More generally, $\mathcal{T}_\mathcal{R}(X)$ has the following universal property: Given an $\mathcal{R}$-system S, each function $F : X \longrightarrow |S|$ extends uniquely to an $\mathcal{R}$-homomorphism $F^\natural : \mathcal{T}_\mathcal{R}(X) \longrightarrow S$.*

As we have already mentioned, the initiality of $\mathcal{T}_\mathcal{R}$ provides a standard model of $\mathcal{R} = (\Sigma, E, L, R)$ satisfying a "no junk, no confusion" version of the closed world assumption. Specifically, $\mathcal{T}_\mathcal{R}$ models a concurrent system in which:

1. The states are exactly those that can be named by the syntax Σ of $\mathcal{R}$;

2. Two states $[t]$ and $[t']$ are equal if and only if $t \equiv_E t'$, that is, if and only if t and t' are provably equal according to the structural axioms E;

3. There is a (possibly complex) transition $[t] \longrightarrow [t']$ in $\mathcal{T}_\mathcal{R}$ if and only if this is provable, that is, if and only if $\mathcal{R} \vdash [t] \longrightarrow [t']$;

4. Two transitions denoted by proof terms $\alpha, \beta : [t] \longrightarrow [t']$ are identical in $\mathcal{T}_\mathcal{R}$ if and only if they denote the same transition in all models of $\mathcal{R}$, that is, in all $\mathcal{R}$-systems.

The fact that, as stated in Theorem 7, a rewrite theory always has an initial model greatly increases the expressive power of rewriting logic, since the closed world assumption in the exact sense explained above can always be imposed simply by giving to a theory $\mathcal{R}$ an initial interpretation. This initial model semantics is the one adopted for Maude modules as explained in Section 2.6 below.

2.6   The Maude and MaudeLog languages

Rewriting logic can be used directly as a wide spectrum language supporting specification, rapid prototyping, and programming of concurrent systems. The Maude language realizes this idea in a particularly modular way in which modules are rewrite theories and in which functional modules with equationally defined data types can also be declared in a functional sublanguage. The examples given later in this paper illustrate the syntax of Maude. Details about the language design, its semantics, its parallel programming and wide spectrum capabilities, and its support of object-oriented programming can be found in [46, 54, 48, 49, 13]. Here we provide a very brief sketch that should be sufficient for understanding the examples presented later.

In Maude there are three kinds of *modules*:

1. *Functional modules*, introduced by the keyword fmod,

2. *System modules*, introduced by the keyword mod, and

3. *Object-oriented modules*, introduced by the keyword omod.

Object-oriented modules can be reduced to a special case of system modules for which a special syntax is used; therefore, in essence we only have functional and system modules, which are respectively of the form

- fmod $\mathcal{E}$ endfm, for an equational theory $\mathcal{E}$, and

- mod $\mathcal{R}$ endm, for a rewrite theory $\mathcal{R}$.

In Maude a module can have *submodules*, which can be imported with protecting, extending, and using qualifications stating (in decreasing order) the degree of integrity enjoyed by the submodule when imported by the supermodule.

The version of rewriting logic used for Maude is *order-sorted*. This means that rewrite theories are typed (types are called *sorts*) and can have subtypes (subsorts), and that function symbols can be overloaded. In particular, functional modules are order-sorted equational theories [21] and they form a sublanguage entirely similar to OBJ [22].

As OBJ, Maude has also *theories* to specify semantic requirements for interfaces and to make high level assertions about modules; they can be functional, system, or object-oriented. Also as OBJ, Maude has *parameterized modules*, again of the three kinds, and *views* that are theory interpretations relating theories to modules or to other theories.

Maude can be further extended to a language called MaudeLog that unifies the paradigms of functional programming, Horn logic programming, and concurrent object-oriented programming. In fact, Maude's design is based on a general axiomatic notion of "logic programming language" which is itself based on a general axiomatic theory of logic. This theory of "general logics" and the associated notions of "mapping between logics" (which systematically translate one logic into another) and of "logic programming language" were developed in [44]. We recall the main ideas about general logics and maps between logics in Section 4.1, and refer the reader to the original paper [44], as well as the more recent [37, 38] for more details and examples. The paper [47] introduces these general concepts, discusses general methods for designing multiparadigm logic programming languages using such concepts, and explains how Maude and MaudeLog were designed according to those methods.

Technically, a unification of paradigms is achieved by mapping the logics of each paradigm into a richer logic in which the paradigms are unified. In the case of Maude and MaudeLog, what is done is to define a new logic (rewriting logic) in which concurrent computations, and in particular concurrent object-oriented computations, can be expressed in a natural way, and then to formally relate this logic to the logics of the functional and relational paradigms, i.e., to equational logic and to Horn logic, by means of maps of logics that provide a simple and rigorous unification of paradigms. As it has already been mentioned, we actually assume an order-sorted structure throughout, and therefore the logics in question are: order-sorted rewriting logic, denoted *OSRWLogic*, order-sorted equational logic, denoted *OSEqtl*, and order-sorted Horn logic, denoted *OSHorn*.

The logic of equational programming can be embedded within order-sorted rewriting logic by means of a map of logics

$$OSEqtl \longrightarrow OSRWLogic.$$

The details of this map of logics are discussed in Appendix B of [47], and a different map is defined in Section 4.1 of [37]. At the programming language level, such a map corresponds to the inclusion of Maude's *functional modules* (essentially identical to OBJ modules) within the language.

Since the power and the range of applications of a multiparadigm logic programming language can be substantially increased if it is possible to solve queries involving *logical variables* in the sense of relational programming, as in the Prolog language, we are naturally led to seek a unification of the three paradigms of functional, relational and concurrent object-oriented programming into a single multiparadigm logic programming language. This unification can be attained in a language extension of Maude called MaudeLog. The integration of Horn logic is achieved by a map of logics

$$OSHorn \longrightarrow OSRWLogic$$

that systematically relates order-sorted Horn logic to order-sorted rewriting logic. This map is detailed in Section 4.2 of [37], and briefly discussed in Section 4.3 below (see also Appendix C of [47]).

The difference between the languages Maude and MaudeLog does not consist in any change in the underlying logic; indeed, both languages are based on rewriting logic, and both have rewrite theories as programs. It resides, rather, in an enlargement of the set of *queries* that can be presented, so that, while keeping the same syntax and models, in MaudeLog we also consider queries involving existential formulas of the form

$$\exists \overline{x} \ \ [u_1(\overline{x})] \longrightarrow [v_1(\overline{x})] \wedge \ldots \wedge [u_k(\overline{x})] \longrightarrow [v_k(\overline{x})].$$

Therefore, the sentences and the deductive rules and mechanisms that are now needed require further extensions of rewriting logic deduction. In particular, solving such existential queries requires performing *unification*, specifically, given Maude's typing structure, order-sorted E-unification for a set E of structural axioms [51].

3   SOME PLANNING PROBLEMS

We discuss how the planning problems considered in [10, 23, 29, 39, 40] can all be solved in rewriting logic, taking advantage in particular of the flexibility of the logic thanks to its user-definable logical connectives. Although in what follows we treat the concept of plan in an intuitive way, in our framework a plan corresponds to a proof in rewriting logic. One advantage of this point of view is that plans are automatically endowed with a notion of parallelism; moreover, the categorical semantics of rewriting logic provides an equational axiomatization characterizing when two plans are essentially the same, abstracting away unnecessary details in the representation and thus giving a truly concurrent semantics for the execution of plans. ¿From this point of view, plans can be thought of as concurrent processes, as in [15].

3.1   Conjunctive planning

We have noted in Section 2.3 the fact that the rewrite rules corresponding to the transitions of a Petri net are ground. In this section, we consider a generalization of tensor theories by allowing in the rules literals built using variables, functions, and predicates instead of propositional constants only (but not explicit quantification), thus obtaining the general framework of conjunctive planning. Note that we need not consider the set of ground instances of the rules as Masseron *et al.* [39, 40], because rewriting logic, via the *Replacement* rule, takes care of the necessary instantiations. We illustrate this case by means of a blocksworld example, borrowed from [29] (see also [39, 40]).

The main module is parameterized by a set of block identifiers, using the parameter theory TRIV with parameter sort BlockId.

```
fth TRIV is
  sort BlockId .
endft

mod BLOCKWORLD[X :: TRIV] is
  sort Prop .
  op table : BlockId -> Prop .       *** block is on the table
  op on : BlockId BlockId -> Prop .  *** block A is on block B
  op clear : BlockId -> Prop .       *** block is clear
  op hold : BlockId -> Prop .        *** robot arm holds the block
  op empty : -> Prop .               *** robot arm is empty
  sort State .
  subsort Prop < State .
  op 1 : -> State .
  op _⊗_ : State State -> State [assoc comm id: 1] .

  vars X Y : BlockId .
  rl pickup(X) : empty ⊗ clear(X) ⊗ table(X) => hold(X) .
  rl putdown(X) : hold(X) => empty ⊗ clear(X) ⊗ table(X) .
  rl unstack(X,Y) : empty ⊗ clear(X) ⊗ on(X,Y)
     => hold(X) ⊗ clear(Y) .
  rl stack(X,Y) : hold(X) ⊗ clear(Y)
     => empty ⊗ clear(X) ⊗ on(X,Y) .
endm
```

In order to create a world with three blocks $\{a, b, c\}$, we consider the functional module

```
fmod BLOCKS3 is
  sort BlockId .
  ops a b c : -> BlockId .
endfm
```

and instantiate the parameterized module BLOCKWORLD[X] using the default view TRIV → BLOCKS3:

```
make WORLD is BLOCKWORLD[BLOCKS3] endmk
```

Now consider the states described in Figure 1. The state I on the left is the initial one, described by the following term of sort State in the rewrite theory (Maude program) WORLD

$$empty \otimes clear(c) \otimes clear(b) \otimes table(a)$$
$$\otimes\ table(b) \otimes on(c,a).$$

Analogously, the final state F on the right is described by the term

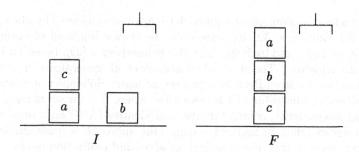

Figure 1. Two states in a world with three blocks.

empty ⊗ clear(a) ⊗ table(c) ⊗ on(a,b) ⊗ on(b,c).

The fact that the sequential plan

unstack(c,a);putdown(c);pickup(b);
  stack(b,c);pickup(a);stack(a,b)

moves the blocks from state I to state F corresponds directly to the following WORLD-rewrite (proof in rewriting logic), where we also show the use of the structural axioms of associativity and commutativity:

empty ⊗ clear(c) ⊗ clear(b) ⊗ table(a) ⊗ table(b) ⊗ on(c,a)
=

empty ⊗ clear(c) ⊗ on(c,a) ⊗ clear(b) ⊗ table(a) ⊗ table(b)
⟶   *Cong* [*Repl* [unstack(c,a)] , *Refl*]
hold(c) ⊗ clear(a) ⊗ clear(b) ⊗ table(a) ⊗ table(b)
⟶   *Cong* [*Repl* [putdown(c)] , *Refl*]
empty ⊗ clear(c) ⊗ table(c) ⊗ clear(a) ⊗ clear(b)
                                      ⊗ table(a) ⊗ table(b)
=

empty ⊗ clear(b) ⊗ table(b) ⊗ clear(c) ⊗ table(c)
                                        ⊗ clear(a) ⊗ table(a)
⟶   *Cong* [*Repl* [pickup(b)] , *Refl*]
hold(b) ⊗ clear(c) ⊗ table(c) ⊗ clear(a) ⊗ table(a)
⟶   *Cong* [*Repl* [stack(b,c)] , *Refl*]
empty ⊗ clear(b) ⊗ on(b,c) ⊗ table(c) ⊗ clear(a) ⊗ table(a)
=

empty ⊗ clear(a) ⊗ table(a) ⊗ clear(b) ⊗ on(b,c) ⊗ table(c)
⟶   *Cong* [*Repl* [pickup(a)] , *Refl*]
hold(a) ⊗ clear(b) ⊗ on(b,c) ⊗ table(c)
⟶   *Cong* [*Repl* [stack(a,b)] , *Refl*]
empty ⊗ clear(a) ⊗ on(a,b) ⊗ on(b,c) ⊗ table(c)
=

empty ⊗ clear(a) ⊗ table(c) ⊗ on(a,b) ⊗ on(b,c)

The reader can compare our approach to the ones considered by Masseron, Tollu, and Vauzeilles [39, 40], based on (the tensor fragment of) propositional linear logic, and by Hölldobler and Schneeberger [29], based on Horn logic with equality. The work of Masseron *et al.* generalizes in a sense the connection between Petri nets and tensor logic. Hölldobler and Schneeberger develop plans using SLDE-resolution, where E is the set of equations imposing associativity, commutativity, and identity (ACI) on a binary operator corresponding to multiset union. Our approach is quite similar to the latter. Indeed, their use of logical variables and unification modulo ACI in order to look for a plan is very similar to the use of E-unification in MaudeLog in order to search for a rewriting logic proof. The approaches can be made even more similar if we modify our rewrite rules by adding a new proposition so that a state records the rules that have been applied in reaching it. For example, the rewrite rule

```
empty ⊗ clear(X) ⊗ table(X) ⊗ plan(P)
                    => hold(X) ⊗ plan(P;pickup(X))
```

would correspond to the following clause in the framework of [29]:

```
PLAN(S, P;pickup(X), hold(X) ⊗ R)
    <= PLAN(S, P, empty ⊗ clear(X) ⊗ table(X) ⊗ R)
```

Note the use of the variable R in this clause, necessary in order to match "the rest of a state." Again, we do not need such a variable in our rewrite rules, because rewriting logic, via the *Congruence* rule (and *Reflexivity* if necessary, see the rewrite above for example), takes care of the context.

Große, Hölldobler, and Schneeberger prove in [23] (see also [24, 28]) that, in the framework of conjunctive planning, there is an equivalence between plans generated by Bibel's linear connection method [8], linear logic proofs as used by Masseron *et al.* [39, 40], and the equational logic programming approach of Hölldobler and Schneeberger [29]. Without going into details, a conjunctive planning problem can be presented as a set of actions A, an initial state I, and a final state F, where these states are assumed to be ground; we can also view it as a generalized (in the sense of allowing predicates and variables) Petri net and two markings. The set of actions can equivalently be presented as a theory in quantifier-free first-order tensor logic.

In our rewriting logic approach, the set of actions of a conjunctive planning problem is represented as a rewrite theory $\mathcal{R}$ consisting (up to renaming of sorts and operators) of:

1. A sort Prop and operators of the form p : s1 ... sn -> Prop, denoting atomic propositions or predicates;

2. An ACI operator ⊗ as follows:

```
sort State .
subsort Prop < State .
op 1 : -> State .
op _⊗_ : State State -> State [assoc comm id: 1] .
```

3. Rewrite rules on the sort State, representing the actions in question.

Then, the initial and final states are two terms $[t]$ and $[t']$ of sort State, and looking for a plan to solve this conjunctive problem is equivalent to looking for a proof in rewriting logic of the statement $\mathcal{R} \vdash [t] \longrightarrow [t']$.

THEOREM 8. *[23] Let $\mathcal{P} = \langle A, I, F \rangle$ be a conjunctive planning problem, and A_{LCM}, A_{ELP}, and A_{LL} denote the representation of the set of actions A in the linear connection method, Horn logic with equality, and linear (tensor) logic, respectively. Then, the following statements about a plan p are equivalent:*

1. *p is a solution of $\mathcal{P}$.*

2. *p is generated by a linear connection proof of the classical first-order formula $A_{LCM} \wedge I \Rightarrow F$.*

3. *p is generated by an SLDE-resolution proof of $PLAN(I, p, F)$ using the equational logic program A_{ELP}.*

4. *p is generated by a linear (tensor) logic proof of the sequent $I \vdash F$ from the (tensor) theory $\mathcal{I}(A_{LL})$, where $\mathcal{I}$ denotes the set of all ground instantiations.*

The equivalences between 1 and 3, and between 1 and 4 were proved in [29] and [40], respectively. Note also that the linear logic proof in 4 is really a tensor logic proof, because $\otimes$ is the only connective that appears in the formulas.

In the light of Theorem 4, the fact that the generalization from Petri nets consists simply in allowing literals built using variables, functions, and predicates instead of propositional constants only, and the motivation above, it is not surprising that we can add to the above equivalence the plans generated by proofs in rewriting logic.

THEOREM 9. *Let $\mathcal{P} = \langle A, I, F \rangle$ be a conjunctive planning problem, and A_{RL} denote the representation of the set of actions as a rewrite theory. Then, a plan p is a solution of $\mathcal{P}$ if and only if it is generated by an A_{RL}-rewrite of the sequent $I \longrightarrow F$.*

An easy way to prove this theorem is to translate rewriting logic proofs to tensor logic proofs and vice versa. We can look at this result as a very particular case of the conservative map of logics from linear logic to rewriting logic discussed later in Section 4.2, and its proof as a particular case of the proof of the general conservativity result in Theorem 12.

3.2   Disjunctive planning

The conjunctive planning approach discussed in the previous section has
been extended to disjunctive planning problems in [10, 40]. Masseron *et
al.* [40] consider theories in the $\{\otimes, \oplus\}$-fragment of linear logic, where the
connective $\oplus$ of additive disjunction is used to interpret nondeterminism.
Brüning *et al.* [10] (see also [24]) generalize the Horn logic with equality
approach of [29] by adding to the ACI operator $\otimes$ (in our notation) a new
binary operator $\oplus$ (in our notation again) that is associative, commutative,
idempotent, has an identity, and such that $\otimes$ distributes over $\oplus$ (note that
the connective $\oplus$ of linear logic satisfies all these properties). In both cases
a term of the form $A \oplus B$ is interpreted as the availability of either the
resources A or the resources B, but without knowing exactly which of them.
In this extended framework, Masseron *et al.* prove the equivalence between
statements 1 and 4 of the corresponding version of Theorem 8. Brüning *et
al.* describe also a generalization of Bibel's linear connection method to the
disjunctive case and prove the equivalence between appropriate versions of
1, 2, and 3 of Theorem 8.

Let us show how rewriting logic subsumes both approaches by means of
the example of the three socks problem. In a drawer there are at least three
socks; they are either black or white, but the drawer is in a dark room and
the person who needs a pair of socks cannot see the color. The question is
how many socks does he need to pick up in order to have a pair of matching
socks. The answer, as the name of the problem implies, is three, and we
want to show the way to reach this solution as a disjunctive plan.

```
mod SOCKS is
   sort Sock .
   ops s b w : -> Sock .   *** sock, black sock, white sock
   sort State .
   subsort Sock < State .
   ops 1 0 : -> State .
   op _⊗_ : State State -> State [assoc comm id: 1] .
   op _⊕_ : State State -> State [assoc comm idem id: 0] .
   op ok : -> State .
   vars A B C : State .
   ax A ⊗ (B ⊕ C) = (A ⊗ B) ⊕ (A ⊗ C) . *** distributivity
   rl pick : s => b ⊕ w .
   rl black : b ⊗ b => ok .
   rl white : w ⊗ w => ok .
   rl end : ok ⊗ A => ok .
endm
```

The initial state, the drawer with at least three socks, is represented by
the following term of sort State:

s $\otimes$ s $\otimes$ s $\otimes$ A

where A is a variable of sort State that represents the rest of the socks. The desired final state is the term ok, as hinted by the rewrite rules black and white. Among others, we have the following SOCKS-rewrite:

s $\otimes$ s $\otimes$ s $\otimes$ A
$\longrightarrow$ $Cong[Repl[pick], Repl[pick], Repl[pick], Refl]$
(b $\oplus$ w) $\otimes$ (b $\oplus$ w) $\otimes$ (b $\oplus$ w) $\otimes$ A
=   (1)
((b $\otimes$ b $\otimes$ b) $\oplus$ (b $\otimes$ b $\otimes$ w) $\oplus$ (b $\otimes$ w $\otimes$ w)
$\oplus$ (w $\otimes$ w $\otimes$ w)) $\otimes$ A
$\longrightarrow$ $Cong[Repl[end], Repl[end], Repl[end], Repl[end], Refl]$
(ok $\oplus$ ok $\oplus$ ok $\oplus$ ok) $\otimes$ A
=   (2)
ok $\otimes$ A
$\longrightarrow$ $Repl[end]$
ok

The module above simplifies the approach in [40], taking advantage of the availability of variables in our framework for the termination rule end. Note that the structural axioms of distributivity and idempotence are essential in steps (1) and (2) of the above SOCKS-rewrite. Notice also that several rewritings can be done at the same time, i.e., we have in this case a concurrent plan, as we have already mentioned in the introduction to this section.

The approach in [24] is even simpler, corresponding to the following simpler rewrite theory that uses instead a more general termination rule. Note, however, that the term rule has the effect of "destroying resources" and therefore it is very dangerous and cannot be applied indiscriminately, but only when needed following a careful strategy.

```
mod SOCKS2 is
    sort Sock .
    ops s b w : -> Sock .
    sort State .
    subsort Sock < State .
    ops 1 0 : -> State .
    op _⊗_ : State State -> State [assoc comm id: 1] .
    op _⊕_ : State State -> State [assoc comm idem id: 0] .
    vars A B C : State .
    ax A ⊗ (B ⊕ C) = (A ⊗ B) ⊕ (A ⊗ C) .
    rl pick : s => b ⊕ w .
    rl term : A ⊗ B => B .
endm
```

The initial state is as before, but the final state is represented more explicitly by the term

(b ⊗ b) ⊕ (w ⊗ w).

In this case, we have the following SOCKS2-rewrite:

s ⊗ s ⊗ s ⊗ A
⟶   Cong[Repl[pick], Repl[pick], Repl[pick], Refl]
(b ⊕ w) ⊗ (b ⊕ w) ⊗ (b ⊕ w) ⊗ A
=
((b ⊗ b ⊗ b) ⊕ (b ⊗ b ⊗ w) ⊕ (b ⊗ w ⊗ w)
                              ⊕ (w ⊗ w ⊗ w)) ⊗ A
⟶   Cong[Repl[term], Repl[term], Repl[term], Repl[term], Refl]
((b ⊗ b) ⊕ (b ⊗ b) ⊕ (w ⊗ w) ⊕ (w ⊗ w)) ⊗ A
=
((b ⊗ b) ⊕ (w ⊗ w)) ⊗ A
⟶   Repl[term]
(b ⊗ b) ⊕ (w ⊗ w)

Again, the plan that we have obtained in this case has a lot of parallelism. Had we applied the rule term carelessly, we could have for example the undesirable rewrite

s ⊗ s ⊗ s ⊗ A ⟶ s.

Our discussion of the three socks example suggests a generalization of Theorem 9 entirely similar to the generalization of Theorem 8 to the disjunctive case provided by Brüning et al. [10] and Masseron et al. [40].

In the disjunctive planning case, the set of actions is represented as a rewrite theory $\mathcal{R}$ consisting (up to renaming of sorts and operators) of:

1. A sort Prop and operators of the form p : s1 ... sn -> Prop, denoting atomic propositions or predicates;

2. Two ACI operators ⊗ and ⊕ as follows:

```
sort State .
subsort Prop < State .
ops 1 0 : -> State .
op _⊗_ : State State -> State [assoc comm id: 1] .
op _⊕_ : State State -> State [assoc comm idem id: 0].
vars A B C : State .
ax A ⊗ (B ⊕ C) = (A ⊗ B) ⊕ (A ⊗ C) .
```

3. Rewrite rules on the sort State, representing the actions in question.

Again, solving a disjunctive planning problem is equivalent to looking for a proof in rewriting logic of the statement $\mathcal{R} \vdash [t] \longrightarrow [t']$, where $[t]$ and $[t']$ are two terms of sort State, denoting the initial and final state, respectively.

THEOREM 10. *Let* $\mathcal{P} = \langle A, I, F \rangle$ *be a disjunctive planning problem, and* A_{RL} *denote the representation of the set of actions as a rewrite theory. Then, a plan* p *is a solution of* $\mathcal{P}$ *if and only if it is generated by an* A_{RL}-*rewrite of the sequent* $I \longrightarrow F$.

As before, this theorem can be seen also as a particular case of the conservative map of logics from linear logic to rewriting logic and Theorem 12 in Section 4.2.

The authors of [24] consider also an example that needs a *non-idempotent* disjunction # (different therefore from the previous operator ⊕), and does not seem to be easily expressible in the linear logic framework. Again, the great flexibility of rewriting logic makes this an easy example in our framework. The idea is to give a very simple model of Mendel's law of genetics for the color of peas, determined by two genes which carry the hereditary factor for either yellow or green. Yellow is recessive, i.e., a pea is yellow if both genes are yellow, whereas green is dominant, i.e., a green gene is enough to determine the green color of the pea. This is described in the following functional module.

```
fmod PEAS is
    sorts Gene Pea .
    ops g y : -> Gene .
    op p : Gene Gene -> Pea [comm] .
    ops yellow green : -> Pea .
    var G : Gene .
    eq p(y,y) = yellow .
    eq p(g,G) = green .
endfm
```

Now we define the effect of crossing two peas. The genes determining the color are split and combined with the genes from the other pea.

```
mod GENETICS is
    extending PEAS .
    sort State .
    subsort Pea < State .
    op 0 : -> State .
    op _#_ : State State -> State [assoc comm id: 0] .
    op c : Pea Pea -> Pea .
    vars W X Y Z : Gene .
    rl c(p(W,X),p(Y,Z)) => p(W,Y) # p(W,Z) # p(X,Y) # p(X,Z) .
endm
```

We want to know the result of crossing two green peas. The following GENETICS-rewrite provides the answer:

```
c(green,green)
  =
c(p(g,G),p(g,J))
  ⟶
p(g,g) # p(g,J) # p(G,g) # p(G,J)
  =
green # green # green # p(G,J)
```

That is, there is a probability of at least 75% that the result of crossing two green peas will be a green pea again. Of course, as Große *et al.* note, had we declared the operator # to be idempotent, we could not get this result at all, because of the identification

```
green # green # green # p(G,J) = green # p(G,J).
```

4 MAPPING LOGICS

The examples in the previous section motivate the idea that rewriting logic subsumes linear logic and Horn logic with equality. This claim is supported by the conservative maps of logics discussed in this section, based on the axiomatic theory of general logics, first introduced in [44].

4.1 General logics

A modular and general axiomatic theory of logics should adequately cover all the key ingredients of a logic. These include: a *syntax*, a notion of *entailment* of a sentence from a set of axioms, a notion of *model*, and a notion of *satisfaction* of a sentence by a model. This section gives a brief review of the required notions; a detailed account with many examples can be found in [44] (see also [37, 38]).

Syntax can typically be given by a *signature* Σ providing a grammar on which to build *sentences*. We assume that for each logic there is a category **Sign** of possible signatures for it, and a functor *sen* assigning to each signature Σ the set $sen(\Sigma)$ of all its sentences. For a given signature Σ in **Sign**, entailment (also called *provability*) of a sentence $\varphi \in sen(\Sigma)$ from a set of axioms $\Gamma \subseteq sen(\Sigma)$ is a relation $\Gamma \vdash \varphi$ which holds if and only if we can prove φ from the axioms Γ using the rules of the logic. This relation must be reflexive, monotone, transitive, and must preserve translations between signatures. These components constitute an *entailment system*.

The axiomatization of a model theory is due to the seminal work of Goguen and Burstall on *institutions* [20]. An institution consists of a category **Sign** of signatures and a functor *sen* : **Sign** → **Set** associating to each signature a set of sentences, as before, together with a functor **Mod** that associates to each signature Σ a category of Σ-*models*, and a binary relation $\models$ between models and sentences called *satisfaction* satisfying appropriate requirements.

DEFINITION 11. [44] A *logic* is a 5-tuple $\mathcal{L} = (\mathbf{Sign}, sen, \mathbf{Mod}, \vdash, \models)$ such that:

- $(\mathbf{Sign}, sen, \vdash)$ is an entailment system,

- $(\mathbf{Sign}, sen, \mathbf{Mod}, \models)$ is an institution,

and the following *soundness condition* is satisfied: for any $\Sigma \in |\mathbf{Sign}|$, $\Gamma \subseteq sen(\Sigma)$, and $\varphi \in sen(\Sigma)$,

$$\Gamma \vdash_\Sigma \varphi \implies \Gamma \models_\Sigma \varphi,$$

where, by definition, the relation $\Gamma \models_\Sigma \varphi$ holds if and only if $M \models_\Sigma \varphi$ holds for any model M that satisfies all the sentences in Γ.

The detailed treatment in [44] includes also a flexible axiomatic notion of a *proof calculus*, in which proofs of entailments, not just the entailments themselves, are first class citizens.

One of the most interesting fruits of the theory of general logics is that it gives us a method for *relating* logics in a general and systematic way, and to exploit such relations in many applications. The general way of relating logics (entailment systems, institutions, etc.) is to consider *maps* that interpret one logic into another. A detailed treatment of such maps is given in [44]; here we just give a brief sketch.

Basically, a map of entailment systems $(\Phi, \alpha) : \mathcal{E} \longrightarrow \mathcal{E}'$ maps the language of $\mathcal{E}$ to that of $\mathcal{E}'$ in a way that respects the entailment relation. This means that signatures of $\mathcal{E}$ are functorially mapped by Φ to signatures of $\mathcal{E}'$, and that sentences of $\mathcal{E}$ are mapped by α to sentences of $\mathcal{E}'$ in a way that is coherent with the mapping of their corresponding signatures. In addition, α must respect the entailment relations $\vdash$ of $\mathcal{E}$ and $\vdash'$ of $\mathcal{E}'$, that is, we must have $\Gamma \vdash \varphi \Rightarrow \alpha(\Gamma) \vdash' \alpha(\varphi)$. The map is *conservative* when this implication is an equivalence. For many interesting applications one needs to map signatures of E to *theories* of E', that is, Σ is mapped by Φ to (Σ', Γ'), with $\Gamma' \subseteq sen'(\Sigma')$. It is this more general notion of *map between entailment systems* that is axiomatized by the definition in [44], and used below for our mappings of linear logic and Horn logic with equality into rewriting logic.

A *map of institutions* $(\Phi, \alpha, \beta) : \mathcal{I} \longrightarrow \mathcal{I}'$ is similar in its syntax part to a map of entailment systems. In addition, for models we have a natural functor $\beta : \mathbf{Mod}'(\Phi(\Sigma)) \longrightarrow \mathbf{Mod}(\Sigma)$ "backwards" from the models in $\mathcal{I}'$ of a translated signature $\Phi(\Sigma)$ to the models in $\mathcal{I}$ of the original signature

Σ, and such a mapping respects the satisfaction relations $\models$ of $\mathcal{I}$ and $\models'$ of $\mathcal{I}'$, in the sense that $M' \models' \alpha(\varphi) \iff \beta(M') \models \varphi$.

A *map of logics* has now a very simple definition. It consists of a pair of maps: one for the underlying entailment systems, and another for the underlying institutions, such that both maps agree on how they translate signatures and sentences.

There is also a notion of *map of proof calculi*, for which we refer the reader to [44].

4.2   Linear logic

Theories in first-order linear logic can be interpreted as rewrite theories, thus greatly generalizing the tensor theories corresponding to Petri nets and conjunctive planning, or the $\{\otimes, \oplus\}$-theories corresponding to disjunctive planning. In this section, we summarize the mapping from propositional linear logic to rewriting logic fully described in [37], and refer to that paper for the complete details and the extension to the first-order case.

The *Congruence* rule of rewriting logic implies that all the operators are monotonic with respect to rewriting. This can create problems with non-monotonic logical operators like negation and implication. In the case of linear logic, as in classical logic, these can be solved by using formulas in negation normal form; that is, using the double negation and De Morgan laws, we can push negation to the atomic level. This is done in a functional theory PROP0[X], omitted here, which includes a sort Prop0 and the following equations among others:

```
eq (A ⅋ B)⊥ = A⊥ ⊗ B⊥ .
eq (A & B)⊥ = A⊥ ⊕ B⊥ .
eq A⊥⊥ = A .
```

The style of our formulation adopts a categorical viewpoint for the proof theory and semantics of linear logic [61, 36]. This style exploits the close connection between the models of linear logic and those of rewriting logic which are also categories, as we have explained in Section 2.5. Without going into details that the reader can find for example in [36] and the references therein, the tensor and linear implication connectives are interpreted in a closed symmetric monoidal category $\langle \mathcal{C}, \otimes, \multimap \rangle$. Negation is interpreted by means of a dualizing object $\perp$ and the definition $A^\perp = A \multimap \perp$ (with this definition of negation, $\mathcal{C}$ becomes a *-autonomous category [6]). The categorical product & interprets additive conjunction. The interpretation of the exponential ! is given by a comonad $(!A, !A \to A, !A \to !!A)$ that maps the comonoid structure $\top \leftarrow A \to A\&A$ into a comonoid structure $1 \leftarrow !A \to !A \otimes !A$ via isomorphisms $!\top \cong 1$ and $!(A\&A) \cong !A \otimes !A$. A category having all the necessary structure is called a *Girard category*.

The dual connectives $\mathbin{⅋}, \oplus$ and $?$ can be defined using negation: $A \mathbin{⅋} B = (A^\perp \otimes B^\perp)^\perp = A^\perp \multimap B$, $A \oplus B = (A^\perp \& B^\perp)^\perp$, $?A = (!A^\perp)^\perp$. Without negation, $\oplus$ needs the presence of coproducts and $?$ is interpreted by means of a monad with a monoid structure. When seeking the minimal categorical structure required for interpreting linear logic, an important question is how to interpret the connective $\mathbin{⅋}$ without using negation, and how to axiomatize its relationship with the tensor $\otimes$. Cockett and Seely answer this question with the notion of a *weakly distributive category* [14]. A weakly distributive category consists of a category $\mathcal{C}$ with two symmetric tensor products $\otimes, \mathbin{⅋}$: $\mathcal{C} \times \mathcal{C} \to \mathcal{C}$, and a natural transformation $A \otimes (B \mathbin{⅋} C) \longrightarrow (A \otimes B) \mathbin{⅋} C$ (weak distributivity) satisfying some coherence equations[6]. Negation is added to a weakly distributive category by means of a function $(\_)^\perp : |\mathcal{C}| \to |\mathcal{C}|$ on the objects of $\mathcal{C}$, and natural transformations $1 \longrightarrow A \mathbin{⅋} A^\perp$ and $A \otimes A^\perp \longrightarrow \perp$ satisfying some coherence equations. Cockett and Seely then prove that the concepts of weakly distributive category with negation and of $*$-autonomous category are equivalent, providing in this way a categorical semantics for linear logic in which the *par* connective $\mathbin{⅋}$ is primitive and is not defined in terms of tensor and negation.

The LINLOG[X] theory below introduces linear logic propositions and the rules of the logic. It is parameterized by a theory ATOM providing atomic formulas. Propositions are of the form [A] for A an expression in Prop0. The purpose of the operation [_] is to transform a formula A into its equivalent negation normal form [A], using the equations in the theory PROP0[X] mentioned before. The rewrite rules for $\otimes, \mathbin{⅋}$, and negation correspond to the natural transformations in the definition of a weakly distributive category, as explained above. The rules for & ($\oplus$, respectively) mirror the usual definition of final object and product (initial object and coproduct, respectively). Finally, the axioms and rules for the exponential ! (?, respectively) correspond to the comonad with a comonoid structure (monad with monoid structure, respectively).

```
fth ATOM is
  sort Atom .
endft
```

```
th LINLOG[X :: ATOM] is
  protecting PROP0[X] .
  sort Prop .
  ops 1 0 ⊥ ⊤ : -> Prop .
  op _⊗_ : Prop Prop -> Prop [assoc comm id: 1] .
  op _⅋_ : Prop Prop -> Prop [assoc comm id: ⊥] .
  op _⊕_ : Prop Prop -> Prop [assoc comm id: 0] .
```

---

[6] Cockett and Seely develop in [14] the more general case in which the tensor products are not assumed to be symmetric.

```
  op _&_ : Prop Prop -> Prop [assoc comm id: T] .
  op !_ : Prop -> Prop .
  op ?_ : Prop -> Prop .
  op [_] : Prop0 -> Prop .

  var A : Prop0 .
  *** Rules for negation
  rl 1 => [A] ⅋ [A⊥] .
  rl [A] ⊗ [A⊥] => ⊥ .

  vars P Q R : Prop .
  *** Rules for ⊗ and ⅋
  rl P ⊗ (Q ⅋ R) => (P ⊗ Q) ⅋ R .

  *** Rules for &
  rl P => T .
  rl P & Q => P .
  crl R => P & Q if R => P and R => Q .

  *** Rules for ⊕
  rl 0 => P .
  rl P => P ⊕ Q .
  crl P ⊕ Q => R if P => R and Q => R .

  *** Structural axioms and rules for !
  ax !(P & Q) = !P ⊗ !Q .
  ax !T = 1 .
  rl !P => P .
  rl !P => !!P .
  rl !P => 1 .
  rl !P => !P ⊗ !P .

  *** Structural axioms and rules for ?
  ax ?(P ⊕ Q) = ?P ⅋ ?Q .
  ax ?0 = ⊥ .
  rl P => ?P .
  rl ??P => ?P .
  rl ⊥ => ?P .
  rl ?P ⅋ ?P => ?P .
endt
```

A linear formula is built from a set of propositional constants using the logical constants and connectives of linear logic. Notice that linear implication $A \multimap B$ is not necessary because it can be defined as $A^{\perp} \, ⅋ \, B$. A linear theory T in propositional linear logic consists of a finite set C of propositional constants and a finite set S of sequents of the form $A_1, \ldots, A_n \vdash B_1, \ldots, B_m$, where each A_i and B_j is a linear formula built from the constants in C. The interpretation of such a theory $T = (C, S)$ in rewriting logic is as follows.

First, we define a functional theory to interpret the propositional constants in C. For example, if $C = \{a, b, c\}$ we would define

```
fth C is
  sort Atom .
  ops a b c : -> Atom .
endft
```

Then, we instantiate the parameterized theory LINLOG[X] with C, so that a linear formula A (with constants in C) is interpreted in LINLOG[C] as the term [A] of sort Prop. For example, the linear formula $(a \otimes b)^\perp \oplus (!(a \& c^\perp))^\perp$ is interpreted as the term

$$[(a \otimes b)^\perp \oplus (!(a \& c^\perp))^\perp]$$

whose negation normal form is

$$([a^\perp] \bindnasrepma [b^\perp]) \oplus ?([a^\perp] \oplus [c]).$$

Finally, we extend the module LINLOG[C] by adding a rule

$$\text{rl } [A1] \otimes \ldots \otimes [An] \Rightarrow [B1] \bindnasrepma \ldots \bindnasrepma [Bm] .$$

for each sequent $A_1, \ldots, A_n \vdash B_1, \ldots, B_m$ in the set S of sequents of T, obtaining in this way a rewrite theory LINLOG(T). The main result is the following conservativity theorem, which is proved in each direction by induction on the proof derivations in the corresponding logic, translating an axiom or rule of deduction in one logic to a derived rule in the other.

THEOREM 12. *[37] A sequent* $A_1, \ldots, A_n \vdash B_1, \ldots, B_m$ *is provable in linear logic from the axioms in a linear theory* T *if and only if the sequent*

$$[A1] \otimes \ldots \otimes [An] \longrightarrow [B1] \bindnasrepma \ldots \bindnasrepma [Bm]$$

is a LINLOG(T)*-rewrite, i.e., it is provable in rewriting logic from the rewrite theory* LINLOG(T).

Finally, in order to complete the map of logics, a model of LINLOG(T) must be mapped to a model of T. In Section 4.3.3 of [37], we show that a LINLOG(T)-system in the sense of (the order-sorted version of) Definition 6 consists of an algebra $\mathcal{A}$ interpreting all the structure of the functional theory PROPO[C], a category $\mathcal{C}$ with all the morphisms necessary to interpret the rewrite rules in the theory LINLOG[C] and the rules corresponding to all the sequents in S, and an inclusion $\mathcal{A} \hookrightarrow \mathcal{C}$. Then, the quotient of the full subcategory of $\mathcal{C}$ generated by $\mathcal{A}$ by a set of equations is a Girard category $\mathcal{L}$ that satisfies a linear sequent if and only if $\mathcal{C}$ satisfies the rewriting logic version of that sequent. In summary, we have a *conservative* map of logics

$$LinLogic \longrightarrow OSRWLogic.$$

As we have already mentioned, the map just described for propositional linear logic can be extended to first-order linear logic at the level of provability of formulas, that is, in terms of entailment systems [37]. The main idea is to internalize as operations in the theory the notions of free variables and substitution that are usually defined at the metalevel. Then, the typical definitions of such notions by structural induction on terms can be easily written down as equations in the theory, but, more importantly, we can consider terms *modulo* these axioms and we can also use the operation of substitution explicitly in the rules introducing or eliminating quantifiers. This equational treatment of quantification is very general and encompasses not only existential and universal quantification, but also lambda abstraction and other such binding mechanisms [31, 37].

There is another conservative map of entailment systems from first-order linear logic to rewriting logic, using a general technique that can be applied to any sequent calculus, be it for intuitionistic, classical, or any other logic [37]. We need an operation

```
op _|-_ : FormMset FormMset -> Sequent .
```

that turns two multisets of formulas (lists, or sets in other cases, depending on the structural rules of the sequent system in question) into a term representing a sequent, and a sort `Configuration` representing multisets of sequents, with a union operator written using empty syntax, that is, as juxtaposition. A sequent calculus rule

$$\frac{G_1 \vdash D_1, \ldots, G_n \vdash D_n}{G \vdash D}$$

then becomes a rewrite rule

```
rl (G1 |- D1) ... (Gn |- Dn) => (G |- D) .
```

on the sort `Configuration`.

We can then apply this method to a sequent presentation of first-order linear logic to obtain our desired conservative map of entailment systems into rewriting logic in this way.

This general method of viewing sequents as rewrite rules can be applied to systems more general than traditional sequent calculi. Thus, a "sequent" can for example be a sequent presentation of natural deduction, a term assignment system, or even any predicate defined by structural induction in some way such that the proof is a kind of tree. The general idea is to map a rule in the "sequent" system to a rewrite rule over a "configuration" of sequents or predicates, in such a way that the rewriting relation corresponds to provability of such a predicate. This idea is illustrated by means of several different examples in [37].

4.3 Horn logic with equality

Horn logic signatures are of the form (F, P), with F a set of function symbols and P a set of predicate symbols. In the order-sorted case such symbols have ranks $f : s_1 \ldots s_n \to s$, and $p : s_1 \ldots s_n$, specified by strings of sorts in the poset of sorts S. Models are F-algebras M together with, for each predicate symbol $p : s_1 \ldots s_n$, a subset $p_M \subseteq M_{s_1} \times \ldots \times M_{s_n}$, which can alternatively be viewed as a characteristic function $p_M : M_{s_1} \times \ldots \times M_{s_n} \longrightarrow Bool$ to the two element Boolean algebra $Bool$. Satisfaction of a Horn clause

$$q_1(\overline{u_1}), \ldots, q_n(\overline{u_n}) \Rightarrow p(\overline{t})$$

in a model M can be expressed as the functional inequality

$$(\dagger) \quad q_1(\overline{u_1})_M \ and \ \ldots \ and \ q_n(\overline{u_n})_M \ \leq \ p(\overline{t})_M$$

between the corresponding interpretations in M as characteristic functions of the conjunction of the premises and of the conclusion.

Horn logic is a particularly simple logic that does not use the full power of classical first order logic; it is therefore reasonable to allow interpretations of the predicate symbols p as "characteristic functions"

$$p_M : M_{s_1} \times \ldots \times M_{s_n} \longrightarrow M_{Prop}$$

into a partially ordered set M_{Prop} of "propositions" which can vary from model to model. We just require of any such poset the structure of having a top element $true : Prop$ and a binary associative and commutative "conjunction" operator $\_,\_: Prop \ Prop \longrightarrow Prop$ that is monotonic and has $true$ as its neutral element. Satisfaction of a Horn clause can then be defined by the functional inequality $(\dagger)$ just as before.

In addition, we can consider the generalization to Horn theories of the form (F, P, E, H) where E is a set of F-equations, and H is a set of Horn clauses involving the predicates in P but not equations (again, equations in E are viewed as structural axioms forming part of the signature). A model satisfies this theory when the underlying F-algebra satisfies all the equations in E and the model satisfies the Horn clauses in H.

A Horn theory $T = (F, P, E, H)$ is mapped to a rewrite theory

$$\Phi(T) = (F \cup P^\circ, E \cup ACI, \{x_{Prop} \longrightarrow true\} \cup H^\circ),$$

where

- $F \cup P^\circ$ is the order-sorted signature that extends F by adding the additional sort *Prop*, a constant *true* : *Prop*, a binary operator $\_ , \_$ on *Prop*, and, for each predicate symbol $p : s_1 \ldots s_n$ in P, an operator $p : s_1 \ldots s_n \longrightarrow$ *Prop*;

- *ACI* is the set of associativity, commutativity, and identity (*true*) structural axioms for the conjunction operator $\_ , \_$;

- H° is a set of rewrite rules such that a Horn clause of the form $p(\bar{t})$ produces the rewrite rule *true* $\longrightarrow p(\bar{t})$ whereas a Horn clause of the form $q_1(\overline{u_1}), \ldots, q_n(\overline{u_n}) \Rightarrow p(\bar{t})$ gives rise to the following rewrite rule: $q_1(\overline{u_1}), \ldots, q_n(\overline{u_n}) \longrightarrow p(\bar{t})$.

As for models, given a Horn theory T, a(n order-sorted) $\Phi(T)$-system consists of a category C_s for each sort s in the poset S, and a category $\mathcal{P}$ for the sort *Prop*, together with a collection of functors satisfying the equations in $\Phi(T)$ and natural transformations interpreting the rewrite rules in $\Phi(T)$. Such a system is mapped by the map of institutions relating Horn logic with equality and rewriting logic to the T-model consisting of the underlying (order-sorted) algebra structure on the family of sets of objects $\{|C_s| \mid s \in S\}$, and a poset obtained as a quotient of the category $\mathcal{P}$. A Horn clause $q_1(\overline{u_1}), \ldots, q_n(\overline{u_n}) \Rightarrow p(\bar{t})$ is satisfied by this T-model if and only if there is a morphism in $\mathcal{P}$ interpreting the rewrite $q_1(\overline{u_1}), \ldots, q_n(\overline{u_n}) \longrightarrow p(\bar{t})$, if and only if this rewriting logic sentence is satisfied by the original $\Phi(T)$-system. Thus, we have a *conservative* map of logics

$$OSHorn \longrightarrow OSRWLogic.$$

5 REPRESENTING CONCURRENT OBJECT-ORIENTED SYSTEMS

Concurrent object-oriented programming is a very active area of research. An important reason for this interest is the naturalness with which this style of programming can model concurrent interactions between objects in the real world. Therefore, from the perspective of logics of change, supporting a concurrent object-oriented modelling style seems a particularly attractive desideratum, because of the great naturalness with which many problems can thus be represented. However, the field of concurrent object-oriented programming seems at present to lack a clear, agreed-upon semantic basis.

Rewriting logic supports a logical theory of concurrent objects that addresses these conceptual needs in a very direct way. In the context of logics of action and change, where acting can often be most naturally conceptualized as changing the internal state of objects, this supports a flexible style of knowledge representation that is both logical and object-oriented. Since, as we have already shown, linear logic can be naturally expressed within rewriting logic, although the approaches are different, there is a connection with the treatment of objects by Andreoli and Pareschi in the Linear Objects language [2, 3].

We summarize here the key ideas regarding Maude's object-oriented modules; a full discussion of Maude's object-oriented aspects can be found in [48, 49].

An *object* in a given state can be represented as a term

```
< O : C | a1 : v1, ... , an : vn >
```

where O is the object's name, belonging to a set OId of object identifiers, C is its class, the ai's are the names of the object's *attributes*, and the vi's are their corresponding values, which typically are required to be in a sort appropriate for their corresponding attribute. The *configuration* is the distributed state of the concurrent object-oriented system and is represented as a multiset of objects and messages according to the following syntax:

```
subsorts Object Message < Configuration .
op __ : Configuration Configuration -> Configuration
                              [assoc comm id: null] .
```

where the operator __ (associative and commutative with identity null) is interpreted as multiset union, and where the sorts Object and Message are subsorts of Configuration and generate data of that sort by multiset union. The system evolves by concurrent ACI-rewriting of the configuration by means of rewrite rules specific to each particular system, whose lefthand and righthand sides may in general involve patterns for several objects and messages. By specializing to patterns involving only one object and one message, we can obtain an abstract, declarative, and truly concurrent version of the Actor model [1] (see [48, Section 4.7]).

Maude's syntax for object-oriented modules is illustrated by the object-oriented module SPREADSHEET below which specifies the concurrent behavior of objects in a very simple class Cell of cells in a spreadsheet, whose unique attribute is the value stored in the cell, set initially to zero. The cells are organized in a grid and are therefore identified by means of pairs (N,M) giving the row and column numbers. Moreover, for each row N there is a cell (N,total) that keeps track of the corresponding total, and similarly for each column M there is a cell (total,M). There is also a cell (total,total) providing the sum of all the values in all the cells in the spreadsheet. The spreadsheet may receive messages add(N,M,V) and sub(N,M,V) for adding or subtracting the amount V to the value stored in cell (N,M). We assume an already defined functional module NAT for natural numbers, with arithmetic operations and an ordering predicate _>=_.

After the keyword class, the name of the class (Cell in this case) is given, followed by a "|" and by a list of pairs of the form a : s separated by commas, where a is an attribute identifier and s is the sort inside which the values of such an attribute identifier must range in the given class. In this example, the only attribute of a cell is val, declared to be a value in Nat. The two kinds of messages involving cells are add and sub, whose user definable syntax is introduced by the keyword msg(s). The rewrite rules specify in a declarative way the behavior associated with these messages. The reader can compare this simple Maude program with the much more complex program developed by Chandy and Taylor in [12], which stimulated our alternative solution.

```
omod SPREADSHEET is
  protecting NAT .
  sort Name .
  subsort Nat < Name .
  op total : -> Name .
  op (_,_) : Name Name -> OId .
  class Cell | val : Nat .
  initially val : 0 .
  msgs add sub : Nat Nat Nat -> Message .
  vars M N V W X Y Z : Nat .

  rl add(N,M,V) <(N,M): Cell | val: W>
       <(total,total): Cell | val: X>
       <(N,total): Cell | val: Y>
       <(total,M): Cell | val: Z>
  => <(N,M): Cell | val: W + V>
       <(total,total): Cell | val: X + V>
       <(N,total): Cell | val: Y + V>
       <(total,M): Cell | val: Z + V> .

  crl sub(N,M,V) <(N,M): Cell | val: W>
       <(total,total): Cell | val: X>
       <(N,total): Cell | val: Y>
       <(total,M): Cell | val: Z>
  => <(N,M): Cell | val: W - V>
       <(total,total): Cell | val: X - V>
       <(N,total): Cell | val: Y - V>
       <(total,M): Cell | val: Z - V>
  if W >= V .
endom
```

The multiset structure of the configuration provides the top level distributed structure of the system and allows concurrent application of the rules. Intuitively, we can think of messages as "travelling" to come into contact with the objects to which they are sent and then causing "communication events" by application of rewrite rules. In rewriting logic, this travelling is accounted for in a very abstract way by the ACI structural axioms. This abstract level supports both synchronous and asynchronous communication and provides great freedom and flexibility to consider a variety of alternative implementations at lower levels. However, the reader should bear in mind that the values in the attributes of an object can also be computed by means of rewrite rules, and this adds yet another important level of concurrency to a concurrent object-oriented system, which might be called intra-object concurrency.

Although Maude provides convenient syntax for object-oriented modules, the syntax and semantics of such modules can be reduced to those of system modules, i.e., we can systematically translate an object-oriented module omod $\mathcal{O}$ endom into a corresponding system module mod $\mathcal{O}\#$ endm, where $\mathcal{O}\#$ is a theory in rewriting logic. A detailed account of this translation process can be found in [48].

Große *et al.* mention in [24] that their approach to planning problems can also be used in object-oriented programming (following some ideas in [2, 3]), and databases. The brief presentation above of object-oriented modules in Maude and the papers [48, 49] show the advantages that rewriting logic can offer in the field of concurrent object-oriented specification and programming. The advantages in the case of object-oriented databases have been investigated in [53].

We conclude this section with an example showing an object-oriented approach to a planning problem. Consider the 8-puzzle problem as presented in [18, p. 283]. There is a set of eight numbered tiles and a blank tile, arranged in a 3×3-grid. By moving the blank tile up, down, left, or right, the goal is to reach the state pictured on the right of the following figure, starting in an arbitrary state, like for example the one pictured on the left.

2	8	3
1		4
7	6	5

1	2	3
8		4
7	6	5

Each tile is represented as an object < (R,C) | value: N >, where R, C denote the row and column, respectively, and N denotes either a natural number between 1 and 8, or the marker blank. Sort constraints [50], which are introduced with the keyword sct and define a subsort by means of a condition, are used to make coordinates range between 1 and 3, and number values in tiles between 1 and 8. Movements are represented as messages sent to the tile configuration.

```
omod 8-PUZZLE is
  protecting NAT .
  sorts NumValue Value Coordinate .
  subsort Coordinate < Nat .
  vars C V : Nat .
  sct C : Coordinate if 3 >= C and C >= 1 .
  subsort NumValue < Nat .
  sct V : NumValue if 8 >= V and V >= 1 .
  subsort NumValue < Value .
  op blank : -> Value .
  op (_,_) : Coordinate Coordinate -> OId .
  class Tile | value : Value .
  msgs left right up down : -> Message .
  vars N M R : Coordinate .
  var P : NumValue .

  crl left < (N,R) | value: blank > < (N,M) | value: P >
      => < (N,M) | value: blank > < (N,R) | value: P >
      if R = M + 1 .
  crl right < (N,R) | value: blank > < (N,M) | value: P >
      => < (N,M) | value: blank > < (N,R) | value: P >
      if R = M - 1 .
  crl up < (R,M) | value: blank > < (N,M) | value: P >
      => < (N,M) | value: blank > < (R,M) | value: P >
      if R = N - 1 .
  crl down < (R,M) | value: blank > < (N,M) | value: P >
      => < (N,M) | value: blank > < (R, M) | value: P >
      if R = N + 1 .
endom
```

The goal is represented by the following term (a picture representation is clearly preferable):

```
< (1,3) | value: 1 > < (2,3) | value: 2 >
< (3,3) | value: 3 > < (1,2) | value: 8 >
< (2,2) | value: blank > < (3,2) | value: 4 >
< (1,1) | value: 7 > < (2,1) | value: 6 >
< (3,1) | value: 5 >.
```

A plan that solves the planning problem in the picture above is of course

```
up;left;down;right
```

The corresponding 8-PUZZLE-rewrite is left as an exercise for the interested reader.

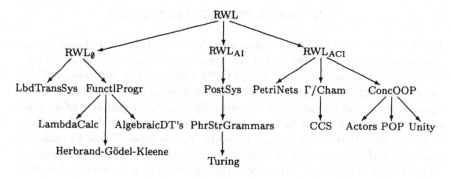

Figure 2. Unification of models of concurrent computation.

5.1 Generality of rewriting logic as a model of concurrent computation

Concurrent rewriting is a very general model of concurrency from which many other models can be obtained by specialization. Except for Petri nets, that were discussed in Section 2.3, and concurrent objet-oriented programming, that has been discussed in Section 5, we refer the reader to [46] for a detailed discussion of the remaining models, and summarize here such specializations using Figure 2, where RWL stands for rewriting logic, the arrows indicate specializations, and the subscripts ∅, AI, and ACI stand for syntactic rewriting, rewriting modulo associativity and identity, and rewriting modulo associativity, commutativity, and identity, respectively.

Within syntactic rewriting we have labelled transition systems, which are used in interleaving approaches to concurrency; functional programming (in particular Maude's functional modules) corresponds to the case of *confluent*[7] rules, and includes the lambda calculus and the Herbrand-Gödel-Kleene theory of recursive functions. Rewriting modulo AI yields Post systems and related grammar formalisms, including Turing machines. Besides the general treatment by ACI-rewriting of concurrent object-oriented programming, briefly described in Section 5, that contains Actors as a special case [1], rewriting modulo ACI includes Petri nets [58], the Gamma language of Banâtre and Le Mètayer [5], and Berry and Boudol's *chemical abstract machine* [7] (which itself specializes to CCS [55]; see [7] and also the treatment in Section 5.3 of [37]), as well as Unity's model of computation [11]; another special case is the POPs and POTs of Engelfriet, Leih, and Rozenberg, which are higher level Petri nets for actors [16].

---

[7]Although not reflected in the picture, rules confluent *modulo* equations E are also functional.

6 THE FRAME PROBLEM REVISITED

Hölldobler reviews in [28] the three approaches to deductive planning discussed in Section 3.1, namely, Bibel's linear connection method, the equational logic programming approach of Hölldobler and Schneeberger, and the linear logic approach of Masseron *et al.*, emphasizing the interest of these approaches in order to solve the frame problem, i.e., the problem of formalizing the assumption that facts are preserved by an action unless the action explicitly says that a certain fact becomes true or false. These formalisms need not explicitly state frame axioms, because they treat facts as resources which are produced and consumed. This question is also discussed in the introduction of [23].

It should be clear from our discussions in previous sections that the advantages of these approaches are also shared by rewriting logic. We have already pointed out ways in which rewriting logic compares favorably with these three formalisms, not only because it subsumes them in a formally precise way by means of conservative maps of logics as explained in Section 4, but also because the rewriting logic rules automatically take care of tasks such as instantiating variables and preserving context. However, even in these approaches, the preservation of certain properties may sometimes have to be made explicit.

Consider the following different representation of the blocksworld, where there is no explicit robot arm to move the blocks around [18, Chapter 11].

```
fth TRIV is
    sort BlockId .
endft

mod BLOCKWORLD2[X :: TRIV] is
    sort Prop .
    op table : BlockId -> Prop .        *** block in on the table
    op on : BlockId BlockId -> Prop . *** block A is on block B
    op clear : BlockId -> Prop .        *** block is clear
    sort State .
    subsort Prop < State .
    op 1 : -> State .
    op _⊗_ : State State -> State [assoc comm id: 1] .
    vars X Y Z : BlockId .
    rl move(X,Y,Z) : clear(X) ⊗ clear(Z) ⊗ on(X,Y)
        => clear(X) ⊗ clear(Y) ⊗ on(X,Z) .
    rl unstack(X,Y) : clear(X) ⊗ on(X,Y)
        =>  clear(X) ⊗ table(X) ⊗ clear(Y) .
    rl stack(X,Y) : table(X) ⊗ clear(X) ⊗ clear(Y)
        => clear(X) ⊗ on(X,Y) .
endm
```

We create a world with three blocks $\{a, b, c\}$ as before

```
fmod BLOCKS3 is
  sort BlockId .
  ops a b c : -> BlockId .
endfm
```

```
make WORLD2 is BLOCKWORLD2[BLOCKS3] endmk
```

Consider the states pictured in the following figure, described by the following two terms

```
clear(c) ⊗ clear(b) ⊗ table(a) ⊗ table(b) ⊗ on(c,a)
```

```
clear(c) ⊗ clear(a) ⊗ table(a) ⊗ table(b) ⊗ on(c,b)
```

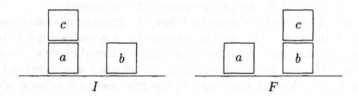

There are several plans that move the blocks from the state I to F, like for example unstack(c,a);stack(c,b). A shorter plan is move(c,a,b) corresponding to the following WORLD2-rewrite:

```
clear(c) ⊗ clear(b) ⊗ table(a) ⊗ table(b) ⊗ on(c,a)
  =
clear(c) ⊗ clear(b) ⊗ on(c,a) ⊗ table(a) ⊗ table(b)
——→      Cong[Repl[move(c,a,b)], Refl]
clear(c) ⊗ clear(a) ⊗ on(c,b) ⊗ table(a) ⊗ table(b)
  =
clear(c) ⊗ clear(a) ⊗ table(a) ⊗ table(b) ⊗ on(c,b)
```

There are two things to point out. First, as discussed above, we do not need frame axioms for the propositions that are not mentioned in a rule. In this example, the *Congruence* and *Reflexivity* rules preserve the subterm table(a) ⊗ table(b) from the description of I to the description of F. However, we have to repeat in the consequent of the rule move(X,Y,Z) the proposition clear(X) that appears as a condition on the antecedent. Otherwise, the resulting term would be

```
clear(a) ⊗ on(c,b) ⊗ table(a) ⊗ table(b)
```

which does not describe completely the state F. Of course, the proposition clear(X) is an essential precondition of the action and needs to be made explicit in the antecedent; otherwise, it would be preserved by the *Congruence* and *Reflexivity* rules as desired, but the rule could also be applied in states in which it should not be allowed, like for example when there is another block on top of block X. The same implicit "frame axioms" for the proposition clear(X) can be seen in the rules stack(X,Y) and unstack(X,Y). Hölldobler and Schneeberger also mention this in [29], with respect to the property red(X).

The problem, therefore, is that, even in a context of resource logics, one may have to make explicit the preservation of some properties. In this sense, a residual of the frame problem remains.

Let us rewrite this blocksworld example in an object-oriented style to consider the question of how to best deal with the preservation of certain properties in a change from another perspective. A block is represented as an object with two attributes, under, saying whether it is under another block or it is clear, and on, saying whether the block is on top of another block or is on the table. Actions are represented as messages.

Maude's object-oriented modules follow the convention that those attributes of an object that are not relevant for a given rule need not be mentioned in that rule. Specifically, in object-oriented modules we allow rules where the attributes appearing in the lefthand and righthand side patterns for an object O mentioned in the rule need not exhaust all the object's attributes, but can instead be in any two arbitrary subsets of the object's attributes. Using the notation $\overline{a : v}$ for a list of attribute-value pairs a1:v1, ... , an:vn, we can picture this as follows

$$\ldots < 0 \; : \; C \; | \; \overline{al : vl}, \; \overline{ab : vb} > \ldots$$
$$\Rightarrow \ldots < 0 \; : \; C \; | \; \overline{ab : vb'}, \; \overline{ar : vr} > \ldots$$

where $\overline{al}$ are the attributes appearing only on the *left*, $\overline{ab}$ are the attributes appearing on *both* sides, and $\overline{ar}$ are the attributes appearing only on the *right*. What this abbreviates by convention is a rule of the form

$$\ldots < 0 \; : \; C \; | \; \overline{al : vl}, \; \overline{ab : vb}, \; \overline{ar : X}, \; Atts > \ldots$$
$$\Rightarrow \ldots < 0 \; : \; C \; | \; \overline{al : vl}, \; \overline{ab : vb'}, \; \overline{ar : vr}, \; Atts > \ldots$$

where the $\overline{X}$ are new "don't care" variables and Atts is a variable matching the remaining attribute-value pairs. The attributes mentioned only on the left are preserved unchanged, the original values of attributes mentioned only on the right don't matter, and all attributes not explicitly mentioned are left unchanged.

For example, the unstack rule

```
rl unstack(X,Y) < X : Block | under: clear, on: Y >
    < Y : Block | under: X >
=> < X : Block | on: table>
    < Y : Block | under: clear > .
```

in the module OOBLOCKWORLD2[X] below is an abbreviation for the following
rule

```
var D : Down .
rl unstack(X,Y) < X : Block | under: clear, on: Y, Atts >
   < Y : Block | under: X, on: D, Atts' >
=> < X : Block | under: clear, on: table, Atts >
   < Y : Block | under: clear, on: D, Atts' > .
```

Note the "don't care" variable D and the attribute under: clear in the
object X. Therefore, this convention allows us to write the rule for the action unstack(X,Y) in a way that makes the "frame axiom" for clear(X)
unnecessary.

```
omod OOBLOCKWORLD2[X :: TRIV] is
  subsort BlockId < OId .
  subsort BlockId < Up .
  subsort BlockId < Down .
  op clear : -> Up .
  op table : -> Down .
  class Block | under : Up, on : Down .
  msg move : OId OId OId -> Message .
  msgs unstack stack : OId OId -> Message .
  vars X Y Z : BlockId .
  rl move(X,Y,Z) < X : Block | under: clear, on: Y >
     < Y : Block | under: X > < Z : Block | under: clear >
  => < X : Block | on: Z > < Y : Block | under: clear >
     < Z : Block | under: X > .
  rl unstack(X,Y) < X : Block | under: clear, on: Y >
     < Y : Block | under: X >
  => < X : Block | on: table>
     < Y : Block | under: clear > .
  rl stack(X,Y) < X : Block | under: clear, on: table>
     < Y : Block | under: clear >
  => < X : Block | on: Y > < Y : Block | under: X > .
endom
```

After the instantiation

```
make OOWORLD2 is OOBLOCKWORLD2[BLOCKS3] endmk
```

the states I and F are described respectively by the following configurations:

```
< a : Block | under: c, on: table >
< c : Block | under: clear, on: a >
< b : Block | under: clear, on: table >
```

```
< c : Block | under: clear, on: b >
< b : Block | under: c, on: table >
< a : Block | under: clear, on: table >
```

Another way in which the object-oriented point of view supported by rewriting logic becomes very helpful in the context of the frame problem is by its support of class inheritance, since this permits a modular and reusable approach to the specification of the axioms for change, which do not have to be redefined each time that new features of objects are introduced. This issue is discussed in detail in [48, 49]; we illustrate it here by means of a simple example. Suppose that the blocksworld is further refined so that now blocks can have colors, say red, blue, and yellow. Of course, we want the rules for manipulating blocks to remain "exactly as before." This is trivially achieved by class inheritance as illustrated by the module

```
omod OOBLOCKWORLD2'[X :: TRIV] is
   extending OOBLOCKWORLD[X] .
   sort Color .
   ops red blue yellow : -> Color .
   class ColoredBlock | color : Color .
   subclass ColoredBlock < Block .
endom
```

The key point is that the rules given for the class Block of blocks also apply without changes to blocks in the subclass ColoredBlock of colored blocks. This is because, thanks to our conventions, extra variables of the form Atts, Atts', etc., matching whatever extra attributes an object may have, were added to the objects in rules once and for all in the expanded version of the rule, when each rule was declared in the superclass. These variables will now match the color attribute of the colored blocks, or any further attributes that might later be declared if other subclasses are defined.

In conclusion, we can say that the rules of rewriting logic together with the conventions and inheritance mechanisms adopted in Maude's object-oriented modules provide a logical framework in which the frame problem disappears. Although we have approached the question from an object-oriented perspective, this intuition was in a sense already present in the original work by McCarthy and Hayes [41], where the frame problem was first articulated, as the following quote shows:

> "We see two ways out of this difficulty. The first is to introduce the notion of frame, like the state vector in McCarthy (1962). A number of fluents are declared as attached to the frame and the effect of an action is described by telling which fluents are changed, all others being presumed unchanged."

7 CONCLUDING REMARKS

We have proposed rewriting logic as a simple, yet very flexible and expressive, logic of concurrent change in which a wide variety of systems can be naturally represented. We have illustrated this flexibility with an ample collection of examples. A variety of logics of change proposed by other authors, including linear logic and Horn logic with equality, have been shown to be subsumed and unified by rewriting logic in natural ways. We have also shown how change in concurrent object-oriented systems can be naturally represented in rewriting logic. Finally, we have argued that rewriting logic provides a satisfactory solution to the frame problem.

Much work remains ahead. Although the language design and object-oriented aspects of Maude are reasonably well advanced, and an interpreter implementation [13] has been demonstrated and is currently used in a number of applications, its modularity and parameterization mechanisms and its specification capabilities, as well as new interpreter features, should all be further developed. We are also developing a compiler for parallel execution of a sublanguage called Simple Maude [32, 33]. The MaudeLog extension will require more detailed study of the deduction and operational semantic aspects as well as extra implementation work. In addition, the precise relationships with other formalisms such as concurrent logic programming [62] and concurrent constraint programming [60] should be investigated.

Narciso Martí-Oliet
Departamento de Sistemas Informáticos y Programación
Facultad de Ciencias Matemáticas
Universidad Complutense de Madrid, Spain

José Meseguer
SRI International, Menlo Park and
Center for the Study of Language and Information, Stanford University

ACKNOWLEDGEMENTS

A first draft of this paper was distributed during an invited lecture by the same title at the ESPRIT Workshop on Logics of Action and Change held in Lisbon, Portugal, in January 1993. We thank the organizers of the workshop and all the participants for the opportunity to discuss our ideas in such a congenial and stimulating environment, and for their valuable suggestions.

We would also like to thank Vladimir Alexiev, Gerd Große, Patrick Hayes, David Israel, Patrick Lincoln, Hitoshi Matsubara, John McCarthy, Hideyuki Nakashima, Carolyn Talcott, and Tomás Uribe for helpful discussions on planning problems, the frame problem, and linear logic, and for their comments on a previous version of this paper.

The work reported in this paper has been supported by Office of Naval Research Contracts N00014-90-C-0086 and N00014-92-C-0518, National Science Foundation Grant CCR-9224005, and by the Information Technology Promotion Agency, Japan, as a part of the Industrial Science and Technology Frontier Program "New Models for Software Architecture" sponsored by NEDO (New Energy and Industrial Technology Development Organization). The first author was supported by a Postdoctoral Research Fellowship of the Spanish Ministry for Education and Science, while he was an International Fellow at the Computer Science Laboratory of SRI International, Menlo Park, and a visiting scholar at the Center for the Study of Language and Information, Stanford University.

REFERENCES

[1] G. Agha, *Actors*, The MIT Press, 1986.

[2] J.-M. Andreoli and R. Pareschi, LO and behold! Concurrent structured processes, in: N. Meyrowitz (ed.), *Proc. OOPSLA-ECOOP'90*, ACM Press, 1990, pages 44–56.

[3] J.-M. Andreoli and R. Pareschi, Linear Objects: Logical processes with built-in inheritance, *New Generation Computing* 9, 1991, pages 445–473.

[4] A. Asperti, *A logic for concurrency*, unpublished manuscript, November 1987.

[5] J.-P. Banâtre and D. Le Métayer, The Gamma model and its discipline of programming, *Science of Computer Programming* 15, 1990, pages 55–77.

[6] M. Barr, *∗-Autonomous Categories*, LNM 752, Springer-Verlag, 1979.

[7] G. Berry and G. Boudol, The chemical abstract machine, *Theoretical Computer Science* 96, 1992, pages 217–248.

[8] W. Bibel, A deductive solution for plan generation, *New Generation Computing* 4, 1986, pages 115–132.

[9] C. Brown, *Relating Petri nets to formulae of linear logic*, Technical report ECS-LFCS-89-87, Laboratory for Foundations of Computer Science, University of Edinburgh, June 1989.

[10] S. Brüning, G. Große, S. Hölldobler, J. Schneeberger, U. Sigmund, and M. Thielscher, Disjunction in plan generation by equational logic programming, in: A. Horz (ed.), *Beiträge zum 7. Workshop Plannen und Konfigurieren*, Arbeitspapiere der GMD 723, 1993, pages 18–26.

[11] K. M. Chandy and J. Misra, *Parallel Program Design: A Foundation*, Addison-Wesley, 1988.

[12] K. M. Chandy and S. Taylor, *An Introduction to Parallel Programming*, Jones and Bartlett Publishers, 1992.

[13] M. Clavel, S. Eker, P. Lincoln, and J. Meseguer, Principles of Maude, in: J. Meseguer (ed.), *Proc. First Int. Workshop on Rewriting Logic and its Applications, Asilomar, California*, Electronic Notes in Theoretical Computer Science 4, Elsevier, September 1996. URL http://www1.elsevier.nl/mcs/tcs/pc/volume4.htm

[14] J. R. B. Cockett and R. A. G. Seely, Weakly distributive categories, in: M. P. Fourman, P. T. Johnstone, and A. M. Pitts (eds.), *Applications of Categories in Computer Science*, Cambridge University Press, 1992, pages 45–65.

[15] P. Degano, J. Meseguer, and U. Montanari, Axiomatizing the algebra of net computations and processes, *Acta Informatica* 33, 1996, pages 641–667.

[16] J. Engelfriet, G. Leih, and G. Rozenberg, Net-based description of parallel object-based systems, or POTs and POPs, in: J. W. de Bakker, W. P. de Roever, and G. Rozenberg (eds.), *Proc. REX School/Workshop on Foundations of Object-Oriented Languages, Noordwijkerhout, The Netherlands, May/June 1990*, LNCS 489, Springer-Verlag, 1991, pages 229–273.

[17] R. E. Fikes and N. J. Nilsson, STRIPS: A new approach to the application of theorem proving to problem solving, *Artificial Intelligence* 2, 1971, pages 189–208.

[18] M. R. Genesereth and N. J. Nilsson, *Logical Foundations of Artificial Intelligence*, Morgan Kaufmann Publishers, 1987.

[19] J.-Y. Girard, Linear logic, *Theoretical Computer Science* 50, 1987, pages 1–102.

[20] J. A. Goguen and R. M. Burstall, Institutions: Abstract model theory for specification and programming, *Journal of the Association for Computing Machinery* 39(1), 1992, pages 95–146.

[21] J. A. Goguen and J. Meseguer, Order-sorted algebra I: Equational deduction for multiple inheritance, overloading, exceptions and partial operations, *Theoretical Computer Science* 105, 1992, pages 217–273.

[22] J. A. Goguen, T. Winkler, J. Meseguer, K. Futatsugi, and J.-P. Jouannaud, *Introducing OBJ*, Technical report SRI-CSL-92-03, Computer Science Laboratory, SRI International, March 1992. To appear in J. A. Goguen and G. Malcolm (eds.), *Software Engineering with OBJ: Algebraic Specification in Practice*, Cambridge University Press.

[23] G. Große, S. Hölldobler, and J. Schneeberger, Linear deductive planning, *Journal of Logic and Computation* 6(2), 1996, pages 233–262.

[24] G. Große, S. Hölldobler, J. Schneeberger, U. Sigmund, and M. Thielscher, Equational logic programming, actions, and change, in: K. Apt (ed.), *Proc. Int. Joint Conf. and Symp. on Logic Programming*, The MIT Press, 1992, pages 177–191.

[25] C. Gunter and V. Gehlot, *Nets as tensor theories*, Technical report MS-CIS-89-68 Logic & Computation 17, Department of Computer and Information Science, University of Pennsylvania, October 1989.

[26] P. J. Hayes, The second naive physics manifesto, in: J. R. Hobbs and R. C. Moore (eds.), *Formal Theories of the Commonsense World*, Ablex Publishing Corp., 1985, pages 1–36. Reprinted in: R. J. Brachman and H. J. Levesque (eds.), *Readings in Knowledge Representation*, Morgan Kaufmann Publishers, 1985, pages 467–485.

[27] P. J. Hayes, What the frame problem is and isn't, in: Z. W. Pylyshyn (ed.), *The Robot's Dilemma: The Frame Problem in Artificial Intelligence*, Ablex Publishing Corp., 1987, pages 123–137.

[28] S. Hölldobler, On deductive planning and the frame problem, in: A. Voronkov (ed.), *Logic Programming and Automated Reasoning, St. Petersburg, Russia, July 1992*, LNAI 624, Springer-Verlag, 1992, pages 13–29.

[29] S. Hölldobler and J. Schneeberger, A new deductive approach to planning, *New Generation Computing* 8, 1990, pages 225–244.

[30] L.-E. Janlert, Modeling change—The frame problem, in: Z. W. Pylyshyn (ed.), *The Robot's Dilemma: The Frame Problem in Artificial Intelligence*, Ablex Publishing Corp., 1987, pages 1–40.

[31] C. Laneve and U. Montanari, Axiomatizing permutation equivalence, *Mathematical Structures in Computer Science* 6(3), 1996, pages 219–249.

[32] P. Lincoln, N. Martí-Oliet, and J. Meseguer, Specification, transformation, and programming of concurrent systems in rewriting logic, in: G. E. Blelloch, K. M. Chandy, and S. Jagannathan (eds.), *Specification of Parallel Algorithms, DIMACS Workshop, May 1994*, DIMACS Series in Discrete Mathematics and Theoretical Computer Science 18, American Mathematical Society, 1994, pages 309–339.

[33] P. Lincoln, N. Martí-Oliet, J. Meseguer, and L. Ricciulli, Compiling rewriting onto SIMD and MIMD/SIMD machines, in: C. Halatsis *et al.* (eds.), *Proc. PARLE'94, Sixth Int. Conf. on Parallel Architectures and Languages Europe, Athens, Greece, July 1994*, LNCS 817, Springer-Verlag, 1994, pages 37–48.

[34] S. Mac Lane, *Categories for the Working Mathematician*, Springer-Verlag, 1971.

[35] N. Martí-Oliet and J. Meseguer, From Petri nets to linear logic, *Mathematical Structures in Computer Science* **1**, 1991, pages 69–101.

[36] N. Martí-Oliet and J. Meseguer, From Petri nets to linear logic through categories: A survey, *International Journal of Foundations of Computer Science* **2**(4), 1991, pages 297–399.

[37] N. Martí-Oliet and J. Meseguer, *Rewriting logic as a logical and semantic framework*, Technical report SRI-CSL-93-05, Computer Science Laboratory, SRI International, August 1993. To appear in D. M. Gabbay (ed.), *Handbook of Philosophical Logic*, Kluwer Academic Publishers.

[38] N. Martí-Oliet and J. Meseguer, General logics and logical frameworks, in: D. Gabbay (ed.), *What Is a Logical System?*, Oxford University Press, 1994, pages 355–392.

[39] M. Masseron, C. Tollu, and J. Vauzeilles, Generating plans in linear logic, in: K. V. Nori and C. E. Veni Madhavan (eds.), *Foundations of Software Technology and Theoretical Computer Science, Bangalore, India, December 1990*, LNCS 472, Springer-Verlag, 1990, pages 63–75.

[40] M. Masseron, C. Tollu, and J. Vauzeilles, Generating plans in linear logic I: Actions as proofs, *Theoretical Computer Science* **113**(2), 1993, pages 349–370.

[41] J. McCarthy and P. J. Hayes, Some philosophical problems from the standpoint of artificial intelligence, in: B. Meltzer and D. Michie (eds.), *Machine Intelligence 4*, Edinburgh University Press, 1969, pages 463–502.

[42] D. McDermott, AI, logic, and the frame problem, in: F. M. Brown (ed.), *Proc. 1987 Workshop on the Frame Problem in Artificial Intelligence*, Morgan Kaufmann Publishers, 1987, pages 105–118.

[43] D. V. McDermott, Logic, problem solving, and deduction, in: J. F. Traub *et al.* (eds.), *Annual Review of Computer Science, Volume 2*, Annual Reviews Inc., 1987, pages 187–229.

[44] J. Meseguer, General logics, in: H.-D. Ebbinghaus *et al.* (eds.), *Logic Colloquium'87*, North-Holland, 1989, pages 275–329.

[45] J. Meseguer, A logical theory of concurrent objects, in: N. Meyrowitz (ed.), *Proc. OOPSLA-ECOOP'90*, ACM Press, 1990, pages 101–115.

[46] J. Meseguer, Conditional rewriting logic as a unified model of concurrency, *Theoretical Computer Science* **96**, 1992, pages 73–155.

[47] J. Meseguer, Multiparadigm logic programming, in: H. Kirchner and G. Levi (eds.), *Proc. Third Int. Conf. on Algebraic and Logic Programming, Volterra, Italy, September 1992*, LNCS 632, Springer-Verlag, 1992, pages 158–200.

[48] J. Meseguer, A logical theory of concurrent objects and its realization in the Maude language, in: G. Agha, P. Wegner, and A. Yonezawa (eds.), *Research Directions in Object-Based Concurrency*, The MIT Press, 1993, pages 314–390.

[49] J. Meseguer, Solving the inheritance anomaly in concurrent object-oriented programming, in: O. M. Nierstrasz (ed.), *Proc. ECOOP'93, 7th European Conf., Kaiserslautern, Germany, July 1993*, LNCS 707, Springer-Verlag, 1993, pages 220–246.

[50] J. Meseguer and J. A. Goguen, Order-sorted algebra solves the constructor-selector, multiple representation and coercion problems, *Information and Computation* **104**, 1993, pages 114–158.

[51] J. Meseguer, J. A. Goguen, and G. Smolka, Order-sorted unification, *Journal of Symbolic Computation* **8**, 1989, pages 383–413.

[52] J. Meseguer and U. Montanari, Petri nets are monoids, *Information and Computation* **88**, 1990, pages 105–155.

[53] J. Meseguer and X. Qian, A logical semantics for object-oriented databases, in: P. Buneman and S. Jajodia (eds.), *Proc. 1993 ACM SIGMOD, Int. Conf. on Management of Data*, *SIGMOD Record* **22**(2), June 1993, pages 89–98.

[54] J. Meseguer and T. Winkler, Parallel programming in Maude, in: J. P. Banâtre and D. Le Métayer (eds.), *Research Directions in High-Level Parallel Programming Languages*, LNCS 574, Springer-Verlag, 1992, pages 253–293.

[55] R. Milner, *Communication and Concurrency*, Prentice Hall, 1989.

[56] N. J. Nilsson, Logic and artificial intelligence, *Artificial Intelligence* **47**, 1991, pages 31–56.

[57] G. Reichwein, J. L. Fiadeiro, and T. Maibaum, Modular reasoning about change in an object-oriented framework, abstract presented at the *Workshop Logic & Change at GWAI'92*, September 1992.

[58] W. Reisig, *Petri Nets: An Introduction*, Springer-Verlag, 1985.

[59] E. Sandewall, *Features and fluents*, Research report LiTH-IDA-R-92-30, Department of Computer and Information Science, Linköping University, Sweden, September 1992.

[60] V. J. Saraswat, *Concurrent Constraint Programming*, The MIT Press, 1992.

[61] R. A. G. Seely, Linear logic, *-autonomous categories and cofree coalgebras, in: J. W. Gray and A. Scedrov (eds.), *Categories in Computer Science and Logic, Boulder, June 1987*, Contemporary Mathematics 92, American Mathematical Society, 1989, pages 371–382.

[62] E. Shapiro, The family of concurrent logic programming languages, *ACM Computing Surveys* **21**, 1989, pages 412–510.

MICHAEL WOLLOWSKI AND ERIC HAMMER

HETEROGENEOUS SYSTEMS FOR MODELING DYNAMIC WORLDS

1 INTRODUCTION

The design of *general* problem solvers and general purpose representations has been a driving force in the field of artificial intelligence since its inception (see for example [26, 1, 24, 29]). While there are valid concerns about generality, an equally important issue is efficiency of inference. Special purpose representations are known to be good at that and have been used widely in Computer Science and Artificial Intelligence. We propose the use of heterogeneous systems for modeling dynamic worlds. A heterogeneous system is one that employs several kinds of representations. In particular, we are interested in systems that use sentential and diagrammatic languages in parallel. Diagrams are common place in communicating information and for problem solving (see newspapers, reports, and papers and books written on planning, qualitative reasoning, etc. [27, 8]. By combining special purpose diagrammatic representations with general purpose sentential representations we hope to get the best of both worlds, generality and efficiency.

There has been some previous work on the use of diagrammatic representations in AI, most notably by [14, 30, 21, 20]. Recently, there has been a renewed interest in those kinds of representations[1] and in particular in integrating several forms of representation [4, 6, 5, 25].

In this paper, we first discuss the benefits and limitations of using special-purpose formalisms to model dynamic worlds where these representations include diagrams, certain types of linguistic representations, and also more causally-charged representations. The benefits include being able to hardwire some of the inferential burden characteristic of reasoning about dynamic worlds into the formalism itself, as discussed by Haugeland [17]. We also briefly discuss the possibility of achieving these benefits in practice.

Throughout the paper we emphasize the importance of "heterogeneity" for the topic of special-purpose formalisms, where this concerns the semantic and syntactic interactions between two or more different types of representations, for example between language and diagrams, between one type of diagram and another, and so on. Heterogeneity is one of the most important topics in the area of representation and computation since by their very definition special-purpose representational systems are limited in their range

---

[1]For example, the 1992 AAAI Spring Symposium on Reasoning with Diagrammatic Representations.

R. Pareschi and B. Fronhöfer (eds.), Dynamic Worlds, 55–72.
© 1999 Kluwer Academic Publishers.

of applicability. Therefore, to be of much practical use, a single such system cannot be used alone; rather, two or more different types of representations must be allowed to work in tandem. Moreover, this must be done in such a way that one can retain the domain-specific advantages of special-purpose formalisms while at the same time handling a large enough range of cases to be of use. There are many theoretical and practical issues that arise in the topic of heterogeneity, a few of which we discuss (see also [4, 7, 16, 25]).

As a case study, we give an analysis of a special-purpose representational system for planning in a dynamic world. The system is a heterogeneous one, including both diagrammatic and linguistic components. We discuss the syntax, semantics, and rules of inference for the system and briefly examine its properties. This sort of formal study of special-purpose representational systems is important for reasons including the following: (1) verifying the correctness or completeness of an implementation of such a system depends first upon having a precise syntax and semantics and thereby a precise definition of such metatheoretic properties; (2) the careful formal analysis of a special-purpose system is a first step towards an implementation of the system in question, since it makes clear what formal properties the implementation must capture; and (3) the complexity of such a system can be studied in a precise manner only in light of such an analysis, since the notion of an inferential "step" will then have been made clear, as will have the complexity of each such step. This sort of formal treatment of diagrams and other special-purpose formalisms also runs contrary to previous work on the topic as in [14, 30, 21, 20] where they are treated as mere heuristic device for reducing search and occasionally eliminating paths inconsistent with a diagram. Even though diagrams have been used in essential ways in these cases, they still were encoded in a sentential language, thereby loosing the structure which is one of the defining marks of diagrams. We claim that one go further and actually use representations that carry over more of the structure of the diagram and thereby alleviating inferential burden. In this context we suggest and investigate the use of bit-matrices and parallel computers.

We finally discuss what seem to be the most pressing and important issues in the area of diagrammatic and other types of special-purpose formalisms. These include the theoretical analysis of heterogeneity. How are different components to interact? How are tasks to be allocated between different components? Should there be some most general component subsuming all the others in expressive power? What is the role of linguistic formalisms with regard to other types? We also discuss the use of diagrams as syntactic representations of semantic objects.

2   MODELING SPATIAL RELATIONSHIPS IN DYNAMIC WORLDS

In an important paper Haugeland [17] argues that diagrammatic representations can avoid certain instances of the frame problem [19]. The sorts of
examples he considers concern the relative spatial locations of objects. Suppose some such information is represented linguistically, say by north(A,B)
∧ west(C,B). Implicit in this information is southwest(C,A). However, if
for some reason the position of A were to change so that south(A,B) were
to hold, southwest(C,A) would then be inconsistent with the new state of
the world, an inconsistency that would have to be explicitly inferred. The
computation of such side effects of an action gives rise to the frame problem
and can become very costly.

Haugeland goes on to point out that a good diagrammatic representation
of the same information can make this sort of extra inference of side effects
unnecessary. Suppose, for example, the information is represented in a
map-like form as in figure 1.

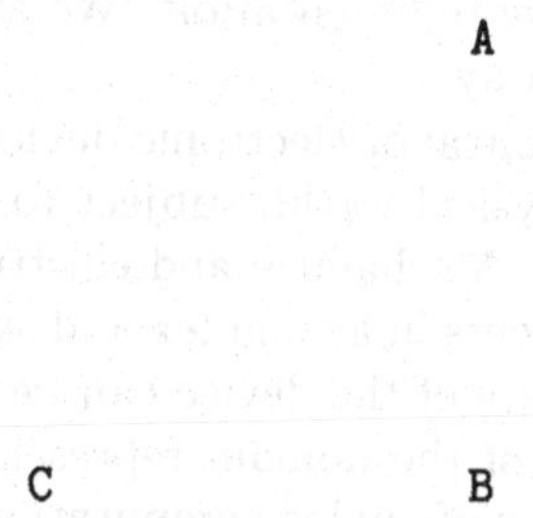

A

C   B

Figure 1. Relative spatial positions of three objects.

With this sort of representation, were A to be moved below of B, one would
have in the process also updated the implicit information that
southwest(C,A); one would not need to explicitly infer that fact.

The desirable properties of this sort of representation are due to the
close connection between the diagram and the domain being represented.
The diagram does not simply describe the domain; it displays it. It serves
to recreate what it is representing. The logical relationships between the
properties of being left of, being right of, being above, and being below
exactly mirror the corresponding relationships between the properties they
represent: being west of, being east of, being north of, and being south of.
Therefore, by manipulating the diagram one is doing the next best thing to
manipulating the domain itself. The spatial side effects of any given action
are had for free.

Representations in which the syntactic structure preserves the structure of what is represented are called "homomorphic" in [4, 7]. People find them very easy to use, as can be seen from the use of diagrams, graphs, pictures, and so on in newspapers, reports, and most of the literature on planning and qualitative reasoning itself [27, 8]. We are arguing in the present paper that such homomorphic representations, also known as "analogical" representations [25, 10], are useful for a large number of different types of domains, that they play an important role in inference, and that they can be beneficial for reasoning about dynamic worlds.

3   MODELING CAUSAL INTERACTION

As Haugeland [17] observes, most instances of the frame problem are not so easily representable as is his example of relative spatial location, since the side effects involved are causal rather than spatial. To get the same benefits as with the above example with these other sorts of cases, one would need a representation such that the *causal* side effects of a given action would fall out of the nature of the representation used, just as changes in relative location fall out of the above representation. We attempt to flesh out this suggestion in the following way.

Just like any other mechanical or electronic device, a computer is a physical entity, a part of the physical world, subject to the usual physical laws extended in time and space. Mechanical and electrical events trigger other mechanical and electrical events in a complex and structured way. For some problems, the causal structure of the device can be so designed that its behavior closely mirrors that of the domain represented, thus providing the well-known gains in efficiency of analog computation (see [10] for example.) For other problems, a more traditional computation of the causal events can be made easier by taking advantage of the structure of the computer. We illustrate these ideas with three examples. The first two are about causally modeling causal events and the last one is about employing the structure of the computer.

If a causally-charged representational system can be constructed in a given case, then whenever an event E in the domain being modeled causes events $E_1, \ldots, E_n$ as (side) effects, E's representation R physically causes (side) effects $R_1, \ldots, R_n$ which are precisely the representations of events $E_1, \ldots, E_n$.

The first example involves finding the distance of the shortest route from some point A to some point F. It is assumed one is given the distances between each branch as in Figure 2.

The brute-force method of solving such a problem involves checking each possibility in turn, clearly a very inefficient procedure. However, it is also possible to represent the problem in such a way that one can causally mimic the properties of the domain, eliminating the need for a costly search. To do

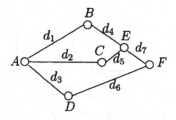

Figure 2. A network of nodes.

this, represent each leg of the problem by means of a delay of appropriate type, perhaps representing an n-mile leg with an n-millisecond delay and connecting the various delays appropriately. So the above problem would be represented as in Figure 3 below,

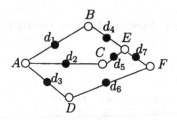

Figure 3. Is there a path of length less than n from A to B?

with the filled circles denoting time delays of length corresponding to the distances indicated. Given such a representation, one simply lets current flow from point A to point F. If it reaches F in n milliseconds, then the shortest path from A to F is n miles. The physical properties of one's representation behave exactly like those of the domain represented. All the possible routes have been tested simultaneously.

The second example concerns a more explicitly causal domain: given a number of objects one juxtaposed next to the other, if the end-block is pushed over one place, so thereby are each of the others also pushed over one place. This is illustrated in figure 4.

To construct a special purpose representation for this domain, represent each location with a device of two possible states, s_0 and s_1. A device at some location in state s_0 represents the location having no object; likewise, state s_1 represents there being an object there. So a row of objects is represented as a row of devices in state s_1. The above example would be

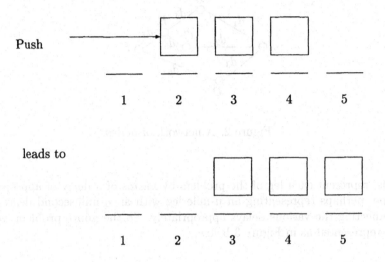

Push

1	2	3	4	5

leads to

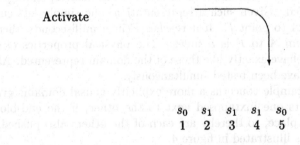

1	2	3	4	5

Figure 4. Moving blocks to the right.

represented as shown:

$$
\begin{array}{ccccc}
s_0 & s_1 & s_1 & s_1 & s_0 \\
1 & 2 & 3 & 4 & 5
\end{array}
$$

The action of pushing an end-block over one place is represented by activating a device at the end of a chain of devices in state s_1, as indicated below.

Activate

$$
\begin{array}{ccccc}
s_0 & s_1 & s_1 & s_1 & s_0 \\
1 & 2 & 3 & 4 & 5
\end{array}
$$

When such an event occurs, the device sends out a pulse to the next device in the row. When a pulse is sent to a device in state s_1, the pulse is simply passed along to the next device. When the pulse finally reaches a device in state s_0, the device switches to state s_1 and the pulse eliminated.

So one has captured the causal side effects of the domain being modeled by appeal to causal properties of the representational mechanism used to model it.

There is a limit to what can be modeled in the described way. We will now have a look at a problem that is not modeled by causal interaction of the device but in which the homomorphic structure of the representation reduces inferential burden. In this example, we will show how local processing, one of the characteristics of diagrams as defined by Larkin and Simon [21], reduces search for potential data to be updated.

This example is about determining side effects in a simple blocks world using diagrams. Consider the following diagram:

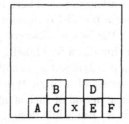

Figure 5. Local Processing in the Blocks World.

Suppose the block marked 'x' is to be moved to the left[2]. One does not have to worry about the blocks to the right of 'x', i.e. blocks D, E, and F. Because of the homomorphic nature of the representation, in determining the (side) effects of moving block 'x' one space to the left, only blocks A, B, and C need to be considered for side effects.

In order to show how to take advantage of local processing let us have a look at how the side effects could be determined. First of all look to the left of block 'x' and determine whether that space is empty. If so, move the block into that space, if not, indicate that 'x's neighbor, C, will also move to the left, and so on recursively until there is an empty space. Once an empty space has been found, the program can actually go about moving the blocks. Since all blocks on top of a moving block move with it, before moving a block the program checks recursively whether there are any blocks on top of a block that is going to be moved.

Sometimes there are no effects of trying to move a block, e.g. when there is an obstructing object such as a wall. This is the case when attempting to move 'x' to the right. On the recursive attempt to move 'x', E, and F, one finds that there is no empty space on the right of F. This result is passed recursively back to 'x' and nothing happens. Another advantage of

---

[2]We will be making the closed-world assumption.

local processing is that the program does not need to check blocks on top of other blocks until it has been determined that the block at the bottom moves indeed. This is the case for block D. For a more detailed description of this algorithm, see [35].

Local processing then means a big gain once the domain gets larger. Because of the nature of determining the (side) effects, only elements of the domain for which there is a potential for being affected are ever considered for updating. For the program, it does not matter whether there are a million blocks to the right of 'x' or none.

One of the problems with diagrams is that computers are set up to process bit-streams but not homomorphic representations. Nevertheless, even a simple bit-matrix representation, even though implemented sequentially, gives us the above described advantages. There are some minor technical advantages if one were to use a parallel computer in which the bit-matrix were implemented by placing the bits in different processors.

Of course there is no such thing as a free lunch. The inferential savings is earned at the price of having constructed a special representational system tailored to the peculiar properties of a single type of problem. There is no point in claiming that the construction of such special purpose formalisms is not a difficult job; certainly it is. But while design costs are large, so can be the payoffs. Namely, if a certain type of problem is encountered frequently and a special representational system can be designed that eliminates a good deal of the inferential demands of the problem, it will likely be worthwhile to spend the extra effort needed to design such a system.

4 LANGUAGE AND HETEROGENEITY

4.1 Language

Although we are arguing for the importance of non-linguistic representations, we are not downplaying the importance of linguistic representations. We are merely urging the importance of level-headed sensitivity to the particular representational mechanism chosen for a given job and the importance of developing a wide range of representational options. If this means sticking with classic first-order languages in a particular case, so much the better. But it also commits one to seeking out formalisms that are radically different from traditional ones if need be as well.

For many tasks, language is the preferred vehicle of representation. It is argued in [4, 7], for example, that operations like disjunction, conjunction, negation, quantification and so forth are best left to linguistic formalisms. Their rich combinatorial power coupled with the lack of good diagrammatic mechanisms for expressing arbitrarily nested Boolean and quantificational operations make language the natural choice. While these sorts of operations can still be diagrammed, as with Peirce's existential graphs [28], the result is hardly an argument in favor of non-linguistic formalisms. These sorts of representational systems do not show any of the desirable properties that make diagrammatic formalisms worth developing; they are simply an equivalent alternative to language.

Diagrams work best when they serve to display or recreate a portion of the world, much like a photograph does; they are useful and efficient when they themselves are very much like what they represent. To the extend that a diagrammatic system leaves this ideal behind, as with existential graphs, it also leaves behind the original advantages and motivations behind developing special purpose representations in the first place.

Even some expressive tasks that obviously *are* well-suited for diagramming can sometimes be equally well represented linguistically. Sometimes, the diagrammatic representations serve to suggest an efficient linguistic representation. For example, problems in the blocks world are often set up diagrammatically [27] for better communication to the reader. However, the same information can be represented in a linguistic representation that is more efficient for some tasks. For example, the use of a variable-placed predicate like stack(A,B,C,D) instead of the simple predicate on(x,y) makes the computation of information concerning "aboveness" much easier (for further examples, see [21]). Doing this, one regains much of the computational advantage of the diagrammatic formalism without having to abandon language (see also [33] for efficient linguistic predicates that are not inspired by diagrams.)

4.2   Heterogeneity

The most important issue with special-purpose formalisms like diagrams seems to concern the nature of the possible interactions between two or more different representational systems. Of particular interest are the relationships between diagrammatic and linguistic representations, between bit-matrix and sentences, between one sort of diagrammatic representation and another, and so forth.

The reason such interaction is so important appears in the very phrase "special-purpose." The power of these formalisms is due to their being expressly designed for a particular, special sort of representational task. Therefore, to gain the expressive range and power needed in any interesting computational or formal system but still get the benefits of these special-purpose formalisms, one must utilize several representational mechanisms simultaneously. One must allow different representational components to work together and to interact. This means that they must be semantically linked together for such interaction to be meaningful and for such things as correctness to be verified. In addition, they must be inferentially linked together for information to be transferable from one form of representation to another and for implementation to be possible [5]. The future of special purpose formalisms hinges entirely on making sense of such interaction.

The most appropriate representational device, even for a given purpose, will most likely be extremely heterogeneous in nature. It will not consist of some single kind of representation which must be adapted by hook or by crook to be uniformly applicable to some huge range of inferential tasks. It will rather consist of a number of components, each designed to handle a particular type of problem efficiently. Heterogeneity gives rise to different types of computational problems. Rather than problems such as determining how to force a homogeneous representational device to handle a huge range of problems efficiently, one will face problems such as determining how to distribute representational tasks to the component best suited to handle it, how to get different representational components to work together in the most efficient manner, and which combinations of representational components can be made to work together in a useful fashion.

5   A HETEROGENEOUS SYSTEM FOR PLANNING IN A DYNAMIC WORLD

We now briefly outline a formal analysis of a heterogeneous system for planning in a dynamic world. One reason for this is simply to show that diagrams can be more than just a source for guiding search. It is possible to define a precise syntax, semantics, and proof theory for diagrams and they can thereby be put on equal footing with sentential representations (see also [25].) In doing so it is to be expected that diagrammatic and in particular homomorphic representations will play a more predominant role in representation.

The heterogeneous system to be presented is about simple *block worlds* The system enables a user to either prove or disprove that there exists a *plan* leading from some *initial situation* satisfying the start state to some final situation satisfying the goal state.

Traditionally, a *block world* consists of a *table* of infinite size and a finite number of equal sized *blocks*. A valid state in a blocks world consists of blocks being stacked singly on top of each other or the table. The valid moves are restricted to moving one block at a time.

We will extend this framework in several ways. First, more than one block can be moved at a time. Whenever a block is moved that has other blocks on top of it, they all move with it. This enables the study of *side-effects* and one form of the *frame problem* (see also section 1.) A big advantage of moving more than one block at a time is that it enables one to find shorter plans. For example, what ordinarily takes a three step solution in the following figure 6 can be turned into a one step solution once the restriction on move size is lifted.

Figure 6. A one step solution when employing side effects.

Second, the number of blocks that can be placed on the table can be limited to some arbitrary number. Some classical problems like the blocks world instantiation of the "variable swapping problem" [27] require that one be able to have a certain number of spaces on the table. However, given that one can move more than one block at a time, two spaces on the table are sufficient. It can be shown that as long as there are two places on the table, one can move at least two blocks at a time, and there are no other restrictions, every situation can be transformed into any other situation [35].

Third, with the help of the predicates of the sentential system, one can place further constraints on plans that enable one to create certain causal connections and temporal restriction. For example, one can specify that some block always has to remain on some other block (which is one way of saying that the block on top can never be moved directly) or that if block x is being moved then also block y has to be moved. Furthermore, one could specify that a block has to be moved a certain number of times or before some other block is being moved. This allows one to recreate the Tower of Hanoi problem, resolution of sets of clauses, and many other complex problems about time and causation.

In order to give a flavor of the system, we will now look at two sample proofs. The first problem (see figure 7) is about showing that there is no plan between the two situations below that satisfies the two constraints "there can never by more than two blocks on the table" and "one can never move more than one block."

The proof will be written down in a tree like manner. This method is inspired by the semantic tree method [32] as well as diagrammatic representations of search spaces in this domain such as found in [27].

For the current example, we need just three rules of inference, *Assume*, *Splitting into cases* and *Close*. The rule of splitting into cases is similar to the *Disjunction elimination* rule in semantic trees. Given a diagram depicting a state of the world at a particular time or "frame" as we will call it, this rule will establish all the immediate and possible successor frames, given the constraints in effect. The cases are written down below the one from which have been derived, with arrows to the new frames. Repeated

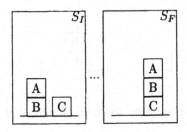

Figure 7. Is there a plan between S_I and S_F, given the sentential constraints?

application of this rule enables us to examine all possible plans and thereby show that there is no plan satisfying the constraints in question. (We will say more about this shortly when we discuss the semantics of the system.) This rule is justified on similar grounds as the rule of disjunction elimination.

The closure rule applies when the only way of validly changing a frame leads to one which we have seen before. In that case, the current frame is just closed off, since any further inferences would be redundant. Even though having seen a frame before is not an inconsistency *per se*, this rule can be motivated on the grounds that for every plan containing a cycle, there is a shorter plan not containing that cycle. A closed case will be marked with the x-symbol.

Now let us have a look at the proof (see figure 8) which shows that there is no a plan leading from the initial situation, S_I, to the final situation, S_F, given the constraints from above. A more explicit syntax would incorporate the constraints in the syntax of the diagrams.

The proof begins by assuming the initial frame, S_I. Given that one can only move one block at a time and not move more than two blocks to the table, there are two successor frames: One in which block A is moved on top of block C and one in which block C is moved on top of block A. The rule of splitting into cases is context sensitive. Had the constraints been different, different successor frames would have been derived. It is easy to verify that the rule of cases exhaustive can be given an entirely explicit and effective formulation.

Frame S_1 can then be transformed into frame S_3 in which block B is moved on top of block A. The other legal move, moving A on top of B is identical to frame S_I and can therefore be disregarded by the cases exhaustive rule. The only legal move in frame S_2 would be back to frame S_I. Therefore, that frame can be closed off too. The same applies to frame S_3.

At this point all paths have been closed off. In addition, none of the

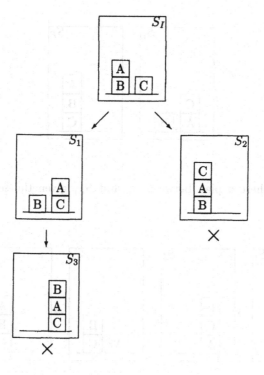

Figure 8. Disproof of the problem from figure 7.

situations that have been generated satisfy the goal state. It is therefore concluded that there is no plan from S_I to S_F satisfying the posed constraints, as desired.

The next example is about showing that there is a plan between two situations satisfying certain constraints.

Here we use two rules of inference, *Assume* and *Frame introduction*. The rule of frame introduction corresponds to the notion of a move in a world.

The problem is defined by the diagram in figure 9 and the sentential information that "there can never be more than two blocks on the table". The proof is depicted in figure 10.

We again begin by assuming the initial situation. Since the goal has block C on the table we may want to achieve that subgoal first. Given that we can only have two blocks on the table, we may want to move block B on top of block C. Then, in situation S_1, move C to the table, which also creates the side-effect of moving block B with it. The proof is completed

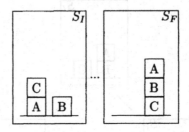

Figure 9. Is there a plan between S_I and S_F, given the sentential constraints?

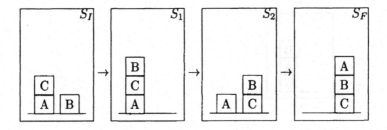

Figure 10. Proof of the problem from figure 9.

by moving block A on top of B.

We will now give a brief sketch of the *syntax* and *semantics* of the system. Diagrams, or "frames" will represent situations, i.e. states of the world at a given time.

A *frame* consists of a horizontal line on which are some labeled or unlabeled squares. The equal-sized squares have to be placed on top of each other or the line in a manner so that they touch but do not intersect each other. It will be assumed that no two squares in a frame are labeled with the same symbol. So the only syntactic concepts needed to adequately define frames are the notion of one block symbol being "immediately above" another block symbol or the table symbol, and the notion of a symbol occurring "within" a rectangle symbol.

Proofs can then be defined as the sorts of tree like structures illustrated above.

What follows is a sketch of the semantics of the system in terms of situations and worlds.

A *situation s* relative to table size c consists of a finite set of equal sized blocks B, a table T, a natural number c, indicating the number of blocks that may be placed on the table, and a set ON of pairs in $B \times B \cup \{T\}$. The relation ON is constrained in the following way. Every block must stand in one and only one relation to either the table or another block, i.e. blocks cannot be suspended in free air. No two blocks may stand in relation ON to one and the same block. Up to c blocks may stand in relation ON to the table. The elements of ON are such that they do not form a cycle.

An "interpretation function" will assign blocks to block squares, and constants, and the table to the line and table constant. Having given the semantics, the notion of truth of a frame in a situation s along with an interpretation function g is as one would expect.

A *world w* relative to table size c and move size m is a finite sequence of situations with the following constraints. All situations in a world have to have the same blocks. No two situations are to be the same, i.e. there will be no cycles. Every two subsequent situations differ only in that some stack of blocks of size smaller or equal to m is on a previously clear block or on the table if there have been fewer than c blocks on it. Truth of a tree of frames in a world w along with an interpretation function is defined as one would expect.

A formal semantics for a special purpose representational system such as the one we have sketched here gives a precise meaning to the question of whether a rule of inference or an implemented planner is sound and also whether it is complete. Furthermore, a precise account of the syntax and semantics of non-linguistic systems allows these systems to be mathematically analyzed in the same way that has been so effective with linguistic systems. The application of powerful mathematical tools to diagrammatic, heterogeneous, and other special purpose formalisms will do a great deal towards promoting them as real and useful possibilities.

6   DISCUSSION

6.1   Diagrams as pseudo-semantic objects

We argued earlier that a good diagram serves to display or picture the domain rather than to make a nested truth-functional or quantificational assertion about it. In this sense, diagrams are (semantically) similar to consistent conjunctions of atomic sentences.

The fact that diagrams serve as partial descriptions of models, as partial descriptions of the domain, suggests that they can also be used for at least some of the purposes usually served by semantics, a point emphasized in [4, 7, 2]. Just as "truth in a model" can be defined between models and well-formed representations, so can "truth in a diagram" be defined between a diagram (i.e. a partial description of a model) and well-formed representations. Roughly, such a relation would hold if and only if every model meeting the description provided by the diagram is such that the representation is true in it. This gives rise to a surrogate notion of "logical consequence" "$\models_{Diagram}$" beyond the standard notion of logical consequence "$\models$." One might call the study of such a notion "pseudo-semantics" since it concerns relationships between different syntactic objects.

Such a notion can be used, for example, to state effective rules of inference allowing one to prove such things as that a representation is *not* a logical consequence of some set of representations or that it is independent of the set or that it is jointly satisfiable with it, etc. All of these things can be done using the system described in [6], for example. So the presence of a diagrammatic component in a formal system affords the possibility of having very useful pseudo-semantic properties that can be appealed to by the rules of inference.

The pseudo-semantic properties of a system, especially a heterogeneous one, are also of interest from a purely mathematical point of view. For example, given a representation ϕ one might compare the class of all diagrams in which ϕ is true, "$Diagram(\phi)$," with the class of all models in which ϕ is true, "$Mod(\phi)$"; or one might determine for which classes Γ of sentences it is true that $Log(Mod(\Gamma)) = Log(Diagram(\Gamma))$, where $Log(K)$ for some class K of models is the set of sentences true in each member of K and $Log(\Delta)$ for some class Δ of diagrams is the set of sentences "true" in each member of Δ. One might also examine how much weaker the relation $\models_{Diagram}$ is than $\models$, or whether the rules are sound and complete with respect to $\models_{Diagram}$, whether or not they are complete with respect to $\models$. There are many other potential properties of interest related to the often close relationships between diagrams and semantics; we leave the analysis of such properties as an open topic.

6.2 Dynamicity

There are worlds that are more dynamic than the ones discussed in this paper and one may wonder whether diagrams and other special-purpose representations are suited to model those more dynamic worlds, such as found in [18, 8]. It appears that in order to model those worlds, and especially their high interdependencies, a diagram is not the best of choices. Among others, a diagram appears to be better suited to represent static situations rather than information about causal interactions or processes enduring over some period of time.

While this may well turn out to be the case, there seems to be a certain place for diagrams, at least when judged by the number of diagrams appearing in papers written on those subjects [18, 8]. Diagrams can well represent interesting start and end states of processes. Furthermore, it is not at all clear whether the causalities have to be represented sententially. If expertise in chess is any indicator, diagrams can be a useful resource for pattern matching, i.e. the analysis of a situation in terms of patterns and the formulation of a next step in terms of patterns. It is estimated [30] that chess masters have the capability to recognize somewhere beyond 50.000 patterns. If it is true that pattern matching is essential to commonsense reasoning, as argued by [11], then diagrammatic processing may give us a shot at cracking the problem of common-sense reasoning (see also [9].)

Indiana University, Bloomington

ACKNOWLEDGEMENTS

We are indebted to the members of the Visual Inference Laboratory at Indiana University for helpful discussions over the past year, especially to Jon Barwise, Ruth Eberle, and Michael Chui who also read and gave many useful comments on earlier versions of this paper.

REFERENCES

[1] James F. Allen. Towards a General Theory of Action and Time. *Artificial Intelligence* **23** (1984) 123-154.

[2] Gerard Allwein, Steve Johnson, and Jon Barwise. *Toward the Rigorous Use of Diagrams in Reasoning about Hardware.* Manuscript, Indiana University. (1993).

[3] Saul Amarel. On Representations of Problems of Reasoning about Actions. in: *Machine Intelligence* **3** D. Mitchie (Ed.). Edinburgh University Press, Edinburgh. (1968) 131-171.

[4] Jon Barwise. Heterogeneous Reasoning. in: *Conceptual Graphs and Knowledge Representation.* G. Mineau, B. Moulin, and J. Sowa. (Eds.). New York: Springer Verlag, to appear.

[5] Jon Barwise and John Etchemendy. Information, Infons, and Inference. *Situation Theory and Its Applications.* Robin Cooper et. al. (Eds.) CSLI, Stanford, CA. (1990).

[6] Jon Barwise and John Etchemendy. *Hyperproof.* Stanford: CSLI, to appear.

[7] Jon Barwise and Eric Hammer. Logical Systems as Models of Inference. *What is a Logical System?* D. Gabbay. (Ed.). Oxford University Press, to appear.

[8] D. G. Bobrow, (Ed.). Special Volume on Qualitative Reasoning and Physical Systems. *Artificial Intelligence* **24(1-3)** (1984).

[9] B. Chandrasekaran and N. H. Narayanan. Towards a theory of commonsense visual reasoning. in: *Lecture Notes in Computer Science 472.* K.V. Nori and C.E. Veni Madhavan (Eds.). Springer-Verlag, Berlin, FRG. (1990) 388-409.

[10] A. K. Dewdney. Computer Recreations. *Scientific American* **250** (1984) 19-26.

[11] Hubert L. Dreyfus and Stuart E. Dreyfus. How to Stop Worrying about the Frame Problem Even though It's Computationally Insoluble. *The Robot's Dilemma.* Zenon Pylyshyn (Ed.) Ablex, Norwood, NJ, (1987).

[12] Brian V. Funt. Problem-Solving with Diagrammatic Representations. *Artificial Intelligence* **13** (1980) 201-230.

[13] George W. Furnas. Reasoning with Diagrams Only. *Working Notes of the AAAI Symposium on Reasoning with Diagrammatic Representations, Stanford, CA.* (1992) 118-123.

[14] Realization of a Geometry-Theorem Proving Machine. *Computers and Though* Edward E. Feigenbaum and Julian Feldman (Eds.) McGraw-Hill, NY, NY. (1963).

[15] Naresh Gupta and Dana S. Nau. On the Complexity of Blocks-World Planning. *Artificial Intelligence* **56** (1992) 223-254.

[16] Eric Hammer. Reasoning with Sentences and Diagrams. *The Notre Dame Journal of Formal Logic.* To appear.

[17] John Haugland. An Overview of the Frame Problem. *The Robot's Dilemma.* Zenon Pylyshyn (Ed.) Ablex, Norwood, NJ, (1987).

[18] Patrick J. Hayes. Naive Physics I: Ontology for Liquids. in: *Formal Theories of the Common-Sense World.* J.R. Hobbs and R.C. Moore (eds.) Ablex, Norwood, NJ, (1985) 1-36.

[19] Patrick J. Hayes. What the Frame Problem Is and Isn't. *The Robot's Dilemma.* Zenon Pylyshyn (Ed.) Ablex, Norwood, NJ, (1987).

[20] Kenneth R. Koedinger and John R. Anderson. Abstract Planning and Perceptual Chunks: Elements of Expertise in Geometry. *Cognitive Science* **14** (1990) 511-550.

[21] Jill H. Larkin and Herbert A. Simon. Why a Diagram is (Sometimes) Worth Ten Thousand Words. *Cognitive Science* **11** (1987) 65-99.

[22] Michael C. Lewis. Visualization and Situations. *Situation Theory and its Applications, Vol.2.* Jon Barwise et.al. (Eds.) CSLI Lecture Notes No. 26, CSLI, Stanford, CA. (1991) 553-580.

[23] John McCarthy. Circumscription - A Form of Non-Monotonic Reasoning. *Artificial Intelligence.* **13** (1980) 27-39.

[24] Drew McDermott. A Temporal Logic for Reasoning About Processes and Plans. *Cognitive Science* **6** (1982) 101-155.

[25] Karen Myers and Kurt Konolige. Reasoning with Analogical Representations. *Proceedings of the Third International Conference on Knowledge Representation.* Bernhard Nebel et. al. (Eds.) Morgan Kaufman, Los Altos, CA. (1992).

[26] Allen Newell and H. A. Simon. GPS, A Program that Simulates Human Thought. in: *Computers and Though* Edward E. Feigenbaum and Julian Feldman (Eds.) McGraw-Hill, NY, NY. (1963).

[27] Nils J. Nilsson. *Principles of Artificial Intelligence.* Tioga, Palo Alto, CA. (1980).

[28] Charles S. Peirce. *The Collected Papers of Charles S. Peirce, volume 4.* Ed. Charles Hartshorne and Paul Weiss. Cambridge: Harvard University Press, 1933.

[29] Yoav Shoham. *Reasoning About Change.* MIT Press, Cambridge, MA (1988).

[30] Herbert A. Simon and William G. Chase. Skill in Chess. *American Scientist* **61** (1973) 394-403.

[31] Aaron Sloman. Interactions Between Philosophy and Artificial Intelligence: The Role of Intuition and Non-Logical Reasoning in Intelligence. *Artificial Intelligence* **2** (1971) 209-225.

[32] Raymond M. Smullyan. *First-order logic.* Springer-Verlag, Berlin, FRG, (1968).

[33] Jeffrey Van Baalen. Automated Design of Specialized Representations. *Artificial Intelligence* **54** (1992) 121-198.

[34] David E. Wilkins. Domain-independent Planning: Representations and Plan Generation. *Artificial Intelligence* **22** (1984) 269-301.

[35] Michael Wollowski. *Planning With Diagrams.* Manuscript, Indiana University. (1993)

CHITTA BARAL, MICHAEL GELFOND
AND RICHARD WATSON

REASONING ABOUT ACTUAL AND HYPOTHETICAL OCCURRENCES OF CONCURRENT AND NON-DETERMINISTIC ACTIONS

1 INTRODUCTION

To perform nontrivial reasoning an intelligent agent situated in a changing domain needs the knowledge of causal laws that describe effects of actions changing the domain, the ability to observe and record occurrences of these actions, and the truth values of fluents[1] at particular moments of time. Discovery of methods of representing this kind of information in a form allowing various types of reasoning about the dynamic world and at the same time tolerant to future updates is one of the central problems of knowledge representation.

Recently, there have been several efforts towards **systematic** development of **provably correct** methods [15, 38, 21] to reason about actions. This paper can be viewed as a continuation of the work started in [15] where the authors introduced the high-level *action description language A* capable of expressing causal laws describing effects of actions as well as statements about values of fluents in possible states of the world.

In the last few years the syntax and semantics of *A* were expanded to allow descriptions of the effects of concurrent and non-deterministic actions as well as descriptions of global constraints expressing time independent relations between fluents [4, 19, 7, 3, 16, 7, 17, 30]. We also have by now a collection of sound and often complete translations from domain descriptions in these languages into disjunctive, abductive, and equational logic programs [11, 9, 17, 41, 2]. This work (together with works based on direct axiomatizations of theories of actions in classical logic and its nonmonotonic extensions [33, 32, 37, 24, 29, 34]) helped increase understanding of the underlying ontological principles of reasoning about actions as well as advantages and limitations of general-purpose non-monotonic formalisms. This work also allowed the establishment of equivalence between some of the previously known theories of actions seemingly based on different intuitions, languages and logics [18] and stimulated work on the theory and implementation of logic programming languages [1, 40, 25, 23].

---

[1] By fluents in this paper we mean propositions whose truth values depend on time.

R. Pareschi and B. Fronhöfer (eds.), Dynamic Worlds, 73–109.
© 1999 *Kluwer Academic Publishers.*

In [6] Baral et al. propose a language inspired by $\mathcal{A}$, called $\mathcal{L}_1$, that can express actual situations, observations of the truth values of fluents in these situations (as opposed to hypothetical values of fluents expressible in $\mathcal{A}$), and observations of actual occurrences of actions. We believe that this adaption[2] significantly improves applicability of action description languages to various areas of AI.

The goal of this paper is to extend $\mathcal{L}_1$ even further to allow representation of concurrent and "non-deterministic" actions. Although our formalization of concurrent action in this paper is based on the language $\mathcal{A}_C$ [4], the proposed language $\mathcal{L}_2$ is not an extension of $\mathcal{A}_C$. This is because we do not allow hypothetical statements in domain descriptions of $\mathcal{L}_2$, while such statements were allowed in the domain descriptions of $\mathcal{A}_C$. On the other hand $\mathcal{L}_2$ allows actual observations. We describe the semantics of the proposed language $\mathcal{L}_2$ (defined as a natural extension of $\mathcal{L}_1$) and demonstrate, by way of examples, that the corresponding entailment allows one to capture various interesting forms of reasoning about actions. Our proposal differs from several other extensions of $\mathcal{A}$ dealing with concurrent and non-deterministic actions in the following way:

1. To the best of our knowledge this is the first proposal which allows reasoning about actual occurrences of concurrent actions.

2. Representation of non-deterministic actions is different (and we believe more natural in many cases) than those presented in the literature.

We also present a translation of domain descriptions in $\mathcal{L}_2$ into disjunctive logic programs [14]. The use of disjunctive logic programs is important because of the availability of interpreters [42, 43] for a large class of disjunctive programs.

We are currently working on investigating applicability of $\mathcal{L}_2$ to the design of architecture for intelligent agents capable of observing, planning, and acting in a changing environment and on discovering efficient methods of computing the corresponding entailment relation. Another direction of research is aimed at combining $\mathcal{L}_2$ with other extensions and dialects of $\mathcal{A}$.

2   SYNTAX OF $\mathcal{L}_2$

We will start with the description of a language $\mathcal{L}_2$ capable of expressing actual observations, compound actions, and hypotheses.

The alphabet of $\mathcal{L}_2$ consists of three disjoint nonempty sets of symbols $\mathcal{F}$, $\mathcal{A}$ and $\mathcal{S}$, called *fluents*, *actions*, and *actual situations*. Elements of $\mathcal{A}$ and

---

[2]It should be noted that $\mathcal{L}_1$ is not an extension of $\mathcal{A}$; mainly because it does not allow hypothetical statements in its domain descriptions.

S will be denoted by (possibly indexed) letters a and s respectively. We will also assume that S contains two special situations s_0 and s_N called *initial* and *current* situations. The 'N' in s_N corresponds to the word 'Now'.

A *fluent literal* is a fluent possibly preceded by $\neg$. Fluent literals will be denoted by (possibly indexed) letters f and p (possibly preceded by $\neg$). $\neg\neg f$ will be equated with f.

By an *action* we mean an arbitrary set of unit actions. A set $\{a_i\}$ where a_i is a unit action will be identified with a_i. Actions of the form $\{a_1,\ldots,a_n\}$ with $n > 1$ are called *compound* and interpreted as sets of actions which are performed concurrently and which start and stop contemporaneously. Unless otherwise specified, by an action we mean a compound action. An expression $[a_1,\ldots,a_n]$ will denote a sequence $a_1,\ldots,a_n$ of actions.

There are three kinds of propositions in $\mathcal{L}_2$; causal laws, facts and hypotheses.

An *effect law* is an expression of the form

(1) a **causes** f **if** $p_1,\ldots,p_n$

where a is an action, and $f,p_1,\ldots,p_n$ $(n \geq 0)$ are fluent literals. $p_1,\ldots,p_n$ are called *preconditions* of (1). We will read this law as "f is guaranteed to be true after the execution of an action a in any state of the world in which $p_1\ldots p_n$ are true". If $n = 0$, we write the effect law as

$$a \text{ \textbf{causes} } f \tag{1a}$$

An atomic *fluent fact* is an expression of the form

(2) f **at** s

where f is a fluent literal and s is a situation. (Unless otherwise stated by situations we will mean actual situations.) The intuitive reading of (2) is "f is observed to be true in situation s".

An atomic *occurrence fact* is an expression of the form

(3) α **occurs_at** s

where α is a sequence of actions, and s is a situation. It states that "the sequence α of actions was observed to have occurred in situation s". (We assume that actions in the sequence follow the next action in the sequence immediately).

An atomic *precedence fact* is an expression of the form

(4) s_1 **precedes** s_2

where s_1 and s_2 are situations. It states that situation s_2 occurred after situation s_1.

Propositions of the type (1) express general knowledge about effects of actions and hence are referred to as *laws*. Propositions (2), (3) and (4) are called *atomic facts* or *observations*. A *fact* is a propositional combination of atomic facts.

A hypothesis is an expression of the form

(5) f **after** $[a_1, \ldots, a_n]$ **at** s

where a_i's are actions and s is a situation. The above expression reads as "Assuming that the sequence of actions $[a_1, \ldots, a_n]$ occurs starting at the situation s, fluent f would be true in the resulting situation."

A collection of laws and facts is called a *domain description* of $\mathcal{L}_2$. (i.e. Domain descriptions do not include hypotheses, but hypotheses can be inferred from a domain description.) The sets of laws and facts of a domain description, D, will be denoted by D_l and D_f respectively. We will only consider domain descriptions whose propositions do not contain the situation constant s_N.

To see how the domain descriptions of $\mathcal{L}_2$ can be used to represent knowledge about actions let us consider the following example:

EXAMPLE 1. Suppose that we are given a series of observations about *Fred*:

(a) when the water pistol was squirted, *Fred* was seen to be *alive* and *dry*,

(b) at the same time a shot was fired at *Fred*.

Suppose also that it is generally known that

(c) *squirting* makes *Fred wet*,   (d) *shooting* makes *Fred dead*

The above information can be represented by a domain description D_1 consisting of the following propositions:

$$
\left.
\begin{array}{ll}
(p1)\ alive \textbf{ at } \ s_0 & (p2)\ dry \textbf{ at } \ s_0 \\
(p3)\ squirt \textbf{ occurs\_at } \ s_0 & (p4)\ s_0 \textbf{ precedes } \ s_1 \\
(p5)\ shoot \textbf{ occurs\_at } \ s_0 & (p6)\ squirt \textbf{ causes } \ \neg dry \\
(p7)\ shoot \textbf{ causes } \ \neg alive &
\end{array}
\right\} D_1
$$

To complete the description of D_1 we need to define its language. For simplicity we assume that this language contains only the fluents and actions explicitly mentioned in the propositions of D_1. Unless stated otherwise the same assumption will be made in other examples throughout this paper. □

Domain descriptions in $\mathcal{L}_2$ are used in conjunction with the following informal assumptions which clarify the description's meaning:

(a) Changes in the values of fluents can only be caused by execution of actions.

(b) There are no actions except those from the language of the domain description.

(c) Effects of an action (possibly compound) are specified by the causal laws in the domain description or inherited from its sub-actions.

(d) No actions occur except those needed to explain the facts in the domain description.

(e) Actions may happen concurrently.

These assumptions give a intuitive understanding of domain descriptions of $\mathcal{L}_2$.

Consider for instance domain description D_1 from Example 1. It is easy to see that D_1 together with assumption (d) implies that *squirt* and *shoot* are the only action which occur between s_0 and s_1. Using D_1 with the assumptions (a) - (e) we can conclude that at the moment s_1 *Fred* is *wet* and *dead*.

Our goal in this paper is to build a mathematical model which will help us to better understand and eventually mechanize these types of arguments. As the first step, we suggest a semantics of domain descriptions of $\mathcal{L}_2$ which precisely specifies the sets of acceptable conclusions which can be reached from such descriptions together with assumptions (a)-(e).

3   SEMANTICS OF $\mathcal{L}_2$

In this section we introduce a semantics of a domain description in $\mathcal{L}_2$. We start with defining causal models of D and proceed by explaining when facts are true in these models.

A *state* is a set of fluent names. A *causal interpretation* is a partial function Ψ from sequences of actions to states such that:

(1) Empty sequence [ ] belongs to the domain of Ψ and   (2) Ψ is prefix-closed[3].

$\Psi([\ ])$ is called the initial state of Ψ. The partial function Ψ serves as an interpretation of the laws of D. If α belongs to the domain of Ψ we say that α is *possible* in the initial state of Ψ.

---

[3]By prefix closed we mean that for any sequence of actions α and action a, if $\alpha \circ a$ is in the domain of Ψ then so is α. (Recall that $\circ$ denotes concatenation, and $\alpha \circ a$ means the sequence of actions where a follows α).

Given a fluent f and a state σ, we say that f *holds* in σ (f is *true* in σ) if $f \in \sigma$; $\neg f$ holds in σ (f is *false* in σ) if $f \notin \sigma$. The *truth* of a propositional formula, C, with respect to σ is defined as usual.

To better understand the role Ψ plays in interpreting domain descriptions let us first use it to define *models* of descriptions consisting entirely of effect laws. To achieve this goal we will attempt to carefully define effects of actions as determined by such a description, D, and our informal assumptions; (a)-(e).

A fluent f is an **immediate effect** of (executing) a in σ if there is an effect law

"a **causes** f **if** $p_1, \ldots, p_n$" in D whose preconditions hold in σ.

For unit actions these are the only effects possible. For compound actions effects may also be determined by the assumption (c) which says that compound actions may inherit effects of their sub-actions. The meaning of this statement however is somewhat ambiguous and needs some refinement. To see the problem consider, for instance, domain description

a **causes** f

$\{a, b\}$ **causes** $\neg f$

and an action $\{a, b, c\}$. Does this action inherit the effect of a, the effect of $\{a, b\}$, both or neither? We follow [4] and opt for the the second alternative on the basis of specificity principle which says that "more specific information overrides less specific information". This leads to the following definition:

DEFINITION 2. A fluent f is an **inherited effect** of (executing) a in σ if there is $b \subset a$ such that
(a) f is an immediate effect of b in σ.
(b) There is no action c such that $b \subset c \subseteq a$ and $\neg f$ is an immediate effect of c in σ. □

DEFINITION 3. f is an **effect** of (executing) a in σ if either f is an **immediate effect** of (executing) a in σ or f is an **inherited effect** of (executing) a in σ. □

Let, $E_a^+(\sigma) = \{f : f$ is an effect of a in $\sigma\}$, $E_a^-(\sigma) = \{f : \neg f$ is an effect of a in $\sigma\}$ and

$$Res(a, \sigma) = \sigma \cup E_a^+(\sigma) \setminus E_a^-(\sigma).$$

The following definition captures the meaning of effect laws of D.

DEFINITION 4. A causal interpretation Ψ **satisfies** the effect laws of D if for any sequence $\alpha \circ a$ from the language of D

$\Psi(\alpha \circ a) = Res(a, \Psi(\alpha))$ if $E_a^+(\Psi(\alpha)) \cap E_a^-(\Psi(\alpha)) = \emptyset$
and undefined otherwise.

We say that Ψ is a **causal model** of D if it satisfies all the effect laws of D □

EXAMPLE 5. Suppose we are given the following general information about effects of actions performed by Mary:
Whenever Mary tries to lift the bowl with one hand, she spills the soup on the table and makes the table wet. When she uses both hands, she does not spill the soup.

To specify these effects by a domain description let us consider an alphabet consisting of a fluent name *spilled* and two unit actions $lift\_l$ and $lift\_r$, and three effect laws:

$\{lift\_l\}$ **causes** *spilled*

$\{lift\_r\}$ **causes** *spilled*

$\{lift\_l, lift\_r\}$ **causes** ¬ *spilled* **if** ¬ *spilled*

The resulting domain description will be denoted by D_1.

It is easy to see that the only causal model of D_1 is defined by a transition function Ψ where

$\Psi(\alpha \circ \{lift\_l\}) = \Psi(\alpha \circ \{lift\_r\}) = \{spilled\}$ if $\Psi(\alpha) = \emptyset$

and for any other action a and sequence α

$\Psi(\alpha \circ a) = \Psi(\alpha)$ □

EXAMPLE 6. Consider a domain description consisting of the following propositions:

a **causes** f
b **causes** $\neg f$

It is easy to see for any α, $\Psi(\alpha \circ \{a, b\})$ is undefined. This is because $E_{\{a,b\}}^+(\Psi(\alpha)) = E_{\{a,b\}}^-(\Psi(\alpha)) = \{f\}$.   □

EXAMPLE 7. Consider a domain description consisting of the following propositions:

$\{a, b\}$ **causes** f
$\{b, c\}$ **causes** g

It is easy to see that for any α, $\Psi(\alpha \circ \{a, b, c\}) = \{f, g\}$. This is because $E_{\{a,b,c\}}^+(\Psi(\alpha)) = \{f, g\}$ and $E_{\{a,b\}}^-(\Psi(\alpha)) = \emptyset$.   □

3.1 Interpreting observations

Let D be an arbitrary domain description and let a causal interpretation Ψ be a causal model of D. To interpret the observations of D we first need to define the meaning of situation constants $s_0, s_1, s_2, \ldots$ from S. To do that we consider a mapping Σ from S to sequences of actions from the language of D. This mapping will be called a *situation assignment of S* if it satisfies the following properties:

1. $\Sigma(s_0) = [\ ]$ 2. for every $s_i \in S$, $\Sigma(s_i)$ is a prefix of $\Sigma(s_N)$.

DEFINITION 8. An *interpretation* M of $\mathcal{L}_2$ is a pair (Ψ, Σ), where Ψ is a causal model of D, Σ is a situation assignment of S and $\Sigma(s_N)$ belongs to the domain of Ψ.   □

$\Sigma(s_N)$ will be called the *actual path* of M and for simplicity will often be denoted by Σ_N.

Now we can define truth of facts of D w.r.t. an interpretation M. Facts which are not true in M will be called *false* in M.

DEFINITION 9. For any interpretation $M = (\Psi, \Sigma)$.

(1) $(f \text{ at } s)$ is *true* in M (or satisfied by M) if f is true in $\Psi(\Sigma(s))$.

(2) atomic fact $([a_1, \ldots, a_n] \text{ occurs\_at } s)$ is true in M if there is a sequence $\beta = [b_1, \ldots b_n]$ of actions such that

(a) The sequence $\Sigma(s) \circ \beta$ is a prefix of the actual path of M, and

(b) for any i, $1 \le i \le n$, $a_i \subseteq b_i$.

(3) $(s_1 \text{ precedes } s_2)$ is true in M if $\Sigma(s_1)$ is a proper prefix of $\Sigma(s_2)$

(4) Truth of non-atomic facts in M is defined as usual.   □

A set of facts is true in interpretation M if all its members are true in M.

To complete the definition of the model we need only to formalize the following underlying assumption of domain descriptions of $\mathcal{L}_2$:

(d) No actions occur except those needed to explain the facts in the domain description.

This is done by imposing a minimality condition on the situation assignments of S which leads to the following definitions.

DEFINITION 10. Let $\alpha = [a_1, \ldots, a_n]$ and $\beta = [b_1, \ldots, b_m]$ be sequences of actions. We say that $\alpha \le \beta$ if there exists a subsequence[4] $[b_{i_1}, \ldots, b_{i_n}]$ of β such that for every $a_k \in \alpha$, $a_k \subseteq b_{i_k}$.   □

---

[4]Given a sequence $X = x_1, \ldots, x_m$, another sequence $Z = z_1, \ldots, z_n$ is a subsequence of X if there exists a strictly increasing sequence $i_1, \ldots, i_n$ of indices of X such that for all $j = 1, 2 \ldots, n$, we have $x_{i_j} = z_j$.

DEFINITION 11. An interpretation $M = (\Psi, \Sigma)$ will be called a *model* of a domain description D in $\mathcal{L}_2$ if the following conditions are satisfied:

(1) Ψ is a causal model of D,
(2) facts of D are *true* in M, and
(3) there is no other interpretation $N = (\Psi, \Sigma')$ such that N satisfies the previous two conditions and $\Sigma'(s_N) \leq \Sigma(s_N)$. $\qquad\square$

The following proposition shows that for a model (Ψ, Σ) of a domain description in $\mathcal{L}_2$, Ψ is completely determined by its initial state.

PROPOSITION 12. Let $M_1 = (\Psi_1, \Sigma_1)$ and $M_2 = (\Psi_2, \Sigma_2)$ be two models of a domain description D in language $\mathcal{L}_2$. If $\Psi_1([\,]) = \Psi_2([\,])$ then $\Psi_1 = \Psi_2$. $\qquad\square$

COROLLARY 13. Let D be a domain description in language $\mathcal{L}_2$. If for all models of D, $\Psi([\,])$ is uniquely defined then Ψ is also uniquely defined. $\qquad\square$

A domain description D is said to be *consistent* if it has a model.

DEFINITION 14. A domain description D entails a fact p (written as $D \models p$) iff p is *true* in all models of D. $\qquad\square$

DEFINITION 15. A domain description D is said to define a unique actual path if for any two situations s_1 and s_2 that are explicitly mentioned in D, $D \models s_1$ **precedes** s_2 or $D \models s_2$ **precedes** s_1. $\qquad\square$

LEMMA 16. Let D be a domain description such that
(1) D defines a unique actual path, and
(2) the only atomic fluent facts which occur in propositions of D are of the form f **at** s_0.
Then situation assignments of all models of D coincide on s_N and on all the situations explicitly mentioned in D. $\qquad\square$

The following proposition shows that the empty set of actions is also an action and it behaves like the wait action with no effects on the fluents. We refer to its as the *wait* action.

EXAMPLE 17. Let D be the following domain description
s_0 **precedes** s_1
s_1 **precedes** s_2
a **occurs_at** s_0
b **occurs_at** s_0

Then $D \models \{\}$ **occurs_at** s_1. $\qquad\square$

3.2 Examples

In this section we illustrate by way of examples how domain descriptions are used to represent information and how the above notion of entailment captures informal arguments based on the information from these descriptions and the informal assumptions (a) - (e). We start with Example 1 from Section 2.

PROPOSITION 18. Consider the domain description D_1 from Example 1. We have

$$D_1 \models ((\neg dry \wedge \neg alive) \text{ at } s_N) \qquad \qquad \Box$$

Proof. Consider a causal interpretation, Ψ, and the situation assignment, Σ, defined as follows:

$$\Psi([\,]) = \{alive, dry\}$$

$$\Psi(\alpha \circ squirt) = \begin{cases} \{alive\} & \text{if } alive \in \Psi(\alpha) \\ \emptyset & \text{otherwise} \end{cases}$$

$$\Psi(\alpha \circ shoot) = \begin{cases} \{dry\} & \text{if } dry \in \Psi(\alpha) \\ \emptyset & \text{otherwise} \end{cases}$$

$$\Psi(\alpha \circ \{squirt, shoot\}) = \emptyset$$

$$\Sigma(s_0) = [\,]$$

$$\Sigma(s_N) = \Sigma(s_1) = [\{squirt, shoot\}]$$

It is easy to check that the interpretation $M = (\Psi, \Sigma)$ satisfies Definition 11 and hence is a model of D_1.

Let us show that it is the only model (i.e. for any model $M_1 = (\Psi_1, \Sigma_1)$ of D_1, $\Psi = \Psi_1$, and $\Sigma = \Sigma_1$). Since by definition any situation assignment maps s_0 into $[\,]$, statements (p1) and (p2) of D_1 will be satisfied only if $\Psi([\,]) = \Psi_1([\,]) = \{alive, dry\}$. Since Ψ and Ψ_1 are causal models of D_1 and causal models are uniquely determined by their initial values, we have that $\Psi = \Psi_1$.

To establish that $\Sigma = \Sigma_1$ notice that to satisfy conditions (p3) - (p5) the actual path $\Sigma_1(s_N)$ of M_1 must start with a compound action which is a superset of $\{squirt, shoot\}$ followed (not necessarily immediately) by another action (possibly $wait$). But then by definition $\Sigma(s_N) \leq \Sigma_1(s_N)$. M_1 is a model of D_1 and hence Σ_1 satisfies the minimality condition 3 from 11. This implies that $\Sigma(s_N) = \Sigma_1(s_N) = [\{squirt, shoot\}]$. Now recall that, by definition of situation assignment, $\Sigma_1(s_1)$ must be a prefix of $[\{squirt, shoot\}]$. Since (p3) and (p5) are true in M_1 we have that $\Sigma(s_1) = \Sigma_1(s_1) = [\{squirt, shoot\}]$.

To complete the proof it suffices to notice that $((\neg dry \wedge \neg alive) \text{ at } s_N)$ is true in M.

EXAMPLE 19 (Reasoning by cases). Let us consider a modification of Example 1 where there is a precondition of being loaded for the shoot action to be deadly and where there are two guns at least one of which is initially loaded.

$(q1)$ *alive* **at** s_0
$(q2)$ *loaded$_1$* **at** s_0 ∨ *loaded$_2$* **at** s_0
$(q3)$ $\{shoot_1, shoot_2\}$ **occurs_at** s_0 $\Big\}$ D_2
$(q4)$ *shoot$_1$* **causes** ¬*alive* **if** *loaded$_1$*
$(q5)$ *shoot$_2$* **causes** ¬*alive* **if** *loaded$_2$*

□

PROPOSITION 20. $D_2 \models$ ¬*alive* **at** s_N. □

EXAMPLE 21 (Explaining observations). Let us now consider a modified version of Example 1 where instead of

(b) At the same moment a shot was fired at *Fred*, we have

(b') In a later moment *Fred* was observed to be dead

and where we assume that our domain contains unit actions $a_1, \ldots, a_n$ different from *squirt* and *shoot*.

The resultant story can be represented by a domain description D_3 consisting of the propositions (p1)–(p4) and (p6) - (p7) of D_1 and the following proposition (p5').

(p5') ¬*alive* **at** s_1 □

PROPOSITION 22.

$D_3 \models ([squirt, shoot]$ **occurs_at** $s_0) \vee ([\{squirt, shoot\}]$ **occurs_at** $s_0)$.
i.e. D_3 entails that either *squirt* occured at s_0 and then *shoot* occured or *squirt* and *shoot* both occured simultaneously at s_0. □

Consider the following three examples which are modifications of example 5. In all three cases we will assume the bowl is initially on the table (i.e. ¬*lifted*) and the soup is not spilled.

EXAMPLE 23. Consider the case when the bowl is lifted by both sides at once. The domain, D_4, can be defined as follows:

$(r1)$ *lift_l* **causes** *spilled*
$(r2)$ *lift_r* **causes** *spilled*
$(r3)$ *lift_l* **causes** *lifted*
$(r4)$ *lift_r* **causes** *lifted*
$(r5)$ $\{lift\_l, lift\_r\}$ **causes** ¬*spilled* **if** ¬*spilled* $\Big\}$ D_4
$(r6)$ $\{lift\_l, lift\_r\}$ **causes** *lifted*
$(r7)$ *initially* ¬*spilled*
$(r8)$ *initially* ¬*lifted*
$(r9)$ $\{lift\_l, lift\_r\}$ **occurs_at** s_0

□

PROPOSITION 24. $D_4 \models \neg spilled$ **at** s_N and $D_4 \models lifted$ **at** s_N.   □

EXAMPLE 25. Next consider the example where first the left side is lifted and then the right side is lifted. Our new domain, D_5, can be represented by propositions (r1) - (r8) from our previous example and three new propositions, (r10) - (r12).

(r10) s_0 **precedes** s_1

(r11) $lift\_l$ **occurs_at** s_0 □

(r12) $lift\_r$ **occurs_at** s_1

PROPOSITION 26. $D_5 \models spilled$ **at** s_N and $D_5 \models lifted$ **at** s_N □

EXAMPLE 27. Let us now consider the case where we aren't told what actions occured, only that in a later moment we observe that the bowl is lifted and the soup is not spilled. Our new domain, D_6, can be represented by propositions (r1) - (r8), (r10), and two new propositions, (r13) and (r14).

(r13) $lifted$ **at** s_1 □

(r14) $\neg spilled$ **at** s_1

PROPOSITION 28. $D_6 \models \{lift\_l, lift\_r\}$ **occurs_at** s_0 □

3.3   Hypothetical Reasoning

Even though domain descriptions of $\mathcal{L}_2$ can express types of knowledge and reasoning not easily expressible in other variants of $\mathcal{A}$, they lack the ability of the latter to do hypothetical reasoning. To do hypothetical reasoning we allow *hypothesis* of the form (5) in the query language of $\mathcal{L}_2$. Note that —according to these definitions— the query language of $\mathcal{L}_2$ is strictly stronger than that of $\mathcal{A}$ (and $\mathcal{A}_C$) while, as a means of specifying domain descriptions, neither $\mathcal{L}_2$ nor $\mathcal{A}$ is more powerful.

For convenience, we introduce the following additional notation:
If s in (5) is the current situation (i.e. s_N) then we simply write

(6) f **after** $[a_1, \ldots, a_n]$

If n in (6) is 0, then we write

(7)   **currently** f

The notions of model of a domain description of $\mathcal{L}_2$ and of the truth of atomic facts in such models remain unchanged. To define answers to queries from $\mathcal{L}_2$ we need the following:

DEFINITION 29. Let D be a domain description in $\mathcal{L}$ and $M = (\Psi, \Sigma)$ be an interpretation of D. We say that a *hypothesis* (5) *is true in an interpretation* M if f is true in $\Psi(\Sigma(s) \circ [a_1, \ldots, a_n])$.   □

DEFINITION 30. Let D be a domain description and H be a hypothesis in $\mathcal{L}_2$. We say $D \models H$ iff H is true in all models of D. □

Truth of arbitrary queries and sets of queries in $\mathcal{L}$ is defined as usual.

A reasoner with knowledge formulated in a domain description D can use hypothetical queries for various purposes. We believe the most important of them is planning. Suppose that our reasoning agent is given a domain description, D, and a collection of fluent literals, G, viewed as a goal to be achieved by performing actions from D. Hypothetical statements of $\mathcal{L}_2$ and $\mathcal{L}_2$ entailment can be used to define a notion of a plan:

DEFINITION 31. Let D be a domain description in $\mathcal{L}_2$ and G be a set of fluent literals. A sequence, α, of actions is a *plan* for achieving a goal G if $D \models f$ **after** α for every fluent literal $f \in G$. □

A planning program should be able to generate sequences of actions viewed as possible plans and test them using the entailment relation of $\mathcal{L}_2$. Consider for instance the following example.

EXAMPLE 32. Consider a variant D_2' of domain description D_2

$$\left. \begin{array}{l} (q1)\ alive\ \textbf{at}\quad s_0 \\ (q2)\ loaded_1\ \textbf{at}\quad s_0 \vee loaded_2\ \textbf{at}\quad s_0 \\ (q4)\ shoot_1\ \textbf{causes}\quad \neg alive\ \textbf{if}\quad loaded_1 \\ (q5)\ shoot_2\ \textbf{causes}\quad \neg alive\ \textbf{if}\quad loaded_2 \end{array} \right\} D_2'$$

and a goal $G = \{\neg alive\}$ a reasoner can come up with a "candidate plan" $[\{shoot_1, shoot_2\}]$ for achieving this goal. The candidate plan will be tested by proving the (hypothetical) statement "$\neg alive$ **after** $[\{shoot_1, shoot_2\}]$", i.e. by checking whether $D_2' \models \neg alive$ **after** $[\{shoot_1, shoot_2\}]$. It is easy to check that the statement is true and therefore $[\{shoot_1, shoot_2\}]$ is indeed a plan for G. Notice that, the resulting domain description (obtained from D_2' by adding $[\{shoot_1, shoot_2\}]$ **occurs_at** s_0) entails G **at** s_N. □

As in the case of $\mathcal{L}_1$, the entailment relation of $\mathcal{L}_2$ also allows modeling of more sophisticated forms of hypothetical reasoning. This aspect is discussed in [6].

Finally, the following definitions and notations can be useful in our further discussions.

Let H_1 and H_2 be two sets of hypotheses. We say that the premise H_1 entails conclusion H_2 in D if H_2 is true in every model of D in which H_1 is true. We will denote this by $H_1 \models_D H_2$.

PROPOSITION 33. $\emptyset \models_D H$ iff $D \models H$ □

A set of hypotheses H is is *inconsistent* w.r.t. a domain description D if no model of D satisfies H.

It is important to notice that the entailment relation ($\models_D$) defined by a domain description D is *monotonic* - addition of new hypothesis to the set of hypotheses H_1 can only decrease the set of models of D satisfying it and hence can only increase the set of conclusions. Non-monotonicity occurs only when new information about the real world (i.e. new laws or new facts) are added to a reasoner's knowledge.

EXAMPLE 34. Consider the following domain description, D_7, consisting of (p1) and (p2):

(p1) *shoot* **causes** $\neg alive$ **if** *loaded*   (p2) *load* **causes** *loaded*

Suppose that, given the domain description D_7, a reasoner would like to know if Fred would be dead after shooting under the assumption that initially the gun is loaded. Notice that both statements are hypothetical and therefore are naturally represented as follows:

$H_1 = loaded$ **after** $[\,]$ **at** s_0 $H_2 = \neg alive$ **after** $[shoot]$ **at** s_0

The question can be formulated as $H_1 \models_{D_7} H_2$? The answer is obviously *yes*.   □

3.4   Relating $\mathcal{L}_2$ and $\mathcal{L}_1$

It was our goal in this paper to extend the language $\mathcal{L}_1$. We now formally state the relation between $\mathcal{L}_1$ and $\mathcal{L}_2$.

THEOREM 35. Let D be a domain description in $\mathcal{L}_2$ which does not contain any compound actions. For any query Q in $\mathcal{L}_2$ which does not contain compound actions, $\mathcal{L}_2 \models Q$ iff $\mathcal{L}_1 \models Q$. (i.e., $\mathcal{L}_2$ is a conservative extension of $\mathcal{L}_1$).   □

Proof:
Follows trivially from the semantics of $\mathcal{L}_1$ and $\mathcal{L}_2$.   □

4   FROM $\mathcal{L}_2$ TO LOGIC PROGRAMS

4.1   Extended Logic Programs and Disjunctive Logic Programs

In this section we review necessary definitions and results from the theory of declarative logic programming. In addition to negation as failure, *not*, [8] of "classical" logic programming languages we consider two other connectives: classical (strong, explicit) negation, $\neg$, of [13] and epistemic disjunction, *or*, of [14]. Both connectives are needed to allow representation of various forms of incomplete information. There is no complete agreement on the nature and semantics of these connectives and their interrelation with negation as failure. Several different proposals were discussed in the literature. (see, for instance, Minker et al. [22], Pereira et al. [31], Dix [10], Przymusinski [35], Gelfond and Lifschitz [14]). We will follow [14]. Applicability of this approach to representation of incomplete information is discussed in [5, 12].

A disjunctive logic program (DLP) is a collection of rules of the form

$$(8) \quad l_0 \; or \; \ldots \; or \; l_k \leftarrow l_{k+1}, \ldots, l_m, not \; l_{m+1}, \ldots, not \; l_n$$

where each l_i is a literal (i.e. an atom possibly preceded by $\neg$) and *not* is the negation as failure. Expression on the left hand (right hand) side of $\leftarrow$ is called the *head* (the *body*) of the rule. Both the head and the body of (8) can be empty. Intuitively the rule can be read as: if $l_{k+1}, \ldots, l_m$ are believed and it is not true that $l_{m+1}, \ldots, l_n$ are believed then at least one of $\{l_0, \ldots, l_k\}$ is believed. For a rule r of the form (8) the sets $\{l_0, \ldots, l_k\}$, $\{l_{k+1}, \ldots, l_m\}$ and $\{l_{m+1}, \ldots, l_n\}$ are referred to as $head(r)$, $pos(r)$ and $neg(r)$ respectively. $lit(r)$ stands for $head(r) \cup pos(r) \cup neg(r)$. For any DLP Π, $head(\Pi) = \bigcup_{r \in \Pi} head(r)$. For a set if predicates S, $Lit(S)$ denotes the set of literals with predicates from S. For a DLP Π, $Lit(\Pi)$ denotes the set of literals with predicates from the language of Π. When it is clear from the context we write Lit instead of $Lit(\Pi)$. Given a literal, l, of the form a or $\neg a$ (where a is an atom), $\bar{l}$ denotes $\neg a$ if $l = a$ and a if $l = \neg a$. For sets of literals X and Y, we say Y is *complete* in X if for every literal $l \in X$, at least one of the complementary literals $l, \bar{l}$ belongs to Y.

A program determines a collection of *answer sets* – sets of ground literals representing possible beliefs of the program.

DEFINITION 36. [14] Let Π be a disjunctive logic program without variables. For any set S of literals, let Π^S be the logic program obtained from Π by deleting

(i) each rule that has a formula *not l* in its body with $l \in S$, and

(ii) all formulas of the form *not l* in the bodies of the remaining rules. $\square$

DEFINITION 37. An *answer set* of a disjunctive logic program Π not containing *not* is a smallest (in a sense of set-theoretic inclusion) subset S of Lit such that

(i) for any rule $l_0 \; or \; \ldots \; or \; l_k \leftarrow l_{k+1}, \ldots, l_m$ from Π, if $l_{k+1}, \ldots, l_m \in S$, then for some i, $0 \leq i \leq k$, $l_i \in S$;

(ii) if S contains a pair of complementary literals, then $S = Lit$.

A set, S, of literals is an answer set of an arbitrary disjunctive logic program, Π, if

S is an answer set of Π^S $\square$

A program[5] is consistent if it has an answer set not containing contradictory literals. As was shown in [12] if a program is consistent then all of its answer sets are consistent. A ground literal l is *entailed* by a DLP if it belongs to all of its answer sets. When all the rules in a DLP have $k = 0$ then it is referred to as an extended logic program [13, 36].

In our further discussion we will need the following proposition about DLPs:

PROPOSITION 38. *[5]* For any answer set S of a disjunctive logic program Π:

(a) For any ground instance of a rule of the type (8) from Π, if
$$\{l_{k+1} \ldots l_m\} \subseteq S \text{ and}$$
$$\{l_{m+1} \ldots l_n\} \cap S = \emptyset$$
then there exists an i, $0 \leq i \leq k$ such that $l_i \in S$.

(b) If S is a consistent answer set of Π and $l_i \in S$ for some $0 \leq i \leq k$ then there exists a ground instance of a rule from Π such that
$$\{l_{k+1} \ldots l_m\} \subseteq S, \text{ and}$$
$$\{l_{m+1} \ldots l_n\} \cap S = \emptyset, \text{ and}$$
$$\{l_0 \ldots l_k\} \cap S = \{l_i\}. \qquad \Box$$

4.2   *Approximating the Entailment Relation of $\mathcal{L}_2$*

Our methodology for computing the entailment relation of $\mathcal{L}_2$ is based on translating a domain description D of $\mathcal{L}_2$ into a declarative logic program ΠD and proving soundness (and if possible completeness) of this translation w.r.t. entailment in D.

In this section we limit ourself to domain descriptions in which all facts are atomic, occurrence facts do not contain action sequences, and which have an explicit actual path. The following definition clarifies what is meant by an explicit actual path.

DEFINITION 39. Let D be a consistent domain description with situation constants $s_0, \ldots, s_k$. We will say that D has an *explicit actual path* if for any $0 < i \leq k$ and any compound or unit action a

$(s_{i-1} \text{ precedes } s_i) \in D$

$D \models (a \text{ occurs\_at } s_i)$ iff $(a \text{ occurs\_at } s_i) \in D$ and $i < k$.
$\qquad \Box$

It is easy to see that any D satisfying these conditions contains the statements

---

[5] Henceforth by "program" we mean a disjunctive logic program.

a_0 **occurs_at** $s_0, \ldots, a_{k-1}$ **occurs_at** s_{k-1} and has a unique actual path, i.e. for any model (Ψ, Σ) of D and for every $0 < i \leq k$, $\Sigma(s_i) = [a_0, \ldots, a_{i-1}]$ and $\Sigma(s_N) = \Sigma(s_k)$.

Now we will assume that D has explicit actual path and describe a program ΠD approximating the entailment relation of D.

The alphabet of ΠD consists of symbols for actions, fluent literals and situations from the language of D, and predicates *holds, occurs_at, causes, imm_follows, undefined, cancels, noninh, subset, eq, subseteq, member*, and *atomic*. We will use the following typed variables:

S for situations
A for actions
F, G for fluent literals
P for lists of fluent literals

All the variables can be indexed. The corresponding lower case letters will denote constants of respective types.

Let D be a domain description with the explicit actual path $a_0, \ldots a_k$. The logic programming approximation ΠD of entailment of D will consists of the following rules:

1. **Domain Dependent Axioms**

   (a) **(AL) Description of Actual Path**

   $$imm\_follows(s_1, s_0) \leftarrow$$

   $$\vdots$$

   $$imm\_follows(s_k, s_{k-1}) \leftarrow$$

   $$occurs\_at(a_0, s_0) \leftarrow$$

   $$\vdots$$

   $$occurs\_at(a_{k-1}, s_{k-1}) \leftarrow$$

   (b) **(BC) Boundary Conditions** Each atomic fluent fact, f **at** s in D, is translated as a rule of the form $h(f, s_i) \leftarrow$

   where, for any literal g, the atom $h(g, s)$ denotes the literal $holds(g, s)$ if g is a positive literal and the literal $\neg holds(|g|, s)$ if g is a negative literal; and for any fluent f, $|f| = f$ and $|\neg f| = f$.

   (c) **(CL) Causal Laws**
   The translation of an effect law "a **causes** f if $p_1, \ldots, p_n$" consists of

   $$causes(a, f, S) \leftarrow h(p_1, S), \ldots, h(p_n, S)$$

   Intuitively, $causes(a, f, s)$ means that if action a is executed in situation s then f will be true as a direct effect of the action a.

2. Domain Independent Axioms

(a) (EA) Effects of actions

The *Effect Axioms* are defined as follows:

(i) $h(F, Result(A, S)) \leftarrow causes(A, F, S), not\ undefined(A, S)$
(ii) $undefined(A, S) \leftarrow causes(A, F, S), causes(A, \overline{F}, S)$
(iii) $undefined(A, res(B, S)) \leftarrow undefined(B, S)$

The effect axiom allows us to prove that f will hold after a, if the preconditions are satisfied.

The first axiom differs from the one suggested in [15] only by allowing terms for compound actions and by using the predicate "undefined". The next axioms are new. They describe how the effects of individual actions are related to the effects of these actions performed concurrently.

(b) (IA) Inheritance Axioms

(i) $h(F, result(A, S)) \leftarrow subsetof(B, A), h(F, result(B, S)),$
$\quad\quad not\ noninh(F, A, S),$
$\quad\quad not\ undefined(A, S)$

(ii) $cancels(X, Y, F, S) \leftarrow subsetof(X, Z), subseteq(Z, Y),$
$\quad\quad causes(Z, \overline{F}, S)$

(iii) $noninh(F, A, S) \leftarrow subseteq(U, A), causes(U, \overline{F}, S),$
$\quad\quad not\ cancels(U, A, \overline{F}, S)$

(iv) $undefined(A, S) \leftarrow noninh(F, A, S), noninh(\overline{F}, A, S)$

Intuitively, $cancels(x, y, f, s)$ means that an action z, $x \subset z \subseteq y$ causes $\overline{f}$ thus cancelling the inheritance of the effect f by the action y from its sub-action x .

Intuitively, $noninh(f, x, s)$ means that the action x does not inherit the effect f from its sub-actions in situation s.

The non-inheritance axioms are essential for the correct treatment of concurrent actions.

According to these axioms the effects of compound actions are normally inherited from the effects of their components.

(c) (FI) First Inertia Axiom

$h(F, result(A, S)) \leftarrow h(F, S), not\ causes(A, \overline{F}, S),$
$\quad\quad atomic(A), not\ undefined(A, S)$

This rule is motivated by the "common-sense law of inertia," [28] according to which fluents normally are not changed by actions. The rule allows us to apply the law of inertia in reasoning "from the past to the future." The auxiliary predicate *causes* is essentially an "abnormality predicate" [27]. The axiom differs from those suggested in [15] only in the use of predicate "atomic" to restrict the inertia rules to unit actions and the predicate "undefined" to restrict inertia rules to executable actions.

(d) **(SI) Second Inertia Axiom**

$$h(F, S2) \leftarrow imm\_follows(S2, S1),$$
$$occurs\_at(A1, S1),$$
$$h(F, result(A1, S1))$$

The second inertia axiom assures that the effects of actions and inertia are passed to named situations.

3. **(FA) Full Awareness of Initial State Axiom**

Turner [41] called it "complete initial situations rule". We prefer to call it "full awareness about the initial situation rule" which means that the program is aware of all fluents of the language in the initial situation.

$$holds(F, s_0) \quad or \quad \neg holds(F, s_0) \leftarrow$$

4. **(LA) Library Axioms**

$$\neg subset(A, B) \leftarrow member(X, A), not \ member(X, B)$$
$$subset(A, B) \leftarrow not \ \neg subset(A, B)$$
$$\neg atomic(X) \leftarrow member(Y, X), member(Z, X), not \ eq(Y, Z)$$
$$atomic(X) \leftarrow not \ \neg atomic(X)$$
$$eq(X, X)$$
$$subseteq(X, Y) \leftarrow subset(X, Y)$$
$$subseteq(X, Y) \leftarrow eq(X, Y)$$
$$member(X, [X|\_])$$
$$member(X, [\_|T]) \leftarrow member(X, T)$$

4.3   Properties of ΠD

In this section we prove various relationships between D and ΠD. The main results are given as propositions and theorems, and lemmas are used in the proofs of the propositions and theorems.

It should be noted that rules of ΠD are ground instantiations of the schemas describing ΠD in the previous subsection, where substitutions of variables by ground terms are done in accordance with definitions of their types.

We first give an overview of "splitting sets" and show a result that will allow us to ignore the "Library Axioms" in our later proofs.

DEFINITION 40. (Splitting set) [25]
A *splitting set* for a program Π is any set U of literals such that, for every rule $r \in \Pi$, if $head(r) \cap U \neq \emptyset$ then $lit(r) \subset U$. If U is a splitting set for Π, we also say that U splits P. The set of rules $r \in \Pi$ such that $lit(r) \subset U$ is called the *bottom* of Π relative to the splitting set U and denoted by $b_U(\Pi)$. The subprogram $\Pi \setminus b_U(\Pi)$ is called *the top of* Π relative to U. $\square$

DEFINITION 41. (Partial evaluation) [25]
The partial evaluation of a program Π with splitting set U w.r.t. a set of literals X is the program $e_U(\Pi, X)$ defined as follows. For each rule $r \in \Pi$ such that:

$$(pos(r) \cap U) \subset X \ \wedge \ (neg(r) \cap U) \cap X = \emptyset$$

put in $e_U(\Pi, X)$ all the rules r' that satisfy the following property:

$$head(r') = head(r), \ pos(r') = pos(r) \setminus U, \ neg(r') = neg(r) \setminus U$$

$\square$

DEFINITION 42. (Solution) [25]
Let U be a splitting set for a program Π. A solution to Π w.r.t. U is a pair $\langle X, Y \rangle$ of literals such that:

- X is an answer set for $b_U(\Pi)$;

- Y is an answer set for $e_U(\Pi \setminus b_U(\Pi), X)$;

- $X \cup Y$ is consistent. $\square$

LEMMA 43. *(Splitting Lemma) [25]*
Let U be a splitting set for a program Π. A set A of literals is a consistent answer set for Π if and only if $A = X \cup Y$ for some solution $\langle X, Y \rangle$ to Π w.r.t. U. $\square$

OBSERVATION 44. The program ΠD can be split (see Definition 40) using the splitting set consisting of $Lit(\{atomic, subset, \neg subset, \neg atomic, subseteq, eq, member\})$. It is easy to see that the bottom part consists of the rules (LA) and the top part consists of the rest. It is easy to see that the bottom part has a unique answer set. Hence by virtue of Lemma 43 in the rest of the paper we only consider the top part of the program ΠD partially evaluated w.r.t. the unique answer set of the bottom part. $\square$

LEMMA 45. Let Π be an extended logic program, $\mathcal{D}$ be a set of disjunctions, and A be a set of literals. If for every disjunction of the form a_1 or ... or a_n in $\mathcal{D}$ there exists an i such that $a_i \in A$, then $\Pi \cup \mathcal{D} \cup A$ and $\Pi \cup A$ have the same answer sets. □

Proof: Follows immediately from the definition of answer sets. □

We now introduce some notations for the forthcoming proofs.

Notation

1. A set of fluent literals $p = \{p_1, \ldots, p_n\}$ is said to hold in a state σ if every p_i holds in σ. Otherwise, we say that p does not hold in σ.

2. For a set of fluent literals $p = \{p_1, \ldots, p_n\}$ we denote the set $\{h(p_1, s), \ldots, h(p_n, s)\}$ by $H(p, s)$.

3. $direct_a^+(\sigma) = \{f : f$ is an immediate effect of a in $\sigma\}$.

4. $direct_a^-(\sigma) = \{f : \overline{f}$ is an immediate effect of a in $\sigma\}$.

5. $inherited_a^+(\sigma) = \{f : f$ is an inherited effect of a in $\sigma\}$.

6. $inherited_a^-(\sigma) = \{f : \overline{f}$ is an inherited effect of a in $\sigma\}$.

7. Given a model, $M = (\Psi, \Sigma)$, an actual situation, s_i, and a sequence of actions, $\alpha_n = [a_1, \ldots, a_n]$, we denote the state $\Psi(\Sigma(s_i))$ by σ_{s_i} and the state $\Psi(\Sigma(s_i) \circ \alpha_n)$ by σ_{s_i, α_n}.

8. Given a sequence of actions $\alpha_n = [a_1, \ldots, a_n]$, we denote the situation $result(a_n, result(a_{n-1}, \ldots, result(a_1, s_i) \ldots))$ by $\alpha_n(s_i)$.

Note that, $E_a^+(\sigma) = direct_a^+(\sigma) \cup inherited_a^+(\sigma)$ and $E_a^-(\sigma) = direct_a^-(\sigma) \cup inherited_a^-(\sigma)$.

PROPOSITION 46. Let D be a domain description. The logic program $(\Pi D)^+$ [6] is locally stratified. □

Proof(sketch)
For a sequence of actions, $\alpha = a_1, \ldots, a_m$, and an actual situation s_i its level is defined as the pair $(m + i, k)$ where k is $|a_m|$, i.e. the cardinality of a_m. We say $(m + i, k) < (m' + i', k')$ iff $m + i < m' + i'$ or $m + i = m' + i'$ and $k < k'$.

---

[6]For an extended logic program Π the normal logic program Π^+ denotes the program obtained by replacing each occurrence of a literals $\neg l$ in Π by l'. See [13] for relation between answer sets of an extended logic program Π and the stable models of the corresponding normal logic program Π^+.

It is easy to see that any assignment of strata to atoms which satisfies the following conditions gives us a local stratification:

(i) Atoms of the form $imm\_follows(s2, s1)$ and $occurs\_at(a, s)$ belong to the lowest strata.

(ii) For atoms $holds(f, \alpha(s_i))$ and $holds(f, \alpha'(s_i'))$ where α and α' are sequence of actions and s_i and s_i' are actual situations, if $level(\alpha', s_i') < level(\alpha, s_i)$ then $strata(holds(f, \alpha'(s_i'))) < strata(holds(f, \alpha(s_i)))$.

(iii) $strata(holds^+(f, \alpha(s_i))) = strata(causes(a, f, \alpha(s_i))) = strata(cancels(X, Y, f, \alpha(s_i))) < strata(noninh(f, X, \alpha(s_i))) = strata(undefined(a, \alpha(s_i))) < strata(holds^+(f, (\alpha \circ b)(s_i)))$

$\square$

LEMMA 47. Let D be a domain description and let A be a set of literals in the language of ΠD. A is a consistent answer set of ΠD iff A is the consistent answer set of
$[\Pi D]_A = \Pi D \cup \{holds(f, s_0) \; : \; holds(f, s_0) \in A\} \cup \{\neg holds(f, s_0) \; : \; \neg holds(f, s_0) \in A\}$.

$\square$

Proof:

$\Longrightarrow$

Let A be a consistent answer set of ΠD. By definition, A is a consistent answer set of $(\Pi D)^A$. It is easy to see that if a program Π does not contain not, then if A is an answer set of Π then A is an answer set of $\Pi \cup B$ for any $B \subseteq A$. Hence, A is a consistent answer set of $([\Pi D]_A)^A$. Therefore, by definition A is a consistent answer set of $([\Pi D]_A)$.

$\Longleftarrow$

Let A be the consistent answer set of $[\Pi D]_A$. It is easy to see that A satisfies $(\Pi D)^A$. Suppose A is not the minimal set that satisfies $(\Pi D)^A$. Let $A' \subset A$ satisfy $(\Pi D)^A$.
(case 1) A and A' differ on facts about the initial state.
Consider the case when $holds(f, s_0) \in A$ and $holds(f, s_0) \notin A'$. (The arguments for the other case is similar.) But then, since either $holds(f, s_0) \in A'$ or $\neg holds(f, s_0) \in A'$ we conclude that $\neg holds(f, s_0) \in A'$. By consistency of A we have $\neg holds(f, s_0) \notin A$. This contradicts our assumption that $A' \subset A$.
(case 2) A and A' do not differ on facts about the initial state. But then A' will satisfy $([\Pi D]_A)^A$ contradicting our assumption that A is an answer set of $[\Pi D]_A$.
Hence, A is the minimal set that satisfies $(\Pi D)^A$ and therefore is an answer set of ΠD.

$\square$

Let D be a domain description with explicit actual path $s_0, \ldots, s_k$. Consider ground instantiations of all the rules of ΠD except the Second Inertia Axiom

(SI), the Description of Actual Path (AL), and the Full Awareness Axiom (FA). The set of all such instantiations not containing any other situation constants except s_i will be denoted by H_i. It is easy to see that Π_D consists of the union of the sets $H_0, \ldots, H_k$ together with ground instantiations of SI, AL, and FA.

LEMMA 48. **Models of D vs Answer sets of H_i**
Let $M = (\Psi, \Sigma)$ be a model of D and for some $0 \leq i \leq k$, let A_i be a consistent answer set of $H_i \cup I$ where $I = \{h(f, s_i) : M \models f \text{ at } s_i\}$

1. If $a_1, \ldots, a_n$ is executable from s_i in M then

   (a) $f \in direct_{a_n}{}^+(\sigma_{s_i, \alpha_{n-1}})$ iff $causes(a_n, f, \alpha_{n-1}(s_i)) \in A_i$.

   (b) $f \in direct_{a_n}{}^-(\sigma_{s_i, \alpha_{n-1}})$ iff $causes(a_n, \overline{f}, \alpha_{n-1}(s_i)) \in A_i$.

   (c) $f \in inherited_{a_n}{}^+(\sigma_{s_i, \alpha_{n-1}})$ iff $noninh(\overline{f}, a_n, \alpha_{n-1}(s_i)) \in A_i$.

   (d) $f \in inherited_{a_n}{}^-(\sigma_{s_i, \alpha_{n-1}})$ iff $noninh(f, a_n, \alpha_{n-1}(s_i)) \in A_i$.

   (e) $undefined(a_n, \alpha_{n-1}(s_i)) \notin A_i$.

   (f) $f \in \sigma_{s_i, \alpha_n} \Leftrightarrow holds(f, \alpha_n(s_i)) \in A_i$.

   (g) $f \notin \sigma_{s_i, \alpha_n} \Leftrightarrow \neg holds(f, \alpha_n(s_i)) \in A_i$.

2. If $a_1, \ldots, a_n$ is not executable from s_i in M then
   $holds(f, \alpha_n(s_i)) \notin A_i$ and $\neg holds(f, \alpha_n(s_i)) \notin A_i$
   and $undefined(a_n, \alpha_{n-1}(s_i)) \in A_i$. $\quad\square$

Proof:
We will prove this theorem using induction on the level of sequence of actions.

Base case: level = (i,0)
Directly from the conditions of the theorem.

Induction Hypothesis: *level* $< (n + i, m)$
Let us assume that by IH

1. If $a_1, \ldots, a_k$ is executable from s_i in M then

   (a) $f \in direct_{a_k}{}^+(\sigma_{s_i, \alpha_{k-1}})$ iff $causes(a_k, f, \alpha_{k-1}(s_i)) \in A_i$.

   (b) $f \in direct_{a_k}{}^-(\sigma_{s_i, \alpha_{k-1}})$ iff $causes(a_k, \overline{f}, \alpha_{k-1}(s_i)) \in A_i$.

   (c) $f \in inherited_{a_k}{}^+(\sigma_{s_i, \alpha_{k-1}})$ iff $noninh(\overline{f}, a_k, \alpha_{k-1}(s_i)) \in A_i$.

   (d) $f \in inherited_{a_k}{}^-(\sigma_{s_i, \alpha_{k-1}})$ iff $noninh(f, a_k, \alpha_{k-1}(s_i)) \in A_i$.

   (e) $undefined(a_k, \alpha_{k-1}(s_i)) \notin A_i$

(f) $f \in \sigma_{s_i, a_n} \Leftrightarrow holds(f, \alpha_k(s_i)) \in A_i$.

(g) $f \notin \sigma_{s_i, a_n} \Leftrightarrow \neg holds(f, \alpha_k(s_i)) \in A_i$.

2. If $a_1, \ldots, a_k$ is not executable from s_i in M then for any fluent atom f,
$holds(f, \alpha_k(s_i)) \notin A_i$ and $\neg holds(f, \alpha_k(s_i)) \notin A_i$
and $undefined(a_k, \alpha_{k-1}(s_i)) \in A_i$.

Induction: level = (n+i,m)

1. Let $a_1, \ldots, a_n$ be executable from s_i in M. Then,

(a) $f \in direct_{a_n}{}^+(\sigma_{s_i, a_{n-1}})$
iff
there is an effect law $(a_n \textbf{ causes } f \textbf{ if } p)$ in D such that p holds
in $\sigma_{s_i, a_{n-1}}$ (by definition)
iff
$H(p, \alpha_{n-1}(s_i)) \subset A_i$ (by IH)
iff
$causes(a_n, f, \alpha_{n-1}(s_i)) \in A_i$ (By consistency of A_i, rule CL, and
Proposition 38).

(b) similar to 1 (a).

(c) $f \in inherited_{a_n}{}^+(\sigma_{s_i, a_{n-1}})$
iff
$\exists b \subset a_n$ s.t. an effect law $b \textbf{ causes } f \textbf{ if } q \in D$, q holds in
$\sigma_{s_i, a_{n-1}}$, and there is no $b \subset c \subseteq a_n$ where there is an effect law
$c \textbf{ causes } \overline{f} \textbf{ if } r \in D$ s.t. r holds in $\sigma_{s_i, a_{n-1}}$ (by definition)
iff
$\exists b \subset a_n$ s.t. $f \in direct_b{}^+(\sigma_{s_i, a_{n-1}})$ and $\neg \exists c : b \subset c \subseteq a_n$ s.t.
$f \in direct_c{}^-(\sigma_{s_i, a_{n-1}})$ (by definition)
iff
$\exists b \subset a_n$ s.t. $causes(b, f, \alpha_{n-1}(s_i)) \in A_i$ and $\neg \exists c : b \subset c \subseteq a_n$ s.t.
$causes(c, \overline{f}, \alpha_{n-1}(s_i)) \in A_i$ (by IH)
iff
$\exists b \subset a_n$ s.t. $causes(b, f, \alpha_{n-1}(s_i)) \in A_i$ and
$cancels(b, a_n, f, \alpha_{n-1}(s_i)) \notin A_i$
(Using consistency of A and applying Proposition 38 to rule
IA(ii).)
iff
$noninh(\overline{f}, a_n, \alpha_{n-1}(s_i)) \in A_i$. (By applying Proposition 38 to
rule IA(iii))

(d) similar to 1 (c).

(e) $a_1, \ldots, a_n$ is executable from s_i in M $\Rightarrow$
$E_{a_n}{}^+(\sigma_{s_i,\alpha_{n-1}}) \cap E_{a_n}{}^-(\sigma_{s_i,\alpha_{n-1}}) = \emptyset$ $\Rightarrow$
$direct_{a_n}{}^+(\sigma_{s_i,\alpha_{n-1}}) \cap direct_{a_n}{}^-(\sigma_{s_i,\alpha_{n-1}}) = \emptyset$ and
$inherited_{a_n}{}^+(\sigma_{s_i,\alpha_{n-1}}) \cap inherited_{a_n}{}^-(\sigma_{s_i,\alpha_{n-1}}) = \emptyset$ $\Rightarrow$
There does not exist f such that both $causes(a_n, f, \alpha_{n-1}(s_i))$ and
$causes(a_n, \bar{f}, \alpha_{n-1}(s_i))$ are in A_i, and there does not exist f such that both $noninh(f, a_n, \alpha_{n-1}(s_i))$ and $noninh(\bar{f}, a_n, \alpha_{n-1}(s_i))$ are in A_i (Using 1(a) to 1(d) of Lemma 48.) $\Rightarrow$
$undefined(a_n, \alpha_{n-1}(s_i)) \notin A_i$ (Using Proposition 38 on rules EA(ii) and IA(iv) of the program.)

(f) $\Longrightarrow$ Let $f \in \sigma_{s_i,\alpha_n}$ $\Rightarrow$
$f \in \sigma_{s_i,\alpha_{n-1}} \cup E_{a_n}{}^+(\sigma_{s_i,\alpha_{n-1}}) \setminus E_{a_n}{}^-(\sigma_{s_i,\alpha_{n-1}})$ $\Rightarrow$
At least one of the following cases is true.

   i. a_n is atomic and $f \in \sigma_{s_i,\alpha_{n-1}} \setminus E_{a_n}{}^-(\sigma_{s_i,\alpha_{n-1}})$

   ii. a_n is not atomic and
$f \in \sigma_{s_i,\alpha_{n-1}} \setminus E_{a_n}{}^+(\sigma_{s_i,\alpha_{n-1}}) \setminus E_{a_n}{}^-(\sigma_{s_i,\alpha_{n-1}})$

   iii. $f \in direct_{a_n}{}^+(\sigma_{s_i,\alpha_{n-1}})$

   iv. a_n is not atomic and
$f \in inherited_{a_n}{}^+(\sigma_{s_i,\alpha_{n-1}}) \setminus E_{a_n}{}^-(\sigma_{s_i,\alpha_{n-1}})$

   i. a_n is atomic and $f \in \sigma_{s_i,\alpha_{n-1}} \setminus E_{a_n}{}^-(\sigma_{s_i,\alpha_{n-1}})$ $\Rightarrow$
$holds(f, s_{n-1}) \in A_i$ (by IH) and $causes(a_n, \bar{f}, \alpha_{n-1}(s_i)) \notin A_i$ (by 1(b)) and $undefined(a_n, \alpha_{n-1}(s_i)) \notin A_i$ (by 1(e)) $\Rightarrow$
$holds(f, \alpha_n(s_i)) \in A_i$ (by using Proposition 38 on rule FI. Note that we can use rule FI only because a_n is atomic.).

   ii. a_n is not atomic and
$f \in \sigma_{s_i,\alpha_{n-1}} \setminus E_{a_n}{}^+(\sigma_{s_i,\alpha_{n-1}}) \setminus E_{a_n}{}^-(\sigma_{s_i,\alpha_{n-1}})$ $\Rightarrow$
From $f \notin E_{a_n}{}^+(\sigma_{s_i,\alpha_{n-1}})$ and $f \notin E_{a_n}{}^-(\sigma_{s_i,\alpha_{n-1}})$ we can conclude that there exists an atomic action b in a_n such that there is no effect axioms of the form b **causes** $\bar{f}$ **if** p where p holds in $\sigma_{s_i,\alpha_{n-1}}$; It is easy to see that α_{n-1}, b is executable from s_i in M and $f \in \sigma_{s_i,\alpha_{n-1},b}$. By IH this implies that $holds(f, res(b, \alpha_{n-1}(s_i))) \in A_i$. From $f \notin inherited_{a_n}{}^-(\sigma_{s_i,\alpha_{n-1}})$ using 1(d) we can conclude that $noninh(f, a_n, \alpha_{n-1}(s_i)) \notin A_i$.
By 1(e) we have $undefined(a_n, \alpha_{n-1}(s_i)) \notin A_i$. Hence using Proposition 38 on the rule IA(i) we can conclude that $holds(f, \alpha_n(s_i)) \in A_i$.

   iii. $f \in direct_{a_n}{}^+(\sigma_{s_i,\alpha_{n-1}})$ $\Rightarrow$
$causes(a_n, f, \alpha_{n-1}(s_i)) \in A_i$ (from 1(a)) $\Rightarrow$

$holds(f, \alpha_n(s_i)) \in A_i$ (Using 1(e) and applying Proposition 38 to rule EA(i)).

iv. a_n is not atomic and
$f \in inherited_{a_n}{}^+(\sigma_{s_i, \alpha_{n-1}}) \setminus E_{a_n}{}^-(\sigma_{s_i, \alpha_{n-1}})$ $\Rightarrow$
From $f \in inherited_{a_n}{}^+(\sigma_{s_i, \alpha_{n-1}})$ it is easy to show that, there exists an action $b \subset a_n$ such that $a_1, \ldots, a_{n-1}, b$ is executable from s_i in M and $f \in direct_b{}^+(\sigma_{s_i, \alpha_{n-1}})$; from which we can conclude by (iii) that
$holds(f, res(b, \alpha_{n-1}(s_i))) \in A_i$. From $f \notin E_{a_n}{}^-(\sigma_{s_i, \alpha_{n-1}})$ we can conclude (by 1(d)) that $noninh(f, a_n, \alpha_{n-1}(s_i)) \notin A_i$. Hence, using Proposition 38, 1(e), and rule IA(i) we can conclude that $holds(f, \alpha_n(s_i)) \in A_i$.

$\Longleftarrow$ Let $holds(f, \alpha_n(s_i)) \in A_i$ $\Rightarrow$
By Proposition 38 at-least one of the following three cases must be true. (Note that $undefined(a_n, \alpha_{n-1}(s_i)) \notin A_i$ in all the three cases)

i. $holds(f, \alpha_{n-1}(s_i)) \in A_i$, a_n is atomic and
$causes(a_n, \bar{f}, \alpha_{n-1}(s_i)) \notin A_i$. (Using rule FI)

ii. There exists an effect law (a_n **causes** f **if** p), such that $H(p, \alpha_{n-1}(s_i)) \subset A_i$. (Using rule EA(i)).

iii. There exists an action $b \subset a_n$ such that
$holds(f, res(b, \alpha_{n-1}(s_i))) \in A_i$ and
$noninh(f, a_n, \alpha_{n-1}(s_i)) \notin A_i$. (using rule IA(i)).

i. By IH, $holds(f, \alpha_{n-1}(s_i)) \in A_i$ implies $f \in \sigma_{s_i, \alpha_{n-1}}$. From $causes(A_n, \bar{f}, \alpha_{n-1}(s_i)) \notin A_i$ using 1(b) we can conclude that $f \notin direct_{a_n}{}^-(\sigma_{s_i, \alpha_{n-1}})$. Since a_n is atomic, $inherited_{a_n}{}^-(\sigma_{s_i, \alpha_{n-1}}) = \emptyset$. Hence, $f \notin E_{a_n}{}^-(\sigma_{s_i, \alpha_{n-1}})$. Hence, $f \in \sigma_{s_i, \alpha_n}$.

ii. There exists an effect law (a_n **causes** f **if** p), such that $H(p, \alpha_{n-1}(s_i)) \subset A_i$. By IH we have p holds in $\sigma_{s_i, \alpha_{n-1}}$. Hence, $f \in E_{a_n}{}^+(\sigma_{s_i, \alpha_{n-1}})$. Since, $a_1, \ldots, a_n$ is executable we have that $f \notin E_{a_n}{}^-(\sigma_{s_i, \alpha_{n-1}})$. Hence, $f \in \sigma_{s_i, \alpha_n}$.

iii. There exists an action $b \subset a_n$ such that
$holds(f, res(b, \alpha_{n-1}(s_i))) \in A_i$ and
$noninh(f, a_n, \alpha_{n-1}(s_i)) \notin A_i$.
We will first show that $f \notin direct_{a_n}{}^-(\sigma_{s_i, \alpha_{n-1}})$. Suppose it is not the case. Using arguments similar to (iii) of ($\Longrightarrow$) we will have $\neg holds(f, \alpha_n(s_i)) \in A_i$. This makes A_i inconsistent and we have a contradiction.
From $noninh(f, a_n, \alpha_{n-1}(s_i)) \notin A_i$ we conclude (using 1(d)) $f \notin inherited_{a_n}{}^-(\sigma_{s_i, \alpha_{n-1}})$. Hence, $f \notin E_{a_n}{}^-(\sigma_{s_i, \alpha_{n-1}})$.

From $holds(f, res(b, \alpha_{n-1}(s_i))) \in A_i$ using IH we can conclude that $f \in \sigma_{s_i, \alpha_{n-i}}$ or $f \in E_b^+(\sigma_{s_i, \alpha_{n-1}})$. If $f \in \sigma_{s_i, \alpha_{n-i}}$, then, since we showed $f \notin E_{a_n}^-(\sigma_{s_i, \alpha_{n-1}})$, we have $f \in \sigma_{s_i, \alpha_n}$.

Now suppose $f \in E_b^+(\sigma_{s_i, \alpha_{n-1}}) \setminus \sigma_{s_i, \alpha_{n-1}}$. This means there exists an action $b_1 \subset a_n$ such that $f \in direct_{b_1}^+(\sigma_{s_i, \alpha_{n-1}})$. Let b_2 be the maximal sub-action of a_n such that $f \in direct_{b_2}^+(\sigma_{s_i, \alpha_{n-1}})$; i.e. there does not exist an action c, $b_2 \subset c \subseteq a_n$ such that $f \in direct_c^+(\sigma_{s_i, \alpha_{n-1}})$.
We now claim that

(*) for all actions g, $b_2 \subset g \subseteq a_n$, if ($g$ **causes** $\overline{f}$ **if** q) in D then q does not hold in $\sigma_{s_i, \alpha_{n-1}}$.

Suppose our claim is false. Then there exists an action g, $b_2 \subset g \subseteq a_n$, such that $f \in direct_g^-(\sigma_{s_i, \alpha_{n-1}})$. From maximality of b_2 we have $f \in inherited_{a_n}^-(\sigma_{s_i, \alpha_{n-1}})$. By 1(d) we have $noninh(f, a_n, \alpha_{n-1}(s_i)) \in A_i$. This contradicts our original assumption that
$noninh(f, a_n, \alpha_{n-1}(s_i)) \notin A_i$. Hence our claim (*) is true.

Therefore, by definition $f \in E_{a_n}^+(\sigma_{s_i, \alpha_{n-1}})$ and hence $f \in \sigma_{s_i, \alpha_n}$.

(g) Similar to the proof of 1(f).

2. $a_1, \ldots a_n$ is not executable from s_i in M $\Rightarrow$
There are two cases:

(case 1) $a_1, \ldots, a_{n-1}$ is executable from s_i in M.
(case 2) $a_1, \ldots, a_{n-1}$ is not executable from s_i in M.

(case 1) $E_{a_n}^+(\sigma_{s_i, \alpha_{n-1}}) \cap E_{a_n}^-(\sigma_{s_i, \alpha_{n-1}}) \neq \emptyset$ $\Rightarrow$
(case 1.1) $direct_{a_n}^+(\sigma_{s_i, \alpha_{n-1}}) \cap direct_{a_n}^-(\sigma_{s_i, \alpha_{n-1}}) \neq \emptyset$ or
(case 1.2) $inherited_{a_n}^+(\sigma_{s_i, \alpha_{n-1}}) \cap inherited_{a_n}^-(\sigma_{s_i, \alpha_{n-1}}) \neq \emptyset$
(The other two cases are not possible.)

(case 1.1) $direct_{a_n}^+(\sigma_{s_i, \alpha_{n-1}}) \cap direct_{a_n}^-(\sigma_{s_i, \alpha_{n-1}}) \neq \emptyset$ $\Rightarrow$
Similar to the case 1 (a) we can show that for some f,
$causes(a_n, f, \alpha_{n-1}(s_i)) \in A_i$ and $causes(a_n, \overline{f}, \alpha_{n-1}(s_i)) \in A_i \Rightarrow$
$undefined(a_n, \alpha_n(s_i)) \in A_i$ (by rule EA(ii).)

(case 1.2) $inherited_{a_n}^+(\sigma_{s_i, \alpha_{n-1}}) \cap inherited_{a_n}^-(\sigma_{s_i, \alpha_{n-1}}) \neq \emptyset$ $\Rightarrow$
There exists $a, a' \subset a_n$ such that $f \in direct_a^+(\sigma_{s_i, \alpha_{n-1}})$, $f \in direct_{a'}^-(\sigma_{s_i, \alpha_{n-1}})$, and there does not exist b and b' where $a \subset b \subseteq a_n$, $a' \subset b' \subseteq a_n$, $f \in direct_b^-(\sigma_{s_i, \alpha_{n-1}})$ and $f \in direct_{b'}^+(\sigma_{s_i, \alpha_{n-1}})$.

Similar to the case 1 (a) we can show that $causes(a, f, \alpha_{n-1}(s_i)) \in A_i$, $causes(a', \overline{f}, \alpha_{n-1}(s_i)) \in A_i$, $cancels(a, a_n, f, \alpha_{n-1}(s_i)) \notin A_i$ and $cancels(a', a_n, f, \alpha_{n-1}(s_i)) \notin A_i$. By using IA(iii) and Proposition 38 we have

$noninh(f, a_n, \alpha_{n-1}(s_i)) \in A_i$ and $noninh(\overline{f}, a_n, \alpha_{n-1}(s_i)) \in A_i \Rightarrow$ $undefined(a_n, \alpha_n(s_i)) \in A_i$ (by Proposition 38 and rules IA(iv).).

(case 2) Using IH and rule EA(iii) we get $undefined(a_n, \alpha_n(s_i)) \in A_i$.

Since for any f, all rules with either $holds(f, \alpha_n(s_i))$ or $\neg holds(f, \alpha_n(s_i))$ in their head, have $not\ undefined(a_n, \alpha_{n-1}(s_i))$ in their body, $holds(f, \alpha_n(s_i)) \notin A_i$ and $\neg holds(f, \alpha_n(s_i)) \notin A_i$.

This ends the proof of this lemma.   □

LEMMA 49. For every model $M = (\Psi, \Sigma)$ of a consistent domain description D, there exists a consistent answer set A_i of $H_i \cup I$ where $I = \{h(f, s_i) : M \models f$ **at** $s_i\}$ s.t.

1. $A_i \models h(f, s_i) \Leftrightarrow M \models f$ **at** s_i.

2. $A_i \models h(f, \alpha(s_i)) \Leftrightarrow M \models f$ **after** α **at** s_i.   □

Proof:
From Proposition 46, it can be seen that $[H_i \cup I]^+$ is locally stratified. Note that since $[H_i \cup I]^+$ also contains complete information about the initial state and has no disjunctions, it will have a unique answer set, say A_i^+. We will first show that A_i^+ is coherent.[7] Incoherency is possible if we derive both $holds(F, S)$ and $holds'(F, S)$ from $[H_i \cup I]^+$. $holds(F, S)$ and $holds'(F, S)$ can be derived using FI, EA(i), and IA(i). Using induction on the level of S, it can be easily shown that
(i) to derive both $holds(F, S)$ and $holds'(F, S)$ using FI the previous situation would have to be incoherent, violating the inductive hypothesis.
(ii) FI and EA(i) can not lead to incoherency. If the body of EA(i) is true for $holds(F, S)$ ($holds'(F, S)$ respectively) then the atom with $causes$ will block FI from deriving $holds'(F, S)$ ($holds(F, S)$ respectively).
(iii) the bodies of FI and IA(i) can not be true at the same time since FI is applicable only for atomic actions, while IA(i) needs the action to be non-atomic.
(iv) we can not have both $holds(f, s)$ and $holds'(f, s)$ derived using EA(i). In that case $undefined$ will block the derivation of both.
(v) EA(i) and IA(i) can not lead to incoherency. If the body of EA(i) is

---

[7] A_i^+ is coherent iff there does not exist an atom, l, such that both l and l' are in A_i^+. For an ELP Π, consistency of answer set of Π corresponds to the coherence of answer sets of Π^+.

true for $holds(F, S)$ ($holds'(F, S)$ respectively) then the atom with $noninh$ will become true blocking IA(i) from deriving $holds'(F, S)$ ($holds(F, S)$ respectively).

(vi) we can not have both $holds(F, S)$ and $holds'(F, S)$ derived from IA(i) at the same time, $noninh$ will block the derivation of at-least one of them. Hence, A_i^+ is coherent and hence [14] A_i is consistent and is the unique answer set of $H_i \cup I$.

Using Lemma 48 w.r.t. D we have that A_i and M agree on all fluent facts and all hypothesis of the form f **after** α **at** s_i in D. □

LEMMA 50. Let D be a consistent domain description with explicit actual path $s_0, \ldots, s_k$ and let Π_1 be obtained from ΠD by replacing (SI) by

$$h(F, s_i) \leftarrow h(F, result(a_{i-1}, s_{i-1}))$$

where $0 < i \leq k$ and $(a_{i-1}$ **occurs_at** $s_{i-1}) \in D$.

Then Π_1 is equivalent to ΠD. □

LEMMA 51. Let D be a consistent domain description with explicit actual path $s_0, \ldots, s_k$, let r_i be the rule $h(f, s_i) \leftarrow h(f, result(a_{i-1}, s_{i-1}))$, let $M = (\Psi, \Sigma)$ be a model of D, and let

$T_m = (H_0 \cup I_0) \cup (r_1 \cup H_1) \cup \ldots \cup (r_m \cup H_m)$ where $I_0 = \{h(f, s_0) : M \models f$ **at** $s_0\}$. For any $0 \leq m \leq k$, the program T_m has a unique consistent answer set A_m s.t.

1. $A_m \models h(f, s_i) \Leftrightarrow M \models f$ **at** s_i.

2. $A_m \models h(f, \alpha(s_i)) \Leftrightarrow M \models f$ **after** α **at** s_i. □

Proof. We use induction on m.

Base: $m = 0$. Conclusion of the Lemma follows immediately from Lemma 49.

Inductive step: Obviously, $T_m = T_{m-1} \cup (r_m \cup H_m)$. By inductive hypotheses T_{m-1} has a unique consistent answer set A_{m-1}. Notice that $head(T_{m-1})$ forms a splitting set [25] for T_m and hence

(i) A_m is an answer set of T_m iff $A_m = A_{m-1} \cup C$ where C is an answer set of the partial evaluation $e(T_m, A_{m-1})$ of T_m w.r.t. A_{m-1}. It is easy to see that

(ii) $e(T_m, A_{m-1}) = H_m \cup I_m$ where

$$I_m = \{h(f, s_m) : A_{m-1} \models h(f, result(a_{m-1}, s_{m-1}))\}$$

By inductive hypotheses, (2) implies that for any fluent literal f s.t. $h(f, s_m) \in I_m$, $M \models f$ **after** a_{m-1} **at** s_{m-1}. Let $\Sigma(s_k)$ be the actual path of D. Then $\Sigma(s_m) = \Sigma(s_{m-1}) \circ a_{m-1}$ and hence $M \models f$ at s_m. Therefore, I_m satisfies the conditions of Lemma 49 and hence $H_m \cup I_m$ has a unique consistent answer set, C, which satisfies conditions (i) and (ii). This, together with (1), implies the conclusion of Lemma 3 for T_m. □

LEMMA 52. For every model $M = (\Psi, \Sigma)$ of a consistent domain description D with explicit actual path $s_0, \ldots, s_k$ there exists a unique consistent answer set, A, of ΠD s.t.

1. $A \models h(f, s_i) \Leftrightarrow M \models f$ at s_i.

2. $A \models h(f, \alpha(s_i)) \Leftrightarrow M \models f$ after α at s_i. □

Proof: By Lemma 50, A is an answer set of ΠD iff A is an answer set of Π_1. Notice that Π_1 can be split using the splitting set $U = Lit(\{imm\_follows, occurs\_at\})$. It can be seen that the bottom contains only the rules describing the actual path, (AL), and the top contains the rest of Π_1. It can easily be seen that the bottom part has a unique answer set, which we will denote as B. Let us consider $e_U(\Pi_1 \setminus b_u(\Pi_1), B)$. Notice that the top and bottom contain no common literals, hence $e_U(\Pi_1 \setminus b_u(\Pi_1), B) = \Pi_1 \setminus (AL)$. We will denote $\Pi_1 \setminus (AL)$ by Π_2. Let $T_k = (H_0 \cup I_0) \cup (r_1 \cup H_1) \cup \ldots \cup (r_k \cup H_k)$ where $I_0 = \{h(f, s_0) : M \models f$ at $s_0\}$ and r_i be the rule $h(f, s_i) \leftarrow h(f, result(a_{i-1}, s_{i-1}))$. By Lemma 51, T_k has a unique answer set which we will denote by, C. Notice that by Lemma 47, C is an answer set of Π_2 iff C is an answer set of $[\Pi_2]_C$. $[\Pi_2]_C$ contains complete information about about the initial state, and hence, by Lemma 45, we can remove the disjunctions, (FA), and still have the same answer sets. But it can easily be seen that, $[\Pi_2]_C \setminus (FA) = T_k$. Following backward through our proof, C is therefore the unique answer set of Π_2 w.r.t M. By Lemma 43, since both B and C are unique, $A = B \cup C$ is the unique answer set of Π_1 for M and hence is the unique answer set of ΠD for M.

□

THEOREM 53. For any consistent domain description D with explicit actual path, its logic programming approximation ΠD is sound w.r.t. D.
□

Proof: Follows directly from Lemma 52. □

The following example shows that, without further restrictions, ΠD is not complete.

EXAMPLE 54. Consider the following domain description D_8:

$$\left.\begin{array}{l} s_0 \textbf{ precedes } s_1 \\ \{a,b\} \textbf{ occurs\_at } s_0 \\ \neg f \textbf{ at } s_0 \\ a \textbf{ causes } f \textbf{ if } p \\ b \textbf{ causes } \neg f \textbf{ if } p \\ \{a,b\} \textbf{ causes } f \textbf{ if } \neg p \\ f \textbf{ at } s_1 \end{array}\right\} D_8$$

There are two candidates for the initial state of a model of D_8:

$\Psi(\Sigma(s_0)) = \{\}$ and $\Psi'(\Sigma(s_0)) = \{p\}$. It is easy to see that $\Psi(\Sigma(s_0) \circ \{a,b\}) = \{f\}$, while $\Psi'(\Sigma(s_0) \circ \{a,b\})$ is undefined. It is easy to show that $M' = (\Psi', \Sigma)$ is not a model of D_8 and hence, $M = (\Psi, \Sigma)$ is the only model of D_8. Hence, $D_8 \models \neg p \textbf{ at } s_0$ and $D_8 \models f \textbf{ after } \{a,b\} \textbf{ at } s_0$.

Now let us consider the program ΠD_8.

It is easy to show that ΠD_8 has two answer sets, A and A', where $\{\neg holds(p, s_0), holds(f, s_1), holds(f, result(\{a,b\}, s_0))\} \subset A$ and $\{holds(p, s_0), holds(f, s_1), undefined(\{a,b\}, s_0)\} \subset A'$.
Since $holds(p, s_0)$ and $holds(f, result(\{a,b\}, s_0))$ each belong to only one of the answer sets of ΠD_8, $\Pi D_8 \not\models \neg p \textbf{ at } s_0$ and $\Pi D_8 \not\models f \textbf{ after } \{a,b\} \textbf{ at } s_0$ and is therefore not complete. □

Now we will show that by adding a stronger condition on the initial state we can achieve both soundness and completeness.

DEFINITION 55. A domain description D is said to be **strongly complete** if for any fluent f in the language either $f \textbf{ at } s_0$ or $\neg f \textbf{ at } s_0$ is in D. □

THEOREM 56. For any strongly complete, consistent domain description D with explicit actual path its logic programming approximation ΠD is sound and complete w.r.t. D. □

Proof: Soundness was proven in Theorem 53.
To prove completeness, notice that it can easily be seen that D has only one model, say M. Since M is unique

1. $D \models f \textbf{ at } s_i \Leftrightarrow M \models f \textbf{ at } s_i$

2. $D \models f \textbf{ after } \alpha \textbf{ at } s_i \Leftrightarrow M \models f \textbf{ after } \alpha \textbf{ at } s_i$

By Lemma 52, there exist a unique answer set, A, of ΠD s.t.

1. $A \models h(f, s_i) \Leftrightarrow M \models f \textbf{ at } s_i$.

2. $A \models h(f, \alpha(s_i)) \Leftrightarrow M \models f \textbf{ after } \alpha \textbf{ at } s_i$.

and therefore

1. $A \models h(f, s_i) \iff D \models f$ **at** s_i.

2. $A \models h(f, \alpha(s_i)) \iff D \models f$ **after** α **at** s_i.

To complete the proof we need to show that A is the only answer set of ΠD. From Proposition 46 ΠD is locally stratified and by Lemma 45 the disjunctions can be removed without changing the answer sets, hence ΠD has a unique answer set, A.   □

5   ACTIONS WITH NON-PREDICTABLE EFFECTS

In this section we discuss another extension of our language which will allow representation of actions with non-predictable (non-deterministic) effects. Let us start with the following example from [39]:

EXAMPLE 57. This is a version of shooting scenario from previous examples. This time the gun is a revolver (to save space we assume that it is a two-shooter, i.e. has two chambers), with a top chamber aligned with the gun's barrel. An action *shoot* is successful (i.e. results in the death of Fred) only if there is a bullet in the top chamber. Action *load* puts the bullet in the top chamber of the cylinder and a new actions, *spin*, rotates the cylinder. As a result of *spin* top chamber may or may not contain a bullet.

Spin is a typical example of an action with non-predictable effects. There are at least two explanations for this phenomena: According to the first one *spin* is a single indivisible action which can cause the chamber containing the bullet to be in any of the possible positions but the actual effect of performing *spin* may be different at different times. This approach seems to be adopted in [19, 39]. Another explanation (see [32]) views *spin* not as a single action, but rather as a collection of actions with precise deterministic effect. Unpredictability of the outcome is caused simply by the lack of knowledge which (unique) action from this collection was actually performed. Our treatment will follow the second view which we find more intuitive in certain cases.   □

To represent knowledge about the occurrences and effects of non-deterministic actions we will augment the syntax and semantics of $\mathcal{L}_2$. First we expand the alphabet of $\mathcal{L}_2$ by a new symbol |. An expression a of the form $a_1 | \ldots | a_n$ (where $a_1 \ldots a_n$ are actions) will be called a *non-deterministic action*, with (possible) *instances* $a_1, \ldots, a_n$. By *generalized actions* we mean deterministic and non-deterministic actions. Propositions of the new language $\mathcal{L}_3$ are defined as follows:

1. Occurrence facts and hypothesis of $\mathcal{L}_3$ are expressions of the form:

$[a_1, \ldots, a_n]$ **occurs_at** s

f **after** $[a_1, \ldots, a_n]$ **at** s

where $a_1, \ldots, a_n (n > 0)$ are **generalized** actions, f is a fluent literal, and s is a situation.

2. All other propositions are exactly the same as in $\mathcal{L}_2$.

Notice that non-deterministic actions can not occur in causal laws. *The effect of executing such action in a particular situation is determined by the effects of its (deterministic) instances.* The semantics of domain descriptions of $\mathcal{L}_3$ refines this intuition.

The notion of interpretation of $\mathcal{L}_3$, i.e. the definition of transition function and situation assignment, is the same as in $\mathcal{L}_2$. To define a model we only need to expand the definition of validity to occurrence facts containing non-deterministic action.

We will say that a sequence $[a_1^*, \ldots, a_n^*]$ of deterministic actions is a (possible) instance of a sequence of generalized actions $[a_1, \ldots, a_n]$ if, for any $1 \leq i \leq n$, $a_i^* = a_i$ or a_i^* is an instance of a_i.

An atomic fact, A, of the form $([a_1, \ldots, a_n]$ **occurs_at** $s)$ is *true* in an interpretation, M, if there is an instance $[a_1^*, \ldots, a_n^*]$ of $[a_1, \ldots, a_n]$ such that $([a_1^*, \ldots, a_n^*]$ **occurs_at** $s)$ is true in M.

To deal with hypothetical reasoning in $\mathcal{L}_3$ we also need to expand the notion of truth for hypothesis containing non-deterministic actions.

We say that A, of the form $(f$ **after** $[a_1, \ldots, a_n]$ **at** $s)$, is *true (false)* in an interpretation, M, if for any instance $[a_1^*, \ldots, a_n^*]$ of $[a_1, \ldots, a_n]$, $(f$ **after** $[a_1^*, \ldots, a_n^*]$ **at** $s)$ is true (false) in M.

Notice that in this formulation, hypothetical queries can be answered as *yes*, *no*, and *unknown* (the latter corresponding to neither true nor false case.)

To illustrate the definition, let us consider the following representation of the above example:

EXAMPLE 58.

$Facts$:
$(f1)$ *alive* **at** s_0
$(f2)$ s_0 **precedes** s_1
$(f3)$ $load(c_1)$ **occurs_at** s_1
$(f4)$ *spin* **occurs_at** s_2

$Laws$:
$(l0)$ $load(X)$ **causes** $bullet\_in(X)$
$(l1)$ $load(X)$ **causes** $top(X)$ D_9
$(l2)$ *shoot* **causes** $dead$ **if** $top(X), bullet\_in(X)$
$(l3)$ *shoot* **causes** $top(c_1)$ **if** $top(c_2)$
$(l3')$ *shoot* **causes** $\neg top(c_1)$ **if** $\neg top(c_2)$
$(l4)$ *shoot* **causes** $top(c_2)$ **if** $top(c_1)$
$(l4')$ *shoot* **causes** $\neg top(c_1)$ **if** $\neg top(c_2)$
$(l5)$ $move\_on\_top(X)$ **causes** $top(X)$

Here variable X ranges over two chambers c_1 and c_2 and *spin* stands for a non-deterministic action $move\_on\_top(c_1)|move\_on\_top(c_2)$.   □

PROPOSITION 59. For the above domain description D_9 we have

1. $D_9 \models (dead$ **after** $[shoot, shoot])$

2. $D_9 \models (bullet\_in(c_1) \wedge top(c_1)$ **at** $s_2)$

3. $D_9 \models (top(c_1) \vee top(c_2)) \wedge bullet\_in(c_1)$ **at** $s_N)$ □

6   CONCLUSION

In this paper we extended the language $\mathcal{L}_1$ to allow compound actions – actions that consist of simultaneous execution of a set of unit actions. The extended language $\mathcal{L}_2$ allows both hypothetical reasoning about effect of actions (by allowing hypothetical statements in the queries), which is useful in planning, and reasoning about actual occurrences of actions, which is useful in formalizing reactive behavior of a robot and in formalizing execution of transactions in databases. Moreover, it can reason with compound actions and elegantly capture the associated frame problem, where we do not want to explicitly specify the effect of all possible compound actions; rather we incorporate inheritance mechanisms such that a compound action normally inherits the effects of its sub-actions.

Some of the recent work that are close to our work in terms of allowing both concurrent actions and actual observations are in [26, 20]. But, it seems like that in both these works the only kind of compound actions that are allowed are the ones where the sub-actions do not conflict with each other or with the overall action. But since both the works are ongoing it is not appropriate at this point to give a detailed comparison between them and our proposal.

University of Texas at El Paso

REFERENCES

[1] K. Apt and M. Bezem. Acyclic programs. *New Generation Computing*, 9(3,4):335–365, 1991.

[2] J Alferes, R. Li, and L Pereira. Concurrent actions and changes in the situation calculus. In H. Geffner, editor, *Proc of IBERAMIA 94*, pages 93–104. McGraw Hill, 1994.

[3] C. Baral. Reasoning about Actions : Non-deterministic effects, Constraints and Qualification. In *Proc. of IJCAI 95*, pages 2017–2023, 1995.

[4] C. Baral and M. Gelfond. Representing concurrent actions in extended logic programming. In *Proc. of 13th International Joint Conference on Artificial Intelligence, Chambery, France*, pages 866–871, 1993.

[5] C. Baral and M. Gelfond. Logic programming and knowledge representation. *Journal of Logic Programming*, 19,20:73–148, 1994.

[6] C. Baral, M. Gelfond, and A. Provetti. Representing Actions : Laws, Observations and Hypothesis. *Journal of Logic Programming (to appear)*, 1996.

[7] S. Bornscheuer and M. Thielscher. Representing concurrent actions and solving conflicts. In *Proc. of German Conference on AI*, 1994.

[8] K. Clark. Negation as failure. In Herve Gallaire and J. Minker, editors, *Logic and Data Bases*, pages 293–322. Plenum Press, New York, 1978.

[9] M. Denecker and D. De Schreye. Representing incomplete knowledge in abductive logic programming. In *Proc. of ILPS 93, Vancouver*, pages 147–164, 1993.

[10] J. Dix. Classifying semantics of logic programs. In *Proceedings of* International Workshop in logic programming and nonmonotonic reasoning, *Washington D.C.*, pages 166–180, 1991.

[11] P. Dung. Representing actions in logic programming and its application in database updates. In D. S. Warren, editor, *Proc. of ICLP-93*, pages 222–238, 1993.

[12] M. Gelfond. Logic programming and reasoning with incomplete information. *Annals of Mathematics and Artificial Intelligence*, 12:19–116, 1994.

[13] M. Gelfond and V. Lifschitz. Logic programs with classical negation. In D. Warren and Peter Szeredi, editors, *Logic Programming: Proc. of the Seventh Int'l Conf.*, pages 579–597, 1990.

[14] M. Gelfond and V. Lifschitz. Classical negation in logic programs and disjunctive databases. *New Generation Computing*, pages 365–387, 1991.

[15] M. Gelfond and V. Lifschitz. Representing actions in extended logic programs. In *Joint International Conference and Symposium on Logic Programming.*, pages 559–573, 1992.

[16] E. Giunchiglia and V. Lifschitz. Dependent fluents. In *Proc. of IJCAI 95*, pages 1964–1969, 95.

[17] S Holldobler and M Thielscher. Actions and specificity. In D. Miller, editor, *Proc. of ICLP-93*, pages 164–180, 1993.

[18] G. Kartha. Soundness and completeness theorems for three formalizations of action. In *IJCAI 93*, pages 724–729, 1993.

[19] G. Kartha and V. Lifschitz. Actions with indirect effects: Preliminary report. In *KR 94*, pages 341–350, 1994.

[20] A. Kakas and R. Miller. A simple declarative language for describing narratives with actions. *Journal of Logic Programming (to appear)*, 1996.

[21] Y. Lesperance, H. Levesque, F. Lin, D. Marcu, R. Reiter, and R. Scherl. A logical approach to high level robot programming – a progress report. In *Working notes of the 1994 AAAI fall symposium on Control of the Physical World by Intelligent Systems (to appear), New Orleans, LA*, November 1994.

[22] J. Lobo, J. Minker, and A. Rajasekar. *Foundations of disjunctive logic programming*. The MIT Press, 1992.

[23] V. Lifschitz, N. McCain, and H. Turner. Automation of reasoning about action: a logic programming approach. In *Posters of the International Symposium on Logic Programming*, 1993.

[24] F. Lin and Y. Shoham. Provably correct theories of actions: preliminary report. In *Proc. of AAAI-91*, 1991.

[25] Vladimir Lifschitz and Hudson Turner. Splitting a logic program. In Pascal Van Hentenryck, editor, *Proc. of the Eleventh Int'l Conf. on Logic Programming*, pages 23–38, 1994.

[26] J. McCarthy. Overcoming an unexpected obstacle. manuscript, 1992.

[27] J. McCarthy. Applications of circumscription to formalizing common sense knowledge. *Artificial Intelligence*, 26(3):89–116, 1986.

[28] J. McCarthy and P. Hayes. Some philosophical problems from the standpoint of artificial intelligence. In B. Meltzer and D. Michie, editors, *Machine Intelligence*, volume 4, pages 463–502. Edinburgh University Press, Edinburgh, 1969.

[29] R. Miller and M. Shanahan. Narratives in the situation calculus. *Journal of Logic and Computation*, 4(5):513–530, October 1994.

[30] N. McCain and H. Turner. Language independence and language tolerance in logic programs. In *Proc. of the Eleventh Intl. Conference on Logic Programming*, pages 38–57, 1994.

[31] L. Pereira, L. Caires, and J. Alferes. Classical negation in logic programs. In *7 Simposio Brasiliero de Inteligencia Artificial*, 1990.

[32] J. Pinto. *Temporal Reasoning in the Situation Calculus*. PhD thesis, University of Toronto, Department of Computer Science, February 1994. KRR-TR-94-1.

[33] J. Pinto and R. Reiter. Temporal reasoning in logic programming: A case for the situation calculus. In *Proceedings of 10th International Conference in Logic Programming, Hungary*, pages 203–221, 1993.

[34] A. Provetti. Hypothetical reasoning about actions: from situation calculus to event calculus. *Computational Intelligence*, 12(3), 1996.

[35] T. Przymusinski. Stationary semantics for disjunctive logic programs and deductive databases. In *North American Conference on Logic Programming*, pages 40–62, 1990.

[36] D. Pearce and G. Wagner. Reasoning with negative information 1 – strong negation in logic programming. Technical report, Gruppe fur Logic, Wissentheorie and Information, Freie Universitat Berlin, 1989.

[37] R. Reiter. The frame problem in the situation calculus: A simple solution (sometimes) and a completeness result for goal regression. In V. Lifschitz, editor, *Artificial Intelligence and Mathematical Theory of Computation*, pages 359–380. Academic Press, 1991.

[38] E. Sandewall. Features and fluents: A systematic approach to the representation of knowledge about dynamical systems. Technical report, Institutionen for datavetenskap, Universitetet och Tekniska hogskolan i Linkoping, Sweeden, 1992.

[39] E. Sandewall. The range of applicability of some non-monotonic logics for strict inertia. *Journal of Logic and Computation*, 4(5):581–616, October 1994.

[40] H. Turner. A monotonicity theorem for extended logic programs. In D. S. Warren, editor, *Proc. of 10th International Conference on Logic Programming*, pages 567–585, 1993.

[41] H. Turner. Signed logic programs. In *Proc. of the 1994 International Symposium on Logic Programming*, pages 61–75, 1994.

[42] R. Watson. An Inference Engine for Epistemic Specifications, 1994. M.S Thesis, Department of Computer Science, University of Texas at El Paso.

[43] D. S. Warren and W. Chen. Query evaluation under well-founded semantics. In *Proc. of PODS 93*, 1993.

DOV M. GABBAY

COMPROMISE UPDATE AND REVISION: A POSITION PAPER

1 INTRODUCTION

We are concerned with the following basic scenario. Let $\mathbb{K}$ be a consistent theory in some underlying logic $\mathbf{L}$. Let C be a consistent Wff of $\mathbf{L}$. We would like to input C into $\mathbb{K}$ to form a new theory, which we denote by $(\mathbb{K}+C)$. If $\mathbb{K} \cup \{C\}$ is consistent, it is clear that $\mathbb{K}+C$ should be $\mathbb{K} \cup \{C\}$. The problem arises when $\mathbb{K} \cup \{C\}$ is inconsistent. In this case, we need to define what $\mathbb{K}+C$ is to be, by using some reasonable mechanisms.

There are many traditional mechanisms for defining $\mathbb{K}+C$. They all share a common philosophy and may differ on the particular details of execution. They are all intolerant of inconsistency and try to restore consistency by adopting one of the following policies:

(a) The non-insistent policy, which rejects the input C and lets $\mathbb{K}+C = \mathbb{K}$.

(b) The insistent policy, which must accept the input C and restore consistency. For this purpose, the mechanisms identify a $\mathbb{K}_C \subseteq \mathbb{K}$ (to be rejected) such that $(\mathbb{K} - \mathbb{K}_C) \cup \{C\}$ is consistent. One then lets $\mathbb{K}+C$ be some consistent theory $\mathbb{K}'$ containing $(\mathbb{K} - \mathbb{K}_C) \cup \{C\}$. The details of how to identify $\mathbb{K}'$ and $\mathbb{K}_C$ depend on the particular approach of the particular system.

(c) A discriminatory policy, that sometimes accepts the new input, and sometimes rejects it, according to certain criteria.

(d) A mixing policy, that accepts part but not all of the input and part but not all of the initial theory.

It is commonly accepted that any insistent revision process should satisfy some rationality postulates. The most well known family of postulates for insistent revision are the AGM postulates [1]. These insist on accepting C as input to obtain a new revised theory $\mathbb{K} \circ C^1$. How to obtain $\mathbb{K} \circ C$ is not specified, as long as the '$\circ$' operation satisfies the postulates.

The underlying philosophy of the above approaches (independently of whether they want to accept or reject the input) is that inconsistency is bad and undesirable and consistency must be restored. So, to be able to

---

[1]We use '$\circ$' for AGM revision and '$+$' for compromise revision. The postulates are listed in Section 4 below.

R. Pareschi and B. Fronhöfer (eds.), Dynamic Worlds, 111–148.
© 1999 Kluwer Academic Publishers.

input C into $\mathbb{K}$ when an inconsistency arises we crucially need to take steps to maintain consistency. Thus either C is rejected or if C is accepted then some part $\mathbb{K}_C$ of $\mathbb{K}$ must be thrown out so that consistency is maintained[2].

Our approach is slightly different. We follow the view of Gabbay–Hunter [6, 7] that inconsistency is not necessarily bad and in many cases it is even desirable. Inconsistency may be welcomed as a trigger for action and as long as the system knows what to do with the inconsistency, we may tolerate it. Thus we may accept the input into the database even though an inconsistency may arise. In fact the database may already be inconsistent!

Following this approach, there are more options available for a system accepting an input and facing an inconsistency.

1. On the one extreme it may proceed to maintain consistency in the traditional manner (Inconsistency Intolerance).

2. On the other extreme it may keep the inconsistent data but know, through some metalevel mechanisms, how to operate an inconsistent database, e.g. how to answer queries from the data (Inconsistency Tolerant).

The mechanisms for giving answers from inconsistent data can vary but they can in principle prove more than what can be got from a revised consistent version of these data. We give an example.

Consider the database

$$C \to B$$

$$C$$

$$\neg C$$

Most reasonable systems of reasoning with inconsistent data can afford to accept B as a conclusion, since B does not clash with $\neg C$, nor does it clash with C. Thus no matter how we would maintain consistency, B can be accepted.

In the spirit above, we offer an alternative mechanism for defining $\mathbb{K} + C$, as a consistent theory, when $\mathbb{K} \cup \{C\}$ is inconsistent. We do not necessarily either reject C or throw out some $\mathbb{K}_C$, but we offer a compromise; we accept some of the logical consequences of C and some of the logical consequences of $\mathbb{K}_C$ and thus form the new consistent theory $\mathbb{K} + C$.

Thus, to summarise, in principle we allow for the following approaches:

---

[2]The AGM postulates actually allow for $\mathbb{K} \circ C$ to have the form $\mathbb{K}' = (\mathbb{K} - \mathbb{K}_C) \cup \mathbb{K}'' \cup \{C\}$.

1. The Inconsistency Intolerant approach:

   (a) Non-insistent input policy,
   (b) Insistent input policy,
   (c) Compromise input policy.

2. The Inconsistency Tolerant approach:

   Input C into $\mathbb{K}$ even if $\mathbb{K} \cup \{C\}$ is inconsistent and use mechanisms for reasoning from inconsistent databases. The best methodology for this is *LDS, Labelled Deductive Systems*, [5].

Our plan for this paper is as follows:

In Section 2 we introduce the idea of compromise revision by giving an example. The basic set up in the example is that we have a theory $\mathbb{K}$ which is consistent and an input C which is also consistent and we want to look at $\mathbb{K} \cup \{C\}$, which is now inconsistent. We know from everyday experience with a multitude of inconsistent data that one can still reason and get consequences from such theories. Thus $\mathbb{K} \cup \{C\}$, although inconsistent, can have a coherent set of consequences. Some of these consequences can be identified as consequences generated by C. Therefore, even if we insist on maintaining consistency and rejecting C, we can still compromise and take some of the consequences of $\mathbb{K} \cup \{C\}$. The particular example of Section 2 illustrates in context how the compromise process works.

We need, however, to present the general mechanism of how to do it in the general case. The problem is, in the general case, how to identify the reasonable consequences of $\mathbb{K} \cup \{C\}$? In classical logic, since $\mathbb{K} \cup \{C\}$ is inconsistent, it can prove anything! So what consequences are 'generated' by C, i.e. what consequences do we take? Obviously we need to present $\mathbb{K}$ in a framework where 'control' over the consequences is possible. The framework for doing so is *Labelled Deductive Systems*, where theories are structures of labelled formulas and full control over proofs and consequences can be exercised using the labels. We cannot use the full theory of labels in this paper and so we need to simplify. The simplest structure where control is possible is the list. We thus develop a labelled formulation and revision mechanisms for theories of the form

$$\mathbb{K} = (A_1, \ldots, A_n),$$

where $\mathbb{K}$ is a list of formulas. If we present $\mathbb{K}$ using labels it will have the form

$$\mathbb{K} = \{t_1 : A_1, \ldots, t_n : A_n\}, \ t_1 < \ldots < t_n,$$

t_i atomic labels. In the sequel we present $\mathbb{K}$ in either form, depending on the needs of the context.

There are many practical applications where such theories arise. For example the list can be a temporal sequence of events, with $t_1 < \ldots < t_n$ representing moments of time or a linearly ordered list of information organised according to the reliability of their sources.

Our choice of theories as lists, turns out to be fortunate from another respect, in the context of revision. We observe that if we have a sequence of inputs, this also gives rise to a list, and so in the context of lists, we can easily consider databases which reflect inside them previous updates and therefore we can define revision mechanisms which are sensitive to the history of past updates ([12]). Thus, the labels can encode list structure of previous updates as well as priorities among data, while at the same time help us maintain full control of proofs and consequences, and thus enabling us to implement our ideas of compromise revision. All in all it seems a wise choice to have our first precise revision mechanism formulated for theories that are lists.

Section 3 deals in detail with such a list model. We present a particular system involving → only and integrity constraints and choose a particular revision mechanism for that.

Section 4 examines the extent that our revision mechanism of Section 3 supports the AGM and other postulates.

Section 5 compares our revision mechanism (which uses lists), with the Lehmann revised system, [12]. Section 6 offers a general theory of revision in the context of *Labelled Deductive System* and we conclude the paper with Section 7 offering a final discussion.

2 A COMPROMISE EXAMPLE

This section deals with an example which will illustrate the idea of the compromise approach. It is adapted from [2].

Let $\mathbb{K} = \{A, A \to B, A \land C \to D \land E, D \to \neg A\}$. $\mathbb{K}$ is our base. Let the input be C. Clearly $\mathbb{K} \cup \{C\}$ is inconsistent, it can prove both A and $\neg A$. If we insist on maintaining consistency, we have several options for $\mathbb{K} + C$.

(a) Reject C (a non-insistent input policy),

(b) Accept C but reject some suitable $\mathbb{K}_C$ (an insistent input policy).

For case (b), depending on the truth maintenance system used, we may throw out any union of

$$\mathbb{K}_C^1 = \{A\},$$

$$\mathbb{K}_C^2 = \{A \wedge C \to D \wedge E\},$$

$$\mathbb{K}_C^3 = \{D \to \neg A\}^3.$$

Looking at this particular example and taking into consideration its meaning given below, it seems reasonable that we either end up with $\mathbb{K}$ (rejecting C) or with $\mathbb{K}_1 = \{C, A \to B, A \wedge C \to D \wedge E, D \to \neg A\}$ (rejecting $\mathbb{K}_C^1$) i.e.

$$\mathbb{K}_1 = (\mathbb{K} - \mathbb{K}_C^1) \cup \{C\}.$$

We now explain what our compromise approach would offer for this example. We consider the two options (a) rejecting C and (b) rejecting A:

(a) We observe that if C were admitted into the database, then $D \wedge E$ can be derived by modus ponens. Although D leads to inconsistency, E does not. So we can compromise and, although we reject C, we can still accept E.

Thus the non-insistent, 'reject C' option would lead to the compromise database $\mathbb{K} \cup \{E\}$.

(b) Similarly, throwing out $\mathbb{K}_C^1 = \{A\}$, would block the deduction of B and of D, E. Since none of $\{B, D, E\}$ lead to any contradiction, we can compromise and take $\mathbb{K}_1 \cup \{B, D, E\}$.

Note that the AGM postulates allow for a revised theory of the form $\mathbb{K}' = (\mathbb{K} - \mathbb{K}_C) \cup \mathbb{K}'' \cup \{C\}$. Thus from the AGM point of view, option (b) above, where we insist on accepting C but keep the consequences of $\mathbb{K}_C = \{A\}$, simply says that we want $\mathbb{K}''$ to be the consequences of A, namely $\mathbb{K}'' = \{B, D, E\}$. We can therefore say that compromise revision for the insistent case (of accepting the input) is a particular way of choosing the AGM compatible revision $\mathbb{K} \circ C$ to contain exactly the consistent consequences of the minimally revised $\mathbb{K}$, (i.e. of what we throw out of $\mathbb{K}$).

Of course, one can compromise by throwing out both C and $\mathbb{K}_C^1$ and keeping in possibly more consequences of $\mathbb{K} \cup \{C\}$. This compromise would

---

[3]Note that the AGM theory pursues an insistent input policy. It gives no details on how to compute $\mathbb{K} \circ C$. It only says that $\mathbb{K} \circ C$ is a consistent theory satisfying the AGM postulates. Thus we can throw out, for example, both $\mathbb{K}_C^1$ and $\mathbb{K}_C^2$ and even add some new X, thus getting $\mathbb{K} \circ C = \mathbb{K} - \mathbb{K}_C^1 - \mathbb{K}_C^2 \cup \{X, C\}$. In this paper we are taking the view that $\mathbb{K} \circ C$ is to be obtained by throwing out a minimal part of $\mathbb{K}$, that is, we throw out as little as possible, just to maintain consistency.

lead to, for example, $\mathbb{K} + C$ being

$$\{A \to B, A \wedge C \to D \wedge E, B, D, E, D \to \neg A\}.$$

Here we pushed both C and A out but accepted their consequences.

Let us give some meaning to the symbols A, B, C, D, E of our example, to see if our compromises make practical sense. Consider the context where John is flying abroad on BA flight 945. He is booked to fly first class but when he shows up he discovers the first class was overbooked. Let

$A =$ John is booked first class.

$B =$ John has double baggage allowance.

$C =$ First class cabin is full.

$D =$ John is seated in economy class.

$E =$ John gets a letter of apology from the airline.

The database $\mathbb{K}$ states (relative to flight BA 945) that John is booked first class, that such passengers get double baggage allowance and that if John is booked first class and the first class is full then John flies economy class, but gets a courtesy bonus. Further, the airline takes pride that no passenger booked first class ever travels economy.

The update is that the first class is full.

We need to be more specific about how we are modelling this airline booking example. Consider a many sorted predicate language L_1 with the following predicates (the sorts are clear from the predicates' English translations).

- $S(x, y, b, t) =$ passenger x is assigned seat y on flight b date t.

- $V_1(y) = y$ is a first class seat.

- $V_2(y) = y$ is an economy class seat.

- $V_3(y) = y$ is not available.

- $A(x, b, t) = x$ is booked first class on flight b date t.

- $B(x, b, t) = x$ has a double baggage allowance on flight b date t.

- $C(b, t) =$ The first class cabin on flight b date t is full. (This predicate can be expressed using S and V_i.)

- $D(x, b, t) = x$ is seated in economy class on flight b date t.

- $E(x, b, t) = $ x gets a letter of apology from the flight b supervisor at date t.

The airline procedures are the following. Up to 60 minutes before the flight departure time booking can be accepted or cancelled according to certain rules. In the last 60 minutes before the flight, passengers with booking and valid tickets are assigned seats (boarding cards).

On the time of the flight, the official "flight database" is closed. It includes a list of passenger names, their booking (economy or first class), their assigned seats (economy or first class) and their baggage allowance. There is also room for comments for each passenger name (apology, medical etc).

The closed database must satisfy the following:

- It must contain either $A(x, b, t_0)$ or $D(x, b, t_0)$ and not both for every passenger x with a boarding card.

- $\forall x \forall t (A \rightarrow B)$.

- $\forall x \forall t (A \wedge C \rightarrow D \wedge E)$.

- $\forall x \forall t (D \rightarrow \neg A)$.

- Some other obvious integrity constraints.

t_0 is the day of the flight. The "input" $C(b, t_0)$ comes in on the day of the flight because, say, a seat was discovered damaged in the first class cabin and so not all passengers booked first class can be assigned first class. Imagine that all other passengers with first class booking have already been assigned seats in the first class cabin. John is the last one and there are no seats to assign to him because the last seat has just been reported damaged. Thus John is assigned an economy seat. The consistency problem from the point of view of the flight supervisor is that if he/she leaves the recorded database as it is, then when it is officially closed it will not satisfy the constraints.

The supervisor is, however, in a position to do something. In logical terms this is revision or consistency maintainance. In practical terms the supervisor can do for example one of the following, in the last minutes before the flight:

(a) Reject C. This can mean in practical terms that the supervisor offers incentives (50% refund) to any passenger who will take the next flight, or that the supervisor quickly repairs the damaged seat.

(b) Take out A. In practical terms this means that the supervisor changes John's first class booking, (with John's consent, of course) and thus will be able to officially record in the closed database an economy booking for John.

The first option makes sense. However, the second option requires some persuation and negotiation. The supervisor can let John enjoy the consequence of his booking (e.g. double baggage allowance) even though he is in economy. But this is the compromise solution!

On the other hand, the compromise solution for the reject C option is a bit cheeky! Had John flown economy (because the first class cabin was full) he would have got a letter of apology. Now that the airline rejected C (i.e. repaired the seat or got some other people off the first class) John need not get a letter of apology.

We see nevertheless that there are circumstances where the compromise solution is most intuitive.

The temporal model we presented above has to do with databases which reflect reality. Certain formula must be maintained to hold in the database. We are free to take some actions in the real world so that formulas can be taken in and out of the database, so that consistency is maintained. There is a period of time before the database is officially "closed" when we take our actions with a view of affecting what the closed database will be.

There are many applications where the data in $\mathbb{K}$ is tied in with programs initiating actions conditional on the data (payroll systems, students exams, etc.). Updates and input signify change of rules or additional information. In such cases a later input has higher priority and may contradict earlier data. However, the consequences of earlier (now possibly rejected) data may have to remain in the database because they were the basis for actions already taken. Each application can decide according to its own needs which consequences to try and keep[4].

I believe that any application involving a language for permission where $\bigwedge x_i \to y$ means that we need to secure permission x_i in order to permit or make true y, would be an application where compromise is meaningful. The integrity constraints of the form $\bigwedge x_i \to \bot$ say that we cannot give too

---

[4]Imagine each first of the month the official data is a list of employees, rank and salary. Thus we may have the following official database in September 97:
(Jan 97, John, Lecturer, £1000)

$\vdots$

(Sep 97, John, Lecturer, £1000).
In October 97 John was promoted retroactively from Jan 97 to a rank of a Reader (Salary £1500). If we just update the database by merely recording our actions in October 97, we may get the following database in October 97.
(Jan 97, John, Reader, £1000)

$\vdots$

(Sep 97, John, Reader, £1000).
(Oct 97, John, Reader, £5500).
The database does not reflect what happened and seems to violate integrity constraints (a reader was underpaid for nine months before it was "detected"). We need two dimensional temporal logic to do this update properly. We need to record both event time and transaction time.

many permissions.

We must clarify the technical machinery used in our compromise procedure: we are given a consistent database $\mathbb{K}$ and an input X. We realise that $\mathbb{K} \cup \{X\}$ is inconsistent. We identify that if X is added to $\mathbb{K}$ then $Y_1, Y_2, Y_3 \ldots$ can be derived. We verify that say $\mathbb{K} \cup \{Y_3, Y_4 \ldots\}$ is indeed consistent and so we *compromise* and take the update $\mathbb{K} + X$ to be $\mathbb{K} \cup \{Y_3, \ldots\}$.

These concepts need to be made precise. If $\mathbb{K} \cup \{X\}$ is inconsistent then (in many logics) it can prove anything, so how do we identify $Y_1, Y_2, \ldots$? Furthermore, what are the applications where such a mechanism is intuitive and makes sense?

The aim of the next section is to deal with these problems.

3   CASE STUDY: COMPROMISE REVISION FOR AN IMPLICATIONAL LANGUAGE

This section will illustrate how to do compromise revision in the case of a propositional language with $\rightarrow$ alone. The connective $\rightarrow$ can be the implicational fragment of a variety of non classical logics, including linear logic, intuitionistic logic and classical logic. We are assuming the language has the connective $\rightarrow$ only to simplify the labelling mechanism. We realise this is a resticted language but our case study is only intended to show how to use labels to enable a compromise mechanism.

Definition 3.1. Let Q be a set of atoms and let $\perp$ be a special atom, possibly not in Q^5. Let S be a set of atomic labels

- A Wff is a formula built up using Q and $\rightarrow$.

- An integrity constraint is a Wff of the form $(A_1, \ldots, A_n) \rightarrow \perp$, where A_i are formulas.

- A database $\mathbb{K}$ is a set of labelled Wffs and integrity constraints, of the form $t_1 : A_1, \ldots, t_k : A_k$ where, t_i are all atomic and pairwise different labels from S.

- We understand $t_1 < t_2$ to indicate that A_1 has a lower priority than A_2. When we input a new C into a database, we put it in with a new

---

[5] $\perp$ does not yet mean *falsity*. We merely use it to write integrity constraints of the form $A \wedge B \rightarrow \perp$, meaning we do not want both A and B to be derivable. Stronger logics will have more properties for $\perp$, for example that $\perp$ proves anything, and these additional properties will turn $\perp$ into *falsity* and $A \rightarrow \perp$ into $\neg A$, for any Wff A. We leave the option open whether to use $\perp$ just as a marker for integrity constraints ($\perp$ not in Q) or allow it to be an atom of the language which has only some of the aspects of *falsity*.

label $a : C$ of the highest priority. Thus

$$\mathbb{K} \cup \{a : C\} = \{t_i : A_i, a : C\} \text{ with } t_1 < t_2 < \ldots < t_n < a.$$

Note that when we maintain consistency, the lower priority formulas will be thrown out first, if we want to ensure that C remains in[6]!

Definition 3.2. We define the notion of $\mathbb{K} \vdash_{\alpha,m,n} A$, for A a Wff or $\perp$ and α a sequence of labels as follows:

1. $\mathbb{K} \vdash_{\alpha,0,0} A$ if $\alpha : A \in \mathbb{K}$.

2. $\mathbb{K} \vdash_{\gamma,m,r} A$ if for some $C, C \to A$, we have that, $\mathbb{K} \vdash_{\alpha,m_1,s_1} C$ and $\mathbb{K} \vdash_{\beta,m_2,s_2} C \to A$, and $\gamma = (\beta\alpha)$ and $r = 1 + s_1 + s_2$ and $m = \max(m_1, m_2)$. Note that in Remark 1 we discuss the option of adding a metalevel condition $\varphi(\beta, \alpha)$ to license this modus ponens).

3. $\mathbb{K} \vdash_{\alpha,m+1,n} A \to B$ if $\mathbb{K} \cup \{x : A\} \vdash_{\beta,m,n} B$ for some n, and where x is a new atom labelling A, and $\alpha = \beta - x$.

4. $\mathbb{K} \vdash_{\alpha,m,n} \perp$ iff for some $(A_1, \ldots, A_n) \to \perp \in \mathbb{K}$, $\mathbb{K} \vdash_{\alpha_i,m_i,n_i} A_i$, and m is $\max(m_i)$, $n = 1 + \Sigma n_i$ and $\alpha = \alpha_1 \ldots \alpha_n$.

Note that there may be more than one triple (α, m, n) such that $\mathbb{K} \vdash_{\alpha,m,n} A$. m counts the maximal number of nested uses of $\to$ introduction and n counts the total number of uses of $\to$ elimination.

REMARK 1. The reader should note that the above definitions actually formulate a *Labelled Deductive System*, [5]. The *LDS* rule for modus ponens is

$$\frac{\alpha : A; \; \beta : A \to B, \; \varphi(\beta, \alpha)}{f(\beta, \alpha) : B}$$

where α is the label for A, β the label for $A \to B$, φ is a (compatibility) licensing metapredicate in the language of labels and f is a function giving the new label.

---

[6]The reader may ask where does the ordering on $\mathbb{K}$ come from? The simplest way of looking at it is to assume that the database was built in stages, by first inputting A_1 into the empty database and then continuing with a sequence of insistent inputs. This will give a natural linear ordering on the database, assuming consistency maintenance is done by throwing out some of the old inputs.

It is important to note that the labels are just atomic dummies. The database $\mathbb{K}$ can be presented as a sequence of Wffs of the form $(A_1, \ldots, A_n)$ together with the integrity constraints.

In our particular case the labels are *resource labels*, tracing the history of the proof. Thus if α and β are sequences of atomic labels, we may choose to define:

$$\frac{\alpha : A; \;\; \beta : A \to B, \;\; \langle \alpha \rangle \cap \langle \beta \rangle = \emptyset}{\beta \alpha : B}$$

The condition $\varphi(\beta, \alpha)$ above, namely $\langle \alpha \rangle \cap \langle \beta \rangle = \emptyset$, ensures that (like in linear logic) each assumption is used at most once!

To define a consequence relation $\vdash$, we need to say when

$$A_1, \ldots, A_n \vdash B$$

we may choose to define, for example

$$A_1, \ldots, A_n \vdash B$$

iff for arbitrary pairwise different atomic labels $t_1, \ldots, t_n$, we have

$$\{t_1 : A_1, \ldots, t_k : A_k\} \vdash_{\alpha, m, n} B$$

such that

$$\langle \alpha \rangle = \{t_1, \ldots, t_n\}.$$

The notion of $\mathbb{K} \vdash_{\alpha, m, n} A$ will have to be modified a bit by adding in item (2) of the definition the meta predicate $\varphi(\beta, \alpha)$ as a necessary license. The logic $\vdash$ just defined is linear logic implication. The reader should therefore note that our revision mechanism equally applies to any logic $\vdash$ definable using labels as above.

Definition 3.3 (Priority ordering). Let $(T, <)$ be a finite linearly ordered set. Assume

$$T = \{t_1, \ldots, t_n\}$$

and that

$$t_1 < t_2 < \ldots < t_n.$$

We want to extend $<$ to pairs of subsets of T. The resulting ordering we call the *compromise priority ordering* on 2^T. The ordering we define will be total. For any T_1, T_2,

$$T_1 < T_2 \text{ or } T_1 = T_2 \text{ or } T_2 < T_1$$

will hold. Assume

$$T_i = \{t_1^i, \ldots, t_{m_i}^i\}, \quad i = 1, 2$$

and assume that

$$t_1^i < t_2^i < \ldots < t_{m_i}^i.$$

We write $m_i = 0$ to mean $T_i = \emptyset$
  we define

$$T_1 < T_2 \quad \text{if} \quad m_1 = 0 \text{ and } m_2 \neq 0$$

$$\text{or} \quad m_1, m_2 \neq 0 \text{ and } t^1_{m_1} < t^2_{m_2}$$

$$\text{or} \quad m_1, m_2 \neq 0 \text{ and } t^1_{m_1} = t^2_{m_2} \text{ and}$$

$$\{t^1_1, \ldots, t^1_{m_1-1}\} < \{t^2_1, \ldots, t^2_{m_2-1}\}.$$

LEMMA 2.

1. *The ordering $<$ on finite subsets of a totally linear set of labels is itself totally linear.*

2. $T_1 \subseteq T_2 \rightarrow T_1 \leq T_2.$

Proof.

(1) By induction. Let
$$T_i = \{t^i_1 < \ldots < t^i_{m_i}\}.$$
Then either $T_i = \emptyset$ $i = 1, 2$ or $T_1 = \emptyset$ and $T_2 \neq \emptyset$, in which case $T_1 < T_2$ or $T_i \neq \emptyset$, $i = 1, 2$ and $t^i_{m_i} < t^j_{m_j}$, $i \neq j$ in which case $T_i < T_j$ or $t^i_{m_i} = t^j_{m_j}$ and $\{t^i_1, \ldots, t^i_{m_i-1}\}$, $i = 1, 2$ are comparable by the induction hypothesis. Thus according to how these sets relate the original sets relate in the same way.

(2) Similar to (1).

■

The ordering of Definition 3.3 can be generated numerically. Let τ be a function associating a number $\tau(t)$ with each label t. For any $S \subseteq T$ let

$$\tau(S) = \{\tau(t) | t \in S\}.$$

$\tau(T)$ is a set of numbers ordered according to magnitude, with the following properties:

- $\tau(t_1) < \ldots < \tau(t_n)$,

- for each $m \leq n$ we have $\tau(t_m) = 2(\tau(t_1) + \ldots + \tau(t_{m-1})).$

Let

$$T_i = \{t_1^i, \ldots, t_{m_i}^i\}, \quad i = 1, 2$$

be two subsets of T. Let

$$\tau_i = \tau(t_1^i) + \ldots + \tau(t_{m_i}^i)$$

(if $m_i = 0$ then $\tau_i = 0$).
We claim the following.

LEMMA 3. $T_1 \leq T_2$ as in Definition 3.3 iff $\tau_1 \leq \tau_2$.

Proof. By induction.

1. Assume $T_1 \leq T_2$ show $\tau_1 \leq \tau_2$.

   We distinguish several cases:

   (a) If $m_1 = m_2 = 0$ then $T_1 = T_2 = \emptyset$ and $\tau_1 = \tau_2 = 0$.

   (b) If $m_1 = 0$ then $\tau_1 = 0$ and $\tau_1 \leq \tau_2$.

   (c) If $m_1, m_2 \neq 0$ and $t_{m_1}^1 < t_{m_2}^2$, assume $t_{m_1}^1 = t_j$ the j-th element of T. Then $t_{m_2}^2 = t_k$, with $j < k$ then we have

   $$\tau_1 = \tau(t_1^1) + \ldots + \tau(t_{m_1}^1) \leq \tau(t_1) + \ldots + \tau(t_j) < \tau(t_{i+1}) \leq \tau(t_k) \leq \tau_2.$$

   (d) Assume $m_1, m_2 \neq 0$ and further assume $t_{m_1}^1 = t_{m_2}^2$.

   Since $T_1 \leq T_2$, this implies that $T_1 - \{t_{m_1}^1\} \leq T_2 - \{t_{m_2}^2\}$.
   We can assume by induction that

   $$\tau_1 - \tau(t_{m_1}^1) \leq \tau_2 - \tau(t_{m_2}^2)$$

   and hence $\tau_1 \leq \tau_2$.

2. Assume $\tau_1 \leq \tau_2$ and show $T_1 \leq T_2$.

   (a) If $\tau_1 = 0$ then $T_1 = \emptyset$ and so $T_1 \leq T_2$.

   (b) If $\tau_1, \tau_2 \neq 0$, then $m_1, m_2 \neq 0$. We claim we cannot have $t_{m_2}^2 < t_{m_1}^1$ because that would imply $\tau_2 < \tau_1$ as in case (1c) above. Hence $t_{m_1}^1 \leq t_{m_2}^2$. If $t_{m_1}^1 < t_{m_2}^2$, we get $T_1 < T_2$. If $t_{m_1}^1 = t_{m_2}^2$, we get that $\tau_1 - \tau(t_{m_1}^1) \leq \tau_2 - \tau(t_{m_2}^2)$ an hence by the induction hypothesis

   $$T_1 - \{t_{m_1}^1\} \leq T_2 - \{t_{m_2}^2\}$$

   and therefore $T_1 \leq T_2$.

This completes the proof of the Lemma.   ∎

It may be helpful to think of $\tau(t_i)$ as the value of the statement A_i. Thus 100:A_i means the information which A_i expresses is worth $100. The database is ordered according to value. When we use modus ponens, say

$$\$10: A$$

$$\underline{\$20: A \to B}$$

$$(\$10, \$20): B$$

The value of B increases since it is derives from a broader base. We shall define later what value we give to B^7.

When we want to throw out some data in order to maintain consistency, we throw out the lesser valued assumptions, so that less money be wasted. The longer the proof of a formula, the more valued it is because we invest effort in proving it.

Example 3.4. To understand the meaning of the ordering assume we can get a contradiction from a labelled database $\{t_1 : A_1, \ldots, t_4 : A_4\}$, in two ways: one by using $\{t_1 : A_1, t_3 : A_3\}$ and the integrity constraints to prove $\bot$, and also by using $\{t_2 : A_2, t_3 : A_3\}$ and the integrity constraints. We want to know which set of assumptions to throw out, $\{A_1, A_2\}$ or $\{A_3\}$, in order to maintain consistency. We assume that $t_1 < t_2 < t_3 < t_4$. To decide we compare

$$T_1 = \{t_1, t_2\} \quad \text{and} \quad T_2 = \{t_3\}.$$

According to the definition of $<$ as extended to sets, we first compare the sets by the highest label. Since $t_2 < t_3$, we throw out A_1 and A_2.

Note that there are other ways of maintaining consistency. The simple minded way is to take out the first n Wffs of lowest priority which restore

---

[7]We can give numerical ordering to infinite sets as well. Consider a sequence of data of the form $A_0, A_1, A_2, \ldots$ ordered by $A_i < A_j$ iff $j < i$. Let $\tau(n) = \frac{1}{2^n}$. Then

$$\sum_{m \geq n+1} \tau(A_m) = \sum_{m \geq n+1} \frac{1}{2^m} = \frac{1}{2^{n+1}} \sum_{m \geq 0} \frac{1}{2^m} = \frac{1}{2^{n+1}} \cdot 2 = \frac{1}{2^n} = \tau(A_n).$$

Thus we set:

$$\tau(Y) = \sum_{X < Y} \tau(X).$$

We can thus define ordering between sets of Wffs

$$T_1 \leq T_2 \text{ iff } \sum_{X \in T_1} \tau(X) \leq \sum_{X \in T_2} \tau(X).$$

consistency. This policy applied to our example will take out $\{A_1, A_2\}$. Compare with [11] and [4].

Definition 3.5. Let $\mathbb{K}$ be a database and let $<$ be a linear ordering of the labels of $\mathbb{K}$. We want to extend the ordering $<$ to all labels of the form (α, m, n). We use the $\$$ value of the labels as guidance. Suppose $\mathbb{K} \vdash_{\alpha,m,n} A$. This means that to prove A we used the set of labels (data) recorded by $\langle \alpha \rangle$ in the order indicated by α. Suppose we want to charge for the information 'A'. First we charge the value $\tau(\langle \alpha \rangle)$. Then we want to charge for the effort of proving A from the data. This means we want to put a price $\tau((m, n))$ associated with the length of proof. We can assume that for long proofs the additional cost of one more proof step is marginal. Thus we give a lower value to proofs of direct modus ponens ($m = 0$) and higher value to proof which use $\rightarrow$ introduction more heavily. This means lexicographic ordering as follows:

$$(\alpha_1, m_1, n_1) < (\alpha_2, m_2, n_2) \text{ iff}$$

(a) $\langle \alpha_1 \rangle < \langle \alpha_2 \rangle$

or (b) $\langle \alpha_1 \rangle = \langle \alpha_2 \rangle$ and $m_1 < m_2$

or (c) $\langle \alpha_1 \rangle = \langle \alpha_2 \rangle$ and $m_1 = m_2$ and $n_1 < n_2$

or (d) $\langle \alpha_1 \rangle = \langle \alpha_2 \rangle$ and $m_1 = m_2$ and $n_1 = n_2$ and α_2 is a longer sequence than α_1

or (e) $\langle \alpha_1 \rangle = \langle \alpha_2 \rangle$ and $m_1 = m_2$ and $n_1 = n_2$ and α_1 and α_2 are of the same length and $\alpha_1 < \alpha_2$ as sequences in the lexicographic ordering.
     Note that $\alpha_1 < \alpha_2$ as sequences in the lexicographic ordering means that α_2 is the first to use a data item of higher value.

REMARK 4.

1. Note that since for $t : A \in \mathbb{K}$ we have $\mathbb{K} \vdash_{t,0,0} A$, the linear ordering defined in Definition 3.5 is compatible with the linear ordering on the labels of $\mathbb{K}$ (through the identification of 't' with '$(t, 0, 0)$' and actually orders linearly all the deductive closure of $\mathbb{K}$).

2. The linear ordering is well ordered, every set of labels $\{(\alpha, m, n)\}$ has a first element. Hence for every A provable from $\mathbb{K}$ there exists a minimal label $\mu_{\mathbb{K},<}(A)$ such that $\mathbb{K} \vdash_{\mu_{\mathbb{K},<}(A)} A$.

Definition 3.6 (Inconsistency).

1. A database $\mathbb{K}$ is said to be inconsistent if for some α, m, n, $\mathbb{K} \vdash_{\alpha,m,n} \perp$.

   $\mu_{\mathbb{K},<}(\perp)$ is the degree of inconsistency.

2. Let $\mathbb{K}$ be a database with data $t_1 : A_1, \ldots, t_n : A_n$, $t_1 < \ldots < t_n$. An input $a : C$ can be inserted anywhere in the sequence i.e.

$$t_1 < \ldots < t_i < a < t_{i+1} \ldots < t_n.$$

We are interested in two cases:

(1) insistent input $t_n < a$,

(2) non-insistent input $a < t_1$.

It may be that C is already provable from $\mathbb{K}$, in which case the input just gives C an additional label. Thus we may have

$$t_1 : C, \; t_2 : A_2, \ldots t_n : A_n, \; a : C.$$

In the general theory of *LDS* one can talk about aggregation of labels and in such a case the label for C can be $t_1 \uplus a$. Thus the input increases the priority of C.

Example 3.7. The example of the previous section can be modified into the following database $\mathbb{K}$ (we represent $\{X \wedge Y \rightarrow U \wedge Z\}$ by $\{X \rightarrow (Y \rightarrow U), X \rightarrow (Y \rightarrow Z)\}$ and $\{\neg X\}$ by $\{X_1, (X, X_1) \rightarrow \perp\}$).

$$
\begin{aligned}
t_1 : &\quad A \\
t_2 : &\quad A \rightarrow B \\
t_3 : &\quad A \rightarrow (C \rightarrow D) \\
t_4 : &\quad A \rightarrow (C \rightarrow E) \\
t_5 : &\quad D \rightarrow A_1
\end{aligned}
$$

$$(A, A_1) \rightarrow \perp.$$

We have

$$\mathbb{K} \vdash_{t_2 t_1, 0, 1} B$$

$$\mathbb{K} \vdash_{t_3 t_1, 0, 1} C \to D$$

$$\mathbb{K} \vdash_{t_4 t_1, 0, 1} C \to E$$

$$\mathbb{K} \cup \{x : C\} \vdash_{t_3 t_1 x, 0, 2} D$$

$$\mathbb{K} \cup \{x : C\} \vdash_{t_4 t_1 x, 0, 2} E$$

$$\mathbb{K} \cup \{x : C\} \vdash_{t_1 t_5 t_3 t_1 x, 0, 3} \perp.$$

Thus although $\mathbb{K} \cup \{x : C\}$ is not consistent, it can prove E with $y_1 = (t_4 t_1 x, 0, 2)$ and prove D with $y_2 = (t_3 t_1 x, 0, 2)$ and we have that $\mathbb{K} \cup \{y_1 : E, y_2 : D\}$ is consistent.

Also $\mathbb{K} \cup \{x : C\} \vdash_{t_2 t_1, 0, 1} B$ and $(\mathbb{K} - \{t_1 : A\}) \cup \{x : C\}$ is consistent with B and D.

Definition 3.8 (Priority consistency maintenance). Let $\mathbb{K}$ be a database and assume that the data in $\mathbb{K}$ has the form $t_1 : A_1, \ldots, t_n : A_n$ with $t_1 < \ldots < t_n$. Assume $\mathbb{K}$ is inconsistent. Our purpose is to use the ordering $<$ to decide on which subset of $\mathbb{K}$ to throw out in order to maintain consistency. We must identify a lowest priority (i.e. $<$) set such that if it is taken out, *all* the proofs of $\perp$ will be blocked. The definitions below lead to this set.

A subset $S \subseteq \{t_1, \ldots, t_n\}$ is said to be inconsistent if for some α, m, n such that $\langle \alpha \rangle = S$ we have $\mathbb{K} \vdash_{\alpha, m, n} \perp$. A set S' is said to be *critical* for $\perp$ if every inconsistent set S intersects it and no proper subset S'' of S' has this property. Critical sets exist. A set $S^\perp$ is said to be minimally critical for $\perp$ if it is critical for $\perp$ and for every other critical set S' we have $S^\perp \leq S'$.

By Lemma 2, $S^\perp$ exists uniquely.

Let $S^\perp$ be the minimal critical set for $\mathbb{K}$ and let $\mathbb{K}^\perp$ be

$$\mathbb{K}^\perp = \{t_i : A_i | t_i \in S^\perp\}.$$

Then $\mathbb{K} - \mathbb{K}^\perp$ is consistent. We let $\mathbb{K}_{cons}$ be this set and this is the result of our priority consistency maintenance. Note that this set may be empty if every member of $\mathbb{K}$ is inconsistent.

Definition 3.9 (∗ Revision). Let $\mathbb{K}$ be a consistent database with data $t_1 : A_1, \ldots, t_n : A_n$ with $t_1 < \ldots < t_n$. Let $a : C$ be a consistent[8] and insistent input into $\mathbb{K}$ and let $\mathbb{K}_1$ be the database $\mathbb{K} \cup \{a : C\}$ with $t_n < a$. Define $\mathbb{K} \ast (a : C)$ as follows:

- If $\mathbb{K}_1$ is consistent let $\mathbb{K} \ast (a : C) = \mathbb{K}_1$.

- If $\mathbb{K}_1$ is not consistent, let $\mathbb{K} \ast (a : C)$ be $(\mathbb{K}_1)_{\text{cons}}$, as defined in Definition 3.8.

Note that since $a : C$ is itself consistent and it has the highest priority in $\mathbb{K}_1$, it will remain in $(\mathbb{K}_1)_{\text{cons}}$ and therefore our ∗ revision does not necessarily contradict the AGM postulates. This matter will be examined in Section 4.

Also note that we can define

$$\mathbb{K} \ast (a_1 : C_1, \ldots, a_m : C_m),$$

for a sequence $a_1 < \ldots < a_m$ in the same manner.

We shall see later that if $a_2 : C_2$ is consistent with $\mathbb{K} \ast (a_1 : C_1)$ then

$$(\mathbb{K} \ast (a_1 : C_1)) \ast (a_2 : C_2) = \mathbb{K} \ast (a_1 : C_1, a_2 : C_2).$$

Since we can regard the labels in as dummies just indicating the order of priority of the assumptions, we can present the data in $\mathbb{K}$ as $(A_1, \ldots, A_n)$ in which case we can present $\mathbb{K} \ast (a : C)$ as $\mathbb{K} \ast C$, or even better as $(A_1, \ldots, A_n) \ast C$, ignoring the integrity constraints of $\mathbb{K}$ (which are assumed to be fixed).

Definition 3.10 (Compromise revision).

Let $\mathbb{K}$ and $\mathbb{K}_1$ be as in Definition 3.9 and assume $\mathbb{K}_1$ is not consistent. Rather than settle for the revised theory $\mathbb{K} \ast C$, which just throws out some of the data in $\mathbb{K}_1$, we would like to rescue some of the consequences of $\mathbb{K}_1$ by compromising.

We now address the machinery needed to achieve this:

Let X be a Wff. We say $S^{\perp}$ is critical for X if for every α, m, n such that $\mathbb{K}_1 \vdash_{\alpha, m, n} X$ we have $\langle \alpha \rangle \cap S^{\perp} \neq \emptyset$. This means that $\mathbb{K}_1 \vdash X$ but $\mathbb{K}_1 - \mathbb{K}_1^{\perp} \nvdash X$.

Let $s_X = (\alpha_0, m_0, n_0)$ be the *minimal* (α, m, n) such that $\mathbb{K}_1 \vdash_{(\alpha, m, n)} X$. Since these labels are lexicographically and linearly ordered, we get a linear ordering of all X such that $S^{\perp}$ is critical for X. First (lower priority) in the

---

[8] When we say that $a : C$ is a consistent input into $\mathbb{K}$, we mean that $a : C$ is consistent relative to the integrity constraints of $\mathbb{K}$. We have to take this view because we are not allowed to revise our integrity constraints, only our data. So for example if $\mathbb{K} = (a, c \to \perp)$, the input c is inconsistent relative to the integrity constraints of $\mathbb{K}$ and hence we will not insist on accepting it. If we ignore the integrity constraints of $\mathbb{K}$ then the input is consistent, but $\mathbb{K}$ and c are inconsistent and we have no way of maintaining consistency.

ordering come $X's$ which can be proved from $\mathbb{K}_1^\perp$ alone and then come the rest.

We now put forward an algorithm which will add to $\mathbb{K}_1 - \mathbb{K}_1^\perp$ as many of these $X's$ as possible.

We must be careful here because we may have in our system axioms of the form

$$(X \to Y) \to (X \to (X \to Y))$$

which will generate an infinite number of formulas of the form $X \to (X \to \dots \to (X \to Y)\dots)$. To avoid that we can limit the formulas we consider to subformulas of the formulas in the database or possibly to a certain length of proof. We can thus assume that we are considering some reasonably chosen set of consequences that we wish to include (compromise on). We order the $X's$ as $X_1, X_2, X_3, \dots$ where X_i has higher priority than X_j for $i > j$. We are now ready to define the Compromise extension,

$$\mathbb{K}_{comp} \supseteq \mathbb{K}_1 - \mathbb{K}_1^\perp,$$

by induction. First we need some renaming of labels. For each $s : A \in \mathbb{K}_1$ we can view the label 's' as '$(s,0,0)$'. This is so because $\mathbb{K}_1 \vdash_{s,0,0} A$. With this identification, the priority label $(s,0,0)$ can be compared with the label s_{X_i} of any X_i in the sequence and we can certainly input $s_{X_i} : X_i$ into the theory $\mathbb{K}_1 - \mathbb{K}_1^\perp$, since its labels are $<$ comparable with s_{X_i}.
We now give the inductive definition:

1. Let $\mathbb{K}_{comp}^\circ = \mathbb{K}_1 - \mathbb{K}_1^\perp$ (with labels $(t_i,0,0)$).

2. Assume $\mathbb{K}_{comp}^m$ has been defined for $m \geq 0$ and is consistent. Let

$$\mathbb{K}_{comp}^{m+1} = \mathbb{K}_{comp}^m \cup \{s_{X_i} : X_i\}$$
$$\text{if consistent and } \mathbb{K}_{comp}^m \text{ otherwise.}$$

Let
$$\mathbb{K}_{comp} = \bigcup_m \mathbb{K}_{comp}^m.$$

We finally define $\mathbb{K} + C$ to be $\mathbb{K}_{comp}$.

Note that we put into $\mathbb{K}_{comp}$ $X's$ of higher priority first. This means that if it takes longer to prove X then it is more likely that X consistent with the data!

Example 3.11.

Let us reconsider the Example 3.7 for the application of our compromise algorithm. We rewrite it as

$(t_1, 0, 0):$ A (data in $\mathbb{K}$)

$(t_2, 0, 0):$ $A \rightarrow B$ (data in $\mathbb{K}$)

$(t_3, 0, 0):$ $A \rightarrow (C \rightarrow D)$ (data in $\mathbb{K}$)

$(t_4, 0, 0):$ $A \rightarrow (C \rightarrow E)$ (data in $\mathbb{K}$)

$(t_5, 0, 0):$ $D \rightarrow A_1$ (data in $\mathbb{K}$)

$(a, 0, 0):$ C (input)

$(A, A_1) \rightarrow$ $\bot$ (integrity constraint)

We are giving the input $a : C$ the highest priority i.e. $t_1 < \ldots < t_5 < a$. This is therefore the case of insistent input policy.

Let us proceed to calculate $\mathbb{K} + C$. The set $\mathbb{K}_1$ is inconsistent. We have

$$\mathbb{K}_1 \vdash_{t_1 t_5 t_3 t_1 a, 0, 3} \bot.$$

The critical subsets of labels for $\bot$ are

$$T_1 = \{(t_1, 0, 0)\}, \quad T_3 = \{(t_3, 0, 0)\}, \quad T_5 = \{(t_5, 0, 0)\},$$

and

$$T_6 = \{(a, 0, 0)\}.$$

The minimally critical set for $\bot$ is T_1. Therefore

$$\mathbb{K}^{\circ}_{comp} = \mathbb{K}_1 - \{(t_1, 0, 0) : A\}.$$

The sequence of $X's$ for which T_1 is also critical is

$$(t_2 t_1, 0, 1) : B$$

$$(t_3 t_1 a, 0, 2) : D$$

$$(t_4 t_1 a, 0, 2) : E$$

The priority order from higher to lower is

$$X_1 = E, \quad X_2 = D, \quad X_3 = B.$$

We add them in stages. D causes inconsistency and is not added, and so the compromise theory $\mathbb{K} + \{a : C\}$ is the following, in order of their labels:

$(t_2, 0, 0):$ $A \to B$

$(t_2 t_1, 0, 1):$ B

$(t_3, 0, 0):$ $A \to (C \to D)$

$(t_4, 0, 0):$ $A \to (C \to E)$

$(t_5, 0, 0):$ $D \to A_1$

$(a, 0, 0):$ C

$(t_4 t_1 a, 0, 2):$ E

$$(A, A_1) \to \perp.$$

Notice that the compromise solution does not have the input C at highest priority. E has highest priority.

Let us now check what happens if we follow a non-insistent input policy. This means we give $a : C$ the lowest priority. Thus the labels are now ordered $a < t_1 < \ldots < t_5$. The critical subsets are the same but the minimal critical subset now is $T_6 = \{(a, 0, 0)\}$.

Therefore in this case the initial compromise set is $\mathbb{K}_1 - \{(a, 0, 0) : C\}$ i.e. it is $\mathbb{K}$. The sequence of $X's$ for which T_6 is also critical now depends on the logic of the labels. Assuming the axiom of commutativity

$$X \to (Y \to Z) \equiv Y \to (X \to Z).$$

We get

$$\mathbb{K}_1 \vdash_{t_3 t_1, 1, 2} A \to D$$

$$\mathbb{K}_1 \vdash_{t_4 t_1, 1, 2} A \to E.$$

The higher priority is the second one. We cannot add $A \to D$ as a compromise because it leads to inconsistency but we can add

$$(t_4 t_1, 1, 2) : A \to E.$$

The final compromise database for the case of non-insistent input policy is

$$\mathbb{K} \cup \{(t_4 t_1, 1, 2) : A \to E\}.$$

$A \to E$ comes in priority after $A \to (C \to E)$ but before $D \to A_1$.

Thus the non-insistent compromise policy does not just reject C but allows for its consequence $A \to E$ to be accepted with an appropriate place in the ordering.

We now proceed with some simplifying theorems for our revision process.

Definition 3.12 ($\star$ Revision). Let $\mathbb{K}$ be a database of the form

$$\mathbb{K} = ((A_1, \ldots, A_n), \mathbb{C}),$$

where $A_1, \ldots, A_n$ are the data and $\mathbb{C}$ the integrity constraints. Let $\mathbb{N}$ be an additional list $(C_1, \ldots, C_m)$ of inputs. Assume that $\mathbb{K}$ is consistent and $\mathbb{N}$ is consistent relative to the integrity constraints of $\mathbb{K}$. We define $\star$ revision by induction as follows:

(1) Let $\mathbb{K}^{\star}_{n+1} = (\mathbb{N}, \mathbb{C})$.

(2) Assume $\mathbb{K}^{\star}_i$ has been defined for all $i > m$. Define $\mathbb{K}^{\star}_m$ to be $\mathbb{K}^{\star}_{m+1}$ if $\mathbb{K}^{\star}_{m+1}$ is inconsistent with A_m. Otherwise let

$$\mathbb{K}^{\star}_m = (A_m, \mathbb{K}^{\star}_{m+1}).$$

(3) Let $\mathbb{K} \star \mathbb{N} = \mathbb{K}^{\star}_1$.

The idea of $\star$ revision is to look at $(A_1, \ldots, A_n, \mathbb{N}, \mathbb{C})$ and go through the list top to bottom, i.e. go through $(A_n, A_{n-1}, \ldots)$, and accept A_i into the revised theory if it is consistent to add it and otherwise skip A_i and consider A_{i-1}, for $i = n, n-1, \ldots, 1$[9].

We now prove that $\star$ revision and $*$ revision are the same.

Theorem 3.13 (Equivalence of $*$ and $\star$). Let $\mathbb{K}$ and $\mathbb{N}$ be as in Definition 3.12. Then

$$\mathbb{K} * \mathbb{N} = \mathbb{K} \star \mathbb{N}.$$

Proof. By induction on the length of the data sequence in $\mathbb{K}$.

For data a one point sequence the equivalence is clear.

Assume the equivalence holds for $\mathbb{K} = (A_1, \ldots, A_k, \mathbb{C})$.

Consider

$$\mathbb{K}_0 = (A_1, \ldots, A_{k+1}, \mathbb{N}, \mathbb{C})$$

---

[9]After this paper was written, Benjamin Grosof visited me in London and I showed him the paper. He told me about the $\star$ revision, which he studied in his thesis [9]. I gave it some thought and found it to be equivalent to $*$ revision, Theorem 3.13 below. Grosof also mentioned that he could handle any upward (i.e. $>$) well ordered sequence of data. This is clear from the $\star$ construction algorithm. Is should be compared with the treatment of infinite sequences in Footnote 7.

and assume that

$$\mathbb{K}_0^\perp = (A_{i_1}, \ldots, A_{i_r}) \; 1 \le i_1 < i_2 < \ldots < i_r < k + 1.$$

This means that $\mathbb{K} * N = \mathbb{K}_0 - \mathbb{K}_0^\perp$.

LEMMA 5. *In $\mathbb{K}_0$, the tail $(A_{i_r}, A_{i_r+1}, \ldots)$ is inconsistent.*

Proof. Otherwise every inconsistent set containing A_{i_r} must contain some B earlier in the sequence. This will make $(A_1, A_2, \ldots, A_{i_r-1})$ a less preferable critical set than $\mathbb{K}_0^\perp$ which is a contradiction. ∎

LEMMA 6. $\mathbb{K}_1^\perp = \mathbb{K}_0^\perp - (A_{i_r})$.

Proof.

(1) First we prove that $\mathbb{K}_0^\perp - (A_{i_r})$ is a critical set in $\mathbb{K}_1$. To show this let B be an inconsistent subset of $\mathbb{K}_1$. It is certainly inconsistent in $\mathbb{K}_0$ and hence it intersects $\mathbb{K}_0^\perp$, and hence it intersects $\mathbb{K}_0^\perp - (A_{i_r})$. Thus $\mathbb{K}_0^\perp - (A_{i_r})$ is a critical set.

(2) We now show that $\mathbb{K}_0^\perp - (A_{i_r})$ is minimal, i.e. it is of less priority than any other critical set. Let M be a minimally critical set for $\mathbb{K}_1$. We want to show $\mathbb{K}^\perp - (A_{i_r}) \le M$. To achieve this we show first that $M \cup (A_{i_r})$ is a critical set for $\mathbb{K}_0$. This will imply that $\mathbb{K}_0^\perp \le M \cup (A_{i_r})$. We second show that $M \le (A_{i_r})$. Together the first and second items imply that $\mathbb{K}_0^\perp - (A_{i_r}) \le M$.

Let B an inconsistent subset of $\mathbb{K}_0$. If A_{i_r} is in B then it intersects $M \cup (A_{i_r})$. Otherwise B is an inconsistent subset of $\mathbb{K}_1$ and so intersects M. Thus

$$\mathbb{K}_0^\perp = (A_1, \ldots, A_{i_r}) \le M \cup (A_{i_r}).$$

We want to show that

$$(A_{i_r}, \ldots, A_{i_r-1}) \le M.$$

To show this it is sufficient to show that A_{i_r} is the top priority element of $M \cup (A_{i_r})$. Otherwise let M be the top element of M. We have $A_{i_r} < M$.

We get a contradiction. We observe (as in Lemma 5) that the tail $(M, \ldots)$ in $\mathbb{K}_1$ is inconsistent. But it is inconsistent in $\mathbb{K}_0$ and therefore should intersect $\mathbb{K}_0^\perp$, which is not possible. Thus the top element of $M \cup \{A_{i_r}\}$ is A_{i_r}, and so we can present this set as (M, A_{i_r}).

Summing up, we have shown that $\mathbb{K}_0^\perp \le (M, A_{i_r})$ and hence $\mathbb{K}_0^\perp - (A_{i_r}) \le M$ which proves that $\mathbb{K}_0^\perp - (A_{i_r})$ is also minimal.

(1) and (2) above yield the statement of the lemma. ∎

We are now ready to conclude the inductive stage of the proof of Theorem 3.13. We need to show that the $\star$ computation process applied to the database

$$\mathbb{K}_0 = (A_1, \ldots, A_{k+1}, \mathbb{N}, \mathbb{C})$$

yields the set $\mathbb{K}_1 - \mathbb{K}_0^\perp$. We know that the tail $(A_{i_r}, A_{i_r+1}, \ldots)$ is inconsistent and that the tail $(A_{i_r+1}, \ldots)$ is consistent. Thus the $\star$ process will accept the tail $(A_{i_r+1} \ldots)$ and reject A_{i_r}, and at this point will continue to examine one by one the elements $A_{i_r-1}, A_{i_r-2}, \ldots$.

By the induction hypothesis, since we proved that the critical set for $\mathbb{K}_1 = \mathbb{K}_0 - (A_{i_r})$ is $\mathbb{K}_0^\perp - (A_{i_r}) = (A_{i_1}, \ldots, A_{i_{r-1}})$, we get that the $\star$ process will exclude exactly $\mathbb{K}_0^\perp - (A_{i_r})$. The total result of the process is therefore to exclude $\mathbb{K}_0^\perp$, which is what the induction step is supposed to prove.

This completes the proof of Theorem 3.13.   ∎

4 COMPARISON WITH AGM REVISION FOR CLASSICAL LOGIC

Let us assume that we are dealing with classical logic and that our Wffs are classical logic formulas with $\rightarrow$ and $\perp$. $\wedge, \vee, \neg$ are therefore definable. For a successful comparison we must use our machinery to define a revision process (which we denote by $*$) which will be acceptable within the AGM approach but at the same time remain within our approach too.

We will not do compromise revision because the way we have done it relied on labelling and the concept $\vdash_{t,m,n}$, which we do not want to get into for the case of classical logic (we shall need a *Labelled Deductive System* formulation of classical logic affording full control on proofs). We thus do $*$ revision as in Definition 3.9. For this the only notion we need is that a subset of the data can prove $\perp$, i.e. a notion of a subset being inconsistent and any traditional formulation of classical logic can give us that.

So let us start!

Definition 4.1.

Let $\sigma = (A_1, A_2, A_3 \ldots)$ be an input stream. Define a sequence of databases by induction as follows:

$$\mathbb{K}_0^* = \emptyset$$
$$\vdots$$
$$\mathbb{K}_{n+1}^* = \mathbb{K}_n^* * A_{n+1}$$

Compare with Definition 6.2 and note that we do not need integrity constraints.

This kind of revision can be presented as follows. A database is a sequence of formulas $\mathbb{K} = (A_1, \ldots, A_n)$. An input is a formula C, forming the new sequence $\mathbb{K}_1 = (A_1, \ldots, A_n, C)$. Deduction is as in classical logic and so the notion of inconsistency is clear. $\mathbb{K}_1$ can be considered as an ordinary classical theory $\{A_1, \ldots, A_n, C\}$. If $\mathbb{K}_1$ is inconsistent in classical logic, we need to perform insistent input revision on $\mathbb{K}_1$. We thus introduce labels (just to do our priority calculations),

$$t_1 : A_1, \ldots, \ t_n : A_n, \ a : C$$

such that $t_1 < \ldots < t_n < a$ and perform the $*$ revision of Definition 3.9. This will give us a new theory $\mathbb{K} * C$, (if we ignore the labels).

Thus we have described a process $\Pi_*(\mathbb{K}, C)$ for going from $\mathbb{K}$ to $\mathbb{K} * C$.

We now check the AGM postulates for this process.

The Katsuno–Mendelzon (update) variant of the AGM postulates includes:

R1: $\mathbb{K} \circ C \vdash C$.

R2: If $\mathbb{K} \cup \{C\}$ is consistent then $\mathbb{K} \circ C = \mathbb{K} \cup \{C\}$.

R3: If C is consistent then so is $\mathbb{K} \circ C$.

R4: If $\mathbb{K}_1$ is equivalent to $\mathbb{K}_2$ and C_1 is equivalent to C_2 then $\mathbb{K}_1 \circ C_1$ is equivalent to $\mathbb{K}_2 \circ C_2$.

R5: $(\mathbb{K} \circ C) \wedge \varphi \vdash \mathbb{K} \circ (C \wedge \varphi)$.

R6: If $(\mathbb{K} \circ C) \wedge \varphi$ is consistent then $\mathbb{K} \circ (C \wedge \varphi) \vdash (\mathbb{K} \circ C) \wedge \varphi$.

Darwiche and Pearl [3] added the following postulates to cover iterated revision[10]

C1: If $\alpha \vdash \beta$ then $(\mathbb{K} \circ \beta) \circ \alpha \equiv \mathbb{K} \circ \alpha$,

C2: If $\alpha \vdash \neg\beta$ then $(\mathbb{K} \circ \beta) \circ \alpha \vdash \mathbb{K} \circ \alpha$,

C3: $\mathbb{K} \circ \alpha \vdash \beta$ implies $(\mathbb{K} \circ \beta) \circ \alpha \vdash \beta$,

C4: If $\mathbb{K} \circ \alpha \nvdash \neg\beta$ then $(\mathbb{K} \circ \beta) \circ \alpha \nvdash \neg\beta$.

We note that there are two main differences between our process and the AGM context:

1. AGM deals with deductively closed theories while we deal with (axiomatic) databases, following [10].

---

[10]There is a bit of fine tuning in whether $\mathbb{K}$ is an epistemic state (as in Darwiche and Pearl) or a belief set (as in Katsuno and Mendelzon). Let us not worry about it.

2. Our databases are a sequence of axioms, ordered according to priority which we can assume reflects the history of previous updates.

This means that certain notions occurring in the AGM context, need to be clarified in our context. Among them are what is meant by $\mathbb{K} \equiv \mathbb{K}'$ (equivalence of two theories) and $\mathbb{K} \wedge \varphi$ (conjunction of a theory and a Wff).

With this in mind, let us start our comparison by checking the postulates one by one.

(R1) $\mathbb{K} * C \vdash C$.

This rule has two parts.

If C is a consistent input, it means that no rejection is allowed. Indeed since the process assigns to C the highest priority we have $C \in \mathbb{K} * C$.

If C is inconsistent our process will reject C. However had we insisted on leaving C in $\mathbb{K} * C$, then it would be inconsistent and since in classical logic an inconsistent theory can prove anything, we still get $\mathbb{K} * C \vdash C$[11].

Thus we can say that Π_* agrees with (R1).

(R2) If $\mathbb{K}_1$ is consistent then it equals $\mathbb{K} * C$.

This holds for our Π_*.

(R3) If C is consistent then so is $\mathbb{K} * C$.

Our revision satisfies this principle.

(R4) $\mathbb{K} \equiv \mathbb{K}'$ and $C \equiv C'$ imply $\mathbb{K} * C \equiv \mathbb{K}' * C'$.

This principle holds but we need a plausible definition of two theories being equivalent, since our theories are sequences of formulas[12]. We can regard the theories as sets and require that $\bigwedge \mathbb{K} \equiv \bigwedge \mathbb{K}'$. This, however, is not sufficient, since the revision process depends on the order. If we examine the revision process we observe that it depends on critical subsets of labels participating in the inconsistency. Thus we need to define a notion which will respect the revision process. The only definition we can give is the obvious one.

$$(A_1, \ldots, A_n) \vdash (B_1, \ldots, B_m)$$

---

[11] Note that in general logics several things can happen. First an inconsistent theory may not prove everything. It makes sense to ask that at least $\mathbb{K} * C$ proves C itself. What can happen, that although C is inconsistent, $\mathbb{K} * C$ can still be consistent and still prove the inconsistent part C. This happens in general labelled theories.

[12] For the case of (R4) formulated for epistemic states, Darwiche and Pearl require identity of states.

iff $n = m$ and for all $i, A_i \vdash B_i$. We let $\mathbb{K} \equiv \mathbb{K}'$ mean $\mathbb{K} \vdash \mathbb{K}'$ and $\mathbb{K}' \vdash \mathbb{K}$. To see why we opt for this definition consider the two databases $\mathbb{K} = (a, p, q)$ and $\mathbb{K}' = (a, p \wedge q)$ and the update $C = \neg(p \wedge q)$ we have

$$\mathbb{K} * C \; = \; (a, q, C)$$
$$\mathbb{K}' * C \; = \; (a, C).$$

We now check $(R5)$ and $(R6)$.

(R5) $(\mathbb{K} * C) \wedge \varphi \vdash \mathbb{K} * (C \wedge \varphi)$.

(R6) If $(\mathbb{K} * C) \wedge \varphi$ is consistent then $\mathbb{K} * (C \wedge \varphi) \vdash (\mathbb{K} * C) \wedge \varphi$.

The above two together say that if φ is consistent with $\mathbb{K} * C$ then

$$(\mathbb{K} * C) \wedge \varphi \equiv \mathbb{K} * (C \wedge \varphi).$$

We need to explain what $(X_1, \ldots, X_n) \wedge \varphi$ means. We take it to mean $(X_1, \ldots, X_{n-1}, X_n, \varphi)$, i.e. we add φ as an input to be the highest priority member of $\mathbb{K}$.

Now assume that $\mathbb{K}$ is the merge of two sequences $\mathbb{K}_a = (A_1, \ldots, A_n)$ and $\mathbb{K}_b = (B_1, \ldots, B_m)$. Let $\mathbb{K}_1 = (\mathbb{K}, C)$ and assume that

$$\mathbb{K} * C = (B_1, \ldots, B_m, C).$$

Thus our consistency maintenance process applied to $\mathbb{K}_1$ yields $\mathbb{K} * C$. If φ is consistent with $\mathbb{K} * C$, we show that the consistency maintenance applied to $\mathbb{K}_2 = (\mathbb{K}, C, \varphi)$ yields $\mathbb{K}_3 = (B_1, \ldots, B_m, C, \varphi)$.

In our proof, we use the fact that $\mathbb{K}_a$ is a critical set of $\mathbb{K}_1$ with lowest priority. Indeed this was the reason it was thrown out. We claim $(A_1, \ldots, A_n)$ is critical in $\mathbb{K}_3$ and is minimal. Let $\mathbb{K}'$ be a set of Wffs leading to inconsistency. If φ is not included in $\mathbb{K}'$ then $\mathbb{K}'$ certainly intersects $(A_1, \ldots, A_n)$. If φ is included $\mathbb{K}'$ and if $\mathbb{K}'$ does not intersect $(A_1, \ldots, A_n)$ then φ is not consistent with $\mathbb{K} * C$, which is contrary to assumption. Now any other critical set $\mathbb{K}_0$, either contains φ, in which case it is of the highest priority or it does not contain φ in which case $\mathbb{K}_a < \mathbb{K}_0$. Thus $\mathbb{K}_a$ is critical and minimal in $\mathbb{K}_2$ and so

$$(\mathbb{K} * (C, \varphi)) = (\mathbb{K} * C) \wedge \varphi.$$

We have actually proved the following.

(R*5) If φ is consistent with $(\mathbb{K} * C)$ then

$$(\mathbb{K} * C) * \varphi = \mathbb{K} * (C, \varphi).$$

Since our process Π_* is a specific algorithmic one, iterated revision is no problem and its properties can be figured out. Let us check the Darwiche–Pearl postulates for our process.

(C1) If $\alpha \vdash \beta$ then $(\mathbb{K} * \beta) * \alpha \equiv \mathbb{K} * \alpha$.

This property does not hold because we perceive our databases as sequences. Let

$$\mathbb{K} = (c \to x \wedge a, x \to \perp), \ \beta = c, \ \alpha = c \wedge x.$$

Then

$$\mathbb{K} * \beta = (x \to \perp, c)$$

$$(\mathbb{K} * \beta) * \alpha = (c, c \wedge x)$$

$$\mathbb{K} * \alpha = (c \to x \wedge a, c \wedge x)$$

which are not the same.

(C2) If $\alpha \vdash \neg \beta$ then $(\mathbb{K} * \beta) * \alpha \vdash \mathbb{K} * \alpha$.

This does not hold either.

Let
$$\mathbb{K} = (a, a \wedge x \to \perp), \ \alpha = \neg x \text{ and } \beta = x.$$

Then

$$\mathbb{K} * \beta \ = \ (a \wedge x \to \perp, x)$$

$$(\mathbb{K} * \beta) * \alpha \ = \ (a \wedge x \to \perp, \neg x)$$

$$\mathbb{K} * \alpha \ = \ (a, a \wedge x \to \perp, \neg x).$$

(C3) $\mathbb{K} * \alpha \vdash \beta$ implies $(\mathbb{K} * \beta) * \alpha \vdash \beta$.

(C4) $\mathbb{K} * \alpha \nvdash \neg \beta$ then $(\mathbb{K} * \beta) * \alpha \nvdash \neg \beta$.

Both (C3) and (C4) hold. In fact we shall prove (C*3,4).

(C*3,4) If $\mathbb{K} * \alpha$ is consistent with β then $(\mathbb{K} * \beta) * \alpha \vdash \beta$.

Assume $\mathbb{K}_\alpha$ is the subdatabase of $\mathbb{K}$ thrown out by the process Π_*. Thus

$$\mathbb{K} * \alpha = (\mathbb{K} - \mathbb{K}_\alpha, \alpha).$$

Assume β is consistent with $\mathbb{K} * \alpha$. Consider $\mathbb{K} * \beta$. Let $\mathbb{K}_\beta$ be what is thrown out, that is

$$\mathbb{K} * \beta = (\mathbb{K} - \mathbb{K}_\beta, \beta).$$

Consider $(\mathbb{K} - \mathbb{K}_\beta, \beta, \alpha)$. We claim the process Π_* does not throw β out, and so

$$(\mathbb{K} * \beta) * \alpha \vdash \beta.$$

Consider the set $\mathbb{K} - \mathbb{K}_\beta$ as a possible critical set. If every proof of inconsistency with α uses some element from $\mathbb{K} - \mathbb{K}_\beta$ then the set we throw out will be a subset of $\mathbb{K} - \mathbb{K}_\beta$ and will not include β.

The other possibility is that there is a proof of inconsistency involving β, α alone. This cannot happen because $\mathbb{K} * \alpha$ includes α and is supposed to be consistent with β.

5   COMPARISON WITH LEHMANN'S REVISED BELIEF REVISION

Daniel Lehmann in IJCAI 95 [12] proposed that revision should take account of the history of previous inputs. He denotes his database by $[\sigma]$, where σ is the sequence of all previous inputs and $[\sigma]$ is the classical theory which is the current database, i.e. if $\sigma = (\sigma_1, \ldots, \sigma_n)$ then

$$[\sigma] = ((\sigma_1 \cdot \sigma_2) \cdot \sigma_3 \ldots) \cdot \sigma_n$$

where $\mathbb{K} \cdot C$ denotes the Lehmann revision. Thus using our notation of Definition 4.1, we can regard

$$\sigma = (\sigma_1, \sigma_2, \ldots, \sigma_n, \top, \top, \ldots)$$

as an infinite input stream, then $[\sigma]$ is $\mathbb{K}_n^*$.

Lehmann gives the following rationality postulates for his belief revision (read $x \in [\sigma]$ as $[\alpha] \vdash x$).

(I1) $[\sigma]$ is a consistent theory.

(I2) $a \in [\sigma \cdot a]^{13}$.

(I3) If $b \in [\sigma \cdot a]$ then $(a \to b) \in [\sigma]$.

(I4) If $a \in [\sigma]$ then $[\sigma \cdot \tau] = [\sigma \cdot a \cdot \tau]$.

(I5) If $b \models a$ then $[\sigma \cdot a \cdot b \cdot \tau] = [\sigma \cdot b \cdot \tau]$.

---

[13] $[\sigma \cdot a]$ really means $[\sigma] \cdot a$.

(I6) If $\neg b \notin [\sigma \cdot a]$ then $[\sigma \cdot a \cdot b \cdot \tau] = [\sigma \cdot a \cdot (a \wedge b) \cdot \tau]$.

(I7) $[\sigma \cdot \neg b \cdot b] \subseteq$ the set of all logical consequence of $[\sigma] \cup \{b\}$.

Before embarking on the task of checking Lehmann's postulates one by one, let us note that the idea of historical remembering of previous inputs is orthogonal to our idea of compromise revision and to the idea of databases being lists. This point is best explained by an example.

Consider the input stream

$$\sigma = (d, d \to e, d \wedge c \to \bot, c, c \to \bot).$$

Apply it to the empty database. We get

$$
\begin{aligned}
\mathbb{K}_0 &= \emptyset \\
\mathbb{K}_1 &= (d) \\
\mathbb{K}_2 &= (d, d \to e) \\
\mathbb{K}_3 &= (d, d \to e, d \wedge c \to \bot) \\
\mathbb{K}_4^* &= (d \to e, d \wedge c \to \bot, c)
\end{aligned}
$$

$\mathbb{K}_4^*$ is the result of a consistency maintenance on the inconsistent database $(\mathbb{K}_3, c)$ by a non compromise revision.

A compromise revision will yield

$$\mathbb{K}_4^+ = (d \to e, e, d \wedge c \to \bot, c).$$

In either case we no longer remember the input history. All we have is the current $\mathbb{K}_4$ database. So when the next input comes in (namely $c \to \bot$) we get

$$\mathbb{K}_5^* = (d \to e, d \wedge c \to \bot, c \to \bot)$$

and

$$\mathbb{K}_5^+ = (d \to e, e, d \wedge c \to \bot, c \to \bot).$$

Had we remembered the history we might have wished to restore the input 'd' which was thrown out at stage 4.

We can therefore define a new history sensitive compromise revision which tries persistently to put back old data thrown out in previous stages, while trying to compromise on all the data it wants to put in.

Definition 5.1 (Historical revision).
Let $\sigma = (A_1, A_2, \ldots)$ be an input stream. Define $\mathbb{K}_n^\sigma$ as follows:

$$\mathbb{K}_0^\sigma = \emptyset$$

$$\vdots$$

$$\mathbb{K}_{n+1}^\sigma = (B_1, \ldots, B_{k_n}, \mathbb{K}_n^\sigma) * A_{n+1}.$$

Where $B_1, \ldots, B_{k_n}$ are the Wffs from previous $\mathbb{K}_i$, $i \leq n$, (ordered according to their historical priority labels) which were thrown out in previous stages of revision. These are appended with low priority to the current database (i.e. $\mathbb{K}_n^\sigma$).

Another way of looking at it is the simultaneous input of $(B_1, \ldots, B_{k_n}, A_{n+1})$ into the slots as indicated [14].

We now check what postulates hold for our $*$ of Definition 4.1.

(I1) holds.

(I2) holds.

(I3) holds.

To show this note that in our notation this means that if $\mathbb{K}_n^* * a \vdash b$ then $\mathbb{K}_n^* \vdash a \to b$.

Assume $\mathbb{K}_n^* = (A_1, \ldots, A_k)$. Then $\mathbb{K}_n^* * a$ is the result of consistency maintenance Π_* applied to $\mathbb{K}' = (A_1, \ldots, A_k, a)$. If $\mathbb{K}'$ is consistent then $\mathbb{K}_n^* * a = \mathbb{K}'$ and so $\mathbb{K}_n^* \vdash a \to b$.

Otherwise some $\mathbb{K}_a' = (A_{i_1}, \ldots, A_{i_m})$ are thrown out and

$$\mathbb{K}_n^* * a = (\mathbb{K}_n^* - \mathbb{K}_a', a).$$

Therefore $\mathbb{K}_n^* - \mathbb{K}_a \vdash a \to b$ and hence $\mathbb{K}_n^* \vdash a \to b$.

(I4) In our notation this postulate says the following:

If $\mathbb{K}_n^* \vdash a$ then $(\mathbb{K}_n^* * \tau) \equiv (\mathbb{K}_n^* * a) * \tau$. This does not hold.

Let

$$\mathbb{K}_n^* = (b, b \to a, \alpha, \alpha \wedge a \wedge \tau \to \perp).$$

Then clearly

$$\mathbb{K}_n^* \vdash a.$$

Hence

$$(\mathbb{K}_n^* * a) = (\mathbb{K}_n^*, a).$$

We therefore have that

$$(\mathbb{K}_n^* * a) * \tau = (b, b \to a, \alpha \wedge a \wedge \tau \to \perp, \tau)$$

but

$$\mathbb{K}_n^* * \tau = (b \to a, \alpha, \alpha \wedge a \wedge \tau \to \perp, \tau).$$

Note that we do not have equality but had we thrown out α instead of b in maintaining consistency for $\mathbb{K}_n^* * \tau$, we would have had equality.

---

[14]If we do not do compromise revision we can be specific and define a simple notion of $\mathbb{K}_n^\Pi$ to be the result of consistency maintenance on $(A_1, \ldots, A_n)$.

(I5) If $b \vdash a$ then $((\mathbb{K}_a^*) * b) * \tau = (\mathbb{K}^n * b) * \tau$.

If the above were to hold, then it would hold for $\tau = \top$ and hence

$$(\mathbb{K}_n^* * a) * b = (\mathbb{K}_n^* * b)$$

which is property (C1) of page 138 which does not hold.

(I6) If b is consistent with $\mathbb{K}_n^* * a$ then

$$((\mathbb{K}_n^* * a) * b) * \tau \equiv ((\mathbb{K}_n^* * a) * a \wedge b) * \tau.$$

Assume

$$\mathbb{K}_n^* * a = (\mathbb{K}_n^* - \mathbb{K}_a, a).$$

Since b is consistent with $\mathbb{K}_n^* * a$, we have

$$(\mathbb{K}_n^* * a) * b = (\mathbb{K}_n^* - \mathbb{K}_a, a, b).$$

We also have that $a \wedge b$ is consistent with $\mathbb{K}_n^* * a$.

Hence

$$(\mathbb{K}_n^* * a) * a \wedge b = (\mathbb{K}_n^* - \mathbb{K}_a, a, a \wedge b).$$

These two theories are classically equivalent though not equivalent as sequences.

Assume $\mathbb{K}_n^* = \emptyset$.

Then

$$(\emptyset * a) * b = (a, b)$$

and

$$(\emptyset * a) * a \wedge b = (a, a \wedge b).$$

If we update by $\tau = a \wedge b \to \perp$ we get

$$
\begin{aligned}
(a, b) * \tau &= (b, a \wedge b \to \perp) \\
(a, a \wedge b) * \tau &= (a, a \wedge b \to \perp).
\end{aligned}
$$

Without priority considerations, we could have made the two cases the same.

(I7) holds.

In our notation this postulate says that if $(\mathbb{K}_n^* * \neg b) * b \vdash x$ then $\mathbb{K}_n^* \vdash b \to x$.

Assume $\mathbb{K}_n^*$ is the merge of $\mathbb{K}_1$ and $\mathbb{K}_2$, and that

$$\mathbb{K}_n^* * \neg b = (\mathbb{K}_2, \neg b)$$

$$(\mathbb{K}_n^* * \neg b) * b = (\mathbb{K}_2 - \mathbb{K}_3, b).$$

Thus if x is provable from $(\mathbb{K}_2 - \mathbb{K}_3, b)$ then $b \to x$ is provable from

$$\mathbb{K}_n^* \supseteq (\mathbb{K}_2 - \mathbb{K}_3).$$

We see here the advantage of a particular algorithm over a set of postulates. We do not have to worry about triviality results and we do not have to (necessarily) supply semantics if the algorithm is based on some applied intuition (though we may have semantics as a bonus).

6   A GENERAL SETTING FOR THEORY REVISION FOR ARBITRARY LOGICS

This section will describe the general setting for revision as we see it. We present a theory of revision for arbitrary logics. Our proposed general methodology for revision enjoys the following properties:

1. The principles are based on proof theory. A theory $\mathbb{K}$ is presented as a (structured) collection of assumptions and a deductive mechanism can derive all its consequences. Revision principles apply to $\mathbb{K}$ of this form[15].

2. The principles apply to any logic and are not formulated (dependent on) just for classical logic.

3. They equally apply to monotonic and non-monotonic logics and theories.

4. They should involve the current theory $\mathbb{K}$ and input C and not past theories and past inputs, nor future inputs. (Note that in *Labelled Deductive Systems*, theories are structured and so the theory structure may help recognise past inputs, but then the structure also contributes to inconsistency etc. and it is a whole different setup!)

We see the above principles as essential to any revision theory. Revision is syntactical, it should depend only on proof theoretic considerations and not just semantical considerations. There are applied logics, however, whose semantics come from applications. In such cases semantical considerations are acceptable.

To study revision, we need the following proof theoretical notions:

---

[15] Note that, AGM assumes $\mathbb{K}$ is deductively closed and that the logic is classical logic with $\vee$.

1. A language for the declarative units and theories (databases).

2. The notion of a structured theory in the language. This can be any of the following.

Logic	A theory is a ...
Classical or intuitionistic logic	Set of Wffs.
Linear logic	Multisets of Wffs.
Lambek calculus	Sequence of Wff.
A Labelled Deductive System	Labelled theory (with structure induced by labels).

3. A notion of a controlled proof theory from structured databases which allows us to organise what is provable into priority levels.

4. A notion of a theory being *inconsistent* or (unacceptable, violating integrity constraints, etc.).

5. A notion of input of a Wff A (or a declarative unit) into a theory.

The following are examples of input notions:

Theory	possible input notions.
Set, multiset	inclusion (one or more copies).
Sequence	append at end (beginning) of sequence.
Labelled Theory	include with a new label and in formation on how the new label relates to existing labels.

6. Some notion of priority among substructures of data.

7. An algorithm Π which takes a database and input and produces a new revised database. Π makes use of the priority notion.

The above considerations show that, in general, principles of theory revision must be expressed in a metalanguage involving predicates over theory structure and inputs.

Note that we need not distinguish between non monotonic or monotonic logics. Rationality postulates can be given for the general case. These are expected to simplify and specialise for each particular logic. So for example one can justify and obtain the AGM postulates for the case of classical logic, as a special case of general rationality principles as specialised to the particular properties of classical logic.

Let us now define a general input process for the case of databases which are a sequence of data $(A_1, \ldots, A_n)$ with integrity constraints.

Definition 6.1 (Input functions).

1. Let $0, 1, 2, 3, \ldots$ be the finite ordinals, i.e.

$$n + 1 = \{0, 1, \ldots, n\}.$$

Let I be a function giving for each ordinal n a value $I(n) \in n + 1$. I is called an input function. If n indicates the priority ordering of a database with

$$t_0 : A_0, \ldots, t_{n-1} : A_{n-1}, \ t_0 < t_2 < \ldots < t_{n-1}$$

and we want to input a new data item $a : C$ then $I(n) = k \in n + 1$ indicates the place in the priority of the input C. Namely we will have the new database with priority

$$t_0 : A_0, \ldots, t_{k-1} : A_{k-1}, a : C, t_k : A_k, \ldots t_{n-1} : A_{n-1}.$$

Note that the labels $\{t_i\}$ are just dummies, they help with the calculations.

2. An input function is said to be *insistent* if $I(n) = n$, for all n.

It is said to be non-insistent if $I(n) = 0$, for all n.

Definition 6.2 (General input process).

1. Let I be an input function and let f be a sequence of formulas $f(i) = A_i$, $i = 1, 2, 3, \ldots$. Then (I, f) is called a general input process.

2. Let $\mathbb{C}$ be a set of integrity constraints. We can define two sequences of databases, using $\mathbb{C}$ and (I, f) as follows:

   (1) Let $\mathbb{K}_0^+ = \mathbb{K}_0^* = \mathbb{C}$.

   (2) Assume $\mathbb{K}_k^+$ and $\mathbb{K}_k^*$ are defined and are consistent and contain the data elements

   $$t_1 : X_1, \ldots, t_{m_k} : X_{m_k}$$

   with $t_1 < \ldots < t_{m_k}$, as well as $\mathbb{C}$. Let us input the element $a : A_k$ (where $A_k = f(k)$) into the $I(m_k)$ place to obtain the new databases $\mathbb{K}_{1,k}^+$ and $\mathbb{K}_{1,k}^*$ respectively.

   Let $\mathbb{K}_{k+1}^+$ be the compromise database $(\mathbb{K}_{1,k}^+)_{\text{comp}}$ as defined in Definition 3.10 and let $\mathbb{K}_{k+1}^*$ be the database $(\mathbb{K}_{1,k}^*)_{\text{cons}}$ as defined in Definition 3.9.

   (3) Note that the database sequences are the result of inputting repeatedly A_i, $i = 1, 2, \ldots$ into $\mathbb{C}$ and maintaining consistency. For the case of I being an insistent input function and the $\mathbb{K}_k^*$ sequence we get repeated revision – AGM style.

7 CONCLUSION

I hope this position paper will persuade the reader to take another look at how theory revision might be approached. Current research (by a very active and imaginative community) is focussed around rationality postulates, whether for a single or iterated revision. I would like to urge the reader to think of another, additional approach to theory revision. Think in terms of a stock of typical algorithms for revision applied to structured databases (possibly using *Labelled Deductive System* formulation as a tool), together with a clear understanding of their range of applicability. This is reminiscent of the state of affairs with sorting algorithms, where there is a stock of known algorithms that can be used in different applications. The AGM theory came at a time when 'theories' meant classical theories, inconsistency was not acceptable, and the landscape of logics (classical, non classical, monotonic and non monotonic) was still at its early stages of expansion. AGM was a significant step at the time, and indeed since then much research by the 'AGM-community' was put forward. However, now times have changed. The pressure of applications expanded the landscape of logics to such a degree that the basic motions of 'theory', 'inconsistency', 'input', 'proof theory' and 'truth maintenance' have evolved and generalised so much that it is no longer sufficient and (for iterated revision perhaps impossible) to study theory revision with all the AGM restrictions. There is such a variety of diverse applications and intuitions that the common postulates for the wide area where revision is involved is probably nil.

I find the practice of putting forward postulates and justifying them using words in the case of iterated revision somewhat unsatisfactory. Words are not precise enough and our intuitions are too confused facing the multitude of practical applications and their conflicting demands. There is so much additional structure in databases, so many options for handling inconsistency and iterated revision that we cannot rely on our intuitions. We need a stock of typical concrete constructions for implementing revision, which can serve as an algorithmic toolkit to choose from and modify for each particular application, where its suitability can be tested.

I don't believe the current semantical orderings available today are of real help. They are formulated much too abstractly and are chosen to formally and blindly reflect the revision postulates. Their meaning does not independently arise from applications.

The orderings are only formalities giving no more information about the revision process than the postulates themselves. Witness the formal definition of $\leq_K$ for models w and w' by the clause $w \leq_K w'$ iff $w \Vdash K$ or $w \Vdash K \circ \text{Theory}(w, w')$. The ordering should be meaningful for the application and arises from it. It does not surprise me, therefore, that there seems to be difficulty in revising the ordering to get a new one after an input!

I hope to develop these ideas within the context of *Labelled Deductive Systems* [8] and would welcome the kind reader's criticisms of my position.

Imperial College, London.

148DOV M. GABBAY

ACKNOWLEDGEMENTS

I am grateful to David Makinson, Daniel Lehmann, Odinaldo Rodrigues and Artur Garcez for commenting on the paper.

REFERENCES

[1] C. Alchourrón, P. Gärdenfors and D. Makinson. On the logic of theory change. *JSL* 50: pp. 510–530, 1985.

[2] F.C.C. Dargam. A compromise revision model for reconciling updates. (this volume)

[3] A. Darwiche and I. Pearl. On the logic of iterated belief revision. In *Artificial Intelligence*, 89: pp. 1–29, 1997.

[4] R. Fagin, J.D. Ullman and M.Y. Vardi. On the semantics of updates in databases. *Proceedings of 2nd ACM SIGACT-SIGMOND-SIGART Symposium Principles of Database Systems*, pp. 352–365, 1983.

[5] D. Gabbay. *LDS — Labelled Deductive Systems — Volume 1 Foundations*. Oxford University Press, 1996.

[6] D. Gabbay and A. Hunter. *Making Inconsistency Respectable — Part 1: A Logical Framework for Inconsistency in Reasoning*. In Fundamentals of AI Research, LNCS 535, Springer–Verlag, 1991.

[7] D. Gabbay and A. Hunter. *Making Inconsistency Respectable — Part 2: Meta-level handling of inconsistency*, LNCS 747, Springer–Verlag, 1993.

[8] D. Gabbay. *Labelled Deductive Systems, volume 2*. OUP, forthcoming.

[9] B.N. Grosof. *Updating and Structure in non monotonic theories*. PhD Dissertation 1992, IBM Research Report RC 20683, 1.7.96, pp. 431.

[10] H. Katsuno and A.O. Mendelzon. On the Difference between Updating a Knowledge Base and Revising it. In P. Gärdenfors, editor, *Belief Revision*, Cambridge University Press, pp. 183–203, 1992.

[11] B. Nebel. Syntax-based approaches to belief revision. In P. Gärdenfors, editor, *Belief Revision*, Cambridge University Press, pp. 52–88, 1992.

[12] D. Lehmann. Belief Revision, Revised. In *Proc. IJCAI 95*, Morgan Kaufmann, pp. 1534–1540, 1995.

FÁTIMA C. C. DARGAM

A COMPROMISE REVISION MODEL FOR RECONCILING UPDATES

1 INTRODUCTION

The main objective of this work is to present a revision mechanism for updates in knowledge bases, which involves a *reconciliation* of the conflicting/contradictory inputs with the base without employing strict rejection.[1]

The problem of resolving conflicting updates in knowledge bases, is a critically important problem of real applications. To solve this problem, many revision mechanisms have been proposed in the literature. See for instance [37], [42], [52], and [44]. However, since theory revision is fundamentally dependent on application-specific mechanisms, principles and heuristics, it is not realistic to aim for a generic revision approach [65]. Each different application requires specific revision treatment, in order to provide sucessful and intuitive results.

As a starting point, there is the work of Gabbay and Hunter [31, 32]. They argue that inconsistency should be faced and formalized. They question the way inconsistency is currently being handled in formal logical systems, in view of the way it is actually handled by humans. They claim that there is a need for the development of a framework in which inconsistency can be viewed in a context-dependent way, as a signal for external and/or internal actions, and not necessarily as a bad element which induces the whole system to collapse. In [32], they present a meta-level system, based on first-order linear temporal logic, for handling inconsistent data. In this spirit, and based on the original ideas of compromise revision of [29], the approach proposed here puts forward a compromise reasoning way for dealing with conflicting updates, which ensures less loss of information w.r.t. the data rejected by the revision strategy.

To illustrate the reconciling approach, consider the situation where Δ is a database and A an input. Assume that A is inconsistent with Δ. Current belief revision/update approaches will keep A and maintain consistency by deleting some element from Δ to form a revised database, usually denoted as $\Delta * A$. There is a lot of research in this area, both theorectical, e.g.: the AGM theory of belief revision,[2] and algorithmic re-

---

[1]The material presented in this paper appears in full in [22]. For the sake of simplicity, some modifications were done here in the way the revision postulates are presented.

[2]The AGM theory was first introduced in [1, 2, 3] and [4], and since then gained many followers who apply and modify that theory in various ways, see for instance [47], [51] [56], [43], [52], [58, 59], [44], [9], [10], [49], [61] and [26].

R. Pareschi and B. Fronhöfer (eds.), Dynamic Worlds, 149–194.
© 1999 *Kluwer Academic Publishers.*

search, e.g.: Reason Maintenance Systems.[3] Our aim in this work is to
offer an alternative approach, which is flexible enough to minimize loss of
information from both the original base and the input. In our approach,
the conflicting input A is kept in Δ only in the case that A generates
inconsistency with Δ indirectly,[4] in which case a revision also applies in
order to restore consistency. However, in the case that A is not allowed
to be kept in Δ, its eventual consistent consequences, w.r.t. the existing
data of Δ, are added to the database under the compromise policy of our
approach. This way, instead of preventing updates from being performed,
when they introduce inconsistency, our approach reconciles the conflicting
inputs by making compromises w.r.t. their consequences. We generate the
consequences of the conflicting inputs, and get rid of the inconsistency, via
retraction of a minimal number of those consequences.[5]

Other examples of studies which deal with inconsistency, are the work
by Baral & Subrahmanian [7], Cholvy [14], and Bauval & Cholvy [6] in
the context of theory combination, mainly based on the maximal consistent
subsets of the global theory. The technique of maximal consistent subsets,
supporting the minimal change notion, is also used by Fagin et al [27] and
Kupper et al [46], in the context of database updates. Gärdenfors [35] and
Nebel [51] also use this technique, in the area of belief revision. Ginsberg &
Smith [40], in the area of reasoning about actions. The work of Besnard [8],
which uses paraconsistent logic. The work by Cerro & Herzig [12, 13], which
uses modal logic for reasoning about updates in the presence of contradictory data. And the work by Wagner [63], which considers formalisms which
are closest to defeasible inheritance systems, where contradictory pieces of
information neutralize each other.

1.1 The Compromising Interfering Updates Approach

We refer to this approach as CIU, meaning *Compromising Interfering Updates*. CIU proposes to reconcile conflicting inputs with respect to the underlying theory, and establishes some policies for dealing with the problem of
inconsistency caused by them. CIU provides a revision mechanism which de-
livers compromise solutions. The compromises adopted ensure that as much
as possible of the otherwise rejected data will be kept in the revised base.
In comparison with approaches that require preference between conflicting
inputs, or that simply avoid them by cancelling them out completely, CIU

---

[3] Reason Maintenance Systems were initiated in [24] based on justifications, and in [45]
based on assumptions. More recent research work following this line have also emerged.
Some of them are found in [25], [38], [54], [57] and [62].

[4] By *indirectly* here, we mean that A does not directly violate any of Δ's integrity
constraints.

[5] As we will see later in this paper, the reconciliation strategy for compromise revision
specifies a safe-maximality notion which restricts the notion of maximality on consistent
sets in order to achieve uniqueness.

allows for more data to be kept in the revised base. This way, it provides more informative results. This approach can be viewed as an instance of a metalevel response to inconsistency, within a reasoning system. Therefore, CIU constitutes a step towards a more realistic framework of knowledge base revision. Such a framework is imagined to provide various different application-dependent revision modules.

Following our compromise revision approach, one will possibly not get all of what he/she originally wanted,[6] in the case of a direct input conflict. Instead, he/she will be able to get extra data from the goal's consistent consequences.

By conflicting or interfering updates, we mean either simultaneous updates which interfere with each other, generating inconsistencies as part of their combined effects, or updates which are inconsistent because they conflict with the given database or scenario representation, by violating some of their constraints. The examples below illustrate our ideas.

EXAMPLE 1.

Consider the situation where (A) John is an executive-class passenger of the air-company Wing. As one of his benefits, (B) John has extra baggage allowance, as part of the company's regulations $(A \to B)$. Assume that John calls the office of Wing, and books a trip to Los Angeles in flight W-346. John is informed by a Wing travel agent that (C) if the executive class of flight W-346 is already full, he is offered the alternative option to (D) fly economy class in the same flight, and (E) have a compensation bonus from Wing for other trips. John accepts the alternative. However, by a general rule in Wing, if (D) John travels in the economy class, then he is not considered an executive-class passenger $(\neg A)$. The base $\mathcal{K}$ below represents John's situation described above.

$$\mathcal{K} = \{A,\ A \to B,\ C \to D \wedge E, D \to \neg A\}.$$

When the travel agent learns that the flight W-346's executive class is full (C is a fact), then the situation scenario has to be updated. Wing, however, offers John his executive-class-passenger advantage of having extra baggage allowance. In this situation, compromise revision would provide a satisfactory solution.[7] The results for revising $\mathcal{K}$ by C, are the following:

$$\mathcal{K}' = \{C,\ B,\ A \to B,\ C \to D \wedge E, D \to \neg A\}, \text{ or}$$

$$\mathcal{K}'' = \{C,\ A,\ A \to B,\ D \to \neg A\}.$$

---

[6]The idea of this revision approach conforms with the meaning of the word *compromise*. Quoting from the Oxford's Dictionary: *"Compromise is a settlement of a dispute which each side gives up something it has asked for, and neither gets all it asked for"*.

[7]It is worth noticing that this approach is proposed for a specific range of applications, and not as a general solution for revising knowledge bases. Certainly there are other interpretations of this formal example, where the compromise results do not seem intuitive and acceptable.

Among $\mathcal{K}'$ and $\mathcal{K}''$, $\mathcal{K}'$ would certainly be the preferred result, since it agrees with our intuitions and it does not retract $C \to D \wedge E$, which in fact gives the solution for John to fly to Los Angeles in the flight W-346, as he originally wanted. The compromise is shown in $\mathcal{K}'$, by the proposition B. This means that John can have his extra baggage allowance, even when travelling in the economy class. Notice that if we had applied a TMS-like approach [24], for instance, we would have forced C in, by removing A and all the consequences derived from A, in order to maintain consistency. This would not give us the intuitively expected result.

Our next example is a planning application, where actions are scheduled to be performed. Usually, an action is performed, as part of a plan, in order to realize some goals. In a logical representation, these goals are logical consequences of the post-conditions of the actions (also known as side-effects), and the post-conditions themselves. Compromising on some of these goals, in case of conflict, means allowing other actions yielding some of the consequences while retaining consistency. The following example illustrates the case of inconsistent actions.

EXAMPLE 2.   Consider a scenario in the Blocks World, where we have blocks a, b, c, and d, as shown below:

This scenario is described by $On(a,\ table)$, $On(d,\ table)$, $On(b,\ a)$ and $On(c,\ b)$. Suppose we want to perform the action of placing block d on top of block b. The post-condition of this action is not consistent, since it does not satisfy the constraint of the Blocks World, which says that if a block is not "free" another block cannot be placed on top of it. Nevertheless, if we think of making compromises w.r.t. the consequences, we may notice that having d on top of b cannot be accepted, but we can accept the consequences of having d above b and d above a. These are the resulting consequences of performing this action, since $Above(x,y) \leftrightarrow (On(x,y) \vee (On(x,z) \wedge On(z,y)))$, where $Above$ is transitive. So a possible solution to this problem would be to place d on top of block c. What we are achieving in this case is not the original update with all the consequences of the action. Instead, we are implementing what we can call a compromise solution, by satisfying some of the consequences of the original update, and eliminating the inconsistent consequences because of the existing restrictions.

1.2 Compromise Reasoning & Application Areas

Compromise solutions for conflicting updates and actions reflect our intuitions in several application areas. For instance, we can think of examples in the legal context, where one might want to have some consequences of actions, without performing them as they were originally specified, because they may contradict some laws or some restrictions of the underlying legal system. In this situation, one would go for a compromise solution for the performance of those actions.

Basically, the compromise approach is a suitable way for building up intermediate stages of development processes in general. If we think of applications in the area of *design*, for instance, the extra information that we get, in keeping as many of the consistent consequences of conflicting updates/actions as possible, may help specify an intermediate phase, and so reduce the time needed to conclude the task under consideration.

Consider, for instance, the application of Printed Circuit Board Design, and the task of positioning integrated circuits and other components on a board. Suppose that we want to place a component, say IC1, on a forbidden area of the board, where no components are allowed to be placed. Let us assume that this particular IC invokes the placing of other components, according to some rules and requirements of the board design. Hence, if we allow for the consistent consequences of the action of placing IC1 on the forbidden area, we will end up having the placement of further components, which certainly speeds up the whole process. We will also have more information available for further components placement, than we would have if we simply refused the inconsistent action.

We can also think of compromising consequences in applications where updates or actions are restricted by the availability of common resources. The compromise approach is appropriate when it is preferable to achieve as many of the consequences of all the actions as possible, and not just the consequences of only some of the actions. Such applications are those which involve decisions about distribution of resources among different candidates, where fairness is required. For example, consider a research organization which has the task of deciding the allocation of funds among projects. We assume that it is necessary for the projects to list all the expenses required for each of their phases, allowing for the option of satisfying only partially those phases (compromise solutions). We assume also that the decision makers are not supposed to favour any project in particular. So, if funds are not sufficient to support all the projects' requirements, CIU would be appropriate to be applied in the process of funds allocation. CIU would allow for as many of all the projects' phases as possible, considering the constraints involved in the process.

To characterize more precisely the type of application areas that can benefit from CIU, we list below some features they should have.

- They should view their input data as pieces of information that can be decomposed into smaller units, instead of viewing them as closed working units.
- They should allow for partial performances of the requested updates.
- They should require a high level of data persistence when undergoing revisions on their bases.
- They should be able to use the compromise pieces of information that are left or introduced in their revised bases, for further inferences of their systems.

In general, via the compromise approach, we are able to keep bits of new information, or a subset of the consequences of updates, which could not be totally assimilated, or performed, due to a conflicting situation. These consequences and bits of new information might reveal important facts about the current situation, which might trigger the system into taking specific actions, depending on the application context. Examples in [16, 17], summarized below, illustrate this case in a military defense application.

Consider a defense system in which a knowledge base KB contains information about all the possible threats, in terms of the enemies' weapons, concerning a particular geographic area. Assume that an input from a sensoring unit detects the presence of a threat γ which could not be expected to be at that particular area, according to the current knowledge base. Threat γ then conflicts with some information in KB. Nevertheless, the input comes from a reliable sensoring unit and has to be taken into account. One way of dealing with this situation could be to analyse the consequences of threat γ in KB, and accordingly take a specific counter-attack action which takes the current scenario into consideration. In this case, our approach could be applied as a means of reconciling γ with KB.

Systems with constantly changing rules are also relevant to our approach. Those applications need to cope with the problem of maintaining the consequences of the old rules, when they are replaced by new ones. Suppose that the government dictates some rules for taxation regarding property-buying-schemes. Assume such a scheme offers a certain percentage of tax-relief. When the government changes, or when there is a critical economic situation, the taxation system also changes, so that the tax-relief is reduced. These changes may apply to new contracts. However, it might be illegal if the government changed the rules retrospectively. So, the changes of the scheme rules apply only to new cases. This means the consequences of the old scheme rules would be still valid for the old cases, while the rules themselves would not be supported any longer. In this case our approach of a compromise solution would apply, allowing for non-supported consequences of rules whose premises are not supported any longer, to be kept in the underlying database.

It is clear by now that the proposed approach tries to represent a practical aspect of life, where we try to salvage the most we can get out of a situation, without being able to get everything. By pursuing this approach, we want to put forward the positive aspect of *compromising and going further*, rather than *giving up*, when we face a conflicting situation.

2   CONFLICTING UPDATES AND COMPROMISE REVISION

We propose a formalization of our compromise revision approach, similar to the AGM model [1] [4] [35]. But unlike the AGM approach, we consider our theory representation as a set of sentences which is not closed under logical consequence. We refer to it as *base*. Compromise revision is presented for bases governed by protected integrity constraints. Some postulates for compromise revision are established, and a revision function is specified.

It has already been recognized in the literature, that change operations in real life are always applied to bases. The approach of using bases instead of closed theories in belief revision, has been introduced in the literature by [51] and [42], and since then has gained many followers. Most of the current work on base revision, proposes an alternative to the AGM model. This is not our intention here. Our main concern is to characterize a specific model which applies to the special case of having compromise solutions to conflicting base updates, for specific applications, and not to propose another general belief revision model.

Since we consider bases governed by protected integrity constraints, we account for theory changes in a more realistic way; we do not always accommodate the new input simply because of its information novelty, but allow for the possibility of rejecting it, if it conflicts with the protected part of the base.[8]

In general, by *compromise revision* we mean that an input sentence α, which is inconsistent with a knowledge base $\mathcal{K}$, will either have its consistent consequences w.r.t. the base added to $\mathcal{K}$, or will be itself added to $\mathcal{K}$, provided that the final revised base can be made consistent. If the input α violates directly some of $\mathcal{K}$'s integrity constraints, then α is not present nor implied by the revised base. But if α is indirectly inconsistent with $\mathcal{K}$, then α is in the revised resulting base. In the case that $\mathcal{K}$ has an empty set of integrity constraints, α is only rejected if it is a contradiction of the logical system considered. The subsection to follow illustrates these situations with some examples.

---

[8]In [42], they also support this point by presenting a notion of belief change, which accounts for the issue of receiving new information without giving it special priority due to its novelty. They call it *non-prioritized reception of epistemic input*.

2.1 Different Kinds of Conflicting Inputs

For the examples below, A and B are formulae of the language being considered. We consider classical logic as the underlying logic, including the usual connectives. A database DB is such that $DB = \Delta \cup P_\Delta$, where Δ denotes set of formulae which composes the body of the database, and P_Δ denotes the set of integrity constraints which rules Δ. The language contains the connectives $\{\neg, \wedge, \vee, \rightarrow\}$. We reserve the constant $\perp$ for the special use, which is still compatible with its meaning as falsity. P_Δ can be comprised of two sets. $P_\Delta' \subseteq \Delta$, which is the protected part of Δ of wffs that must remain in Δ; and P_Δ'' which is a set of wffs α which must be excluded from Δ. We present this fact by writing $\alpha \rightarrow \perp$. So, the only place we use $\perp$ is in P_Δ''.

The different kinds of conflicting inputs we can get are the following:

(a) Conflicting inputs within the update (transaction).

  EXAMPLE 3.   Update $= \{A \wedge \neg A\}$

(b) Inputs which conflict directly with some of the integrity constraints which rule the database.

  EXAMPLE 4. $DB = \Delta \cup P_\Delta$
  $P_\Delta = \{A \rightarrow \perp\}$
  Update $= \{A\}$

(c) Inputs which conflict indirectly with some of the integrity constraints which rule the database.

  EXAMPLE 5. $DB = \Delta \cup P_\Delta$
  $P_\Delta = \{A \wedge C \rightarrow \perp\}$
  $\Delta = \{C\}$
  Update $= \{A\}$

(d) Inputs which contradict existing data in the database.

  EXAMPLE 6. $DB = \Delta \cup P_\Delta$
  $\Delta = \{A\}$
  Update $= \{\neg A\}$

Combinations of the kinds of conflict described above are also possible to happen. For instance, we could have a conflict combining case (c) and case (d), in which case the input contradicts the database and conflicts indirectly with integrity constraints.

EXAMPLE 7. $DB = \Delta \cup P_\Delta$
$P_\Delta = \{A \wedge C \rightarrow \perp\}$

$\Delta = \{ C, \neg A\}$
Update $= \{A\}$

2.2   The Adopted Compromises

The aim of the compromise revision is to generate a consistent base, revised by the conflicting input, with minimal loss of information from both the original base and the input. Hence, compromises apply with relation to what is being added to $\mathcal{K}$ and to what is being retracted from it. The compromises adopted by the revision are of two types: (1) In the case that the input sentence cannot be added to the knowledge base $\mathcal{K}$, we compromise by allowing its consistent consequences to be added to $\mathcal{K}$. We refer to this as *"the input compromise case"*. (2) The input can be added to the base, $\mathcal{K}$ is revised and we compromise by allowing the consistent consequences of the retracted sentences to be in the revised base. We refer to this as *"the retracted sentences compromise case"*. By adopting those compromises, we have less loss of information from the requested update of the knowledge base.

EXAMPLE 8.

Consider a negotiation within an argumentation system, where a knowledge base is constrained by some integrity constraints. Take, as a simple example, a propositional base $\mathcal{K} = \{a_1, a_2, a_3, a_4, a_5, a_1 \wedge a_8 \rightarrow c_1, a_4 \wedge a_2 \rightarrow c_2\}$, where each a_i is an argument and each c_j is a conclusion. $\mathcal{I}$ is a set of constraints for the negotiations over $\mathcal{K}$, where $\mathcal{I} = \{a_2 \wedge a_7 \rightarrow \bot, a_8 \rightarrow \bot\}$. Intuitively, they mean that the argument a_8, and the arguments a_2 and a_7 together are not valid arguments for the current negotiations. Imagine that the arguments a_7 and a_8 are new inputs to the system, w.r.t. $\mathcal{K} \cup \mathcal{I}$. In this case, a_8 must not be included in $\mathcal{K}$, since it directly conflicts with an integrity constraint. However, via the *"input compromise case"*, its consequence w.r.t. $\mathcal{K}$, i.e. c_1, is allowed in $\mathcal{K}$. Furthermore, a_7 revises $\mathcal{K}$, and the argument a_2 is taken out in order to retain consistency. Via the *"retracted sentences compromise case"*, the consequence of a_2 w.r.t. $\mathcal{K}$, i.e. c_2, is kept in $\mathcal{K}$.

2.3   The Compromise Revision Steps

We consider the bases to be consistent, prior to any modification. So, if an input causes a base to become inconsistent, then the following steps are taken:

- We add the new input to the base.

- If the base is inconsistent because the input itself is not consistent, then we reject the input.

- If the base is inconsistent because the input directly contradicts some of the sentences of its protected part, then we make the base consistent by rejecting the input, but allowing its consistent consequences to be added to the base.(The input compromise case).

- If the base is inconsistent because the input either contradicts an old sentence of the base (which is not protected), or contradicts together with some other sentences of the base, sentences of the protected part, then we make the base consistent by rejecting some old sentences of the base. For each sentence retracted, we allow its consequences to be added to the base, provided that they do not contradict or cause inconsistency due to the incorporation of the new input to the base. (The retracted sentences compromise case).

EXAMPLE 9.

Consider a base $\mathcal{K}$ composed of a protected subset of integrity contraints $P_{\mathcal{K}}$ and a non-protected subset of sentences $\Delta_{\mathcal{K}}$. Assume that $P_{\mathcal{K}} = \{a \wedge b \wedge c \rightarrow \perp, a \wedge q \rightarrow \perp\}$ and $\Delta_{\mathcal{K}} = \{b, c, q, a \wedge c \rightarrow d\}$. If we want to update $\mathcal{K}$ with the input a, by compromise revision we may end up with one of the following revised bases:

$$\Delta_{\mathcal{K}'} = \{a, c, a \wedge c \rightarrow d\}, \ or \ \Delta_{\mathcal{K}''} = \{a, b, a \wedge c \rightarrow d, d\}.$$

Notice that a together with $\Delta_{\mathcal{K}}$ contradict the integrity constraints in $P_{\mathcal{K}}$. Hence, some old sentences are retracted from $\Delta_{\mathcal{K}}$ to generate $\Delta_{\mathcal{K}'}$ and $\Delta_{\mathcal{K}''}$. Obtaining $\Delta_{\mathcal{K}''}$, for instance, c q are retracted, and d is added as a compromise.[9]

EXAMPLE 10.

Consider a base $\mathcal{K} = P_{\mathcal{K}} \bigcup \Delta_{\mathcal{K}}$, where $P_{\mathcal{K}} = \{a \rightarrow \perp\}$ and $\Delta_{\mathcal{K}} = \{b, c, q, a \wedge c \rightarrow d\}$. If we want to update $\mathcal{K}$ with the input a, we may end up with the following revised base:

$$\mathcal{K}' = \{b, c, q, a \wedge c \rightarrow d, d, a \rightarrow \perp\}.$$

In this case, a contradicts directly the integrity constraint in $P_{\mathcal{K}}$. Hence, $a \notin \mathcal{K}'$ and d is added to $\mathcal{K}'$ as an update compromise.

EXAMPLE 11.

If we consider again the Example 1, we can view the airline company's rule of restricting the possibility of a passenger being an economy-class

---

[9]In the examples given in this section, we have omitted the disjunctive consequences (residuals) from the revised bases, because they do not contribute to the central idea that we want to illustrate. Those disjunctive consequences will not be relevant in the proposed formalization of the compromise revision, since we introduce the notion of a *compromise consequence relation*, which restricts the classical relation notion and avoids those consequences.

(D) and an executive-class passenger (A) at the same time, as an integrity constraint of the system. So, considering $\mathcal{K} = \Delta_{\mathcal{K}} \bigcup P_{\mathcal{K}}$, in the situation of that example we have that $\Delta_{\mathcal{K}} = \{A,\ A \rightarrow B,\ C \rightarrow D \wedge E\}$ and $P_{\mathcal{K}} = \{D \rightarrow \neg A\}$. This new representation, however, would not change the two possible results of revising the base $\mathcal{K}$ with the input C. Nevertheless, if the rule $C \rightarrow D \wedge E$ is also taken as a protected sentence of $\mathcal{K}$, such that $C \rightarrow D \wedge E \in P_{\mathcal{K}}$, then as such it can not be removed from $\mathcal{K}$. In this case the revision would be restricted to the result $\mathcal{K}'$, such that $\mathcal{K}' = \{C,\ B,\ A \rightarrow B,\ C \rightarrow D \wedge E, D \rightarrow \neg A\}$.

In terms of logical consequences, our approach is not so restrictive in comparison with conventional base revision, and not so permissive as closed-theory revision. This is because we do not allow for all the consistent logical consequences of the base to be part of the revised set. However, via the cases of *input compromise* and *retracted sentences compromise*, we do allow the inclusion of some consequences of conflicting inputs, and of the sentences which were rejected from the original base into the revised base. As a result, our revised set loses less information than one obtained by a standard base-revision approach. Moreover, it acquires extra information from the input, via the *input compromise case*. Such a feature has not been provided previously by standard revisions. Hence, a compromise revised set is not necessarily a subset of the revised set obtained by the closed-theory approach.

2.4 Basic Assumptions & Definitions

We consider a finite propositional language L.[10] The underlying logic includes classical propositional logic, so that L is closed under applications of the usual boolean operators, namely $\neg$; $\wedge$; $\vee$; and $\rightarrow$.

The knowledge base, denoted by $\mathcal{K}$, is initially defined as the set $\mathcal{K} = \Delta_{\mathcal{K}} \bigcup P_{\mathcal{K}}$, in which $\Delta_{\mathcal{K}}$ and $P_{\mathcal{K}}$ are assumed to be finite sets of sentences of L, that are not necessarily closed under logical consequence. $P_{\mathcal{K}}$ is a protected part of $\mathcal{K}$. Therefore, its formulae cannot be modified by any update operation in $\mathcal{K}$. $P_{\mathcal{K}}$ represents the integrity constraints ranging over $\Delta_{\mathcal{K}}$. $P_{\mathcal{K}}$ is comprised of two sets of wffs A. Those that must be in $\Delta_{\mathcal{K}}$, i.e. $A\ in\Delta_{\mathcal{K}}$, and those that must remain out. The latter are conveniently written as $A \rightarrow \bot \in P_{\mathcal{K}}$.

Notice that in the special case that the set of integrity constraints is empty, we have the case of conventional bases.

$Cn(\mathcal{K})$ denotes the set of logical consequences of $\mathcal{K}$, such that $Cn(\mathcal{K}) = \{x \mid \mathcal{K} \vdash x\}$, $\mathcal{K} \subseteq Cn(\mathcal{K})$, $Cn(\mathcal{K}) = Cn(Cn(\mathcal{K}))$, and $Cn(\mathcal{K}_1) \subseteq Cn(\mathcal{K}_2)$

---

[10]We understand that a predicate formalization would be more appropriate for the scope of database revision. However, for the sake of simplicity, we restrict the current formalization to the propositional case, since it is only intended to show the mechanism of our compromise reasoning approach.

whenever $\mathcal{K}_1 \subseteq \mathcal{K}_2$. The consequence relation $\vdash$ is assumed to be compact, and closed under the operators $\neg$, $\wedge$, $\vee$, and $\rightarrow$. Also, $\vdash$ is assumed to satisfy the deduction theorem, and if α is a classical tautology then $\vdash \alpha$. By $\mathcal{K} \vdash \alpha$ we mean that $\alpha \in Cn(\mathcal{K})$, where α is a sentence of L. That is, either $\alpha \in \mathcal{K}$, or $\vdash \alpha$; or there exists a β, such that $\beta \wedge \alpha$ or $\beta \rightarrow \alpha$ is in $Cn(\mathcal{K})$, and $\beta \in Cn(\mathcal{K})$. In the usual way, we assume that $\mathcal{K} \vdash \perp$ if $\mathcal{K} \vdash \alpha$ and $\mathcal{K} \vdash \neg\alpha$, or $\mathcal{K} \vdash \beta$ and $\beta \rightarrow \perp$ is in $Cn(\mathcal{K})$ ($\perp \in Cn(\mathcal{K})$). $\mathcal{K}$ is assumed to be initially consistent, i.e. $\mathcal{K} \nvdash \perp$. $\mathcal{K}_\perp$ denotes the inconsistent set, which contains the set of all sentences of L.

We use the symbol $+$ to denote the AGM expansion operator, such that $\mathcal{K} + \alpha$ denotes the expansion of $\mathcal{K}$ by α and its logical consequences. That is, $\mathcal{K} + \alpha = Cn(\mathcal{K} \bigcup \{\alpha\})$.

We introduce in Figure 1 the revision operation $\circledast$ for conventional bases. $\mathcal{K} \circledast \alpha$ denotes the knowledge base which results from the revision of the base $\mathcal{K}$ by α. $\circledast$ is a function which takes a base set $\mathcal{K}$ and a sentence α to another base set $\mathcal{K} \circledast \alpha$. The revision operation $\circledast$ is a variant of the AGM revision operation $*$, adapted for finite bases. We have established a set of postulates for the revision $\circledast$, in order to guide the definition of the compromise revision postulates. The postulates for $\circledast$ have similar intuitions of those defined for the AGM theory.[11]

The symbol " $-$ " used throughout this paper, unless otherwise stated, denotes difference in the set-theoretical sense.

2.5   On the Postulates Definition

Given a base $\mathcal{K} = \Delta_\mathcal{K} \bigcup P_\mathcal{K}$, we assume that α revises $\mathcal{K}$ in a compromise way. We write " $\circledR$ " to denote the operator for compromise revision. We define the postulates $(\circledR 1)$-$(\circledR 10)$ as the basic requirements for achieving the new base $\mathcal{K} \circledR \alpha$, the result of the compromise revision of the knowledge base $\mathcal{K}$ by α. So, $\mathcal{K} \circledR \alpha$ is assumed to satisfy the postulates $(\circledR 1)$-$(\circledR 10)$.

In the postulates $(\circledR 1)$-$(\circledR 10)$ to follow, we note the following assumptions:

- For the *input compromise case*, we assume that $CI(\alpha)$ is the *chosen* set of all the consequences of α w.r.t. $\Delta_\mathcal{K}$, such that $CI(\alpha)$ is inclusion-maximal and the following conditions are satisfied: $CI(\alpha) \bigcup \Delta_\mathcal{K} \nvdash \alpha$ and $CI(\alpha) \bigcup \Delta_\mathcal{K} \nvdash \perp$.[12]

- $MaxCI(\alpha)$ is the set of all inclusion-maximal consistent subsets of $CI(\alpha)$ w.r.t. $\mathcal{K}$, such that for each $maxCI(\alpha)_i \in MaxCI(\alpha)$, for

---

[11]See [21] for more details on the revision operation $\circledast$ and its postulates.

[12]The set $CI(\alpha)$ may not be necessarily unique. For now, it is sufficient to consider a *chosen* $CI(\alpha)$, which satisfies some requirements. In the formalization of the compromise revision function, this notion is made precise.

AGM Revision Postulates and Base Revision Postulates:

The AGM Postulates for Revisions on Closed Theories:

(K is a closed theory. A and B are sentences of the language L).

(K^*1) $K * A$ is a belief set.

(K^*2) $A \in K * A$.

(K^*3) $K * A \subseteq K + A$.

(K^*4)   If $\neg A \notin K$ then $K + A \subseteq K * A$.

(K^*5) $K * A = K_\perp$ if and only if $\vdash \neg A$.

(K^*6)   If $\vdash A \leftrightarrow B$ then $K * A = K * B$.

(K^*7) $K * A \wedge B \subseteq (K * A) + B$.

(K^*8)   If $\neg B \notin K * A$ then $(K * A) + B \subseteq K * A \wedge B$.

Postulates for Revision on Finite Bases:
(adapted from the AGM revision postulates).

($\mathcal{K}$ is a finite base, not closed under the consequence relation. α and β are sentences of the language L).

($\mathcal{K}\circledast 1$) $\mathcal{K} \circledast \alpha$ is a base set.

($\mathcal{K}\circledast 2$) $\alpha \in \mathcal{K} \circledast \alpha$.

($\mathcal{K}\circledast 3$) $\mathcal{K} \circledast \alpha \subseteq \mathcal{K} \bigcup \{\alpha\}$.

($\mathcal{K}\circledast 4$)   If $\mathcal{K} \nvdash \neg\alpha$ then $\mathcal{K} \bigcup \{\alpha\} \subseteq \mathcal{K} \circledast \alpha$.

($\mathcal{K}\circledast 5$) $\mathcal{K} \circledast \alpha \vdash \perp$ if and only if $\vdash \neg\alpha$.

($\mathcal{K}\circledast 6$)   If $\vdash \alpha \leftrightarrow \beta$ then $Cn(\mathcal{K} \circledast \alpha) = Cn(\mathcal{K} \circledast \beta)$.

($\mathcal{K}\circledast 7$) $\mathcal{K} \circledast \alpha \wedge \beta \subseteq (\mathcal{K} \circledast \alpha) + \beta$.

($\mathcal{K}\circledast 8$)   If $\mathcal{K} \circledast \alpha \nvdash \neg\beta$ then $(\mathcal{K} \circledast \alpha) + \beta \subseteq Cn(\mathcal{K} \circledast \alpha \wedge \beta)$.

Figure 1. AGM and Base Revision Postulates

$1 \leq i \leq r$, $maxCI(\alpha)_i \bigcup \mathcal{K} \nvdash \perp$. These conditions involving $maxCI(\alpha)_i$ and $CI(\alpha)$ guarantee that if a $maxCI(\alpha)_i$ is added to $\Delta_{\mathcal{K}}$, the resulting base is consistent, and does not imply the sentence α.

- $maxCI(\alpha)_{\circledR}$ is the final set of compromise consequences of α w.r.t $\Delta_{\mathcal{K}}$, which is obtained from the set $MaxCI(\alpha)$ described above.

- When a sentence β has to be retracted from $\mathcal{K}$ to allow us to admit α in $\mathcal{K} \circledR \alpha$, we say that β is rejected w.r.t. α. R_α denotes the *chosen* set of sentences $\{\beta\} \subseteq \mathcal{K}$, rejected w.r.t. α.[13]

- For the *retracted sentences compromise case*, we assume that $CR(R_\alpha)$ is the set of compromise consequences of the sentences in R_α, w.r.t. $\mathcal{K}$, such that $CR(R_\alpha)$ satisfies the following conditions: $R_\alpha \nsubseteq CR(R_\alpha)$; $\forall y \in CR(R_\alpha)$, $\Delta_{\mathcal{K}} \vdash y$ and $(\Delta_{\mathcal{K}} - R_\alpha) \nvdash y$; and $\forall \beta \in R_\alpha$, $CR(R_\alpha) \bigcup (\Delta_{\mathcal{K}} - R_\alpha) \nvdash \beta$. These conditions guarantee that the sentences in $CR(R_\alpha)$ are consequences of $\mathcal{K}$, which are justified by the sentences in R_α. And that if $CR(R_\alpha)$ is added to $(\Delta_{\mathcal{K}} - R_\alpha)$, the resulting base does not imply any sentence in R_α.[14]

- $MaxCR(R_\alpha)$ is the set of all inclusion-maximal consistent subsets of $CR(R_\alpha)$ w.r.t. $(\Delta_{\mathcal{K}} - R_\alpha) + \alpha$, such that for each $maxCR(R_\alpha)_i \in MaxCR(R_\alpha)$, for $1 \leq i \leq m$, $maxCR(R_\alpha)_i \bigcup (\Delta_{\mathcal{K}} - R_\alpha) \bigcup P_{\mathcal{K}} \bigcup \{\alpha\} \nvdash \perp$.

- $maxCR(R_\alpha)_{\circledR}$ is the final set of compromise consequences of R_α w.r.t $\Delta_{\mathcal{K}}$, which is obtained from the set $MaxCR(R_\alpha)$ described above.[15]

2.5.1 *Proposed Postulates*

(®1) $\mathcal{K} \circledR \alpha$ is a base.

(®2)   If $\vdash \neg\alpha$, then $\mathcal{K} \circledR \alpha = \mathcal{K}$.

---

[13]Notice that R_α may not be necessarily unique, since when adding α to $\mathcal{K}$, it may be possible to re-establish consistency in the new base in many different ways. For the current postulates, it is sufficient to consider a *chosen* R_α which satisfies some requirements. For the revision function definition (section 3), we make this notion precise.

[14]In this formalization, $CR(R_\alpha)$ and $CI(\alpha)$ are defined using the notion of compromise consequence relation, defined later in this paper, in order to avoid unwanted and irrelevant consequences.

[15]Notice that there are many ways in which the set $maxCR(R_\alpha)_{\circledR}$ can be obtained. If it is chosen as one of the sets in $MaxCR(R_\alpha)$, then we are using a choice approach to select the consistent consequences of R_α, without any priority control as done for the maxichoice approach for contraction. If it is the intersection of all the sets in $MaxCR(R_\alpha)$, then a skeptical full meet approach is used, and so on. In our case, we define $maxCR(R_\alpha)_{\circledR}$ under the notion of safe-maximality introduced in [22].

(®3)   If $P_K + \alpha \nvdash \bot$, then $\alpha \in K \circledR \alpha$.

(®4)   If $\alpha \in K$ then $K \circledR \alpha = K$.

(®5)   If $K + \alpha \nvdash \bot$ then $K \circledR \alpha = K \cup \{\alpha\}$.

(®6)   If $\nvdash \neg\alpha$ and $P_K + \alpha \vdash \bot$, then $K \circledR \alpha = \Delta_{K\circledR\alpha} \cup P_K$, $K \circledR \alpha \nvdash \alpha$ and $\Delta_{K\circledR\alpha} = \Delta_K \cup maxCI(\alpha)_\circledR$.

(®7)   If $K + \alpha \vdash \bot$ and $P_K + \alpha \nvdash \bot$, then $K \circledR \alpha = \Delta_{K\circledR\alpha} \cup P_K$, and $\Delta_{K\circledR\alpha} = (\Delta_K - R_\alpha) \cup \{\alpha\} \cup maxCR(R_\alpha)_\circledR$.

(®8) $P_K \subseteq K \circledR \alpha$.

(®9)   For all bases K and sentences α, $K \circledR \alpha \nvdash \bot$.

(®10)   If $\vdash \alpha \leftrightarrow \beta$ then $Cn(K \circledR \alpha) = Cn(K \circledR \beta)$.

Notes:
Postulate (®1) states that the resulting revised knowledge base preserves the structural properties of the original base.[16] It is equivalent to the postulate ($K\circledast1$).

Postulate (®2) guarantees that if the input sentence is a contradiction of the logical system, then no change is made on the original set K.

Postulate (®3) states the condition under which the input sentence is in the revised base. (®10) is a restriction of the postulate ($K\circledast2$), with respect to the consistency checking of the input sentence with the set of integrity constraints.

Postulate (®4) states the vacuousness of the compromise revision.

Postulate (®5) states that compromise revision is reduced to the set-inclusion operation, in the case that the sentence α does not contradict any sentences in K. This postulate is equivalent to the postulate ($K\circledast4$).

Postulate (®6) caters for the case that the input sentence violates some integrity constraints. (®6) introduces the *input compromise case* in compromise revision. In (®6), $maxCI(\alpha)_\circledR$ is obtained from the set of the inclusion-maximal subsets of $CI(\alpha)$. By postulate (®6), we guarantee that the revised base does not entail the input sentence. But it entails all the input's logical consequences, which do not contradict any sentence in the original base.

Postulate (®7) caters for the case that the input sentence contradicts some sentences in Δ_K, without violating any integrity constraint in P_K. (®7) introduces the *retracted sentences compromise case* in compromise revision. In (®7), $maxCR(R_\alpha)_\circledR$ is obtained from the set of the inclusion-maximal subsets of $CR(R_\alpha)$. By postulate (®7), we state that all the consistent consequences of the retracted sentences w.r.t. $K + \alpha$ are added

---

[16]If $K = \langle \Delta_K, P_K \rangle$, then $K \circledR \alpha = \langle \Delta_{K\circledR\alpha}, P_{K\circledR\alpha} \rangle$.

to the revised base. We consider the postulates (®7) and (®6) together, as the *success* postulates in compromise revision.

Postulate (®8) is the *integrity preservation* postulate. It guarantees that all the protected sentences in P_K, which are part of the original knowledge base, remain present in the revised set.

Postulate (®9) claims that the resulting revised base is always consistent.

Postulate (®10) is equivalent to postulate ($\mathcal{K}$⊛6). It guarantees the equality between the closure of the compromise revisions of logically equivalent sentences, w.r.t. the same original bases.

The set composed of the postulates (®1)-(®10) represents the basic set of postulates for compromise revisions of bases with integrity constraints. These postulates express the compromise nature of our revision process, and they should guide the construction of a compromise-revision function for such bases.

When comparing the compromise revision postulates with the general postulates for revision on finite bases presented in Figure 1, we notice that the postulate ($\mathcal{K}$⊛3) is not satisfied in compromise revision, since we might add to $\mathcal{K}$ ® α some consequences of retracted sentences which do not belong to $\mathcal{K} \bigcup \{\alpha\}$. Compromise revision is more strict in terms of consistency than AGM revision. While AGM revision allows the revised base to become inconsistent in the case that the input sentence contradicts a logical tautology, the compromise revision rejects the input. This is shown by postulates ($\mathcal{K}$⊛5) and (®2). Postulate ($\mathcal{K}$⊛7) is not generally satisfied in compromise revision. $\mathcal{K}$ ® $\alpha \wedge \beta \subseteq (\mathcal{K}$ ® $\alpha) +\beta$ would only be satisfied in the case that $R_\alpha \subseteq R_{\alpha \wedge \beta}$. Otherwise, we might add to $\mathcal{K}$ ® $\alpha \wedge \beta$ some consequences of retracted sentences which do not belong to $(\mathcal{K}$ ® $\alpha) + \beta$. Postulate ($\mathcal{K}$⊛8) is also not satisfied in compromise revision, since by postulate (®2), we restrict the case in which the input is inconsistent. So, considering the postulate ($\mathcal{K}$⊛8) in compromise revision, if α is inconsistent, we would have that $Cn(\mathcal{K} \bigcup \beta) \subseteq Cn(\mathcal{K})$, which is not the case.

3　ON FORMALIZING A COMPROMISE REVISION FUNCTION

The set of postulates for compromise revision provides the minimum requirements that a revision function should satisfy. They do not uniquely define a compromise revision function. Like the AGM postulates, they serve only as guidelines for obtaining a revision function. By examining the postulates, we notice that at a few points in the revision process, it is required that we choose among different options for particular sets. Hence, for the formulation of a compromise revision function, some notions still remain to be defined. Among them are the notions of how to select the sentences to be retracted from the base (R_α), how to choose a set of sentences to be added to the base ($CR(R_\alpha)$ and $CI(\alpha)$), and how to deal with maximal consistent subsets.

The notion of maximality for consistency maintenance is very straight-forward. If we cannot have a consistent set of sentences with respect to a particular input, then we want to modify the original set as little as possible, when revising it by that input. This notion of maximality can also apply to different conditions, not only to consistency checking. We might, for instance, want to have a maximal subset of $CR(R_\alpha)$, $maxCR(R_\alpha)$, such that the condition $maxCR(R_\alpha) \bigcup (\Delta_\mathcal{K} - R_\alpha) \nvdash \beta$, for all $\beta \in R_\alpha$, is satisfied. In general, the standard approach using maximal subsets does not consider preferences or restrictions. See for instance [55]. By adopting the skeptical view of taking the intersection of all the maximal subsets as a final result, one might not get an intuitive solution. One loses too much information. In order to express restrictions or preferences, we have to be able to consider a more credulous view of handling not all the maximal sub-sets, but a selection of them. Such a selection should express the essence of the restrictions that we want to make on the sets available.

One method for selecting the sentences to be retracted, can be by using an ordering on $\Delta_\mathcal{K}$. Most of the approaches which deal with preferred maximal subsets of a base, work with an ordering on the base. As an example, we can cite Brewka's work on preferred subtheories [11], among others. As pointed out in [37], it is more natural to work with an ordering of the sentences in the base than with an ordering of the maximal subsets of the base. Furthermore, it seems intuitive to import preferences from the world being modelled. Based on these motivations, we adopt the idea of considering an ordering on the base.[17]

Intuitively, we want to be able to know which elements of $\mathcal{K}$ conflict with α, so that we can build up a set containing these elements, and then determine the set R_α. This way, an ordering on $\Delta_\mathcal{K}$ would help to determine the elements of R_α.[18] This strategy resembles the notion of *safe contraction/revision* introduced in [47], [2]. In safe contraction, an ordering ($<$) which is irreflexive and transitive, is defined on $\mathcal{K}$. In general terms, if α is the sentence to revise $\mathcal{K}$ then $\neg\alpha$ should be the sentence that one wishes to eliminate from among the consequences of $\mathcal{K}$. So, an element x of $\mathcal{K}$ is said to be *safe* w.r.t. $\neg\alpha$ (modulo $<$), if and only if every minimal subset M of $\mathcal{K}$ that implies $\neg\alpha$ either does not contain x, or contains at least one element y that is less relevant, or worse, than x w.r.t. the ordering, $y < x$. In [47], they write as $\mathcal{K}/\neg\alpha$ for the set of all elements of $\mathcal{K}$ that are safe w.r.t. $\neg\alpha$, modulo $<$, and they define the safe contraction

---

[17]More details about the adopted ordering on the sentences of the base, are given later in section 3.1.

[18]The ordering on the sentences of $\Delta_\mathcal{K}$, would also be used to determine a general (not skeptical) approach for dealing with the problem of choosing among various maximal subsets of the base.

$\mathcal{K} \doteq \neg\alpha$ as the set of all elements of $\mathcal{K}$ that are implied by $\mathcal{K}/\neg\alpha$, $\mathcal{K} \doteq \neg\alpha = Cn(\mathcal{K}/\neg\alpha) \cap \mathcal{K}$.

In the case of a compromise revision $\mathcal{K} \circledR \alpha$, concerning the sentences that we might want to eliminate from among the consequences of $\mathcal{K}$, we do not only have to consider $\neg\alpha$, but also all the other elements of $\Delta_{\mathcal{K}}$ that together with α violate some integrity constraints in $P_{\mathcal{K}}$. Based on this idea, we define a set denoted by $\perp_\alpha$, which includes all the inclusion-minimal subsets of $\Delta_{\mathcal{K}}$ containing those elements.

Moreover, we want to be able to perform the necessary retractions, satisfying the conservativity principle. So, the definition of the set R_α has to take into account the minimal elements of the subsets of $\perp_\alpha$, w.r.t. the ordering of $\Delta_{\mathcal{K}}$. Notice that the notion of an ordering does not apply to $P_{\mathcal{K}}$, since $P_{\mathcal{K}}$ is protected.[19] Hence, we assume a partial order $\leqslant$ on the elements of $\Delta_{\mathcal{K}}$. To determine R_α, we first select from the sets of $\perp_\alpha$ the minimal elements which should be retracted from $\Delta_{\mathcal{K}}$. Then, a safe-contraction-like approach is considered, for each element β in the set R_α. As briefly described in the postulates, we adopt a compromise contraction method, which allows for all the consistent consequences of the elements of R_α to be kept in the resulting base.

3.1 The Ordering on the Base

As already discussed, we consider a partial order $\leqslant$, on the elements of $\Delta_{\mathcal{K}}$. We also restrict the types of sentences in $P_{\mathcal{K}}$. We assume that we only have integrity constraints which are of clausal form, with $\perp$ as the conclusion part. This is justified by the fact that here we only want the integrity constraints to extend the notion of keeping consistency in $\mathcal{K}$. So, we change the initial notion of the knowledge base $\mathcal{K}$ from the set $\mathcal{K} = \Delta_{\mathcal{K}} \cup P_{\mathcal{K}}$, to the structure $\mathcal{K} = \langle \Delta_{\mathcal{K}}, P_{\mathcal{K}} \rangle$, as defined below.[20]

DEFINITION 12 ($\mathcal{K} = \langle \Delta_{\mathcal{K}}, P_{\mathcal{K}} \rangle$).

Given a language L of propositional sentences, let $\mathcal{K}$ be a knowledge base given by the structure $\mathcal{K} = \langle \Delta_{\mathcal{K}}, P_{\mathcal{K}} \rangle$, such that $P_{\mathcal{K}}$ is a protected set of sentences of L of the type $\bigwedge_{i=1}^{i=n} \alpha_i \rightarrow \perp$, where α_i is an atomic proposition or its negation, and $\Delta_{\mathcal{K}}$ is a partially ordered set of sentences of L, w.r.t. $\leqslant$.

The ordering $\leqslant$ on $\Delta_{\mathcal{K}}$ is supposed to give the intuitive meaning of relevance to the elements of $\Delta_{\mathcal{K}}$, according to the requirements of the

---

[19] We are not interested in ordering the sentences in $P_{\mathcal{K}}$, since they are not changed.

[20] When we state the union of $\mathcal{K} \cup \{\alpha\}$, for instance, we implicitly mean that α is added to $\Delta_{\mathcal{K}}$, such that $\mathcal{K} \cup \{\alpha\} = \langle \Delta_{\mathcal{K}} \cup \{\alpha\}, P_{\mathcal{K}} \rangle$. Concerning the ordering, whenever not explicitly stated, α receives the highest priority in $\Delta_{\mathcal{K}}$. Also, for the sake of notation simplicity, we sometimes say that $\alpha \in \mathcal{K}$ whenever $\alpha \in \Delta_{\mathcal{K}}$ or $\alpha \in P_{\mathcal{K}}$. We also sometimes write $\Delta_{\mathcal{K}} \subseteq \mathcal{K}$ and $P_{\mathcal{K}} \subseteq \mathcal{K}$, by abuse of notation.

application area to which the system is applied. Since $\leqslant$ is a partial order, it allows a high level of expressivity on the knowledge base representation. The user has the option to define the relevance order among the elements of the set Δ_K, considering also that some elements might not be related by $\leqslant$. When this happens, it means that the elements are mathematically incomparable w.r.t. their relevance levels. If the application requires, Δ_K can also be defined as a chain, i.e. as a totally ordered set, simplifying quite a lot the revision process.

When we say that x, $y \in \Delta_K$, we mean that x and y are sentences of L ordered by $\leqslant$ in Δ_K. We say that a sentence x has at least the same relevance as another sentence y, whenever $y \leqslant x$. As usual, $y < x$ means $y \leqslant x$ and $x \not\leqslant y$. Also, the notations $y \leqslant x$ and $y < x$, are equivalent to $x \geqslant y$ and $x > y$, respectively. For any sentences α, β, γ in Δ_K, the ordering $\leqslant$ on Δ_K satisfies *reflexivity*, *transitivity*, and *antisymmetry*.

Some Assumptions involving the Ordering

In compromise revision, when the input sentence α is present in the revised base $K \circledR \alpha$, we assume that α gets the highest priority w.r.t. the ordering $\leqslant$ on Δ_K. So, when $\alpha \in K \circledR \alpha$, $\forall x \in \Delta_K$, $x < \alpha$. The idea of giving α the highest priority, is motivated by the fact that since α is accepted in $K \circledR \alpha$, then its relevance reflects its novelty. Hence, α gets the highest priority w.r.t. $\leqslant$, since α is the newest piece of information which updates K.

In the cases of *input compromise* and *retracted sentences compromise*, we add to a revised base $K \circledR \alpha$ some consequences of either the input, taken from $CI(\alpha)$, or of the retracted sentences, taken from $CR(R_\alpha)$. Hence, we need to define which levels of relevance w.r.t. $\leqslant$, those consequences get when added to $K \circledR \alpha$. Moreover, the ordering on the candidate consequences to be added to $K \circledR \alpha$, helps the selection of the ones which are effectively going into $K \circledR \alpha$. Such selection is needed, in order to avoid that the consequences introduce inconsistency into the revised base. So, we assume that for an arbitrary set X ordered by $\leqslant$, the notion of propagation of the ordering $\leqslant$ on the elements of X to its logical consequences, relates each consequence y of X to the premises in X, which are necessary to derive y. This way, we state that a logical consequence y of X has at least the same relevance of the sentences in X, which contribute to its derivation. The definition below captures the ordering propagation notion.

DEFINITION 13 (Propagation of $\leqslant$).

Given a consistent set of propositional sentences X, ordered by the partial order $\leqslant$, if $y \in Cn(X)$ and $y \notin X$, then there exists a set

Z, such that Z is an inclusion-minimal subset of X that derives y $(Z \vdash y)$, and $x \leqslant y$ in the ordering of $Cn(X)$, for each element $x \in Z$. In the case that Z is not unique, then for all Z_i such that Z_i is an inclusion-minimal subset of X that derives y, $x \leqslant y$ for all $x \in \bigcup Z_i$. The expanded set $X \cup y$ is then ordered by $\leqslant$, as a subset of $Cn(X)$.

EXAMPLE 14 ($\leqslant$ Propagation).

Consider a set X ordered by $\leqslant$, such that $X = \{a, b, c, c \to d, a \to e\}$, and $\leqslant_X$ is a set of ordered pairs of elements of X, where $\leqslant_X = \{(a,b), (a,c), (c,c \to d), (a,a \to e)\}$, such that for each pair $(x,y) \in \leqslant_X$, it means that $x \leqslant y$. Assume that $Con(X)$ is a subset of $Cn(X)$, such that $Con(X) = \{a, b, c, c \to d, a \to e, d, e\}$. Hence, the ordering on $Con(X)$ is given by $\leqslant_{Con(X)} = \{(a,b), (a,c), (c,c \to d), (a,a \to e), (c,d), (c \to d,d), (a,e), (a \to e,e)\}$. We notice that the consequences d and e are related to their premises $\{c, c \to d\}$ and $\{a, a \to e\}$, repectively, such that in the ordering $\leqslant_{Con(X)}$, $c \leqslant d, c \to d \leqslant d$, $a \leqslant e$, and $a \to e \leqslant e$.

3.2   Problems in Compromise Revision

The revision to be employed by CIU faces the following two problems, which we need to address: **the irrelevant-consequences problem**, that is the problem of keeping in the revised knowledge base derivations which are not relevant to the changes that have been applied to the base; and **the non-uniqueness problem**, that is the problem of coping with non-uniqueness of maximal consistent sets. These problems also occur in standard revision approaches. Some solutions to them are presented in the literature.[21] However, in our approach the solutions for such problems have to account for some compromise reasoning criteria. Then, it is the reponsibility of our proposed solutions, to express such compromise notion within our revision method.

3.2.1   The Problem of Irrelevant Consequences

We face the problem of irrelevant consequences by distinguishing the wanted and the unwanted among the consequences of the retracted formulae, to be

---

[21] Concerning the *irrelevant-consequences problem*, Ryan in [60] has proposed the notion of a "Natural Consequence Relation". Such a relation is defined as a sub-relation of ordinary consequence, which selects relevant consequences from unwanted ones by preventing the addition of irrelevant disjuncts as conclusions. Ryan's Natural Consequence Relation is shown to be substructural, but it satisfies reflexivity, weak monotonicity and weak cut. Concerning the *non-uniqueness problem*, many solutions were proposed in belief revision based on the definition of special contraction functions to obtain the revision of a base. Those contraction functions usually make use of selection mechanisms to get a unique final resulting set. See [4] and [35] for details.

added to the database as a consequence of the compromise revision. The simple example below illustrates this problem.

EXAMPLE 15.

Consider a database $DB = \{a, a \to b\}$ and we want to update DB with "$\neg a$". It seems clear that in a compromise revision approach, we want to keep "b" in the revised database. However, depending on the language and on the derivation mechanism of the underlying logic, we may end up with a great number of unwanted disjunctive compromise consequences and not only with the ones that we consider to be relevant. If we formalize compromise revision under propositional classical logic, for instance, and we update DB with "$\neg a$", we get $\{\neg a, b, b \vee p, ...\}$, for any arbitrary p in the language. This is certainly not what we want!

Notice that if one is dealing with a formalization based on an implicational language, say relevant or linear implication,[22] then the consequences can be obtained by repeated application of the *modus ponens* rule as defined below. In this case, the problem of irrelevant consequences may not occur, since most of those consequences appear as unwanted disjunctions.[23] Since we deal with a more general language in our approach formalization, we have to provide a general solution to the problem of irrelevant consequences.

3.2.2   A Proposed Solution to the Irrelevant-Consequences Problem

From the example given above, it is clear that not all the consequences of the retracted (or rejected) formulae from the base, should be added to it as compromise consequences. However, specifying which compromise consequences to keep is not an easy task.

The syntactical concept of *Natural Consequence* introduced in [60], achieves the goal of preventing the addition of irrelevant disjuncts as conclusions. For example, the sequents below which are ordinarily valid, are not valid under Ryan's *Natural Consequence*.

(1) $p \models p \vee q$ (3) $p \models q \to p$ (5) $p \wedge q \models p \leftrightarrow q$
(2) $p \models p \vee \neg q$ (4) $\neg p \models p \to q$

Examining the non-valid natural consequences above, we see that in (1) and (2), the premise p does not give us any information about q, to justify the conclusions $p \vee q$ or $p \vee \neg q$. By avoiding (1) and (2), we can already prevent the unwanted disjuncts. As pointed out in [60], resource logics, like linear and relevance logics, already reject (3) and (4), as they represent the well-known "inelegancies" of material implication. Finally, (5) implies that the fact that both p and q are valid, corresponds to having them somehow

---

[22]For more details about relevance and linear logics refer to [5] and [39], respectively.

[23]This case includes planning applications, where an implication like "$A \to B$", would mean "*pre-condition* $\to$ *post-condition*".

bound together. This does not seem to be a natural conclusion. Hence, it is not valid under *Natural Consequence*.

In the formalization of the compromise revision method, we adapt the notion of Ryan's *Natural Consequence* to give a *Compromise Consequence Relation*. This relation imposes some logical restrictions on the ordinary notion of classical consequence, by taking into account a set of sentences and a particular sentence which is involved in the compromise.

The *Compromise Consequence Relation* is of particular importance in compromise revision, when we generate the consequences of the retracted (or rejected) formulae to be added to the base. Basically, this consequence relation notion guarantees that, for a given base $\mathcal{K}$ and a sentence α which is the object of a compromise,[24] the following holds:

(1) If $\alpha \notin \mathcal{K}$, then the set of compromise consequences of α w.r.t. $\mathcal{K} \bigcup \{\alpha\}$ is such that:

  (i) α is not in the set of compromise consequences;

  (ii) For any sentence β which together with the base $\mathcal{K}$ derives (classically speaking) α, β is not in the set of compromise consequences;

  (iii) For any disjunctive sentence γ such that γ contains the disjunct α, e.g. $\gamma \equiv \beta \vee \alpha$ for any β in the language, if $\gamma \notin \mathcal{K}$, then γ is not in the set of compromise consequences;

  (iv) Analogously to *(iii)*, for any sentence γ such that γ is of the form $\gamma \equiv \beta \to \alpha$ or $\gamma \equiv \neg\alpha \to \beta$ for any β in the language, if $\gamma \notin \mathcal{K}$, then γ is not in the set of compromise consequences;

  (v) Any classical consequence γ of $\mathcal{K} \bigcup \{\alpha\}$ which is not constrained by conditions *(i)*-*(iv)*, is in the set of compromise consequences of α w.r.t. $\mathcal{K} \bigcup \{\alpha\}$.

(2) If $\alpha \in \mathcal{K}$, then the set of compromise consequences of α w.r.t. $\mathcal{K}$ is supposed to satisfy the conditions *(i)*-*(iv)*, described above.[25] Also, any classical consequence γ of $\mathcal{K}$ which is not constrained by the conditions *(i)*-*(iv)*, is in the set of compromise consequences of α w.r.t. $\mathcal{K}$.

Condition (1) above caters for the situation which deals with the compromise consequences of the non-allowed updating input α. Condition (2) caters for the situation where we have to deal with the compromise consequences of the retracted sentences from the base, to accomplish a revision. Notice that the item *(iii)* above, takes care of preventing unwanted disjuncts

---

[24] By this we mean that α is either rejected or retracted in a compromise-based way.
[25] In condition *(ii)*, we consider the base $\mathcal{K} - \{\alpha\}$, instead of $\mathcal{K}$, for the case that $\alpha \in \mathcal{K}$.

as conclusions. And item *(iv)* prevents irrelevant derivations involving the implicational operator.

The *Compromise Consequence Relation* is then defined as a restricted version of the classical consequence relation, in order to capture the requirements of (1) and (2). By doing so, the proposed consequence relation is able to express the notion of compromise reasoning, without allowing introduction to the base of consequences which are considered irrelevant for finite bases applications. In comparison with Ryan's notion of *Natural Consequence*, the only sequent among (1)-(5) validated by the *Compromise Consequence Relation*, is the one in (5). The *Compromise Consequence Relation*, denoted as $\vdash$, imposes some logical restrictions to the ordinary notion of classical consequence, identifying syntactically the origin of the sentences proved in the case that they are of the forms $\gamma \vee \alpha$, or $\gamma \rightarrow \alpha$, or $\neg\alpha \rightarrow \gamma$.

DEFINITION 16 (Compromise Consequence Relation $\vdash$).

Given a base $\mathcal{K}$, the classical consequence relation $\vdash$, and the sentences α, β and γ of the language L, we say that β is a consequence of $\mathcal{K}$, with respect to a compromise on α, denoted by $\mathcal{K} \vdash_\alpha \beta$, if and only if $\beta \neq \alpha$ and the following conditions hold:

1. $\mathcal{K} \vdash \beta$ and $(\mathcal{K} - \{\alpha\}) \cup \{\beta\} \nvdash \alpha$, if $\alpha \in \mathcal{K}$; otherwise, if $\alpha \notin \mathcal{K}$, $\mathcal{K} \cup \{\alpha\} \vdash \beta$ and $\mathcal{K} \cup \{\beta\} \nvdash \alpha$; and

2. If $\beta \equiv \gamma \vee \alpha$, or $\beta \equiv \gamma \rightarrow \alpha$, or $\beta \equiv \neg\alpha \rightarrow \gamma$, then either $\beta \in \mathcal{K}$, or there is a $\psi \in L$ such that $\nvdash \psi$ and either $\beta \wedge \psi \in Cn(\mathcal{K})$, or $\psi \rightarrow \beta \in Cn(\mathcal{K})$ and $\psi \in Cn(\mathcal{K})$.

REMARK 17.

The above definition of the $\vdash$ consequence relation always refers to a particular sentence (α), which is the object of a compromise in the base. Condition *1* above caters for establishing the compromise on the consequences of α, both for the input case and for the case of retracting old sentences from $\mathcal{K}$. Condition *2* caters for avoiding the derivation of unwanted and irrelevant consequences. When we constrain in condition *2* the derivations equivalent to formulae of the form $\gamma \vee \alpha$, $\gamma \rightarrow \alpha$ and $\neg\alpha \rightarrow \gamma$, we want to express that the sequents of the forms: $\alpha \models \gamma \vee \alpha$, $\alpha \models \gamma \rightarrow \alpha$ and $\alpha \models \neg\alpha \rightarrow \gamma$, are not valid under this notion of consequence. So, in proof theorectical terms, the formulae of the forms stated in *2*, are not entailed via $\vdash$ by $\mathcal{K}$, with relation to the compromise on α. Unless they are justified by reflexivity, or by derivations originated by mechanisms like modus ponens or and-elimination. The restriction of $\nvdash \psi$ was imposed in order to ensure that condition *2* is not trivially satisfied when ψ is logically valid.

EXAMPLE 18.

Consider a base $\mathcal{K} = \langle \Delta_\mathcal{K}, P_\mathcal{K} \rangle$, where $\Delta_\mathcal{K} = \{b, c, \neg a, a \to p, a \lor d\}$, and $P_\mathcal{K} = \{\neg b \to \bot\}$. When the input $\neg a$ revises the base $\mathcal{K}$, the sentence a has to be retracted from $\mathcal{K}$. In this case, we have that $\mathcal{K} \nvdash_a p$ and $\mathcal{K} \nvdash_a a \lor d$. So, the consequence p is added to the resulting revised base as a compromise. (As expected, $a \lor q$ for an arbitrary q, is not included, since it is not a consequence of $\vdash$ in this case).

As Ryan's natural consequence relation, the compromise consequence relation $\vdash$ is substructural, i.e. it fails to satisfy the properties of *inclusion*, *monotonicity*, and *cut*. But it is transitive and it satisfies a conditioned version of reflexivity, weak monotonicity and weak cut.

PROPOSITION 19.

Given a base $\mathcal{K}$ and the sentences α, β and γ of the language L, $\mathcal{K} \vdash_\alpha \beta$ satisfies the following properties:

1. *Conditioned Reflexivity:* $\mathcal{K} \vdash_\alpha \beta$, *where* $\beta \in \mathcal{K}$ *and* $\beta \to \alpha \notin Cn(\mathcal{K})$, *in the case that* $\alpha \in \mathcal{K}$.

2. *Weak (Restricted) Monotonicity:*
$$\frac{\mathcal{K} \vdash_\alpha \beta \quad \mathcal{K} \vdash_\alpha \gamma}{\mathcal{K} \cup \{\beta\} \vdash_\alpha \gamma}$$

3. *Weak Cut:*
$$\frac{\mathcal{K} \vdash_\alpha \beta \quad \mathcal{K} \cup \{\beta\} \vdash_\alpha \gamma}{\mathcal{K} \vdash_\alpha \gamma}$$

3.2.3   The Non-Uniqueness Problem

The notion of maximal consistent sets states that when we cannot have a consistent set of sentences with respect to a particular input, we need to revise the original set, by modifying it as little as possible.

In compromise revision, whenever we need to give up some sentences in order to get an inclusion-maximal subset of the base, which satisfies a particular condition, we adopt the notion of *safe-maximality*. This notion requires that an ordering is employed in the database. Our compromise revision approach is designed to work on partially ordered knowledge bases, which are finite data presentations. We refer to the set which results from the safe-maximality procedure as "safe-maximal", and we view it as a cautious restriction of a maximal set. A safe-maximal set does not choose arbitrarily the elements to retract from the original base. Instead, it discards a convenient subset of the minimal elements which fail to accomplish the condition given. The selection of those minimal elements is performed in a unique way. For this reason, a safe-maximal subset is not necessarily inclusion-maximal. By adopting the safe-maximal subset solution, we are led to a more impartial (fair) position, when we have to choose among some elements to discard from a base.

3.2.4 The Safe-Maximality Notion

Let us consider an arbitrary partially ordered set X, and a condition $c(X)$ which depends on X. Let $Fail(X)_c = \{F_1, F_2, \cdots, F_n \mid \neg c(F_i)$ holds and F_i is inclusion minimal$\}$. $Fail(X)_c$, if not empty, contains all the inclusion-minimal subsets $F_1, F_2, \cdots, F_n$ of X, which fail to satisfy condition c, when F_i substitutes X in c, for $i = 1, \cdots, n$. Since X is ordered by $\leqslant$, we have that all the $F_i \in Fail(X)_c$ are also ordered by $\leqslant$, as a subset of X. Each set $F_i \in Fail(X)_c$ is an inclusion-minimal subset of X, w.r.t. the failure of the condition c. So, we know that if we get rid of at least one of the elements of each F_i, then the condition c w.r.t. $F_i - \{x\}$, where $x \in F_i$, does not fail.[26]

EXAMPLE 20.

Consider a base $\mathcal{K}$ which is composed of $\Delta_\mathcal{K} \bigcup P_\mathcal{K}$, where $\Delta_\mathcal{K} = \{b, e, q, a \wedge e \to d\}$, and $P_\mathcal{K} = \{a \wedge b \wedge e \to \bot, a \wedge q \to \bot\}$, and we want to update $\mathcal{K}$ with the input a. Considering the update consistency condition to be: $c = \Delta_\mathcal{K} \bigcup P_\mathcal{K} \bigcup \{a\} \nvdash \bot$, we have that $Fail(\Delta_\mathcal{K})_c = \{\{b,e\}, \{q\}\}$, such that $\{b,e\} \bigcup \{a\} \bigcup P_\mathcal{K} \vdash \bot$ and $\{q\} \bigcup \{a\} \bigcup P_\mathcal{K} \vdash \bot$. So, by retracting one element from the non-single sets in $Fail(\Delta_\mathcal{K})_c$, we should be able to satisfy c. This is easily seen, considering $\{b,e\}$, since $\{e\} \bigcup \{a\} \bigcup P_\mathcal{K} \nvdash \bot$ and $\{b\} \bigcup \{a\} \bigcup P_\mathcal{K} \nvdash \bot$.

In the example above, in order to have a minimal change of $\mathcal{K}$ to input a, we would have to remove from $\mathcal{K}$ either $\{b,q\}$ or $\{e,q\}$. Hence, our next goal is to try to obtain a set which selects one element from each set F_i of $Fail(X)_c$, by using the ordering $\leqslant$ of those sets. Such a set would then be used to form the maximal subset of X. To obtain this set, we define first the set $min(Fail(X)_c)$, which contains for each set $F_i \in Fail(X)_c$, a set $m(F_i)$ of the minimal elements of F_i, w.r.t. the ordering $\leqslant$. So, we have that $m(F_i) = \{x \mid x$ is $\leqslant$-minimal in F_i, where $F_i \in Fail(X)_c\}$.

EXAMPLE 21.

For some partially ordered set S and condition c, involving S, assume that we get the set $Fail(S)_c = \{\{a,d\}, \{f,g\}, \{b,a,e\}\}$, where from $\leqslant_S$ we know that $a \leqslant d$, $a \leqslant f$, $e \leqslant g$, $f \leqslant e$, and $b \leqslant e$. So the set $min(Fail(S)_c) = \{\{a\}, \{f\}, \{b,a\}\}$. We notice that the elements a and b are not related, so they are both minimal elements in the set $\{b,a,e\}$ of $Fail(S)_c$.

---

[26]Proposition 3.5.1 in [22] states formally this result.

As shown in the example above, since we are dealing with partial orders, we may have more than one minimal element in the sets $m(F_i)$ of $min(Fail(X)_c)$. So, by taking the union of the sets $m(F_i) \in min(Fail(X)_c)$, we do not achieve our goal of getting one only element of each set $F_i \in Fail(X)_c$, to form the set of sentences that should be retracted from X to obtain a maximal subset of X that satisfies condition c. However, we have to admit that dealing with the union of the sets $m(F_i)$, is already better in terms of minimal change of X, when we make $X - \bigcup_{i=1}^{i=n} m(F_i)$, than considering the union of the sets $F_i \in Fail(X)_c$. We refer to the union $\bigcup_{i=1}^{i=n} m(F_i)$ as $Min(Fail(X)_c)$. The drawback of taking the set $Min(Fail(X)_c)$ to get $X - Min(Fail(X)_c)$, comes when there are many elements in the set X that are not related by the ordering $\leqslant$. In this case, $X - Min(Fail(X)_c)$ would discard many more sentences than the minimal number needed to satisfy the condition c. Hence the need of refining the set $Min(Fail(X)_c)$.

As a refined alternative to the set $Min(Fail(X)_c)$, we propose to consider the common elements of the sets $m(F_i) \in min(Fail(S)_c)$, so that fewer elements of the original ordered set X are retracted from it to obtain a maximal subset conditioned to c. From here onwards, we will refer to the refined alternative for $Min(Fail(X)_c)$ as $RMin(Fail(X)_c)$. A priori, we know that the singletons in $min(Fail(X)_c)$ will be used to form the set $RMin(Fail(X)_c)$, as the main requirement is that $RMin(Fail(X)_c)$ contains one element of each set $m(F_i) \in min(Fail(S)_c)$. We refer to the set cointaining the single elements of the singletons of $min(Fail(X)_c)$, as $min(Fail(X)_c)^1$. And to the set of non-single sets of $min(Fail(X)_c)$, as $min(Fail(X)_c)^+$. Since all the elements in $min(Fail(X)_c)^1$ are already going to be in $RMin(Fail(X)_c)$, we can assume that the non-single sets in $min(Fail(X)_c)^+$, which have at least one element that is also in $min(Fail(X)_c)^1$, are not going to be considered to form $RMin(Fail(X)_c)$. We denote as $min(Fail(X)_c)^{++}$ the set that contains the sets in $min(Fail(X)_c)^+$, which have at least one element in common with $min(Fail(X)_c)^1$. That is, the $min(Fail(X)_c)^{++}$ contains the sets $m(F_i)$ in $min(Fail(X)_c)^+$, such that $m(F_i) \bigcap min(Fail(X)_c)^1 \neq \emptyset$. In fact, we have to consider the set which includes the result from the difference $min(Fail(X)_c)^+ - min(Fail(X)_c)^{++}$, in order to work out how to select only one element of each of its remaining sets. We refer to this set-difference as $Dif(Fail(X)_c)$. At this point, we would like to be able to single out the common elements of the sets in $Dif(Fail(X)_c)$, in order to form a refined version, $RDif(Fail(X)_c)$, which contains one element of each set in $Dif(Fail(X)_c)$. However, such a set can only be obtained in an unique way, if all sets in $Dif(Fail(X)_c)$ satisfy the covering property, such that for all sets $D_j \in Dif(Fail(X)_c)$, for $j = 1, \cdots, m$, $\bigcap_{i=1}^{i=m} D_i \neq \emptyset$.[27] This

---

[27]If we try to identify the common elements in each set $D_j \in Dif(Fail(X)_c)$, we

would be the most desirable solution for obtaining the set $RDif(Fail(X)_c)$. Alternatively, if $\bigcap_{i=1}^{i=m} D_i = \emptyset$, then the other way to obtain a unique solution for $RDif(Fail(X)_c)$, is to make it as the union of all the sets $D_j \in Dif(Fail(X)_c)$. We can then form the alternative refined version of the set $Min(Fail(X)_c)$, the set $RMin(Fail(X)_c)$, which contains the union of the sets $min(Fail(X)_c)^1$ and $RDif(Fail(X)_c)$.

EXAMPLE 22.

Assume that for some partially ordered set S and condition c, involving S, we obtain the set $min(Fail(S)_c) = \{\{a\}, \{a,d\}, \{j\}, \{f,g\}, \{a,e\}, \{f,b\}, \{c,h\}, \{c,i\}, \{a,f,c\}, \{j,l\}\}$. So, we have that:
$min(Fail(S)_c)^1 = \{a, j\}$;
$min(Fail(S)_c)^+ = \{\{a,d\}, \{f,g\}, \{a,e\}, \{f,b\}, \{c,h\}, \{c,i\}, \{a,f,c\}, \{j,l\}\}$;
$min(Fail(S)_c)^{++} = \{\{a,d\}, \{a,e\}, \{a,f,c\}, \{j,l\}\}$; and
$Dif(Fail(S)_c) = \{\{f,g\}, \{f,b\}, \{c,h\}, \{c,i\}\}$.
In this case $RDif(Fail(S)_c) = \{f,g,b,c,h,i\}$.
So, $RMin(Fail(S)_c) = min(Fail(S)_c)^1 \bigcup RDif(Fail(S)_c)$, that is $RMin(Fail(S)_c) = \{a, b, c, f, g, h, i, j\}$.

From the example above, we notice that in general, the process of getting $RMin(Fail(X)_c)$ does not produce from the original set X an inclusion-minimal subset, in order to satisfy the condition c. For instance, the set $\{a, c, f, j\}$ would also be accepted as a result in that example, and $\{a, c, f, j\} \subset RMin(Fail(S)_c)$. But, as noticed before, such an inclusion-minimal set is not guaranteed to be obtained in an unique way. Hence, when we retract the set $RMin(Fail(X)_c)$ from X, we do not get a maximal subset of X which satisfies the condition c. Instead, we get a set which we call the *"safe-maximal"* subset of X, that satisfies the condition c and is uniquely determined. We denote this *safe maximal* subset of X as $Smax(X)_c$. Figure 2 summarizes the definitions of the sets $Fail(X)_c$; $min(Fail(X)_c)$; $Min(Fail(X)_c)$; $min(Fail(X)_c)^1$; $min(Fail(X)_c)^+$; $min(Fail(X)_c)^{++}$; as well as $Dif(Fail(X)_c)$; $RDif(Fail(X)_c)$; $RMin(Fail(X)_c)$; and $Smax(X)_c$.

3.3   The Input Compromise Case

In this compromise case, the input sentence conflicts directly with protected part of the base, i.e. $P_K + \alpha \vdash \perp$. Then, we have to define the set of consequences of the input α w.r.t. Δ_K, which are consistent with K, that will be inserted to Δ_K as a revision compromise.

We denote as $CI(\alpha)$, the set of all consequences of the input α w.r.t. Δ_K. Our goal is to define $CI(\alpha)$, such that $CI(\alpha) \bigcup \Delta_K \bigcup P_K$ is

---

might not necessarily get a unique result. Since there may be many common elements allowing for different combinations of acceptable results.

Safe-Maximality

Considering a set X ordered by $\leqslant$, and a condition c which involves the set X, we denote as $c(X/F)$ the fact that the set F substitutes the set X in c.

$$Fail(X)_c = \begin{cases} \emptyset & \text{if } c \text{ is satisfied;} \\ \{F \mid F \text{ is a } \subseteq\text{-minimal} \\ \text{subset of } X, \\ \text{such that } c(X/F) \text{ fails}\} & \text{otherwise.} \end{cases}$$

$$min(Fail(X)_c) = \begin{cases} \emptyset & \text{if } X = \emptyset; \\ \{m(F_i) \mid \forall \alpha \in m(F_i), \\ \alpha \text{ is } \leqslant\text{-minimal in } F_i, \\ \text{where } F_i \in Fail(X)_c\} & \text{otherwise.} \end{cases}$$

$$Min(Fail(X)_c) = \bigcup_{i=1}^{i=n} m(F_i), \text{ where } m(F_i) \in min(Fail(X)_c).$$

$$min(Fail(X)_c)^1 = \{\alpha \mid \alpha \in m(F_i)_j, m(F_i)_j \in min(Fail(X)_c), \\ \text{and } |m(F_i)_j| = 1\}.$$

$$min(Fail(X)_c)^+ = \{m(F_i)_j \mid m(F_i)_j \in min(Fail(X)_c), \text{and} |m(F_i)_j| > 1\}.$$

$$min(Fail(X)_c)^{++} = \{(M_i)_j \mid (M_i)_j \in min(Fail(X)_c)^+, \\ \text{and for some } \alpha \in min(Fail(X)_c)^1, \alpha \in (M_i)_j\}.$$

$$Dif(Fail(X)_c) = min(Fail(X)_c)^+ - min(Fail(X)_c)^{++}.$$

$$RDif(Fail(X)_c) = \begin{cases} \bigcap_{i=1}^{i=r} D_i \in Dif(Fail(X)_c), & \text{if } \bigcap_{i=1}^{i=r} D_i \neq \emptyset; \\ \bigcup_{i=1}^{i=r} D_i \in Dif(Fail(X)_c), & \text{otherwise.} \end{cases}$$

$$RMin(Fail(X)_c) = min(Fail(X)_c)^1 \cup RDif(Fail(X)_c).$$

$$Smax(X)_c = \begin{cases} X & \text{if } c \text{ is satisfied;} \\ X - RMin(Fail(X)_c) & \text{otherwise.} \end{cases}$$

Figure 2. Summary of the Definitions for Safe-Maximality

consistent. We adopt the *safe-maximality* notion in the following way:

- First we get the safe-maximal subset $Smax(\Delta_K)_{c_1}$ of Δ_K, w.r.t. the condition $c_1 = \Delta_K \cup \{\alpha\} \nvdash \bot$, via the auxiliary sets $Fail(\Delta_K)_{c_1}$ and $RMin(Fail(\Delta_K)_{c_1})$ to create $Smax(\Delta_K)_{c_1}$. As a result, we get that $Smax(\Delta_K)_{c_1} \cup \{\alpha\} \nvdash \bot$. This step is justified by the fact that $\Delta_K \cup \{\alpha\}$ can also be inconsistent when $P_K \cup \{\alpha\} \vdash \bot$, since the set of postulates defined in section 2.5.1 does not restrict this case. So, in the case that $\Delta_K \cup \{\alpha\} \vdash \bot$, in order to generate the consistent consequences of α w.r.t. Δ_K, we first have to consider a maximal subset of Δ_K such that α does not introduce inconsistency to it.[28]

- Then we define $CI(\alpha)$ in relation to $Smax(\Delta_K)_{c_1}$. We use the compromise consequence relation $\overset{\vdash}{}$ to avoid that irrelevant consequences of α w.r.t. $Smax(\Delta_K)_{c_1}$ be in $CI(\alpha)$, such that
$$CI(\alpha) = \{y \mid Smax(\Delta_K)_{c_1} \nvdash y \text{ and } Smax(\Delta_K)_{c_1} \cup \{\alpha\} \overset{\vdash}{}_\alpha y\} .$$

- In the case that the condition $CI(\alpha) \cup \Delta_K \nvdash \bot$ is not satisfied, we have to retract from $CI(\alpha)$ the minimal elements w.r.t. $\leqslant$, which contribute to the failure of the condition above. From $CI(\alpha)$, we get the safe-maximal subset $Smax(CI(\alpha))_{c_2}$, w.r.t. the condition $c_2 = CI(\alpha) \cup \Delta_K \nvdash \bot$. The auxiliary sets $Fail(CI(\alpha))_{c_2}$ and $RMin(Fail(CI(\alpha))_{c_2})$ are used to create $Smax(CI(\alpha))_{c_2}$. And as a result, we get that $Smax(CI(\alpha))_{c_2} \cup \Delta_K \nvdash \bot$.

- In the case that the conditions $CI(\alpha) \cup \Delta_K \nvdash \alpha$ and $CI(\alpha) \cup \Delta_K \cup P_K \nvdash \bot$ are not fulfilled, we have to retract from $CI(\alpha)$ the minimal elements w.r.t. $\leqslant$, which make the condition above fail. Hence, in order to guarantee consistency, we get the safe-maximal subset of $Smax(CI(\alpha))_{c_2}$, denoted as $Smax(Smax(CI(\alpha))_{c_2})_{c_3}$, w.r.t. the condition $c_3 = Smax(CI(\alpha))_{c_2} \cup \Delta_K \cup P_K \nvdash \bot$. This set is obtained using the auxiliary set $Fail(Smax(CI(\alpha))_{c_2})_{c_3}$ and the set $RMin(Fail(Smax(CI(\alpha))_{c_2})_{c_3})$. As a result, we get that $Smax(Smax(CI(\alpha))_{c_2})_{c_3} \cup \Delta_K \cup P_K \nvdash \bot$.

So, $Smax(Smax(CI(\alpha))_{c_2})_{c_3}$ is the safe-maximal version of the set $CI(\alpha)$, such that it can be inserted in K without causing inconsistency.

3.4 The Retracted Sentences Compromise Case

In this compromise case, the input sentence α does not violate any integrity constraint in P_K, but it contradicts some existing sentences in Δ_K. So,

---

[28] Notice that this measure is only for the sake of generating a consistent set $CI(\alpha)$ to be added to Δ_K. Because, as defined in the postulates, in this input compromise case no sentence is retracted from Δ_K within the revision process.

when $P_K + \alpha \not\vdash \bot$ and $K + \alpha \vdash \bot$ we have to achieve two milestones, described as follows:

- Obtain the set R_α, which contains the elements to retract from Δ_K, such that $\alpha \in K \circledR \alpha$. And guarantee that by retracting the set R_α from Δ_K, we do not derive any element of R_α from $(\Delta_K - R_\alpha)$, i.e. for all elements x in R_α, $(\Delta_K - R_\alpha) \not\vdash x$.

- Introduce the non-conflicting set of consequences of R_α, denoted as $CR(R_\alpha)$, to Δ_K as a compromise of $K \circledR \alpha$. Within this step, we have to verify the following conditions:

  1. For every element x in R_α, $(\Delta_K - R_\alpha) \bigcup CR(R_\alpha) \not\vdash x$; and

  2. $(\Delta_K - R_\alpha) \bigcup CR(R_\alpha) \bigcup P_K \bigcup \{\alpha\} \not\vdash \bot$.

To obtain the set R_α, we create the set $\bot_\alpha$, which includes all the minimal subsets of Δ_K, whose elements together with the input sentence α and the set of integrity constraints P_K, generate inconsistency. In fact, the set $\bot_\alpha$ has the same notion of the set $Fail(\Delta_K)_{c_4}$, where condition c_4 is $\Delta_K \bigcup P_K \bigcup \{\alpha\} \not\vdash \bot$.

EXAMPLE 23.

Consider a base $K = \langle \Delta_K, P_K \rangle$, where $\Delta_K = \{b, c, d, q\}$, and from $\leqslant_{\Delta_K}$ we know that $c \leqslant d$, $d \leqslant q$, and $b \leqslant d$. Assume that $P_K = \{a \wedge b \wedge c \wedge d \rightarrow \bot, a \wedge q \rightarrow \bot\}$. If we consider the update input a and the condition $\Delta_K \bigcup P_K \bigcup \{a\} \not\vdash \bot$, we have that $\bot_a = \{\{b, c, d\}, \{q\}\}$.

Since $\leqslant$ is a partial order on Δ_K, we might have more than one minimal element in the sets F_i of the family $\bot_\alpha$, i.e. $Fail(\Delta_K)_{c_4}$. In the example above, for instance, $min(\bot_a) = \{\{b, c\}, \{q\}\}$, where b and c are both minimal elements (non-comparable by $\leqslant$). However, we can guarantee that it is sufficient to retract only one element of each set of $\bot_\alpha$ from Δ_K, in order to achieve consistency (i.e. to satisfy condition c_4). So, in order to retract a minimum number of sentences from Δ_K, to accomplish the inclusion of the input sentence α in the revised set $K \circledR \alpha$, we would like to be able to define a choice mechanism, in which only one minimal element out of each set F_i of $\bot_\alpha$ could be chosen. In most cases, such mechanisms are based on empiric premises which are often non-justified for a general framework.

The option of a safe-maximal subset of Δ_K, $Smax(\Delta_K)_{c_4}$ relative to the same condition of $\bot_\alpha$, as defined previously, is not yet the ideal approach. Via the safe-maximality notion, we do not guarantee a maximal consistent set. However, one can argue that this option is justified by the fact that, since the minimal elements are not related (or comparable) by the ordering $\leqslant$, there is no criterion which allows us to choose a particular one among them for retraction. Here we call the safe-maximality option as *"the impartial-choice for safe-minimal change"*.

An alternative to the safe-maximality option would be to allow the current application to define which elements to retract from $\Delta_{\mathcal{K}}$. This option is free from a non-justifiable general choice mechanism. Instead, it can be viewed as a user-choice approach, since it allows the user to decide which minimal element to discard from each set of minimals of F_i of $\perp_\alpha$, which are available in the set $Dif(\perp_\alpha)$, in the case that $\bigcap_{i=1}^{i=r} D_i = \emptyset$, for $D_i \in Dif(\perp_\alpha)$. By doing so, we can have that only one minimal element from each set of minimals of F_i is going to be retracted from $\Delta_{\mathcal{K}}$. Consequently, within this option, the conservativity principle can be fully satisfied.[29] We call this option *"the user-choice for minimal change"*.

To implement this option in the *retracted sentences compromise case*, we define the set R_α by adopting a combined approach, with both *"the impartial-choice for safe-minimal change"* and *"the user-choice for minimal change"* options. We assume that the set R_α selects the minimal elements to be retracted from $\Delta_{\mathcal{K}}$, in order to accomplish $\mathcal{K} \circledR \alpha$, having *"the user-choice for minimal change"* as the main option, when it applies, and *"the impartial-choice for safe-minimal change"* as default. To do this, we consider the sets $\perp_\alpha$, $min(\perp_\alpha)$, $Min(\perp_\alpha)$, $min(\perp_\alpha)^1$, $min(\perp_\alpha)^+$, $min(\perp_\alpha)^+$, $Dif(\perp_\alpha)$, $RDif(\perp_\alpha)$, and $RMin(\perp_\alpha)$; and we define a function which caters for the choice of retraction, combining *"the impartial-choice for safe-minimal change"* and *"the user-choice for minimal change"*. We call such a function *Choice*. It is defined, having as input parameters the *option* from the user and an *entry-set*, and as output it supplies the set of chosen sentences. The parameter *option* can be given two possible inputs by the user: u for user-choice, or d for default-choice. It is obtained via a user-request function *Req*, where $Req(\{d, u\}) = option$. Hence, when the function *Choice* is invoked, we assume that an option u or d is already available from the user. When the set $min(\perp_\alpha)^+$ is empty, there is no need to request the user for the choice of one of the minimal elements of each set S_i, since all the $min(S_i)$ sets of $min(\perp_\alpha)$ are unitary. In this case, the default-choice is applied directly. Also, when we have that $\bigcap_{i=1}^{i=r} D_i \neq \emptyset$ for $D_i \in Dif(\perp_\alpha)$, then this means that the choice of the minimal elements is done automatically via the impartial safe-minimal change approach.

In the case that *"the impartial-choice for safe-minimal change"* is invoked, the user has to have the set $Dif(\perp_\alpha)$ available, to choose one element among the minimal elements from each of its sets. We define the resulting set as the *chosen* set. $Choice(option, \perp_\alpha) = $ chosen-set, where:

---

[29]This principle is supported by the compromise revision, in the sense that it is defined to maintain as many as possible of the old sentences and of their consequences in $\Delta_{\mathcal{K}}$.

$$\text{chosen-set} = \begin{cases} RMin(\perp_\alpha) & \text{if } option = \{d\}; \\ \\ \bigcup_{i=1}^{i=r}\{x_i\}, \text{ such that} \\ \text{each } x_i \text{ is a chosen element} \\ \text{from each } D_i \text{ in } Dif(\perp_\alpha)\} & \text{if } option = \{u\}. \end{cases}$$

Then we define the set R_α, which contains the selected elements to be retracted from $\Delta_\mathcal{K}$, such that $R_\alpha = \text{chosen-set} \cup min(\perp_\alpha)^1$. However, we still need to guarantee that retracting R_α from $\Delta_\mathcal{K}$, we cannot derive from $(\Delta_\mathcal{K} - R_\alpha)$ any element of R_α. To do so, we get a safe-maximal subset of $(\Delta_\mathcal{K} - R_\alpha)$. First, we obtain the set $Fail(\Delta_\mathcal{K} - R_\alpha)_{c_5}$, where c_5 is the condition $(\Delta_\mathcal{K} - R_\alpha) \nvdash x, \forall x \in R_\alpha$. Then, we get the safe-maximal subset of $(\Delta_\mathcal{K} - R_\alpha)$, $Smax(\Delta_\mathcal{K} - R_\alpha)_{c_5}$, relative to condition c_5.

As described previously, the contraction for compromise revision allows the consistent consequences of the sentences to be retracted, to become available in the resulting revised base. Hence, we have to cater for introducing the consequences of the elements of R_α w.r.t. $\Delta_\mathcal{K}$, provided that they do not conflict with the base $\langle(\Delta_\mathcal{K} - R_\alpha), P_\mathcal{K}\rangle$. We use the notion of propagation of the ordering $\leqslant$, as in Definition 13, for defining the ordering of the set of consequences of the elements that should be retracted from $\Delta_\mathcal{K}$. We call such a set $CR(R'_\alpha)$, where R'_α is the union of R_α and the set $RMin(Fail(\Delta_\mathcal{K} - R_\alpha)_{c_5})$. So, we have that $CR(R'_\alpha) = \{y \mid \Delta_\mathcal{K} \overset{\vdash}{\ }_x y \text{ and } Smax(\Delta_\mathcal{K}-R_\alpha)_{c_5} \overset{\vdash}{\ }_x y, \text{ for all } x \in R'_\alpha\}$. By considering R'_α for obtaining $CR(R'_\alpha)$, we get the consequences of all the elements effectively retracted from $\Delta_\mathcal{K}.^{30}$

Our interest at this point is to include the set $CR(R'_\alpha)$ in $Smax(\Delta_\mathcal{K} - R_\alpha)_{c_5}$, without deriving any element of R_α from the resulting base. To do so, some points need to be observed. Notice that it is not guaranteed that $CR(R'_\alpha) \cup Smax(\Delta_\mathcal{K} - R_\alpha)_{c_5} \nvdash x, \forall x \in R'_\alpha$. We still need to specify a safe-maximal subset of $CR(R'_\alpha)$ that satisfies this condition. However, we do not need to check for consistency of the base $\langle Smax(\Delta_\mathcal{K}-R_\alpha)_{c_5} \cup CR(R'_\alpha), P_\mathcal{K}\rangle$, since the original base, $\mathcal{K} = \langle \Delta_\mathcal{K}, P_\mathcal{K}\rangle$, is assumed to be consistent and as $R'_\alpha \subseteq \Delta_\mathcal{K}$, $CR(R'_\alpha) \subset Cn(\Delta_\mathcal{K})$, and $Cn(\Delta_\mathcal{K}) \neq \mathcal{K}_\perp$. Then, we define the set $Smax(CR(R'_\alpha))_{c_6}$ relative to condition $c_6 = CR(R'_\alpha) \cup Smax(\Delta_\mathcal{K} - R_\alpha)_{c_5} \nvdash x, \forall x \in R'_\alpha$. From $Smax(CR(R'_\alpha))_{c_6}$ we construct the set $Smax(Smax(CR(R'_\alpha))_{c_6})_{c_7}$, satifying the condition c_7, which states that $Smax(CR(R'_\alpha))_{c_6} \cup (Smax((\Delta_\mathcal{K}-R_\alpha)_{c_5} \cup \{\alpha\}) \cup P_\mathcal{K} \nvdash \perp$.

As a result of the *retracted sentences compromise case*, considering an update α and a base $\mathcal{K} = \langle \Delta_\mathcal{K}, P_\mathcal{K}\rangle$, we would have that the resulting revised base would be given by adding α and $Smax(Smax(CR(R'_\alpha))_{c_6})_{c_7}$ to $\Delta_\mathcal{K}$, while retracting R'_α from it.

---

[30]We also apply here the notion of the compromise consequence relation $\overset{\vdash}{\ }$ used to define $CI(\alpha)$.

3.4.1 Compromise Contraction & Revision

We state below the definition of compromise contraction of the set R_α from $\mathcal{K}$ to achieve $\mathcal{K} \circledR \alpha$.

DEFINITION 24 (Compromise Contraction).

Given a base $\mathcal{K} = \langle \Delta_\mathcal{K}, P_\mathcal{K} \rangle$, an input sentence α, and a set R_α, we assume that $[\, \mathcal{K} \ominus R'_\alpha \,]_\alpha$ is the compromise contraction of R'_α from $\mathcal{K}$, for the achievement of the revision of $\mathcal{K}$ by α. So, $[\mathcal{K} \ominus R'_\alpha]_\alpha = \langle \Delta_{[\mathcal{K}-R'_\alpha]_\alpha}, P_\mathcal{K} \rangle$, and $\Delta_{[\mathcal{K}-R'_\alpha]_\alpha}$ is obtained in the following way:

$$\Delta_{[\mathcal{K}-R'_\alpha]_\alpha} = Smax(\Delta_\mathcal{K} - R_\alpha)_{c_5} \cup Smax(Smax(CR(R'_\alpha))_{c_6})_{c_7}.$$

Now, we can build up our compromise revision function. But first, we re-describe the compromise revision steps, more specifically now, by taking into account the definitions stated so far:

- We add the new input α to the non-protected part $\Delta_\mathcal{K}$ of the base $\mathcal{K} = \langle \Delta_\mathcal{K}, P_\mathcal{K} \rangle$, such that $x \leqslant \alpha, \forall x \in \Delta_\mathcal{K}$. The ordered set $\Delta_\mathcal{K}$ augmented by α is then referred to as $\Delta'_\mathcal{K}$.

- If the base is inconsistent because α is a contradiction of the logical system, then we make the base consistent by rejecting the input. If $\vdash \neg\alpha$, then $\mathcal{K} \circledR \alpha = \mathcal{K}$.

- If the base is inconsistent because $P_\mathcal{K} \cup \{\alpha\} \vdash \bot$, then we make the base consistent by rejecting α, but allowing its consistent consequences to be added to the base. That is, we get $CI(\alpha)$ and $Smax(Smax(CI(\alpha))_{c_2})_{c_3}$, and our compromise result is given by the knowledge base
$\mathcal{K} \circledR \alpha = \langle (\Delta_\mathcal{K} \cup Smax(Smax(CI(\alpha))_{c_2})_{c_3}), P_\mathcal{K} \rangle$.

- If the base is inconsistent because $\Delta'_\mathcal{K} \cup P_\mathcal{K} \vdash \bot$ when $P_\mathcal{K} \cup \{\alpha\} \nvdash \bot$, then we make the base consistent by keeping α in it and rejecting from it some old sentences. We also introduce to $\Delta_\mathcal{K}$ the consistent consequences of the retracted sentences. This is done in the following way:

    First we obtain the sets $\bot_\alpha$; R_α; $Smax(\Delta_\mathcal{K} - R_\alpha)_{c_5}$; $CR(R'_\alpha)$ and $Smax(Smax(CR(R'_\alpha))_{c_6})_{c_7}$.

    Then, we make the compromise contraction
    $[\, \mathcal{K} \ominus R'_\alpha \,]_\alpha = \langle \Delta_{[\mathcal{K}-R'_\alpha]_\alpha}, P_\mathcal{K} \rangle$, where
    $\Delta_{[\mathcal{K}-R'_\alpha]_\alpha} = Smax(\Delta_\mathcal{K} - R_\alpha)_{c_5} \cup Smax(Smax(CR(R'_\alpha))_{c_6})_{c_7}$.

    Finally, we perform the compromise revision of the base $\mathcal{K}$ by α, such that: $\mathcal{K} \circledR \alpha = \langle (\Delta_{[\mathcal{K}-R'_\alpha]_\alpha} \cup \{\alpha\}), P_\mathcal{K} \rangle$.

We formalize now the definition of the compromise revision function considering the steps described above.

DEFINITION 25 (Compromise Revision Function).

Given a base $\mathcal{K} = \langle \Delta_{\mathcal{K}}, P_{\mathcal{K}} \rangle$ and an input sentence α, let $\mathcal{K} ® \alpha$ denote the compromise revision of $\mathcal{K}$ by α. We denote by $\Delta_{\mathcal{K} ® \alpha}$ the resulting non-protected part of $\mathcal{K} ® \alpha$, such that $\mathcal{K} ® \alpha = \langle \Delta_{\mathcal{K} ® \alpha}, P_{\mathcal{K}} \rangle$. And $\Delta_{\mathcal{K} ® \alpha}$ is obtained, such that one of the following conditions holds:

(Case 1) If $\alpha \in \Delta_{\mathcal{K}}$ or $\vdash \neg\alpha$, then $\Delta_{\mathcal{K} ® \alpha} = \Delta_{\mathcal{K}}$.

(Case 2) If $\mathcal{K} + \alpha \nvdash \perp$ [31], then $\Delta_{\mathcal{K} ® \alpha} = \Delta_{\mathcal{K}} \bigcup \{\alpha\}$.

(Case 3) If $P_{\mathcal{K}} + \alpha \vdash \perp$,
then $\Delta_{\mathcal{K} ® \alpha} = \Delta_{\mathcal{K}} \bigcup Smax(Smax(CI(\alpha))_{c_2})_{c_3}$.

(Case 4) If $\mathcal{K} + \alpha \vdash \perp$ and $P_{\mathcal{K}} + \alpha \nvdash \perp$, then
$\Delta_{\mathcal{K} ® \alpha} = Smax(\Delta_{\mathcal{K}} - R_\alpha)_{c_5} \cup Smax(Smax(CR(R'_\alpha))_{c_6})_{c_7} \bigcup \{\alpha\}$.

The compromise revision function is defined, considering the four basic cases which are implicitly described in the proposed postulates. Case 1 represents the *vacuity* of the revision process. Case 2 expresses the *inclusion* property of the revision. Case 3 represents the *input compromise* case, and Case 4 is the *retracted sentences compromise* case.

3.5   Main Properties of Compromise Revision

The compromise revision satisfies the consistency property and a version of the persistence notion, as shown below. The proofs of the theorems and propositions presented here are found in [19, 22].

Consistency

THEOREM 26.
    Given a base $\mathcal{K} = \langle \Delta_{\mathcal{K}}, P_{\mathcal{K}} \rangle$, *for any input sentence* α, $\mathcal{K} ® \alpha \nvdash \perp$.

Persistence

Intuitively, the persistence notion - a well-established notion within belief revision approaches, states that as much of the former base should survive a revision as possible. Hence, by revising a base $\mathcal{K}$ with a sentence α and then retracting α, we should be able to derive from the resulting base, all the consequences of $\mathcal{K}$ that do not directly contradict α.

---

[31] By $\mathcal{K} + \alpha \nvdash \perp$, we mean that $\Delta_{\mathcal{K}} \bigcup P_{\mathcal{K}} \bigcup \{\alpha\} \nvdash \perp$.

As we would already expect, our system does not satisfy the original notion of persistence. In our compromise approach to revision, it is not enough to say that we should be able to derive from the revised base, all the consequences of the original base which do not contradict the revised sentence α. Since we have extended the consistency notion of our system with the presence of integrity constraints in the base, we should also take them into account at this point. So, we need to adjust the notion of persistence, to cater for our specific requirements of compromise revision.

The proposition below presents a compromise version of the persistence notion, considering that we should be able to derive from $(K \circledR \alpha) \ominus \{\alpha\}$, all the consequences of K that do not directly contradict α, and also that do not violate integrity contraints in K.

PROPOSITION 27 (Compromise Persistence).

Given a base $K = \langle \Delta_K, P_K \rangle$ if we revise it by a sentence α, such that it is not the case that $\vdash \neg\alpha$, then $\forall x$ such that $K \vdash x$, $(K \circledR \alpha) \ominus \{\alpha\} \vdash x$, provided that $x \neq \alpha$ and that $x \notin R'_\alpha$.

Correspondence between the Postulates and the Revision Function

The theorems to follow state the correspondence between the compromise revision function formalization and the proposed postulates for compromise revision.

THEOREM 28.

If a contraction function is defined as a compromise contraction $\ominus$, then the revision function $\circledR$ satisfies the postulates $(\circledR 1)$ to $(\circledR 10)$.

THEOREM 29.

Given a compromise contraction function $\ominus$, for any knowledge base $K = \langle \Delta_K, P_K \rangle$, and any sentence α, a revision function is a compromise revision $\circledR$, if and only if it satisfies the postulates $(\circledR 1)$ to $(\circledR 10)$.

Below we consider again the airline example discussed previously, taking into account the compromise revision definitions presented in this section.

EXAMPLE 30.

Consider the airline Example 1, where: (A) John is an executive-class passenger Wing; (B) John has extra baggage allowance, as part of the company's rules $(A \rightarrow B)$; (C) The executive class of the flight John wants to travel is already full; (D) John flies economy class; (E) John gets a compensation bonus. The airline also adopts a rule which instanciates that $A \wedge D \rightarrow \bot$. Let us assume that the base $K = \langle \Delta_K, P_K \rangle$ is given by:

$$\Delta_K = \{A \rightarrow B, A, C \rightarrow D \wedge E\} \text{ and}$$
$$P_K = \{A \wedge D \rightarrow \bot\},$$

where the ordering on Δ_K is given by $\leqslant_{\Delta_K} = \{(A, A \rightarrow B), (A, C \rightarrow D \wedge E)\}$, such that for each pair $(x, y) \in \leqslant_{\Delta_K}$, $x \leqslant y$. The update α

to be considered in this case is the sentence C. $P_K \bigcup \{C\}$ is consistent, however, $\Delta_K \bigcup P_K \bigcup \{C\} \vdash \bot$. In this case, the resulting base $K \circledR C$ is obtained by allowing C into Δ_K, and rejecting from it some old sentences to maintain consistency. The set $\bot_\alpha$ which includes all minimal subsets of Δ_K whose elements together with P_K and the update generate consistency, is such that $\bot_\alpha = \{A, C \to D \wedge E\}$. According to the ordering in Δ_K, $min(\bot_\alpha) = \{A\}$ and $min(\bot_\alpha)^1 = \{A\}$. The sets $min(\bot_\alpha)^+$, $min(\bot_\alpha)^{++}$, $Dif(\bot_\alpha)$, and $RDif(\bot_\alpha)$ are empty, and $RMin(\bot_\alpha) = min(\bot_\alpha)^1 = \{A\}$. Hence, the actual set of elements to be retracted from Δ_K is given by: $R_\alpha = \{A\}$. Since $Fail(\Delta_K - R_\alpha)_{c_5}$ is empty, $Smax(\Delta_K - R_\alpha) = \Delta_K - R_\alpha$, and $R_\alpha = R_\alpha'$. So, $Smax(\Delta_K - R_\alpha) = \{A \to B, C \to D \wedge E\}$. The set $CR(R_\alpha)$ of compromised consequences of R_α, is such that $CR(R_\alpha) = \{B\}$. Since $CR(R_\alpha)$ is a singleton, $Smax(Smax(CR(R_\alpha'))_{c_6})_{c_7} = CR(R_\alpha)$. The compromised contraction of K by R_α is given by $[K \ominus R_\alpha']_\alpha = \langle \Delta_{[K - R_\alpha']_\alpha}, P_K \rangle$, where $\Delta_{[K - R_\alpha']_\alpha} = Smax(\Delta_K - R_\alpha)_{c_5} \bigcup Smax(Smax(CR(R_\alpha'))_{c_6})_{c_7}$. That is, $\Delta_{[K - R_\alpha']_\alpha} = \{A \to B, C \to D \wedge E, B\}$. Hence, the result for revising K by C is the following:

$$K \circledR C = \langle \Delta_{K \circledR C}, P_K \rangle, \text{ where}$$
$$\Delta_{K \circledR C} = \{A \to B, C \to D \wedge E, B, C\}.$$

In $\Delta_{K \circledR C}$, the sentence B is a compromise consequence of the retraction of A. This result agrees with our intuitions, since it does not retract $C \to D \wedge E$, which in fact gives the solution for John to fly to Los Angeles in the flight W-346, as he originally wanted.

3.6 Discussions

The compromise revision was designed based on a user-oriented choice for a minimal loss of information of the original base K, and on an impartial solution via the notion of safe-maximality. Our motivation to allow the user to choose a minimal element from each set of $Dif(\bot_\alpha)$ to be retracted from the set Δ_K, is grounded on the following arguments: (1) In the case that the sentences on the base Δ_K are not comparable by the partial ordering, according to the application's requirements, we lack the application background knowledge in order to design a selection function for choosing one of the minimal elements. (2) By allowing the user to make the choice, we are not imposing that the contraction function of our system is the only option to retract conflicting data. Instead, we are offering a combined choice between the function and the application-oriented option, hoping for a more adequate result. (3) The high persistence results that the user-option brings to our system, meets our basic goals of contracting the former base minimally when revising it, without having to apply unjustified selection mechanisms w.r.t. the current application.

In order to build the sets of compromise consequences in the input compromise case and in the retracted sentences compromise case, $CI(\alpha)$ and $CR(R_\alpha)$, respectively, we have introduced the notion of the compromise consequence relation $\vdash$. This consequence relation has been defined by imposing some logical restrictions on the ordinary notion of the classical consequence relation. It avoids the derivation of consequences that are considered irrelevant for finite base applications. Consequently, those unwanted consequences are not introduced in both sets $CI'(\alpha)$ and $CR'(R_\alpha)$.

The safe-maximality notion adopted in this work restricts the notion of a maximal subset, relative to a certain condition. The major advantage of the safe-maximality option is that it provides uniqueness in the result. As a consequence, it allows for revision iterations. Also, it does not count on unjustified orderings for selecting a particular minimal element to be retracted from a set of many $\leqslant$-minimals. A drawback of the safe-maximality solution comes when we have many elements in the base which are not related by the ordering. In this case, such a solution could discard many more sentences than the minimal number needed from the set of compromise consequences, to satisfy the required condition. Nevertheless, even in such a case, we believe that we would not underestimate the system's revision as a whole. Because we would be restricting only the number of compromise consequences to be added to the revised base in both compromise cases of input and retracted sentences. In fact, this is the special feature that our approach proposes as a compromise solution, in relation to other revision methods for finite bases. In the retracted sentences compromise case, we keep more information when retracting data, and in the input compromise case we allow for partial acquisition of inputs.

4   COMPROMISE UPDATES IN LABELLED DATABASES

The work presented in this paper is part of the research work in [22], based on the ideas presented in [29], whose initial specifications appeared in [23]. [19] presents in full the belief revision characterization of compromise revision. In [20], the problem of dealing with inconsistency after the performance of a database transaction, within the context of deductive databases is addressed. In [18, 21], we present a concrete specific realization of a compromise interfering update system for labelled databases (CIU_{LDS}), based on the framework of Labelled Deductive Systems (LDS) [30]. We devote this section to describe briefly the system CIU_{LDS}.

The framework of LDS deals with labelled formulae as its basic units of information, where the labels can be of arbitrary form, belonging to a given *labelling algebra*. In LDS, derivation rules act on the labels as well as on the formulae. These rules include some prescribed ways, given by the labelling algebra, to propagate the labels. The handling of labelled formulae allows standard proof systems to be extended with non-standard features. The system CIU_{LDS} takes advantage of LDS's labelling facility, to control the derivation process of the compromise consequences. We embed in the labelling propagation conditions, which act on the inference rules, part of the control mechanism for the compromise revision approach. This mechanism allows the update operations to perform the reconciliation of conflicting inputs. The update operations invoke the compromise revision presented in this paper, in order to achieve the revised labelled database, whenever conflicts arise.

The labelled formula are denoted as declarative units and written as $\gamma : \alpha$, where γ is a label and α is a logical formula. The intended meaning of $\gamma : \alpha$ in our database representation is to provide the structural information of the database, i.e. to express the nature of each of the formulae available in and from the database. The system's language $\mathcal{L}_{CIU}$ is defined as the ordered pair: $\langle \mathcal{L}_{\gamma}, \mathcal{L} \rangle$, composed of a propositional logical language $\mathcal{L}$, and a distinct language for the labels $\mathcal{L}_{\gamma}$. The logical language $\mathcal{L}$ provides propositional well formed formulae (wff), considering a countable number of propositional letters, A, B, C, $D, \cdots$, including $\top$ and $\bot$; and the logical connectives $\neg$, $\wedge$, and $\rightarrow$. The labelling language $\mathcal{L}_{\gamma}$ comprises a finite set of typed constants symbols T, where $T = \{$ E, I, P, N $\}$, used to qualify the label nature, and the binary function symbols '$\copyright_{\uplus}$', '$\copyright_{\Xi}$', '$\copyright_{\wedge I}$', '$\copyright_{\rightarrow I}$', '$\copyright_{\rightarrow E}$', and '$\copyright_{\bot I}$', which are used to define how labels propagate in relation to the derivation rule being applied. The label types E, I, P, and N express the types of data that they may qualify in the database. Borrowing the conceptual presentation of deductive databases, we distinguish in the labelled database $\mathcal{D}$ the explicit facts from the rules. In deductive database terms, we distinguish between the extensional (explicit facts) and the intensional components (deductive rules and the derivable data). CIU_{LDS}, however, requires two more formulae identifications. One which refers to the protected data, and another which addresses the non-supported consequences generated by the compromise solutions of our revision policy. Those consequences have non-supported label type and are subject to continuous checking by the proof system, as the database is further modified. Hence, E; I; P; and N, correspond to extensional data; intensional data; protected data; and non-supported data, respectively. The functions '$\copyright_x$', where $x \in \{\uplus, \Xi, \wedge I, \rightarrow I, \rightarrow E, \bot I\}$, combine two label types of $\mathcal{L}_{\gamma}$ and return another label type as result, in the case that the combination succeeds. This combination expresses the possible applications of the inference rules and update operations represented by x. See [21, 22] for more details.

We consider a labelled database as the tuple $\mathcal{D} = \langle \Delta_{\mathcal{D}}, \preccurlyeq \rangle$, where $\Delta_{\mathcal{D}}$ is a set of declarative units of the form $\gamma : \alpha$, and $\preccurlyeq$ is an ordering on the declarative units of $\Delta_{\mathcal{D}}$. The ordering relation $\preccurlyeq$ is not part of the language $\mathcal{L}_{CIU}$, but it is used to compare the declarative units of this language on a meta-level. We leave the interpretation of the ordering $\preccurlyeq$ open, since we do not specify which database application our formalization is dealing with. However, we assume that $\preccurlyeq$ is a pre-order, and that the protected data in $\Delta_{\mathcal{D}}$ are equivalent in the ordering, and that $\preccurlyeq$ propagates to newly inserted declarative units in $\Delta_{\mathcal{D}}$ in the same way described in section 3.1.

The derivation mechanism of CIU_{LDS} is sensitive to the presence of the non-supported declarative units. By this we mean that it applies some restrictions, in the case that a non-supported declarative unit is involved in a derivation process. The proof system defined for CIU_{LDS} is given by a set of inference rules; some labelling conditions, which have to be satisfied by the inference rules in order to define the labelling propagation in the derivable declarative units; the notion of proof of a declarative unit; and the notion of the system's consequence relation. The notion of consequence is stated as a binary relation between a database and a declarative unit, denoted as $\mathcal{D} \vdash_{CIU_{LDS}} \gamma : \alpha$, (or $\mathcal{D} \vdash \gamma : \alpha$ for short). The intended meaning is to determine if we can exhibit a proof of $\gamma : \alpha$, denoted as $\rho[\gamma : \alpha]$, from $\mathcal{D}$. $\rho[\gamma : \alpha]$ is a pair $\langle P_{\rho}, k \rangle$, where P_{ρ} is a finite sequence of the pairs (or sub-derivations) A/C, $P_{\rho} = \{A_1/C_1, A_2/C_2, \cdots, A_n/C_n\}$, where $n > 0$, and each A_i, for $1 \leq i \leq n$, is a set of declarative units used as premises by a CIU_{LDS} inference rule IR, in order to reach the consequent C_i which is a single declarative unit. And k is a mapping from the set $\{1, \cdots, n\}$, to the set of inference rules IR_{CIU}, where $IR_{CIU} = \{\text{CR}, \wedge\text{I}, \wedge\text{E}, \rightarrow \text{I}, \rightarrow \text{E}, \neg\text{E}, \perp\text{I}\}$ as shown in Figure 3. IR_{CIU} is a convenient subset of the set of inference rules relative to each connective defined in the language, presented in the natural deduction style. Given a database $\mathcal{D}$, an inference rule IR is defined as a tuple $\langle A_{\text{IR}}, \varphi_{\text{IR}}, C_{\text{IR}} \rangle$, where A_{IR} indicates a set of declarative units, in or derived by $\mathcal{D}$, used as premises of the rule; φ_{IR} denotes the labelling condition which needs to be satisfied by the application of the IR inference rule; and C_{IR} represents the declarative unit derived from A_{IR} via the inference rule IR, provided that φ_{IR} holds. The labelling conditions φ apply to the inference rules as well as to the update operations of CIU_{LDS}. They act on pairs of labels, depending on the operations $\copyright_x$ and on some specific conditions involving the label types, for the inference rules that are not dealt with by $\copyright_x$. If a labelling condition holds, then it belongs to the algebra of labels $\mathcal{A}$, such that $\mathcal{A} = \{\varphi_x(\gamma_1, \gamma_2) \mid \varphi_x(\gamma_1, \gamma_2) \text{ holds}\}$.

The inputs of the CIU_{LDS} system are update requests, which invoke an update function of the form $U(\mathcal{D}, \sigma, \delta) \Rightarrow \mathcal{D}'$, where $\mathcal{D}$ and $\mathcal{D}'$ are labelled databases before and after the update, respectively. σ is the type of update to be performed, and δ is the data involved in the update. $\sigma = \{\text{U}_+, \text{U}_-\}$, where ' U_+ ' implies that the update requests an addition of the argument δ, and ' U_- ' implies that the update operation requested

CIU_{LDS} Inference Rules:

Conditional Reflexivity: $\langle A_{CR}, \varphi_{CR}, C_{CR} \rangle$,

where $A_{CR} = \{\, \gamma : \alpha \,\}$, $C_{CR} = \gamma' : \alpha$, and $\varphi_{CR}(\gamma, \gamma_i) \in \mathcal{A}$, for any γ_i, such that $\mathcal{D}' \vdash \gamma_i : \alpha$, where $\mathcal{D}' = \mathcal{D} - \{\gamma : \alpha\}$.

$\wedge$ Introduction: $\langle A_{\wedge I}, \varphi_{\wedge I}, C_{\wedge I} \rangle$, where $\varphi_{\wedge I}(\gamma_1, \gamma_2) \in \mathcal{A}$,

$$\frac{\gamma_1 \; : \; \alpha_1 \qquad\qquad \gamma_2 \; : \; \alpha_2}{\gamma_3 \; : \; \alpha_1 \; \wedge \; \alpha_2}$$

$\wedge$ Elimination: $\langle A_{\wedge E}, \varphi_{\wedge E}, C_{\wedge E} \rangle$, where $\varphi_{\wedge E}(\gamma_1, \gamma_2) \in \mathcal{A}$,

$$\frac{\gamma_1 \; : \; \alpha_1 \; \wedge \; \alpha_2}{\gamma_2 \; : \; \alpha_1} \qquad\qquad \frac{\gamma_1 \; : \; \alpha_1 \; \wedge \; \alpha_2}{\gamma_2 \; : \; \alpha_2}$$

$\rightarrow$ Introduction: $\langle A_{\rightarrow I}, \varphi_{\rightarrow I}, C_{\rightarrow I} \rangle$, where $\varphi_{\rightarrow I}(\gamma_1, \gamma_2) \in \mathcal{A}$,

$$\frac{\mathcal{D}, \; \gamma_1 \; : \; \alpha_1 \; \vdash \; \gamma_2 \; : \; \alpha_2}{\gamma_3 \; : \; \alpha_1 \; \rightarrow \; \alpha_2}$$

$\rightarrow$ Elimination: $\langle A_{\rightarrow E}, \varphi_{\rightarrow E}, C_{\rightarrow E} \rangle$, where $\varphi_{\rightarrow E}(\gamma_1, \gamma_2) \in \mathcal{A}$,

$$\frac{\gamma_1 \; : \; \alpha_1 \qquad\qquad \gamma_2 \; : \; \alpha_1 \; \rightarrow \; \alpha_2}{\gamma_3 \; : \; \alpha_2}$$

$\neg$ Elimination: $\langle A_{\neg E}, \varphi_{\neg E}, C_{\neg E} \rangle$, where $\varphi_{\neg E}(\gamma_1, \gamma_2) \in \mathcal{A}$,

$$\frac{\gamma_1 \; : \; \neg\neg\alpha}{\gamma_2 \; : \; \alpha}$$

$\perp$ Introduction: $\langle A_{\perp I}, \varphi_{\perp I}, C_{\perp I} \rangle$, where $\varphi_{\perp I}(\gamma_1, \gamma_2) \in \mathcal{A}$,

$$\frac{\gamma_1 \; : \; \neg\alpha_1 \qquad\qquad \gamma_2 \; : \; \alpha_1}{\gamma_3 \; : \; \perp}$$

Figure 3. Inference Rules.

is a deletion. The δ argument denotes a declarative unit $\gamma : \alpha$.

The update function invokes the update operations of conditional addition $\uplus$, and compromised retraction Ξ, such that: $Up(\mathcal{D}, \text{U}_+, \gamma : \alpha) = \mathcal{D} \uplus \gamma : \alpha$; and $Up(\mathcal{D}, \text{U}_-, \gamma : \alpha) = \mathcal{D} \Xi \gamma : \alpha$. These operations carry the reconciling flavour of our approach. The conditional inclusion $\uplus$ invokes the compromise revision function, when a compromise solution for the update applies. In this case, both *the input compromise* and *the retracted sentences compromise* cases can be performed. The compromise retraction operation Ξ embeds the mechanism for allowing consequences of retracted declarative units to be added to the database as non-supported data. This operation uses the notion of safe-maximality when a choice is needed among the compromise consequences.

Some basic properties were investigated for CIU_{LDS} in relation to the consequence relation, the revision function, and the update operations. As expected, the consequence relation does not follow the classical standards. It relaxes both reflexivity and monotonicity. However it satisfies the deduction property: $\mathcal{D} \vdash \gamma_3 : \alpha \rightarrow \beta$ iff $\mathcal{D}, \gamma_1 : \alpha \vdash \gamma_2 : \beta$, where γ_3 is given by $\gamma_1 \, \copyright_{\rightarrow_1} \gamma_2$, γ_2 is given by the labelling conditions of the inference rules applied in the derivation of $\gamma_2 : \beta$, and α is not a clausal formula.[32]. It also satisfies restricted reflexitivity, as long as it satisfies the application of the conditional reflexivity inference rule CR, as well as restricted monotonicity:

$$\frac{\mathcal{D} \vdash \gamma_1 : \alpha \quad \mathcal{D} \vdash \gamma_2 : \beta}{\mathcal{D}, \gamma_1 : \alpha \vdash \gamma_2 : \beta},$$

strong transitivity (unitary cut):

$$\frac{\mathcal{D} \vdash \gamma_1 : \alpha \quad \mathcal{D}, \gamma_1 : \alpha \vdash \gamma_2 : \beta}{\mathcal{D} \vdash \gamma_2' : \beta},$$

where γ_2' is given by the labelling conditions of the inference rules used for the derivation of $\gamma_2' : \beta$, and non-explosiveness. Some of those properties also hold for the case that the conditional inclusion operation of the system is considered, in place of the conventional set-theoretical inclusion. The notion of non-explosiveness is considered by some pragmatic formalisms, when dealing with contradictory information and conflicting data in general. In traditional logical approaches, the system is forced to collapse when inconsistency is detected. As pointed out in [64], *"It seems to be an unnatural overreaction to abandon a knowledge base once it is discovered to be inconsistent. Rather, one should accomodate it by means of a logic which continues to function plausibly under inconsistency."* CIU_{LDS} supports this viewpoint, and the consequence relation $\vdash_{CIU_{LDS}}$ satisfies Non-explosiveness, such that when $\mathcal{D}, \gamma : \alpha \vdash \gamma^* : \bot$, we do not have that $\mathcal{D}, \gamma : \alpha \vdash \gamma' : \alpha'$, for any $\gamma' : \alpha' \in \mathcal{L}_{CIU}$. The update and the revision functions of CIU_{LDS} are shown to be consistent and to preserve the structural properties of the original labelled database. See [18, 21, 22] for more details.

---

[32] α is constrained from being a clausal formula, because the system does not support embedded implications.

The system CIU_{LDS} can be considered as a propositional prototype of a database system, which shows how compromise revisions can be achieved from updates in labelled databases when conflicts occur. Our main motivation for formalizing CIU in LDS, was to have a convenient representation at the object level of extra-logical information relevant to our compromise reasoning approach. This feature in CIU_{LDS} allowed that the labelling conditions, applied to the inference rules and to the update operations, controlled both the derivation and the reconciliation processes of the system.

5   FINAL REMARKS

In this paper, the notion of compromise reasoning was presented, and the approach of compromise revision was introduced. We specified a base-theory change operator ® for specific applications which allow for compromise solutions, based on some established postulates. We defined a compromise contraction for revision and established some relevant correspondence theorems and propositions among the functions and postulates of this formalization. We also described briefly the logical update system CIU_{LDS}, which used the compromise revision approach. The CIU_{LDS} system re-enforced the fact that the LDS framework is suitable for formalizations which combine logical and extra-logical reasoning.

There are some important points which were not covered by this work, but left for further investigation. Among those points, we can cite the problem of the computational tractability of compromise revisions. We understand, however, that the problem of achieving base revisions is a difficult problem to cope with. It is at least as hard as the problem of determining consistency of a set.

It is worth pointing out that the main concern with the compromise revision formalization, was to characterize a specific model for compromise solutions to conflicting base updates, and not to propose another general belief revision model. The specific revision method proposed here, re-enforces the importance of having different theory change operators available for specific applications, in order to promote the construction of a more realistic framework for theory revision. It would be interesting to investigate the relationship of compromise revision with existing approaches of base revision; as well as the behaviour of compromise solutions for modelling simultaneous occurrence of actions. In this area, we have to tackle problems which arise when reasoning about possible conflicts and combined effects of those actions. We hope that the basic ideas of this paper will stimulate further work on compromise revision.

SimTech Simulation Technology, Graz and

Institute of Logics and Theory of Science (ILTC), Rio de Janeiro

ACKNOWLEDGEMENTS

The development of this work was supported by CNPq-Brazil, under the grant 202078/90.6, while the author was at Imperial College in the Logic and Automated Reasoning Section, Department of Computing. The author is very grateful to Dov Gabbay for his supervision in this research project. Thanks to Doris Aragon; Gerd Brewka; Krysia Broda; Sanjay Modgil; Hans Jürgen Ohlbach; and Odinaldo Rodrigues, for important comments and suggestions on this work. Thanks also to anonymous referees, for their constructive comments and suggestions on an earlier version of this paper.

REFERENCES

[1] C. Alchourrón; D. Makinson, *"The Logic of Theory Change: Contraction functions and their associated functions"*, Theoria 48, 1982.

[2] C. Alchourrón; D. Makinson, *"On the Logic of Theory Change: Safe Contractions"*, Studia Logica, 44, 1985.

[3] C. Alchourrón; D. Makinson, *"Maps between some different kinds of contractions functions"*, Studia Logica, 45, 1986.

[4] C. Alchourrón; P. Gärdenfors; D. Makinson, *"On the Logic of Theory Change: partial meet functions for contraction and revision"*, Journal of Symbolic Logic, 50, 1985.

[5] A. R. Anderson; N. D. Belnap, *"Entailment: The Logic of Relevance and Necessity"*, vol 1, Princeton University Press, 1975.

[6] A. Bauval; L. Cholvy, *"Automated Reasoning in case of Inconsistency"*, in Proceedings of the 1st World Conference on Fundamentals of AI, 1991.

[7] C. Baral; J. Minker; S. Kraus; V. S. Subrahmanian, *"Combining Knowledge Bases consisting of First Order Theories"*, Computational Intelligence, 8(1), 1992.

[8] P. Besnard, *"Logics for Automated Reasoning in case of Inconsistency"*, in Proceedings of AI: Methodology, Systems and Applications, 1990.

[9] C. Boutilier, V. Becher, *"Abduction as Belief Revision: A Model of Preferred Explanation"*, in Proceedings of AAAI, pp 642-648, 1993.

[10] C. Boutilie; M. Goldszmidt, *"Revision by Conditionals Beliefs"*, in Proceedings of AAAI, 1993.

[11] G. Brewka, *"Non-Monotonic Reasoning: Logical Foundations of Common Sense"*, Cambridge University Press, 1991.

[12] L. Farinas del Cerro; A. Herzig, *"Reasoning about Database Updates"*, in Proceedings of the Workshop on Foundations of Deductive Databases and Logic, 1986.

[13] L. Farinas del Cerro; A. Herzig, *"Constructive Minimal Changes"*, in Report IRIT, 1992.

[14] L. Cholvy, *"Querying an Inconsistent Database"*, in Proceedings of AI: Methodology, Systems and Applications, 1990.

[15] L. Cholvy, *"Proving Theorems in a Multi-Source Environment"*, in Proceedings of IJCAI-93, Chambery, vol.1 , pp 66-71, 1993.

[16] F.C.C. Dargam, *"Sistema Especialista Aplicado a Guerra Eletronica"*, (An Expert System applied to Electronic Warfare), Masters Thesis (in Portuguese), IME-RJ SE/9, Instituto Militar de Engenharia, Rio de Janeiro, Brasil, 1989.

[17] F.C.C. Dargam; E.L. Passos; F.R. Pantoja, *"Decision Support Systems for Military Applications"*, European Journal of Operational Research (EJOR), (special issue on DSS), 1991.

[18] F.C.C. Dargam, *"On Compromising Updates in Labelled Databases"*, Imperial College - Department of Computing Research Report DoC-96/1, UK, 1996.

[19] F.C.C. Dargam, *"A Compromised Characterization to Belief Revision"*, Imperial College - Department of Computing Research Report DoC-96/2, UK, 1996.

[20] F.C.C. Dargam, *"Compromised Updates in Deductive Databases"*, Research Report, Department of Computing, Imperial College, UK, 1996.

[21] F.C.C. Dargam, *"Compromised Updates in Labelled Databases"*, in Proceedings of the 3rd International Conference on Artificial Intelligence and Symbolic Mathematical Computations AISMC-3, LNCS 1138, Springer-Verlag, 1996.

[22] F.C.C. Dargam, *"On Reconciling Conflicting Updates: A Compromise Revision Approach"*, PhD. Thesis, Department of Computing, Imperial College, UK, 1996.

[23] F.C.C. Dargam; D. Gabbay, *"Resolving Conflicting Actions and Updates- Extended Abstract"*, in Proceedings of the Compulog Net - Knowledge Representation and Reasoning CNKRR'93, 1993.

[24] J. Doyle, *"A Truth Maintenance System"*, Artificial Intelligence 12, pp 231-272, 1979.

[25] C. Elkan, *"A Rational Reconstruction of Non-monotonic Truth Maintenance Systems"*, Artificial Intelligence 43(2), pp 219-234, 1990.

[26] M. Freund; D. Lehmann, *"Belief Revision and Rational Inference"* Technical Report, TR94-16, Institute of Computer Science, The Hebrew University of Jerusalem, Israel, 1994.

[27] R. Fagin; J.D. Ullman; M. Vardi, *"On the Semantics of updates in Databases"*, in Proceedings of ACM-PODS, 1983.

[28] R. Fagin; G. Kupper; J.D. Ullman; M. Vardi, *"Updating Logical Databases"*, in Advances in Computer Research, P. Kanellakis (ed.), Morgan-Kaufman, 1988.

[29] D. Gabbay, *"Compromise Update and Revision: A Position Paper"*, (this volume).

[30] D. Gabbay, *"LDS - Labelled Deductive Systems - Volume I Foundations"*, Oxford University Press, 1996.

[31] D. Gabbay; A. Hunter, *"Making Inconsistency Respectable - Part 1: A Logical Framework for Inconsistency in Reasoning"*, in Fundamentals of AI Research, LNCS 535, Springer-Verlag, 1991.

[32] D. Gabbay; A. Hunter, *"Making Inconsistency Respectable - Part 2: Meta-level handling of inconsistency"*, LNCS 747, Springer-Verlag, 1993.

[33] D. Gabbay; O. Rodrigues, *"A Methodology for Iterated Theory Change"*, in Proceedings of the International Conference on Formal and Applied Practical Reasoning, FAPR'96, Bonn. Edited by D. Gabbay and H.J. Ohlbach. LNAI 1085, Springer, 1996.

[34] J. Galliers, *"The Positive Role of Conflict in Cooperative Multiagent Systems"*, in Decentralized AI, edited by Y. Demazeau and J.P. Muller, pp 33-46 ,1990.

[35] P. Gärdenfors, *"Knowledge in Flux: Modeling the Dynamics of Epistemic States"*, Bradford Books, Cambridge, MA: The MIT Press, 1988.

[36] P. Gärdenfors, *"The Dynamics of Belief Systems: Foundations x Coherence Theories"*, Revue Internationale de Philosophie, vol. 44, n. 172, 1/1990.

[37] P. Gärdenfors; D. Makinson, *"Revisions of Knowledge Systems using Epistemic Entrenchment"* in Proceedings of the 2nd Conference on Theorectical Aspects of Reasoning about Knowledge, edited by M. Vardi, 1988.

[38] L. Giordano; A. Martelli, *"An Abductive Characterization of the TMS"*, ECAI-90, LNAI 515, Springer-Verlag, 1990.

[39] J.Y. Girard, *"Linear Logic"*, Theoretical Computer Science. 50, pp 1-102, 1987.

[40] M.L. Ginsberg; D.E. Smith, *"Reasoning About Action I: A Possible Worlds Approach"*, Artificial Intelligence, 35:165-195, 1988.

[41] A. Guessoum; J.W. Lloyd, *"Updating Knowledge Bases"*, in New Generation Computing, 8(1), 71-89, 1990.

[42] S. Hansson, *"In Defense of Base Contraction"*, Synthese, 1991.

[43] P.Jackson; J. Pais, *"Semantic Accounts of Belief Revision"*, ECAI-90, LNAI 515, Springer-Verlag, 1990.

[44] H. Katsuno; A.O. Mendelzon, *"On the Difference between Updating a Knowledge Base and Revising it"*, in Belief Revision, edited by P.Gärdenfors, Cambridge University Press, pp 183-203, 1992.

[45] J.de Kleer, *"An Assumption-based TMS"*, Artificial Intelligence 28, pp 127-162, 1986.

[46] G.M. Kupper; J.D. Ullman; M. Vardi, *"On the Equivalence of Logical Databases"*, in Proceedings of ACM-PODS, 1984.

[47] D. Makinson, *"How to give it up"*, Synthese 62, 1985.

[48] D. Makinson, *"General Theory of Cumulative Inference"*, in Nonmonotonic Reasoning, edited by Reinfrank et al., LNAI 346, Springer-Verlag, 1989.

[49] D. Makinson, *"Five Faces of Minimality"*, Studia Logica, vol.53, n.3, 1993.

[50] S. Naqvi; F. Rossi, *"Reasoning in Inconsistent Databases"*, in Proceedings of the North American Conference on Logic Programming, pp 255-272, 1990.

[51] B. Nebel, *"A Knowledge level Analysis of Belief Revision"*, in Proceedings of the 1st Conference on Principles of Knowledge Representation and Reasoning, 1989.

[52] B. Nebel, *"Reasoning and Revision in Hybrid Representation Systems"*, LNAI 422, Springer-Verlag, 1990.

[53] B. Nebel, *"Belief Revision and Default Reasoning: Syntax-Based Approaches"*, in Proceedings of the 2nd. International Conference on Principles of Knowledge Representation and Reasoning, 1991.

[54] S. G. Pimentel; J. L. Cuadrado, *"A Truth Maintenance System Based on Stable Models"*, in Proceedings of the North American Conference on Logic Programming NACLP, pp 274-290, 1989.

[55] D. Poole, *"A Logical Framework for Default Reasoning"*, Artificial Intelligence, 36, 1988.

[56] A. Rao, N. Foo, *"Minimal Change and Maximal Coherence: A Basis for Belief Revision and Reasoning about Actions"*, in Proceedings of the 11th International Joint Conference on Artificial Intelligence, pp 966-971, 1989.

[57] W. Rodi; S. Pimentel, *"A Nonmonotonic Assumption-Based TMS using Stable Bases"*, in Proceedings of KR'91, pp 485-495, 1991.

[58] H. Rott, *"Two Methods of Constructing Contractions and Revisions of Knowledge Systems"*, Jounal of Philosophical Logic, 20, 1991.

[59] H. Rott, *"On the Logic of Theory Change: more maps between different kinds of contractions functions"* in Belief Revision, edited by P.Gärdenfors, Cambridge University Press, pp 122-141, 1992.

[60] M. Ryan, *"Ordered Presentations of Theories - Default Reasoning and Belief Revision"*, Ph.D. Thesis, Department of Computing, Imperial College, London, UK, 1991.

[61] S. Sripada, *"A Temporal Approach to Belief Revision in Knowledge Bases"*, in Proceedings of the 9th. IEEE Conference on AI for Applications CAIA, 1993.

[62] X. Wang; H. Chen, *"On the Semantics of TMS"*, in Proceedings of IJCAI '91, pp 306-309, 1991.

[63] G. Wagner, *"Reasoning with Inconsistency in Extended Deductive Databases"*, in Proceedings of the 2nd International Workshop on Logic Programming and Non-monotonic Reasoning, Pereira & Nerode editors, 1993.

[64] G. Wagner, *"Vivid Logic"*, LNAI 764, Springer Verlag, 1994.

[65] M. Winslett, *"Updating Logical Databases"*, Cambridge University Press, 1990.

JINXIN LIN AND ALBERTO O. MENDELZON

KNOWLEDGE BASE MERGING BY MAJORITY

1 INTRODUCTION

In many fields such as heterogeneous databases [1] or genomic information systems [9] we are often confronted with multiple and conflicting sources of information. Systems organized around reasoning agents [12, 6] face the similar problem of resolving conflicts among contradictory knowledge or beliefs[1] held by different agents. At the same time, these systems want to extract additional knowledge that is not locally held by any agent, but collectively by all of them (called *implicit knowledge* in [12]). For example, if an agent knows a and another agent knows $a \to b$, then combining their knowledge yields b, even though neither one of them individually knows b.

Assume each agent is associated with a knowledge base and the agent reasons about the world according to the knowledge base. Then the problem of how to merge the knowledge of multiple agents is the same as how to merge multiple knowledge bases. One simple method for knowledge base merging is to take the disjunction of the maximal consistent subsets of the union of the knowledge bases. This is essentially the approach adopted by Baral *et al.* [3], who also consider merging knowledge bases in the presence of integrity constraints and priorities over the knowledge bases. However, such an approach does not take into account the "popularity" of a belief among a group of agents. There are many situations (but of course not all) where the number of agents who hold a particular belief is important, and sometimes it may be the only practical way of resolving a conflict. For example, suppose there are three agents with knowledge bases $T_1 = \{a\}, T_2 = \{a\}$ and $T_3 = \{\neg a\}$. The approach of Baral *et al.* yields $a \lor \neg a$, a tautology, which does not support either a or $\neg a$, even though two out of the three agents support a. In contrast, our approach in this paper will produce a, which reflects the view of the majority. Furthermore, our approach is independent of the particular syntax of the knowledge bases to be merged, while the method of Baral *et al.* is syntax-dependent. The method of Revesz [20] also does not take majority into account. For the above example, it returns the same result as the one of Baral *et al.*

Borgida and Imielinski [2] proposed several approaches to resolve a conflict in beliefs held by a collection of experts (which they called a "committee"). However, using their protocols, committees may remain indecisive or contradictory on the conflicting issues. One protocol they defined is that a committee supports a sentence α if all members support (imply) α. This

---

[1]We do not distinguish between *knowledge* and *belief* in this paper.

R. Pareschi and B. Fronhöfer (eds.), Dynamic Worlds, 195–218.

protocol is equivalent to taking the disjunction of the knowledge bases. This does not take majority into account, and the committee remains indecisive on conflicting issues. In the example above this method produces the same result as the one of Baral *et al.*, $a \vee \neg a$. Among other protocols they defined, the "democracy" protocol seems closest to the principle of majority. Under the democracy protocol, a committee C is defined to support α if: (1) some subcommittee supports α, and (2) if some other subcommittee S supports $\neg\alpha$ then there is a subcommittee S' such that S' supports α and cardinality$(S') >$ cardinality(S), where a subcommittee is a subset of C and is defined to support a sentence if every member in the subcommittee supports the sentence. Then it is not difficult to verify that the committee consisting of $T_1 = \{a\}, T_2 = \{b\}$ and $T_3 = \{\neg a \vee \neg b\}$ supports a and b and $\neg a \vee \neg b$, which is a contradiction! In the method we describe here, the result of merging is always consistent; in fact this property is one of the basic conditions we postulate for all knowledge merge operators.

Halpern and Moses [12] defined the notion of *implicit knowledge* in a group of agents. But their formulation of implicit knowledge applies only to agents who do not have conflicting views; if there is a conflict, the implicit knowledge of the agents is every sentence in the language.

Majority rule is used in many other fields, notably social choice theory (see, e.g., [14]). However, the majority postulate we formalize in this paper is specifically designed for knowledge merging and is different from the majority rule in the other fields. This is due to the fact that our postulate includes a notion of 'partial support' defined in the paper. We show that the simple majority rule commonly used in other fields, i.e., given two alternatives, select the one that has more supporters, will lead to contradiction when applied to knowledge merging, as in the case of the above "democracy" protocol. On the other hand, various voting schemes studied in social choice theory [14] cannot accomplish the purpose of knowledge merging. For example, we would like to achieve new knowledge b by merging two knowledge bases $\{a\}$ and $\{a \rightarrow b\}$. But since neither knowledge base supports b, b cannot be obtained through "voting" by the knowledge bases.

The rest of this paper is organized as follows. In Section 2 we define the language and basic notation used in the paper. In Section 3, we formally propose a set of four postulates for knowledge merging by majority. We show that our formalization of majority postulate is reasonable such that a stronger version will lead to contradiction, and a weaker version will not capture the requirement of knowledge base merging. We then present in Section 4 a model-theoretic characterization of the postulates, which demonstrates how the set of postulates captures the 'minimal criterion'. In Section 5 we review several previous approaches and show how those approaches fail to satisfy some of the postulates. Then in Section 6, we propose a majority merging operator *CMerge* and give a syntactic characterization of it. We conclude the paper in Section 7 by pointing out some topics for future research. The proofs of some theorems and lemmas are given in the Appendix.

2   PRELIMINARIES

In this paper, we consider the language L of propositional logic formed from a finite set of atoms $\mathcal{P}$ in the usual way. And we use the standard terminology of propositional logic except for the definitions given below.

A *knowledge base* is a finite set of L sentences. We sometimes refer to a knowledge base as an *agent* and use the two terms interchangeably. A *possible world* is a function from $\mathcal{P}$ to $\{t, f\}$. The set of all possible worlds is denoted $\mathcal{W}$. Logical equivalence is denoted by $\equiv$. A *literal* is an atom or negation of an atom. For convenience, if a literal l denote one of p and $\neg p$ (where p is an atom) then $-l$ denote the other of p and $\neg p$. And $\mathcal{P}(l)$ denotes the atom appearing in l. Given a possible world w, we denote w_l^- to be the possible world that agrees with w on every atom except the atom $\mathcal{P}(l)$, in which case w_l^- maps $\mathcal{P}(l)$ to t if w maps it to f, and maps $\mathcal{P}(l)$ to f if w maps it to t.

A *model* of a propositional formula ψ is a possible world where ψ is true in the usual sense. The set of all the models of ψ is denoted by $[\![\psi]\!]$.

A *pre-order* over the set of possible worlds $\mathcal{W}$ is a reflexive and transitive relation on $\mathcal{W}$. For a pre-order $\leq$, we define $<$ as: $w < w'$ iff $w \leq w'$ and $w' \not\leq w$. Let W be a subset of $\mathcal{W}$. We say a possible world w is *minimal* in W with respect to $\leq$ if $w \in W$ and there is no $w' \in W$ such that $w' < w$. Let $Min(W, \leq)$ denote the set of possible worlds that are minimal in W with respect to $\leq$.

3   POSTULATES FOR MAJORITY MERGING

In this section, we propose a set of four *postulates* that knowledge merging operators are expected to satisfy. The first three postulates apply to any merge operator; the fourth one is specific to operators that obey majority rule.

Suppose the knowledge bases under consideration are $T_1, \ldots, T_n$. A merging function *Merge* is a mapping from the set of knowledge bases to a new knowledge base $Merge(\{T_1, \ldots, T_n\})$. Our basic postulates for knowledge merging are as follows:

MM1 $Merge(\{T_1, \ldots, T_n\})$ is consistent.

MM2 If $T_1 \wedge \cdots \wedge T_n$ is consistent then $Merge(\{T_1, \ldots, T_n\}) \equiv T_1 \wedge \cdots \wedge T_n$.

MM3 If $T_1 \equiv T_1', \ldots, T_n \equiv T_n'$, then

$$Merge(\{T_1, \ldots, T_n\}) \equiv Merge(\{T_1', \ldots, T_n'\}).$$

Postulate MM1 assures that the result of merging is consistent since we do not want the conflicts among the knowledge bases to remain unresolved. Postulate MM2 takes care of one limiting case, saying that if there is no conflict among the knowledge bases then the result of merging is simply the union of the knowledge bases. This provides "cooperation" among the knowledge bases, meaning that the group obtains the maximum amount of knowledge from each knowledge base and new knowledge is created by this combination. Postulate MM3 requires the merging function to be independent of the syntax of each knowledge base, as we are considering merging the *knowledge* from the knowledge bases and two knowledge bases have the same knowledge if they are logically equivalent. Note also that the order of the knowledge bases is irrelevant since we take the *set* of knowledge bases as the argument of *Merge*.

We now formalize, in terms of a postulate, the "majority principle" in the context of knowledge base merging. Let us discuss possible ways of doing this.

We say a knowledge base T_i *supports* a sentence α if T_i implies α ($T_i \models \alpha$), and *opposes* α if T_i implies $\neg\alpha$ ($T_i \models \neg\alpha$). One possible formalization of majority rule is to have the merged knowledge base support a sentence α if there are over half (or some fixed percentage) of members in the group of knowledge bases to be merged supporting α. But this postulate is too weak. Consider the following operator that satisfies the postulate: the merged knowledge base is defined to support a sentence α if over half of members support α. Then consider three knowledge bases $T_1 = \{a\}$, $T_2 = \{b, c\}$, and $T_3 = \{\neg c\}$. Intuitively the conflict among the knowledge bases centers on c and we want a and b to be in the merge result, but fewer than half of the knowledge bases support a or b.

A more appealing formalization of majority rule is to require the merged knowledge base to support α whenever there are more members supporting α than $\neg\alpha$. But this can produce contradictory results. For example, suppose $T_1 = \{a\}$, $T_2 = \{\neg a \lor \neg b\}$ and $T_3 = \{b, c\}$. Then the merged knowledge base supports a, b and $\neg a \lor \neg b$.

The problem is that the principle we just proposed applies not only to atomic sentences such as a or b but also to compound ones such as $\neg a \lor \neg b$. In order to avoid inconsistent results, we have to restrict the principle to atomic sentences. We can justify this with a metaphor: in a decision-making committee, members vote on single issues instead of disjunctions or more complex combinations of issues.

Suppose we now restrict our proposal as follows. If there are more members supporting a literal l than its negation $-l$, then the result should support l. Then for the example $T_1 = \{a\}$, $T_2 = \{\neg a \lor \neg b\}$ and $T_3 = \{b, c\}$, the merged knowledge base supports a and b. But there is still a problem with this proposal: it ignores knowledge encoded in compound sentences such as T_2. In fact, merging T_1, T_2 and T_3 has the same result as merging T_1 and

T_3, which seems undesirable. On closer examination of the agent T_2, we note that he has some "partial" support for $\neg a$ and for $\neg b$, i.e., he knows that one of $\neg a$ and $\neg b$ must be true but does not know which one. In fact this knowledge ($\neg a \vee \neg b$) denies the sentence $a \wedge b$. It seems therefore that we should not conclude $a \wedge b$, ignoring T_2's partial support for $\neg a$ and $\neg b$.

To state our final proposal for formalizing the principle of majority, we first define what we mean by a knowledge base "partially supporting" a literal. We say a knowledge base T_i *partially supports* literal l (denoted $T_i \triangleright l$) if there is a β, which mentions no atom appearing in l, such that $T_i \models l \vee \beta$ but $T_i \not\models l$ and $T_i \not\models \beta$. That is, the agent believes either l or β is true without knowing which one is. We restrict this β to be a proposition that mentions no atom appearing in l, for the purpose of excluding the cases that $\beta = -l \vee \ldots$. Otherwise, knowledge of the tautologies would be sufficient to have partial knowledge of any literal. This notion of partial support has a simple model-theoretic description.

PROPOSITION 1. *A knowledge base ψ partially supports a literal l if and only if $[\![\psi \wedge -l]\!] \neq \emptyset$ and there exists $w \in [\![\psi \wedge l]\!]$ such that $w_l^- \notin [\![\psi]\!]$.*

Proof.: 'If' direction: Let ψ be a knowledge base and l be a literal such that $[\![\psi \wedge -l]\!] \neq \emptyset$ and there exists $w \in [\![\psi \wedge l]\!]$ such that $w_l^- \notin [\![\psi]\!]$. Since $w_l^- \notin [\![\psi]\!]$, for each $u \in [\![\psi]\!] - \{w\}$ we can find an atom $p_u \in \mathcal{P}$ such that $p_u \neq \mathcal{P}(l)$ and $u(p_u) \neq w(p_u)$. Define β to be:

$$\beta = \bigvee_{u \in ([\![\psi]\!] - \{w\})} \begin{cases} p_u & \text{if } u(p_u) = t \\ \neg p_u & \text{if } u(p_u) = f. \end{cases}$$

We have for every $u \in [\![\psi]\!] - \{w\}$, $u \models \beta$. Then since $w \models l$, $\psi \models l \vee \beta$. It is clear from the construction of β that β mentions no atom appearing in l and $w \not\models \beta$. Hence $\psi \not\models \beta$. Since $[\![\psi \wedge -l]\!] \neq \emptyset$, we have $\psi \not\models l$. This means that ψ partially supports l.

'Only-If' direction: Let ψ partially support l. Then $[\![\psi \wedge -l]\!] \neq \emptyset$. Otherwise $\psi \models l$ and it follows that $\psi \models l \vee \beta$, for any β, which means that ψ does not partially support l.

From the definition of 'partial-support', we know that there exists β, which mentions no atom appearing in l, such that $\psi \models l \vee \beta$ but $\psi \not\models l$ and $\psi \not\models \beta$. From $\psi \not\models \beta$ we also know that there exists $w \in [\![\psi]\!]$ such that $w \not\models \beta$. Then we have $w_l^- \not\models \beta$ as well since β mentions no atom appearing in l and w and w_l^- assigns the same valuation to every atom except the atom appearing in l. Since $\psi \models l \vee \beta$, we have $w \models l \vee \beta$. But $w \not\models \beta$, so we have $w \models l$. Thus, $w \in [\![\psi \wedge l]\!]$. Since $w \models l$ it is obvious that $w_l^- \not\models l$. It follows from $w_l^- \not\models \beta$ that $w_l^- \not\models l \vee \beta$. Then clearly, $w_l^- \notin [\![\psi]\!]$ since $\psi \models l \vee \beta$, from which the 'Only-If' direction follows. $\square$

The following property about partial support is instructional.

PROPOSITION 2. *For a knowledge base ψ and a literal l, if $\psi \models l$ or $\psi \models -l$ or ψ is inconsistent then ψ does not partially supports l.*

Proof.: Immediate from the definition of partial support. $\square$

We return to the example $T_1 = \{a\}$, $T_2 = \{\neg a \vee \neg b\}$ and $T_3 = \{b, c\}$. As we mentioned, there seems no reason to conclude a and b since T_2 opposes $a \wedge b$; and obviously no reason as well to conclude $\neg a \vee \neg b$. But there is no question that c should be supported. From these observations, we formalize the majority principle as: a group of knowledge bases supports a literal sentence l if there are more members supporting l than members supporting $-l$ or partially supporting $-l$. We do not count members who partially support l, since they may turn out not to support l, but we count the members who partially support $-l$ since they may turn out to support $-l$. That is, support for l should be stronger than opposition to l, including potential opposition.

Formally, let $|T_i \models l|$ denote the number of T_i's that support l, and $|T_i \triangleright l|$ denote the number of T_i's that partially support l, where $i \in [1, n]$. Then the postulate is:

MM4 For a literal sentence l, if

$$(1) \quad |T_i \models l| > |T_i \models -l| + |T_i \triangleright -l|$$

then $Merge(\{T_1, \ldots, T_n\})$ implies l.

We note that if a T_i is inconsistent then $T_i \models l$, $T_i \models -l$ and T_i does not partially support $-l$ according to Proposition 1. Hence any inconsistent T_i makes no difference to the inequality $|T_i \models l| > |T_i \models -l| + |T_i \triangleright -l|$. We can just count those T_i's that are consistent, and rephrase MM4 as:

For a literal l, if there are more consistent T_i's supporting l than supporting or partially supporting $-l$ then $Merge(\{T_1, \ldots, T_n\})$ implies l.

Normally, for a $Merge$ that abides by MM4, the condition of $|T_i \models l| > |T_i \models -l|$ does not guarantee the result of $Merge$ to support l. But in the following case, it suffices:

PROPOSITION 3. *Let Merge be a merging function that abides by MM4. If every member of $\{T_1, \ldots, T_n\}$ supports either l or $-l$ and $|T_i \models l| > |T_i \models -l|$ then $Merge(\{T_1, \ldots, T_n\}) \models l$.*

This is due to the fact that there is no member partially supporting $-l$ in this case.

The following is a simple consequence of the definition of MM4, which relates MM4 and the "strict majority rule"; we omit its proof.

PROPOSITION 4. *Let Merge be a merging function that abides by MM4. If there are over half of the members supporting l but not $-l$ then*

$$Merge(\{T_1, \ldots, T_n\}) \models l.$$

In the case that there is no conflict among the knowledge bases, MM2 alone subsumes all the other postulates. This is shown by the following proposition whose proof is trivial and is omitted.

PROPOSITION 5. *If $T_1 \wedge \cdots \wedge T_n$ is consistent and $Merge(\{T_1, \ldots, T_n\})$ satisfies MM2 then $Merge(\{T_1, \ldots, T_n\})$ satisfies MM1-4.*

So the postulates MM1 and MM3-4 are particularly useful when there are conflicts among the knowledge bases.

The set of postulates MM1-4 is consistent, since the merge function *CMerge* (presented in a later section) satisfies them for any given set of knowledge bases.

4   A MODEL-THEORETIC CHARACTERIZATION OF MERGE OPERATORS

The class of all knowledge base merge operators that satisfy MM1-4 can be characterized in model-theoretic terms. Briefly describing, for each merge operator that complies with the postulates and for each set of knowledge bases $\{T_1, \ldots, T_n\}$ there is a metric that orders the possible worlds in W in terms of their closeness to $\{T_1, \ldots, T_n\}$, so that the result of the merge operation is defined by the set of worlds that are "closest" to the knowledge bases according to this metric. Conversely, each well-behaved metric can be used to define a merge operator that complies with MM1-4.

We say a function that assigns to every set of knowledge bases $\{T_1, \ldots, T_n\}$ a pre-order $\leq_{\{T_1, \ldots, T_n\}}$ over the set of possible worlds W is a *majority* assignment if the following conditions hold:

1. If $[\![T_1]\!] = [\![T_1']\!], \ldots, [\![T_n]\!] = [\![T_n']\!]$ then $\leq_{\{T_1, \ldots, T_n\}} = \leq_{\{T_1', \ldots, T_n'\}}$.

2. Let $W = [\![T_1]\!] \cap \ldots \cap [\![T_n]\!]$. Then for all $w \in W$ and $w' \in \mathcal{W}$, $w \leq_{\{T_1, \ldots, T_n\}} w'$; In particular, $w <_{\{T_1, \ldots, T_n\}} w'$ if $w' \notin W$.

3. Let l be a literal that satisfies the inequality (1), then for all $w \in [\![l]\!]$, $w <_{\{T_1, \ldots, T_n\}} w_l^-$.

The first condition says that the order for $\{T_1, \ldots, T_n\}$ should be independent of the syntax of each T_i ($i = 1, \ldots, n$). The second condition says that all models of $T_1 \wedge \ldots \wedge T_n$ are equally close to the knowledge bases and are strictly closer to them than any non-model. The third one says that if there are more knowledge bases supporting l than supporting or partially supporting $-l$, then given any two possible worlds that agree on every atom except the atom $\mathcal{P}(l)$, the world that satisfies l is strictly closer to the knowledge bases than the one that does not satisfy l. We now take $Min(\mathcal{W}, \leq_{\{T_1, \ldots, T_n\}})$ to be the set of possible worlds in $\mathcal{W}$ that are closest to $\{T_1, \ldots, T_n\}$.

THEOREM 6. *A merging function Merge satisfies postulates MM1-4 iff there exists a majority assignment that maps each set of knowledge base* $\{T_1, \ldots, T_n\}$ *to a partial pre-order* $\leq_{\{T_1, \ldots, T_n\}}$ *such that*

$$[\![Merge(\{T_1, \ldots, T_n\})]\!] = Min(\mathcal{W}, \leq_{\{T_1, \ldots, T_n\}}).$$

Proof.: For convenience in the proof, let $T = \{T_1, \ldots, T_n\}$.

(If-part) Let *Merge* be a merging function and there exists a majority assignment that maps the set of knowledge base T to a partial pre-order $\leq_T$ such that $[\![Merge(T)]\!] = Min(\mathcal{W}, \leq_T)$. We now prove that *Merge* satisfies MM1-4.

MM1: Assume $Merge(T)$ is inconsistent. This means $Min(\mathcal{W}, \leq_T)$ is empty. It follows that for any $w_1 \in \mathcal{W}$ there is $w_2 \in \mathcal{W}$ such that $w_2 <_T w_1$. Similarly, for w_2, there exists $w_3 \in \mathcal{W}$ such that $w_3 <_T w_2$. Hence there is an infinite sequence such that $\cdots <_T w_i <_T w_{i-1} <_T \cdots <_T w_2 <_T w_1$. We now prove that every world in the sequence is distinct. Assume to the contrary that there are two worlds w_i and w_j $(i > j)$ in the sequence such that $w_i = w_j$. Then $w_i <_T \cdots <_T w_{j+1} <_T w_j$ $(i = j + 1$ is allowed). Since $\leq_T$ is transitive it follows that $w_i \leq_T w_{j+1}$. Since $w_i = w_j$ we can substitute w_i with w_j in $w_i \leq_T w_{j+1}$ and we have $w_j \leq_T w_{j+1}$, contradicting the fact that $w_{j+1} <_T w_j$. Hence every world in the sequence is distinct.

As the language we are concerned with is finite, the set of all possible worlds $\mathcal{W}$ is finite. However in the infinite sequence $\cdots <_T w_i <_T w_{i-1} <_T \cdots <_T w_2 <_T w_1$ every world is distinct. This means there are infinite number of possible worlds, a contradiction. Hence $Merge(T)$ is consistent. MM1 is satisfied.

MM2: If $T_1 \wedge \ldots \wedge T_n$ is consistent, $[\![T_1 \wedge \ldots \wedge T_n]\!]$ is not empty. We prove $Min(\mathcal{W}, \leq_T) = [\![T_1 \wedge \ldots \wedge T_n]\!]$. Let $w \in Min(\mathcal{W}, \leq_T)$. Assume $w \notin [\![T_1 \wedge \ldots \wedge T_n]\!]$. Since $[\![T_1 \wedge \ldots \wedge T_n]\!]$ is not empty there is at least a possible world $w' \in [\![T_1 \wedge \ldots \wedge T_n]\!]$. We have $w' <_T w$ according to the second condition of majority assignment. This contradicts the fact that $w \in Min(\mathcal{W}, \leq_T)$.

Let $w \in [\![T_1 \wedge \ldots \wedge T_n]\!]$. Assume $w \notin Min(\mathcal{W}, \leq_T)$. Then there is $w' \in \mathcal{W}$ such that $w' <_T w$. However we have $w \leq_T w'$ by the second condition of majority assignment. This is a contradiction. Hence $Min(\mathcal{W}, \leq_T) = [\![T_1 \wedge \ldots \wedge T_n]\!]$. It follows that $[\![Merge(T)]\!] = [\![T_1 \wedge \ldots \wedge T_n]\!]$. MM2 is satisfied.

MM3: is satisfied by the first condition of majority assignment.

MM4: Let l be a literal such that $|T_i \models l| > |T_i \models -l| + |T_i \rhd -l|$. Assume $Merge(T) \not\models l$. Then there is $w \in [\![Merge(T)]\!]$ such that $w \models -l$. It follows that $w \in Min(\mathcal{W}, \leq_T)$ and $w_l^- \models l$. But then by the third condition of majority assignment, $w_l^- <_T w$, contradicting the fact that $w \in Min(\mathcal{W}, \leq_T)$. Hence $Merge(T) \models l$. MM4 is satisfied.

(Only-if part) Assume that *Merge* satisfies MM1-4. We define a relation $\leq_T$ as $w \leq_T w'$ if and only if one of the following conditions holds:

C1 $w = w'$.

C2 w is a model of $Merge(T)$.

C3 $w \in [\![l]\!]$ and $w' = w_l^-$ for some literal l such that $|T_i \models l| > |T_i \models -l| + |T_i \triangleright -l|$.

C4 There is $w^* \in W$ such that $w \leq_T w^*$ and $w^* \leq_T w'$.

For the order such defined, we have the following lemma that will be needed later.

LEMMA 7. *For two possible worlds w and w', if $w \models Merge(T)$ and $w' \not\models Merge(T)$ then $w <_T w'$.*

Proof.: Since $w \models Merge(T)$, we have $w \leq_T w'$ according to (C2). Then to prove $w <_T w'$ we need to prove $w' \not\leq_T w$. Assume to the contrary that $w' \leq_T w$. Then there must exist some sequences using (C1-4) to define $w' \leq_T w$. Among them, we assume the shortest to be $w^1 \leq_T w^2 \leq_T \cdots \leq_T w^m$ where $w^1, w^2, \ldots, w^m$, $m \geq 2$ are possible worlds, and $w^1 = w'$ and $w^m = w$. Since $[\![\neg Merge(T)]\!]$ and $[\![Merge(T)]\!]$ are disjoint and $w^1 \in [\![\neg Merge(T)]\!]$ but $w^m \in [\![Merge(T)]\!]$, there must be some w^i and w^{i+1} ($i \in [1, m]$) in the sequence such that $w^i \in [\![\neg Merge(T)]\!]$ and $w^{i+1} \in [\![Merge(T)]\!]$ and $w^i \leq_T w^{i+1}$. Since the sequence is the shortest, $w^i \leq_T w^{i+1}$ is defined using (C1-3) only. It is clear that (C1) does not apply, as one is the model of $Merge(T)$ and the other is not. Condition (C2) does not apply either since w^i is not a model of $Merge(T)$. It follows that $w^i \leq_T w^{i+1}$ is defined using (C3) only. Then from the definition of (C3), we have $w^i \models l$ and $w^{i+1} = (w^i)_l^-$, for some literal l such that $|T_i \models l| > |T_i \models -l| + |T_i \triangleright -l|$. As *Merge* satisfies MM4, $Merge(T) \models l$. But $w^{i+1} \not\models l$, which contradicts the fact that $w^{i+1} \in [\![Merge(T)]\!]$. Hence $w <_T w'$. $\square$

To prove the (only-if) part, we need to show two things: (1) $\leq_T$ is a partial pre-order and the assignment mapping the set of knowledge bases to $\leq_T$ is a majority assignment. (2) $[\![Merge(T)]\!] = Min(W, \leq_T)$.

(1). It is easy to see that $\leq_T$ is a partial pre-order. We now show that the assignment mapping the set of knowledge bases to $\leq_T$ is a majority assignment. The first condition of majority assignment is satisfied trivially. We now show the remaining conditions.

- For the second condition, if there exists $w \in [\![T_1 \wedge \ldots \wedge T_n]\!]$ then $T_1 \wedge \ldots \wedge T_n$ is consistent. And since *Merge* satisfies MM2, it follows that $w \in [Merge(T)]$. By (C2) we have $w \leq_T w'$, for all $w' \in \mathcal{W}$. In particular, if $w' \notin [T_1 \wedge \ldots \wedge T_n]$, then $w' \notin [Merge(T)]$. By Lemma 7 we have $w <_T w'$. Hence the second condition of majority assignment is satisfied.

- For the third condition, suppose there exists l such that $|T_i \models l| > |T_i \models -l| + |T_i \triangleright -l|$. Let $w \in [l]$. We want to prove $w <_T w_l^-$. From MM4 we have $Merge(T) \models l$. Thus according to (C3), $w \leq_T w_l^-$. It remains to be shown that $w_l^- \not\leq_T w$. Assume to the contrary that $w_l^- \leq_T w$. Then there must exist some sequences using (C1-4) to define $w_l^- \leq_T w$. Among them, we assume the shortest to be $w^1 \leq_T w^2 \leq_T \cdots \leq_T w^m$ where $w^1, w^2, \ldots, w^m$ ($m \geq 2$) are possible worlds, and $w^1 = w_l^-$ and $w^m = w$. Since $[-l]$ and $[l]$ are disjoint and $w^1 \in [-l]$ but $w^m \in [l]$, there must be some w^i and w^{i+1} ($i \in [1, m]$) in the sequence such that $w^i \in [-l]$ and $w^{i+1} \in [l]$ and $w^i \leq_T w^{i+1}$. Since this sequence is the shortest, $w^i \leq_T w^{i+1}$ is defined using (C1-3) only. It is clear that (C1) does not apply, as w^{i+1} satisfies l but the other does not. Assume Condition (C2) is satisfied. Then w^i is a model of $Merge(T)$, and since w_l^- is not a model of $Merge(T)$, we have $w^i <_T w_l^-$ by Lemma 7. But by the transitivity of $\leq_T$, we know $w^1 \leq_T w^i$. That is, $w_l^- \leq_T w^i$ since $w^1 = w_l^-$, contradicting $w^i <_T w_l^-$. Hence $w^i \leq_T w^{i+1}$ is defined using (C3) only. From the definition of (C3), we have $w^i \models l'$ and $w^{i+1} = (w^i)_{l'}^-$ for some literal l' such that $|T_i \models l'| > |T_i \models -l'| + |T_i \triangleright -l'|$. Then w^i and w^{i+1} assign the same valuations to all atoms except the one appearing in l'. However, $w^i \models -l$ and $w^{i+1} \models l$. Hence we have $l' = -l$. It follows that $|T_i \models -l| > |T_i \models l| + |T_i \triangleright l|$. This contradicts our assumption from the beginning that $|T_i \models l| > |T_i \models -l| + |T_i \triangleright -l|$ (note that $|T_i \triangleright l|$ and $|T_i \triangleright -l|$ are non-negative numbers). Hence $w_l^- \leq_T w$ does not hold. Hence $w_l <_T w_l^-$. The third condition of majority assignment is satisfied.

(2). We now prove $[Merge(T)] = Min(\mathcal{W}, \leq_T)$. Let $w \in [Merge(T)]$. Assume $w \notin Min(\mathcal{W}, \leq_T)$. Then there exists $w' \in \mathcal{W}$ such that $w' <_T w$. However, since w is a model of $Merge(T)$ and according to (C2), we have $w \leq_T w'$. This is a contradiction.

To prove the other direction, let $w \in Min(\mathcal{W}, \leq_T)$ and $w \notin [Merge(T)]$. Then by MM1, $Merge(T)$ is consistent, and hence there exists $w' \in \mathcal{W}$ such that $w' \in [Merge(T)]$. From Lemma 7, we have $w' <_T w$. This contradicts the fact that $w \in Min(\mathcal{W}, \leq_T)$.

Therefore we have $[Merge(T)] = Min(\mathcal{W}, \leq_T)$. □

Note the similarity of this theorem to the representation theorems of Katsuno and Mendelzon for theory change operators such as revision and update [16, 15]. In theory change, we have a knowledge base T and a sentence α

that *must* be incorporated into T; the operators select from all models of α those that are closest to T in a certain sense. In knowledge base merge, we are not restricted to choosing models of any given sentence, but rather we try to compromise among multiple theories to come up with a result that combines as much local knowledge as possible into global knowledge, using majority rule to resolve conflicts.

5   REVIEW OF PREVIOUS PROPOSALS

We have described in the introductory section several previous approaches for resolving conflicts in a group of agents. We review in this section those approaches in light of postulates MM1-4. In the following, the result of merging is usually a set of sentences. For the first three approaches, the result can be viewed as the set of all sentences that the protocol supports.

5.1   *"All Support" Protocol*

In [2], Borgida and Imielinski discuss a protocol where a group of agents is defined to support a sentence α if every agent in the group support α. Let us call this "All support" protocol.

It is easy to see that the result of "All support" can be described as the disjunction of the knowledge bases. That is, a set of knowledge bases $T_1, \ldots, T_n$ supports a sentence α according to the "All support" protocol iff $T_1 \vee \ldots \vee T_n \models \alpha$. With respect to the postulates MM1-4, we have:

PROPOSITION 8. *The "All support" protocol satisfies MM3, but not MM1, MM2, and MM4.*

Proof.: MM3 can easily be seen to hold, which shows that the method has a semantic nature rather than syntactic. When all the knowledge bases to be merged are inconsistent, the disjunction of the knowledge bases is also inconsistent. Hence MM1 is violated. However, the disjunction is consistent if at least one of the knowledge bases is consistent. So for most interesting cases, particularly when each knowledge base to be merged is consistent by itself but inconsistent with other knowledge bases, the result of the protocol is consistent. This means that conflict is sure to be resolved by the protocol for most interesting cases.

The protocol violates MM2. Consider two knowledge bases $\{a\}$ and $\{a \rightarrow b\}$. Then the merge result is $a \vee (a \rightarrow b)$, a tautology that does not support anything else. This means that there is no cooperation among the agents and no new knowledge (such as b in this example) is ever achieved, even when there is no conflict among the agents. In other words, the resulting knowledge base of the protocol is more ignorant than any knowledge base before.

For MM4, consider $T_1 = \{a\}, T_2 = \{a\}$ and $T_3 = \{\neg a\}$. Then the result of the protocol is also a tautology $a \vee \neg a$. The conflict on a is not resolved by majority. $\Box$

5.2   "Democracy" Protocol

Borgida and Imielinski [2] also propose a "Democracy" protocol described as follows. A set of agents is said to support a sentence α iff: (1) some sub-committee supports α, and (2) if some other subcommittee S supports $\neg\alpha$ then there is a subcommittee S' such that S' supports α and cardinality(S') > cardinality(S), where a subcommittee is a subset of agents and is defined to support a sentence if every member in the subcommittee supports the sentence.

PROPOSITION 9. *The "Democracy" protocol satisfies MM2-4, but not MM1.*

Proof.: See the following "More proponents than opponents" protocol. $\Box$

5.3   "More Proponents than Opponents" Protocol

In Section 3, we mentioned a proposal that defines a group of agents to support a sentence if there are more members supporting the sentence than members supporting its negation. Let us call this "More proponents than opponents" protocol. It turns out that the protocol is equivalent to the "Democracy" protocol in the previous subsection.

PROPOSITION 10. *The "More proponents than opponents" protocol is equivalent to the "Democracy" protocol and it satisfies MM2-4, but not MM1.*

Proof.: The equivalence follows from the fact that in the "Democracy" protocol, a subcommittee is a subset of agents and is defined to support a sentence if every member in the subcommittee supports the sentence.

It is easy to see that the protocol satisfies MM2-3. For MM4, just note that for any literal l, if there are more members supporting l than members supporting or partially supporting $-l$ then there are more members supporting l than members supporting $-l$. From this we also see that the postulate MM4 sets a weaker requirement to merge operators than the "More proponents than opponents" rule applying to literal sentences.

MM1 is violated by the example given in the introductory section. That is, for $T_1 = \{a\}, T_2 = \{b\}$ and $T_3 = \{\neg a \vee \neg b\}$, the protocol supports a and b and $\neg a \vee \neg b$, contradictory. $\Box$

5.4 "Maximal Consistent Subsets" Protocol

Baral *et al.* [3] consider how to combine knowledge bases by manipulating the maximal consistent subsets of the union of the knowledge bases. Although they also consider integrity constraints and priorities, the basic idea is to define the merged result as the disjunction of all the maximal consistent subsets. Let us call this "Maximal consistent subsets" protocol, denoted by *MCS*.

DEFINITION 11. $MCS(\{T_1, \ldots, T_n\}) = \bigvee \{C \mid C \subseteq U$ is consistent, and $\not\exists C' \subseteq U$ such that C' is consistent and $C \subset C'$ $\}$, where $U = T_1 \cup \cdots \cup T_n$.

PROPOSITION 12. *MCS satisfies MM1 and MM2, but not MM3 and MM4.*

Proof.: MM1 and MM2 are satisfied trivially. For MM3, let $T_1 = \{a, b\}$ and $T_2 = \{\neg b\}$ then the merged result is equivalent to a. But if $T_1 = \{a \wedge b\}$ and $T_2 = \{\neg b\}$ then the result is equivalent to $a \vee \neg b$. Thus the *MCS* depends on the particular syntax of the knowledge bases, violating MM3. The problem with syntactic merging is that an agent cannot contribute to the merge his knowledge by reasoning independently with his own knowledge base.

   MCS violates MM4 by the example given in the introductory section. That is, for $T_1 = \{a\}, T_2 = \{a\}$ and $T_3 = \{\neg a\}$, the merged result is $a \vee \neg a$, which does not support a. $\square$

6   A MAJORITY MERGING OPERATOR

In this section, we propose a merging operator *CMerge* that satisfies MM1-4. By Theorem 6, all we have to do is define the pre-order $\leq_{\{T_1, \ldots, T_n\}}$ which is used to measure the distance between a possible world and the set of knowledge bases $\{T_1, \ldots, T_n\}$. We will define the distance between a possible world and a set of knowledge bases as the sum of the distances between the world and each knowledge base, where the distance to a single knowledge base is defined using the method of Dalal's [5], which is simply the minimum number of atoms on which the world differs from some model of the knowledge base.

6.1   The Definition

Let the distance between two possible worlds w_1 and w_2, $dist(w_1, w_2)$, be the number of atoms whose valuations differ in the two possible worlds; and let the distance between a possible world w and a knowledge base T be

$$dist(w,T) = \min_{w' \in [\![T]\!]} dist(w,w').$$

For the boundary case where T is inconsistent, we define $dist(w,T) = 0$.

There may be some possible worlds that are close to a particular knowledge base but distant from others in the set. Since we want the views of the majority to be reflected, we try to select those worlds that are closest *overall* to the set of knowledge bases.

One simple way of defining *overall distance* between a possible world w and $\{T_1,\ldots,T_n\}$ is to take the sum of the distances between the world and each T_i. Hence we say w is *closer to or at the same distance from* $\{T_1,\ldots,T_n\}$ than w' (denoted by $w \preceq_{\{T_1,\ldots,T_n\}} w'$) if $\sum_{i=1}^n dist(w,T_i) \leq \sum_{i=1}^n dist(w',T_i)$.

Finally, *CMerge* is defined as:

DEFINITION 13. $[\![CMerge(\{T_1,\ldots,T_n\})]\!] = Min(W, \preceq_{\{T_1,\ldots,T_n\}})$.

That is, a possible world is a model of *CMerge* if and only if its overall distance to the set of knowledge bases is minimum. We have the following property.

LEMMA 14. *CMerge satisfies MM1-4.*

Proof.: In view of Theorem 6, all we need is to prove that $\preceq_{\{T_1,\ldots,T_n\}}$ is a pre-order and the assignment that maps $\{T_1,\ldots,T_n\}$ to $\preceq_{\{T_1,\ldots,T_n\}}$ is a majority assignment. It is easy to see $\preceq_{\{T_1,\ldots,T_n\}}$ is a pre-order, and it is also obvious that the assignment which maps $\{T_1,\ldots,T_n\}$ to $\preceq_{\{T_1,\ldots,T_n\}}$ satisfies the first and the second conditions of majority assignment.

We now show the third condition of majority assignment. Let l be a literal such that $|T_i \models l| > |T_i \models -l| + |T_i \rhd -l|$, and $w \in [\![l]\!]$. We want to prove that $w \prec_{\{T_1,\ldots,T_n\}} w_l^-$. That is, we want to prove $\sum_{i=1}^n dist(w,T_i) < \sum_{i=1}^n dist(w_l^-,T_i)$.

First of all, there must be some T_i ($i \in [1,n]$) that is consistent. Otherwise, each T_i ($i \in [1,n]$) supports both l and $-l$ and hence $|T_i \models l| = |T_i \models -l|$, contradicting the assumption that $|T_i \models l| > |T_i \models -l| + |T_i \rhd -l|$.

Without loss of generality, we assume T_i ($i \in [1,m], m \leq n$) to be the consistent T_i. Note that there are more T_i ($i = 1,\ldots,n$) that support l than support or partially support $-l$, and each inconsistent T_i ($i = m+1,\ldots,n$) supports both l and $-l$ but does not partially support $-l$. Hence, there are more T_i ($i = 1,\ldots,m$) that support l than support or partially support $-l$.

For $i \in [1,m]$, T_i either supports l, or supports $-l$, or partially supports $-l$, or neither of the above three. We consider these cases in the following:

1. For the T_i that supports l, we prove $dist(w,T_i) = dist(w_l^-,T_i) - 1$. Let $u \in [\![T_i]\!]$ such that $dist(w,T_i) = dist(w,u)$, i.e., $dist(w,u) = \min_{v \in [\![T_i]\!]} dist(w,v)$. From $T_i \models l$ we have $u \models l$, and it follows from

$w \models l$ that $dist(w, u) = dist(w_l^-, u) - 1$. Then to prove $dist(w, T_i) = dist(w_l^-, T_i) - 1$, it suffices to prove $dist(w_l^-, T_i) = dist(w_l^-, u)$.

Assume to the contrary that $dist(w_l^-, T_i) \neq dist(w_l^-, u)$. Then there is $v \in [\![T_i]\!]$ such that $dist(w_l^-, v) < dist(w_l^-, u)$. From $T_i \not\models l$ we have $v \models l$. Then it is easy to see $dist(w, v) = dist(w_l^-, v) - 1$ and $dist(w, u) = dist(w_l^-, u) - 1$ since $w \models l$ and $u \models l$. It follows that $dist(w, v) < dist(w, u)$. But since $v \in [\![T_i]\!]$, this contradicts that $dist(w, u) = \min_{v \in [\![T_i]\!]} dist(w, v)$. Therefore, $dist(w_l^-, T_i) = dist(w_l^-, u)$ and it follows that $dist(w, T_i) = dist(w_l^-, T_i) - 1$.

2. For the T_i that supports $-l$, we have $dist(w, T_i) = dist(w_l^-, T_i) + 1$ accordingly.

3. For the T_i that partially supports $-l$, it is easy to see $dist(w, T_i) \leq dist(w_l^-, T_i) + 1$ since w and w_l^- differs only on the atom $\mathcal{P}(l)$.

4. For the remaining T_i, they do not supports l or $-l$ or partially supports $-l$. We prove $dist(w, T_i) \leq dist(w_l^-, T_i)$. Let $u \in [\![T_i]\!]$ such that $dist(w, u) = dist(w, T_i)$, and $v \in [\![T_i]\!]$ such that $dist(w_l^-, v) = dist(w_l^-, T_i)$. Then to prove $dist(w, T_i) \leq dist(w_l^-, T_i)$, it suffices to prove $dist(w, u) \leq dist(w_l^-, v)$. Assume to the contrary that $dist(w, u) > dist(w_l^-, v)$. We have two cases: $v \models -l$ or $v \models l$.

   - $v \models -l$. Since T_i does not supports l, $[\![T_i \wedge l]\!] \neq \emptyset$. Then since T_i does not partially supports $-l$, it follows from the Proposition 1 that for all $y \in [\![T_i \wedge -l]\!]$, $y_l^- \in [\![T_i]\!]$. Therefore, $v_l^- \in [\![T_i]\!]$. It is clear that $dist(w, v_l^-) = dist(w_l^-, v)$. Then from the assumption we have $dist(w, u) > dist(w, v_l^-)$. But since $v_l^- \in [\![T_i]\!]$, this contradicts that $dist(w, u) = dist(w, T_i)$.

   - $v \models l$. Then since $w \models l$, $dist(w_l^-, v) = dist(w, v) + 1$. It follows from the assumption that $dist(w, u) > dist(w, v)$. But since $v \in [\![T_i]\!]$, this also contradicts that $dist(w, u) = dist(w, T_i)$.

In both cases we derive a contradiction. So $dist(w, u) \leq dist(w_l^-, v)$ and it follows that $dist(w, T_i) \leq dist(w_l^-, T_i)$.

Since there are more T_i $(i = 1, \ldots, m)$ that support l than support or partially support $-l$, it is easy to see that for the T_i $(i = 1, \ldots, m)$ that supports l or supports $-l$ or partially supports $-l$, the sum of $dist(w, T_i)$ is smaller than the sum of $dist(w_l^-, T_i)$. For the T_i $(i = 1, \ldots, m)$ that does not support l or $-l$ or partially support $-l$, the sum of $dist(w, T_i)$ is equal to or smaller than the sum of $dist(w_l^-, T_i)$. Thus, $\sum_{i=1}^{m} dist(w, T_i) < \sum_{i=1}^{m} dist(w_l^-, T_i)$. For the inconsistent T_i $(i \in [m+1, n])$, we have $dist(w, T_i) = dist(w_l^-, T_i) = 0$ by the definition of $dist$. It follows that $\sum_{i=1}^{n} dist(w, T_i) < \sum_{i=1}^{n} dist(w_l^-, T_i)$. Thus, $w \prec_{\{T_1, \ldots, T_n\}} w_l^-$ and the assignment which maps

$\{T_1, \ldots, T_n\}$ to $\preceq_{\{T_1, \ldots, T_n\}}$ satisfies the third condition of majority assignment, from which the theorem follows. $\square$

The following result makes sure that if there are some inconsistent knowledge bases in the group, they do not prevent *CMerge* from obtaining the knowledge from the other consistent knowledge bases.

PROPOSITION 15. $CMerge(\{T_1, \ldots, T_n\}) \equiv CMerge(\{T'_1, \ldots, T'_m\})$, *where* $T'_1, \ldots, T'_m$ *are the consistent knowledge bases in* $\{T_1, \ldots, T_n\}$.

Proof.: It suffices to prove $\preceq_{\{T_1, \ldots, T_n\}} = \preceq_{\{T'_1, \ldots, T'_m\}}$. This means to prove $w \preceq_{\{T_1, \ldots, T_n\}} w'$ iff $w \preceq_{\{T'_1, \ldots, T'_m\}} w'$, where $w, w' \in \mathcal{W}$. That is, to prove $\sum_{i=1}^{n} dist(w, T_i) \leq \sum_{i=1}^{n} dist(w', T_i)$ iff $\sum_{i=1}^{m} dist(w, T'_i) \leq \sum_{i=1}^{m} dist(w', T'_i)$. Note that if T_i is inconsistent, $dist(w, T_i) = 0$. Hence

$$\sum_{i=1}^{n} dist(w, T_i) = \sum_{i=1}^{m} dist(w, T'_i)$$

and

$$\sum_{i=1}^{n} dist(w', T_i) = \sum_{i=1}^{m} dist(w', T'_i).$$

It follows that $w \preceq_{\{T_1, \ldots, T_n\}} w'$ iff $w \preceq_{\{T'_1, \ldots, T'_m\}} w'$. $\square$

When T_i is inconsistent for every $i \in [1, n]$, all worlds in $\mathcal{W}$ are equally close to $\{T_1, \ldots, T_n\}$ and consequently $[CMerge(\{T_1, \ldots, T_n\})] = \mathcal{W}$, i.e., the result of *CMerge* is a tautology.

6.2 A Syntactic Characterization of CMerge

The result of *CMerge* can be obtained by a syntactic transformation of the knowledge bases to be merged, without recourse to any model-theoretic construction.

First, we assume the knowledge base is put in the disjunctive normal form known as *dual clause form*, where a *dual clause* is a set of literals among which $\wedge$ is implied, and the knowledge base is equivalent to the disjunction of all the clauses. We use $DNF(\alpha)$ to denote the dual clause form of α. We require all the dual clauses in $DNF(\alpha)$ to be satisfiable if α is satisfiable. If α is unsatisfiable, we define $DNF(\alpha) = \{\emptyset\}$.

We will use the structure called *multiset* in the syntactic characterization. A *multiset* is a data structure similar to *set* except that duplicate elements are allowed in a multiset. We express a multiset like a set, e.g., a multiset $C = \{a, b, a\}$. We define the operation *combination* ($\sqcup$) between two sets A and B as: $A \sqcup B$ results in a multiset containing all the elements of A

and all the elements of B. *Combination* is similar to the operation *union* of sets, except that during the operation of combination duplicate elements are not removed. The membership predicate 'in' ($\in$) between an element and a multiset is as in set theory.

We say a multiset C of literals contains an *inconsistent pair* $\langle l, -l \rangle$ if both l and $-l$ are in C. Given a multiset C, we can break it into two sub-multisets: one is $f(C)$, which contains all the inconsistent pairs that could be found in C; the other one is $t(C)$, which contains the remaining elements of C after $f(C)$ is removed. For example, suppose $C = \{a, a, a, \neg a, \neg a, b, \neg b, c\}$. Then $f(C) = \{a, \neg a, a, \neg a, b, \neg b\}$ and $t(C) = \{a, c\}$. It is useful to notice that $t(C)$ is always satisfiable, and $f(C)$ is unsatisfiable unless it is empty. We can call $t(C)$ the *consistent part* of C and $f(C)$ the *inconsistent part* of C. Let $|C|$ denote the cardinality of C, where C is a set or multiset.

THEOREM 16. *(Syntactic equivalence of CMerge)*

$$CMerge(\{T_1, \ldots, T_n\}) \equiv$$

$$\bigvee \{\bigwedge t(C) \mid C \in S, \text{ and } \nexists C' \in S \text{ such that } |f(C')| < |f(C)|\},$$

where $S = \{D_1 \sqcup \ldots \sqcup D_n \mid D_i \in DNF(T_i), i = 1, \ldots, n\}$.

Proof.: For a possible world w and a set of literals D, let $diff(w, D)$ denote the number of literals in D that are not supported by w, i.e., $diff(w, D) = |\{l \in D \mid w \not\models l\}|$. Then we have the following lemma:

LEMMA 17. *Let w be a possible world and T be a knowledge base. Then*

$$dist(w, T) = \min_{D \in DNF(T)} diff(w, D).$$

Proof.: If T is inconsistent (unsatisfiable) then $DNF(T) = \{\emptyset\}$ and $dist(w, T) = 0$. It is easy to see that the lemma holds. Hence we assume T is satisfiable.

Assume $dist(w, T) > \min_{D \in DNF(T)} diff(w, D)$. Let $D' \in DNF(T)$ such that $diff(w, D') = \min_{D \in DNF(T)} diff(w, D)$. Then $dist(w, T) > diff(w, D')$. From the definition of DNF, we know that all the dual clauses in $DNF(T)$ is satisfiable and hence D' is satisfiable. Thus there is not $p \in D'$ such that $\neg p \in D'$. We let w' be a possible world such that $w'(p) = t$ if $p \in D'$, $w'(p) = f$ if $\neg p \in D'$, and $w'(p) = w(p)$ otherwise. Then it is obvious that $w' \models D'$ and therefore $w' \in [\![T]\!]$. It is also easy to see $dist(w, w') = diff(w, D')$. Then from $dist(w, T) > diff(w, D')$ it follows that $dist(w, T) > dist(w, w')$. But since $w' \in [\![T]\!]$, this contradicts the fact that $dist(w, T) = \min_{u \in [\![T]\!]} dist(w, u)$.

Conversely, assume $dist(w, T) < \min_{D \in DNF(T)} diff(w, D)$. Let $w' \in [\![T]\!]$ such that $dist(w, w') = dist(w, T)$. Then

$$dist(w, w') < \min_{D \in DNF(T)} diff(w, D).$$

Since $w' \in [T]$, $w' \models D'$ for some $D' \in DNF(T)$. Then $w' \models l$ for all $l \in D'$. Hence we have $\textit{diff}(w, D') \leq \textit{dist}(w, w')$. Then from $\textit{dist}(w, w') < \min_{D \in DNF(T)} \textit{diff}(w, D)$ it follows that

$$\textit{diff}(w, D') < \min_{D \in DNF(T)} \textit{diff}(w, D).$$

But since $D' \in DNF(T)$, this is a contradiction.

Therefore $\textit{dist}(w, T) = \min_{D \in DNF(T)} \textit{diff}(w, D)$. $\square$

LEMMA 18.

$$\sum_{i=1}^{n} \textit{diff}(w, D_i) = \textit{diff}(w, t(D_1 \sqcup \ldots \sqcup D_n)) + |f(D_1 \sqcup \ldots \sqcup D_n)|/2,$$

where w is any possible world and $D_1, \ldots, D_n$ are any sets of literals.

Proof.: Follows from the definitions of $\textit{diff}$ and $t(D_1 \sqcup \ldots \sqcup D_n)$ and $f(D_1 \sqcup \ldots \sqcup D_n)$. $\square$

We now proceed to prove the main theorem.

Since both RHS and LHS are consistent, we let $w \models RHS$ and $w' \models LHS$. Then $w \models \bigwedge t(D_1 \sqcup \ldots \sqcup D_n)$, for some $D_1 \in DNF(T_1), \ldots, D_n \in DNF(T_n)$ such that $|f(D_1 \sqcup \ldots \sqcup D_n)| \leq |f(C)|$ for all $C \in S$. Let $Q_i \in DNF(T_i)$ ($i = 1, \ldots, n$ respectively) such that $\textit{diff}(w', Q_i) = \min_{D \in DNF(T_i)} \textit{diff}(w', D)$. Then the first thing we get is:

(2) $|f(D_1 \sqcup \ldots \sqcup D_n)| \leq |f(Q_1 \sqcup \ldots \sqcup Q_n)|.$

For the later development, we prove two inequalities, one concerning w:

(3) $\displaystyle\sum_{i=1}^{n} \textit{dist}(w, T_i) \leq |f(D_1 \sqcup \ldots \sqcup D_n)|/2,$

and another concerning w':

(4) $\displaystyle\sum_{i=1}^{n} \textit{dist}(w', T_i) \geq |f(Q_1 \sqcup \ldots \sqcup Q_n)|/2.$

We first prove (3). From the fact that $w \models \bigwedge t(D_1 \sqcup \ldots \sqcup D_n)$ we have $\textit{diff}(w, t(D_1 \sqcup \ldots \sqcup D_n)) = 0$. It follows from Lemma 18 that $\sum_{i=1}^{n} \textit{diff}(w, D_i) = |f(D_1 \sqcup \ldots \sqcup D_n)|/2$. By Lemma 17 we have $\sum_{i=1}^{n} \textit{dist}(w, T_i) = \sum_{i=1}^{n} \min_{D \in DNF(T_i)} \textit{diff}(w, D)$. So to prove (3), it suffices to prove $\sum_{i=1}^{n} \min_{D \in DNF(T_i)} \textit{diff}(w, D) \leq \sum_{i=1}^{n} \textit{diff}(w, D_i)$. Assume to the contrary that $\sum_{i=1}^{n} \min_{D \in DNF(T_i)} \textit{diff}(w, D) > \sum_{i=1}^{n} \textit{diff}(w, D_i)$. Then there must be at least an $i \in [1, n]$ such that $\min_{D \in DNF(T_i)} \textit{diff}(w, D)$

$> diff(w, D_i)$. But since $D_i \in DNF(T_i)$, this is a contradiction. Therefore $\sum_{i=1}^{n} \min_{D \in DNF(T_i)} diff(w, D) \le \sum_{i=1}^{n} diff(w, D_i)$, from which (3) is established.

Next we prove (4). By Lemma 17 and the definition of Q_i ($i = 1, \ldots, n$) we have

$$(5) \quad \sum_{i=1}^{n} dist(w', T_i) = \sum_{i=1}^{n} \min_{D \in DNF(T_i)} diff(w', D) = \sum_{i=1}^{n} diff(w', Q_i).$$

By Lemma 18 we know $\sum_{i=1}^{n} diff(w', Q_i) \ge |f(Q_1 \sqcup \ldots \sqcup Q_n)|/2$, from which together with the equation (5) we obtain (4).

Then the proof of the main theorem is by contradiction and is carried out in the following two steps:

(a). Assume $w \not\models LHS$. Then since $w' \models LHS$, we have

$$\sum_{i=1}^{n} dist(w', T_i) < \sum_{i=1}^{n} dist(w, T_i).$$

Then using (3) and (4), we get $|f(Q_1 \sqcup \ldots \sqcup Q_n)| < |f(D_1 \sqcup \ldots \sqcup D_n)|$. This contradicts (2).

Hence, $w \models LHS$.

(b). Assume $w' \not\models RHS$. Our goal is to derive a contradiction by proving

$$\sum_{i=1}^{n} dist(w, T_i) < \sum_{i=1}^{n} dist(w', T_i).$$

As $|f(D_1 \sqcup \ldots \sqcup D_n)| \le |f(Q_1 \sqcup \ldots \sqcup Q_n)|$, there are two cases:

- $|f(D_1 \sqcup \ldots \sqcup D_n)| < |f(Q_1 \sqcup \ldots \sqcup Q_n)|$. Then using (3) and (4), we obtain $\sum_{i=1}^{n} dist(w, T_i) < \sum_{i=1}^{n} dist(w', T_i)$.

- $|f(D_1 \sqcup \ldots \sqcup D_n)| = |f(Q_1 \sqcup \ldots \sqcup Q_n)|$. Then $|f(Q_1 \sqcup \ldots \sqcup Q_n)| \le |f(C)|$ for all $C \in S$. It must be the case that $w' \not\models t(Q_1 \sqcup \ldots \sqcup Q_n)$ otherwise $w' \models RHS$ which contradicts our assumption. This means $diff(w', t(Q_1 \sqcup \ldots \sqcup Q_n)) > 0$. Then by Lemma 18, we have $\sum_{i=1}^{n} diff(w', Q_i) > |f(Q_1 \sqcup \ldots \sqcup Q_n)|/2$. Then from equation (5) we obtain $\sum_{i=1}^{n} dist(w', T_i) > |f(Q_1 \sqcup \ldots \sqcup Q_n)|/2$.

  Then using (3) and the fact that $|f(D_1 \sqcup \ldots \sqcup D_n)| = |f(Q_1 \sqcup \ldots \sqcup Q_n)|$, we establish $\sum_{i=1}^{n} dist(w', T_i) > \sum_{i=1}^{n} dist(w, T_i)$.

In both cases we have $\sum_{i=1}^{n} dist(w', T_i) > \sum_{i=1}^{n} dist(w, T_i)$. This contradicts the fact that $w' \models LHS$.

The theorem follows from (a) and (b). $\square$

The idea of the syntactic equivalence is to select from each DNF knowledge base a dual clause such that the combination of the dual clauses has minimum number of inconsistent pairs; and the result of *CMerge* is the disjunction of the consistent parts of these combinations. Notice that any direct manipulation or storage of complete models of the knowledge bases is not required for the syntactic equivalence of *CMerge*. Based on this syntactic equivalence, efficient algorithms can be developed to compute the result of merging multiple DNF knowledge bases with *CMerge*. Of course, converting the knowledge base to DNF may itself require exponential time, and the problem of computing *CMerge* on arbitrary knowledge bases is easily seen to be NP-hard.

6.3   Examples

We now look at some examples of *CMerge*. This first one shows an example of transformation as described in Theorem 16.

EXAMPLE 19. Given three knowledge bases $T_1 = \{a, c\}$, $T_2 = \{a \rightarrow b, \neg c\}$ and $T_3 = \{c\}$. Their disjunctive normal forms $DNF(T_1) = \{\{a, c\}\}$, $DNF(T_2) = \{\{\neg a, \neg c\}, \{b, \neg c\}\}$ and $DNF(T_3) = \{\{c\}\}$.

Then $S = \{C_1, C_2\}$ where $C_1 = \{a, c, \neg a, \neg c, c\}$ and $C_2 = \{a, c, b, \neg c, c\}$.

We have $f(C_1) = \{a, \neg a, c, \neg c\}$ and $t(C_1) = \{c\}$, while $f(C_2) = \{c, \neg c\}$ and $t(C_2) = \{a, b, c\}$. Since C_1 has two inconsistent pairs while C_2 has only one inconsistent pair,

$$
\begin{aligned}
CMerge(\{T_1, T_2, T_3\}) &\equiv t(C_2)\\
&= \{a, b, c\}\\
&\equiv \{a, a \rightarrow b, c\}.
\end{aligned}
$$

EXAMPLE 20. Let $T_1 = \{a, c\}$, $T_2 = \{a \rightarrow b, \neg c\}$ and $T_3 = \{b \rightarrow e, c\}$. Then $CMerge(\{T_1, T_2, T_3\}) \equiv \{a, a \rightarrow b, b \rightarrow e, c\}$.

We observe that the conflict among the knowledge bases centers on c. Since there are two knowledge bases who support c while only one opposes c, the result supports c, reflecting the opinion of the majority. The result also implies the other propositions irrelevant to c, from the three knowledge bases allowing the derivation of the implicit knowledge b and e.

EXAMPLE 21. Suppose in the last example, a fourth knowledge base $T_4 = \{\neg c\}$ is added into the group. Then $CMerge(\{T_1, T_2, T_3, T_4\}) \equiv \{a, a \rightarrow b, b \rightarrow e\}$.

Now in the group there are two knowledge bases supporting c and two supporting $\neg c$. Therefore, c is left undecided. But as in the last example, the propositions irrelevant to c are preserved.

Suppose another knowledge base $T_5 = \{\neg c\}$ is added into the group. Then $CMerge(\{T_1, T_2, T_3, T_4, T_5\}) \equiv \{a, a \rightarrow b, b \rightarrow e, \neg c\}$. The result supports $\neg c$ since now $\neg c$ has a majority of supporters.

EXAMPLE 22. Suppose $T_1 = \{b\}$
$T_2 = \{a, a \to b\}$
$T_3 = \{\neg b\}$.
Then $CMerge(\{T_1, T_2, T_3\}) \equiv \{a, a \to b\} \equiv a \wedge b$.

The result supports b since the majority of knowledge bases support b. The result also supports a since T_2 supports a and the other knowledge bases have no opinion about a. Note if we change T_2 to $\{a, b\}$, the result is the same. $CMerge$ is independent of the syntax of the knowledge bases.

EXAMPLE 23. Suppose $T_1 = \{a\}$
$T_2 = \{a \to b\}$
$T_3 = \{a, \neg b\}$.
Then $CMerge(\{T_1, T_2, T_3\}) \equiv \{a, a \to b\} \vee \{a, \neg b\} \equiv a$.

One way to interpret the result is as follows. The merged knowledge base keeps T_1 and eliminates T_2 and T_3 since T_2 and T_3 are mutually exclusive – one of T_2 and T_3 is logically equivalent to the negation of the other (i.e., $\neg(a \to b) \equiv a \wedge \neg b$).

Another way to look at the result is as the following. The merged knowledge base supports a since the majority support a. For b it is a striking of balance between $a \to b$ and b: one knowledge base (T_3) opposes b, but because the majority support a, T_2 generates support for b using its rule $a \to b$. The opposing and supporting forces are in balance, and hence the issue of b is undecided – the result of merging supports neither b nor $\neg b$.

EXAMPLE 24. Suppose in the last example, a fourth knowledge base $T_4 = \{\neg b\}$ is added into the group. Then $CMerge(\{T_1, T_2, T_3, T_4\}) \equiv \{a, \neg b\}$. The resulting knowledge base opposes b since now the opposing force is stronger than the supporting force for b.

Suppose instead that $T_4 = \{a \to b\}$. Then $CMerge(\{T_1, T_2, T_3, T_4\}) \equiv \{a, a \to b\} \equiv a \wedge b$. The merged knowledge base supports b since now the supporting force for b is stronger than the opposing force.

Table 1 compares the results of $CMerge$ and the results produced by other methods.

7   CONCLUSION

We have proposed a set of four postulates that knowledge merging operators are expected to satisfy, within which the fourth postulate formalizes the principle of majority in the context of knowledge base merging. We then investigated the model-theoretic characterization of the set of postulates and proposed the particular knowledge merging operator, $CMerge$, that satisfies the postulates and that appears to resolve conflicts among the knowledge bases in a plausible way.

It is can be noticed that it is possible to generalize our result to merging

Table 1. A Comparison of *CMerge* and Other Methods

	Knowledge bases	All support	More proponents than opponents (Democracy)	Maximal consistent subsets	*CMerge*
1	$\{a\}$, $\{a\}$, $\{\neg a\}$	$a \vee \neg a$. a tautology	supports $a, \neg a \vee p, \neg a \vee \neg p$. Contradictory	$a \vee \neg a$. Tautology	a
2	$\{a,c\},\{a \to b, \neg c\}$, $\{b \to d,c\}$	$\{a,c\}\vee\{a \to b, \neg c\}\vee\{b \to d,c\}$. Not imply b, d, or c.	supports c, $\neg c \vee p, \neg c \vee \neg p$. Contradictory	$\{a, a \to b, b \to d\}$. Implies b and d, but not c.	$\{a, a \to b, b \to d, c\}$. Implies c, b, d.
3	$\{a,c\},\{a \to b, \neg c\},\{b \to d, c\},\{\neg c\}$	$\{a,c\}\vee\{b \to d,c\} \vee \{\neg c\}$. Not imply b, or d.	supports $c \vee p, c\vee\neg p, \neg c\vee p, \neg c \vee \neg p$. Contradictory	same as (2)	$\{a, a \to b, b \to d\}$
4	$\{b\},\{a,a \to b\}, \{\neg b\}$	$b \vee (a \wedge b) \vee \neg b$. Tautology	supports b, $\neg b \vee p, \neg b \vee \neg p$. Contradictory	$\{a, a \to b, b\}\vee\{a, \neg b\}\vee \{\neg b, a \to b\}$. Not imply a, or b	$\{a, a \to b\}$
5	$\{b\}, \{a,b\}, \{\neg b\}$	same as (4)	same as (4)	$\{a,b\} \vee \{a, \neg b\}$. Differs from (4). Syntax dependent	same as (4)
6	$\{a\},\{a \to b\}, \{a, \neg b\}$	$a\vee(a \to b)\vee (a \wedge \neg b)$. A tautology	supports $a, \neg b, \neg a \vee b \vee p$, $\neg a \vee b \vee \neg p$. Contradictory	$\{a, a \to b\}\vee\{a, \neg b\}\vee \{\neg b, a \to b\}$.	a
7	$\{a\},\{a \to b\}, \{a, \neg b\},\{\neg b\}$	$a\vee(a \to b)\vee (a\wedge\neg b)\vee\neg b$. A tautology	supports sentences in (6). Contradictory	same as (6)	$a \wedge \neg b$
8	$\{a\},\{a \to b\}, \{a, \neg b\}, \{a \to b\}$	$a\vee(a \to b)\vee (a \wedge \neg b)$. A tautology	supports sentences in (6). Contradictory	same as (6)	$\{a,a \to b\}$

Note: in the result of "More proponents than opponents", p is any symbol that does not appear in any of the given knowledge bases.

knowledge bases with weights. In that case the merge result should reflect the views of the knowledge bases with higher weights, but for the knowledge bases with the same weights, majority principle should still govern the merging process. The result in this extension is reported in [18].

Another obvious research direction is to extend the result to first-order case, which is practically appealing. It is also interesting to consider merging the knowledge including 'meta-knowledge' of the agents, e.g., an agent's knowledge about some other agents. The situation can quickly become complicated as 'meta-knowledge' is added in.

University of Toronto

ACKNOWLEDGMENTS

We thank Anthony Bonner, Hector Levesque, Fangzhen Lin and Ray Reiter for helpful discussions on the subject. We are grateful to the Institute for Robotics and Intelligent Systems of Canada for providing funding to this research.

REFERENCES

[1] M.W. Bright, A.R.Hurson, and S.H. Pakzad. A taxonomy and current issues in multidatabase systems. *Computer*, 25(3):50–59, 1992.

[2] A. Borgida and T. Imielinski. Decision making in committees-a framework for dealing with inconsistency and non-monotonicity. In *Proceedings Nonmonotonic Reasoning Workshop*, pages 21–32, 1984.

[3] C. Baral, S. Kraus, J. Minker, and V. S. Subrahmanian. Combining knowledge bases consisting of first-order theories. *Computational Intelligence*, 8:45–71, 1992.

[4] C. Boutilier. Revision sequences and nested conditionals. In *Proceedings of International Joint Conference on Artificial Intelligence (IJCAI)*, 1993.

[5] Mukesh Dalal. Investigations into a theory of knowledge base revision: preliminary report. In *Proceedings of the 7th National Conference of the American Association for Artificial Intelligence*, pages 475–479, 1988.

[6] R. Fagin and J. Halpern. Belief, awareness, and limited reasoning. *Artificial Intelligence*, 34:39–76, 1988.

[7] R. Fagin, J. Halpern, and M. Vardi. A model-theoretic analysis of knowledge. *Journal of the ACM*, 38(2):382–428, 1991.

[8] R. Fagin, G. M. Kuper, J. D. Ullman, and M. Vardi. Updating logical databases. *Advances in Computing Research*, 3:1–18, 1986.

[9] K. A. Frenkel. The human genome project and informatics. *Communications of the Association for Computing Machinery*, 34:42, 1991.

[10] R. Fagin, J. D. Ullman, and M. Vardi. On the semantics of updates in databases. In *2nd ACM SIGACT-SIGMOD Symposium on Principles of Database Systems*, pages 352–365, 1983.

[11] J. Halpern. Reasoning about knowledge: an overview. In *Proceedings of the Conference on Theoretical Aspects of Reasoning about Knowledge*, 1986.

[12] J. Halpern and Y. Moses. A guide to the modal logics of knowledge and belief. In *Proceedings IJCAI-85*, pages 480–490, 1985. A complete version appears in *Artificial Intelligence*, 54(3):319-379, 1992, under the title "A guide to completeness and complexity for modal logics of knowledge and belief".

[13] J. Halpern and Y. Moses. Knowledge and common knowledge in a distributed environment. *Journal of the ACM*, 37(3):549-587, 1990.

[14] Jerry S. Kelly. *Social Choice Theory: An Introduction*. Springer-Verlag, 1988.

[15] H. Katsuno and A. O. Mendelzon. On the difference between updating a knowledge base and revising it. In *Proceedings of the 2nd International Conference on Principles of Knowledge Representation and Reasoning*, pages 387-394, 1991.

[16] H. Katsuno and A. O. Mendelzon. Propositional knowledgebase revision and minimal change. *Artificial Intelligence*, 52:263-294, 1991.

[17] Hector J. Levesque. A logic of implicit and explicit belief. FLAIR Texh. Rept. 32, Fairchld Lab. for AI Research, Palp Alto. A preliminary version appears in *Proc. of the 4th National conference of the American Association for Artificial Intelligence*, pages 198-202,1984, 1984.

[18] Jinxin Lin. Integration of weighted knowledge bases. *Artificial Intelligence*, 83/2:363-378, 1996.

[19] P. Revesz. On the semantics of theory change: arbitration between old and new information. In *Proceedings of the Twelfth ACM SIGACT-SIGMOD-SIGART Symposium on Principles of Database Systems*, pages 71-82, 1992.

[20] P. Revesz. On the semantics of arbitration. *International Journal of Algebra and Computation*, 7(2):133-160, 1997.

ELISA BERTINO, GIOVANNA GUERRINI
AND LUCA RUSCA

OBJECT EVOLUTION IN OBJECT DATABASES

1 INTRODUCTION

There are many aspects related to evolution in object-oriented databases. Not all of them have been investigated in sufficient depth. Generally speaking, one can distinguish between evolution of schemas - for example, modifying a class definition - and of instances - for example, the migration of an instance from one class to another. In the latter kind of evolution, an instance modifies its own structure while maintaining the same identity. In this paper we discuss instance evolution in the context of the Chimera object-oriented data model [11, 18]. However, though developed with reference to the Chimera data model, the discussion is applicable to any object-oriented database system. Chimera[1] is an object-oriented, deductive, active data model developed as part of ESPRIT Project Idea P6333. Chimera provides all concepts commonly ascribed to object-oriented data models, such as: object identity, complex objects and user-defined operations, classes, inheritance; it provides capabilities for defining deductive rules, that can be used to define views and integrity constraints, to formulate queries, to specify methods to compute derived information; it supports a powerful language for defining triggers.

The object-oriented model introduces different kinds of evolution for objects. In addition to modifications to the values of an object's attributes (state evolution), other kinds of evolution are possible, by which individual objects can modify their own structure and behavior, while maintaining their own identity constant. Whereas state evolution finds its relational counterpart in modifications to the values of the attributes of a tuple, other kinds of evolution exist which are specific to object systems. In particular, the structure and/or behavior of an object can be modified because of:

- migrations of the object to different classes;

- dynamic addition of classes, even not related by inheritance, to the object, thus leading to multiple class direct membership[2];

- specialization of the object, leading to exceptional instances.

---

[1] A Chimera is a monster of Greek mythology with a lion's head, a goat's body, and a serpent's tail; each of them represents one of the three components of the language.

[2] An object belonging to a class C is a *direct member* of C if it does not belong to any subclass of C. An object is a *member* of a class C if it is a direct member of C or is a direct member of some subclass of C.

R. Pareschi and B. Fronhöfer (eds.), Dynamic Worlds, 219–246.
© 1999 *Kluwer Academic Publishers.*

It should be noted that the migration of an object to a new class is different from adding a new class to the object. In the first case, the class to which the instance belonged is lost, whereas in the second case it is not. In the latter of these two options, an object must be able to be a direct member of several classes at the same time. The specialization of an object allows an object to have additional features (attributes and methods) in addition to those of the classes it belongs to. The specialized object is also called an exceptional instance.

These kinds of evolution are not as yet supported by many systems, as they introduce problems for both implementation and consistency. Chimera supports both object migration and dynamic addition of classes, leading to multiple class direct membership. By contrast, Chimera does not support exceptional instances, which is a peculiarity of the O_2 object-oriented database system [14].

Moreover, Chimera supports derived (or predicative) classes. That is, classes whose extents are not explicitly manipulated; rather those classes are implicitly populated in that a population predicate is associated with the class specifying sufficient and necessary conditions for an object to belong to the extent of the class. In models supporting derived classes, it is difficult to ensure that an object belongs to a unique most specific class, because it depends on the population predicates being disjoint. In such a situation, when a new object is inserted in the database, the object may be classified as instance of several most specific classes and the user may even not realize this fact. Note that also modifications to the values of an object's attributes may result in the addition of one or more classes to the object or in the removal of the object from the extent of one or more classes.

Another important aspect concerning instance evolution is that when an object is able to migrate to different classes, or to dynamically acquire and loose classes, appropriate constraints must be imposed to ensure that correct evolutions are defined. Semantically meaningful migrations depend from the application domain. One option is to specify special integrity constraints [36]. Such constraints include:

- specifying a class as *essential*

  a class C is essential if an object which is a member of C cannot at a subsequent point in time migrate to another class and stop belonging to the set of members of C. This means that migrations of an object which is a member of C are confined to the inheritance hierarchy having C as root. Note that an object can have several essential classes, if the model has multiple inheritance.

- specifying a class as *exclusive*

  a class is exclusive if an object that belongs to this class as a direct member cannot belong at the same time to other classes. This constraint can be refined by introducing the notion of exclusiveness of one class with respect to another.

The fact that a class is essential does not imply it is exclusive. An essential class C can be added to an object O, even if the object already has essential classes. The only constraint is that O cannot later loose class C. Conversely, an object can loose an exclusive class.

In this paper we elaborate on all the aspects concerning object evolution in Chimera, presenting also a survey of instance evolution capabilities provided by other systems and discussing relevant open research issues. The paper is organized as follows. The remainder of this section introduces an example that will be used to illustrate the various kinds of object evolution throughout the paper. Section 2 discusses the main issues related to object migration, whereas Section 3 deals with implicit object migration, that is, with state-based dynamic object classification and derived classes. Section 4 is devoted to multiple class direct membership, while Section 5 presents some additional examples. Finally, Section 6 surveys the forms of instance evolution supported in other object-oriented systems, and Section 7 concludes the paper.

1.1 An Example

Figure 1 illustrates a portion of a database schema handling data related to teams in a national football championship. The graphic representation is similar to that used in [7]. Each class is represented by a rectangle, divided in a number of slots, representing the attributes and the methods of the class. Attribute names are in plain text, while method names are in italics. With each rectangle a name is moreover associated (bold), representing the name of the class. Two kinds of arc are used: plain arcs represent aggregation relationships between classes, whereas bold arcs represent inheritance relationships. Thus, a plain arc from an attribute a of a class C to a class C' denotes that C' is the domain of attribute a in class C. By contrast, a bold arc from class C to class C' denotes that C is a subclass of (that is, inherits from) C'.

A team is characterized by a name, which identifies the team, and by a division, in which the team plays (teams are organized according to a certain number of divisions, e.g. from first division to fifth division, each corresponding to a different championship). A group can moreover be associated with a team. Indeed, divisions can be organized in different groups. In general the first division consists of a single group, whereas lower divisions are organized around different groups (e.g. corresponding to different regional areas of the country). For each team its current score is recorded.

Teams are partitioned in professional and non-professional teams. For each professional team, the capital and the fiscal registration number are

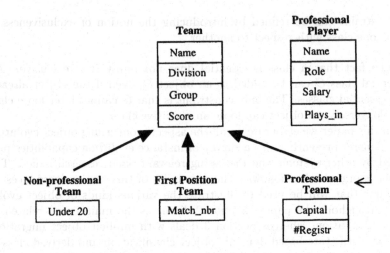

Figure 1. Database schema of our *Teams* example

recorded, whereas for non-professional teams it is recorded whether or not
the team has an associated under-20 team (it is supposed that each professional team has one). A subclass **First Position Team** of the **Team** class
is also defined in the schema. This subclass contains the teams that are
leading their championship (e.g. their group or their division). With each
first position team, the number of matches from which it is leading the
championship is associated.

Finally, the schema includes class **Professional Player**. Each professional player is characterized by a name, a role (e.g., goalkeeper, defender,
mildfielder, forward) and a salary. Moreover, a professional player plays
in a professional team, thus class **Professional Player** has an attribute
Plays_in with domain **Professional Team**.

2   OBJECT MIGRATION

In this section, we first discuss issues and approaches to support object
migration (Subsection 2.1) and then we focus on the approach adopted in
the Chimera data model (Subsection 2.2).

2.1   Issues and Approaches to Object Migration

Migration allows an object to become a direct member of a class which is
different from the class from which the object has been created. Migration
represents an important functionality for object evolution. In particular,

migration allows an object to modify its features, attributes and methods, while retaining its identity.

Referring to our *Teams* example, the change of the status of a team from non-professional to professional is a meaningful evolution. However, despite such a change, teams maintain their identity, and their time-invariant properties, such as the name. In particular, if we restrict the teams playing in divisions one, two, and three to be professional teams, and teams in lower divisions to be non-professional teams, then, at the end of the championship, the teams which are promoted from the fourth to the third division become professional teams, whereas the teams that move from the third to the fourth division become non-professional teams.

This kind of evolution is not supported by many systems, because of implementation and consistency problems. Consistency problems, in particular, arise when an object O, which is a member of a class C, is referred by an object O' as the value of an attribute A, whose domain is C; in such case, the migration of O to a superclass of C violates the integrity constraint established by specifying the domain for A. In other words, object O', after the migration of O, will have as value for attribute A an object which is not a member (neither direct nor indirect) of the class domain of A. Referring to our *Teams* example, the migration of a professional team to the Team class causes that team to no longer be a legal value for attribute Plays_in of a professional player. The situation is similar to the one where the explicit deletion of a referred object is requested. Migration upward in the class hierarchy, indeed, can be seen as a "partial deletion" of the object. Because of those problems, in systems supporting migration, objects are restricted to migrate only into subclasses of the class to which they belong. Here, objects, in a sense, also keep the previous class to which they belonged, since they remain members of this class, despite becoming direct members of a new class.

Before discussing possible solutions for the consistency problems caused by migrations, let us recall that in object-oriented database systems there are two basic deletion policies. Under the first one, referred to as *explicit deletion view*, an object deletion statement is made available at user level[3]. By using such a command, object deletions are explicitly requested by users. Under the second policy, referred to as *garbage collection view*, users can only delete references from an object to another one. An object is then deleted (by the system) when it is no longer referred by any other object. In object systems with explicit deletion, there is the problem of dangling pointers, due to objects containing references to deleted objects. That problem is similar to the referential integrity problem arising in any data model with an explicit deletion operation. Several options to solve that prob-

---

[3]Here and in what follows, the term user should be intended in the broader meaning of an actual user or an application.

lem are available in SQL [9] and have been revisited in an object-oriented context [5], ranging from forbidding the deletion of the referred object, to propagating (that is, cascading) the deletion to the referencing object, and to setting the reference to null. To avoid dangling references, Zdonik [36] proposes to keep a *tombstone object* in place of the deleted object. This solution overcomes the problem of dangling references, since each reference is either to the original object, or to its tombstone object. A main problem of this solution is that each method and query following references from an object to other ones must handle the case in which the referred objects have been deleted. Method code becomes more complicated, because very simple expressions, like the one denoting the value of an object attribute, must handle the exceptions generated by the fact that the object no longer exists (and its tombstone is found, instead).

The problem of upward migrations is similar. If an object O migrates from a class C to a class C', with C subclass of C', an object can exist with a reference to O as an object of class C. There are two different approaches to the migration of an object:

- *Global Type Modification*

  The class modification is performed directly on the object and causes a change in the object state, namely, the deletion of specific attributes defined in the classes from which the object has migrated. If there are other objects referring to object O as a member of C, they must be notified that O is no longer a member of C.

  The problem is similar to that of deletion discussed above and a similar approach can be used. A tombstone can for example be placed in the object to denote that this object used to be a member of class C, but that now the attributes related to C have been deleted. Whenever a method, or a query, tries to access the object's attributes specific to C, it must be prepared to receive a message (exception) denoting that those attributes are no longer available.

- *Local Type Modification*

  Under this approach, the migration operation does not modify the state of the object, rather it creates another *view* of the object. More specifically, upward migration does not delete the information related to the class from which the object migrates. Rather, it creates another view of the object. This view has as type the class to which the object has migrated. Thus, two different references to the object exist, with different types; the reference corresponding to the current object is the most general.

  In a similar way, when dealing with downward migration, the attributes specific to the class to which the object has migrated are not added to the object state. Rather, a new view of the object is created. This view, having as type the lower class, has the additional attributes of the lower class, and shares the state with the original object. Under this approach, the portions of the object state that are no longer referred can be garbage collected.

2.2   Object Migration in Chimera

Object migration in Chimera can be *explicit*, through the invocation of migration commands by users, or *implicit*. Implicit migration arises because Chimera supports predicate classes. A predicate class is a class whose extent is implicitly specified by some predicates, called *population predicates*. All instances of a class C that verify the population predicate of some subclass of C are automatically migrated to this subclass. Because population predicates state conditions against object attribute values, changes to these values trigger automatic migrations. We discuss explicit migrations in the remainder of this subsection, whereas implicit migration is discussed in the following sections.

Chimera provides two operations, supporting upward and downward migrations, respectively. If an existing object in a given class is to be inserted into a more specific subclass or, inversely, moved back to a more general superclass, the OID of the object does not change. Only those attributes that exclusively belong to the more specific class have to be added or removed from the object state. As an example, referring to our *Teams* database, when a team becomes the first in its championship, it is specialized to class First Position Team, and a value for attribute Match_nbr must be provided. By contrast, when the team looses its leadership and it is generalized back to the Team class, the value for attribute Match_nbr is removed from the state of the object.

Specialization of an object to a subclass is performed by the specialize operation, which takes as input parameters two class names, C_1 and C_2, an object identifier O and a record term T. The result of the operation is to insert object O, initially belonging to class C_1, into class C_2 as well. Moreover, the state of O is extended by concatenating its old state (containing values for those attributes that are now inherited) with T, where T specifies values for those attributes that are specific to C_2. Note that O remains a member of C_1 due to the subclass relationship between C_1 and C_2.

The inverse process is performed by the generalize operation, which takes only three parameters: two class names C_1 and C_2, and an identifier O. The result of the operation is to remove object O from class C_1, and to make it a direct member of the superclass C_2 of C_1, which O used to be a member of. Therefore, all attributes specific to C_1 are dropped. Thus, Chimera supports global type modifications. Referential integrity is enforced in Chimera as follows: whenever an object O is deleted from class

C^4, the OID of the deleted object is dropped from all attribute values which refer to O in other objects O'; therefore:

- if C is the type of an atomic attribute of O' (either defined individually or a record component), its value is set to null;

- if C is the type of the element of an attribute of O' built by means of set or list constructors, then O is deleted from the set or list; this may result in producing an empty set or list.

Referring to our *Teams* example, the change of status from non-professional to professional team is performed by the following operations. First, the non-professional team is generalized to class Team (loosing attribute Under_20) through a generalize command, then the team is specialized to class Professional Team (specifying a value for attributes Capital and #Registr) through a specialize command.

Chimera supports multiple inheritance. However the constraint is imposed that for multiple inheritance a common ancestor must exist. Therefore a class C can be defined as a subclass of classes C_1 and C_2 only if a class C' exists from which both C_1 and C_2 inherit from. In Chimera the existence of a common root of the entire class hierarchy is not imposed. Rather the hierarchy is partitioned into multiple strongly connected components. Each strongly connected component is characterized by a single node without incoming edges: this node is called *root* of the strongly connected component. Thus, a class can inherit from multiple classes only if the classes belong to the same strongly connected component, that is, if they have a common ancestor. Therefore, we may think of the set of all classes as partitioned in m distinct hierarchies $\mathcal{H}_1, \ldots, \mathcal{H}_m$, corresponding to the m strongly connected components of the class hierarchy. In Chimera, moreover, an object cannot migrate over different hierarchies. This is reflected by the fact that the only migration primitives supported are generalization to a superclass and specialization to a subclass. Thus, in Chimera, the root of the hierarchy to which the object belong is an *essential* type, with the meaning discussed earlier (see Section 1).

3   OBJECT CLASSIFICATION AND PREDICATE CLASSES

A predicate (or derived) class has all the properties of a usual class, including a name, a set of superclasses, a set of attributes and a set of methods. In addition, a predicate class has a population predicate. A predicate class represents the subset of the members of its superclass(es) that also satisfy the predicate. Whenever an object is a member of the superclasses of the predicate class, and the population predicate evaluates to true on the object,

---

[4]Note that "deleted from class C" also means "generalized to a superclass of C".

the object is automatically considered a member of the predicate class. An object member of a predicate class has all the attributes and methods of this class. If the object state later changes and the population predicate no longer evaluates to true, the object is excluded from the predicate class. The population predicate can test the value or the state of an object, thus supporting a form of implicit classification based on attribute values in addition to explicit classification based on types supported by traditional classes. Predicate classes support indeed a form of automatic, dynamic classification of objects, based on their run-time value, state, or other user-defined properties. In traditional object-oriented models various kinds of static type-based classifications of objects using classes and inheritance are supported; by contrast, the specialization of an object depending on the value of one of its attributes is not allowed.

Referring to our *Teams* example, class First Position Team can be expressed as a derived class. Its population predicate requires, for an object to be member of First Position Team, that the object belongs to the Team class, and that its score is greater than (or equal to) that of each other team in the same championship (that is, in the same group and division). Thus, an object migration between classes Team and First Position Team is induced by a simple modification to attribute Score of an object (not necessarily the one that migrates). Moreover, if we consider that any team playing in division one, two or three must be a professional team, whereas each team playing in a lower division must be a non-professional team, then also classes Non-professional Team and Professional Team can be defined as derived classes, whose population predicates depend on the value of the Division attribute.

In models supporting predicate classes, it is difficult to ensure that an object is a direct member of a unique class, since it depends on population predicates being disjoint. Thus, derived classes lead to the need of supporting a form of multiple class direct membership. The following section discusses how multiple class direct membership is supported in Chimera.

Predicate classes are also the base of *views* in object-oriented data models. View mechanisms for object-oriented databases based on derived classes are presented in [22, 26, 27, 29, 30]. In [29] multiple class direct membership is simulated by *surrogate objects*, that is, each view instance has a special attribute whose value is the identifier of its base object. In [26] the simulation is based on the *object-slicing* approach: the storage structure of a class (or view) object is dispersed through a hierarchy of implementation objects linked to a conceptual object which is a dictionary storing associations of implementation object identifiers and their respective classes.

A form of predicate classes is supported by object-oriented languages with classification facilities [35]. In those languages two kinds of class-like constructs are introduced: primitive concepts, used for explicit classification of objects, and defined concepts, used for implicit property-based classification. An object is member of a primitive concept only when explicitly stated, whereas an object is member of a defined concept whenever its attributes satisfy certain restrictions. Only a few kinds of restrictions are allowed, such as checking for an attribute being an instance of a particular class, being within an integer range, or being an element of some fixed set. In return, the system automatically computes subsumption relationships among concepts (i.e., when a concept "inherits" from another). An object in Yelland's system may be a member of several independently defined concepts. The system creates internal combination subclasses, and uses a single combination subclass to record that an object is a member of several independent concepts simultaneously.

When methods are associated with predicate classes, method dispatching depends not only on the dynamic type of an argument, but also on its dynamic value or state. Among languages supporting predicate classes, Cecil [12] is the only one for which a dispatching mechanism has been developed. Cecil is based on multiple-dispatching. In Cecil, methods are defined by specifying a name, the formal parameters and an implementation. Each formal parameter can, optionally, be associated with an *argument specializer* obj_i, specifying that the method is defined only if the actual parameters (that is, the message arguments) are descendants of object obj_i[5]. For non-specified formal parameters (that is, without argument specializer), any value is legal as actual parameter. Argument specializers are the mean for associating the (multi-)method with specialized objects.

In Cecil methods are dispatched as follows. First, methods applicable to the message, that is, methods with the same name and number of arguments of the message, and whose argument specializers are ancestors of corresponding actual parameters, are determined. Applicable methods are then ordered by their specificity: a method m_1 is more specific than a method m_2 if any argument specializer of m_1 is a descendant of the corresponding argument specializer of m_2 and at least one of the argument specializers of m_1 is a proper descendant of (that is, different from) the corresponding argument specializer of m_2. If a unique most specific applicable method does not exist, an "ambiguous message" error is generated and the message is not dispatched. Cecil does not make use of any ordering on objects or on arguments to solve ambiguities in an automatic way.

Another aspect that must be carefully handled in a system supporting derived classes is type checking. Predicate classes require a new kind of type checking taking into account that the interface exported by an object depends on the current state of the object, as shown by the following example. Referring to the *Teams* example, consider a variable X declared of type First Position Team. If the value of X.Score of the object referenced by

---

[5]Cecil does not support the notion of class, thus inheritance relationships are specified at the object level.

X is modified, the object may not any longer verify the predicate of class **First Position Team**. As a consequence, variable X would reference an object which not consistent with the type of X. To avoid such problem, different solutions can be adopted. Two of them, namely

- disallowing a variable to be declared with a type corresponding to a derived class;

- disallowing updates on the attributes appearing in the population predicate

are conservative solutions. If the population predicate can only be falsified by updates on the object on which it is evaluated[6] that solutions can be refined by allowing a variable to be declared with a type corresponding to a derived class but disallowing updates on the attributes appearing in the population predicate to be applied to that variable. Such an approach prevents, by static checks, a variable of type T from referencing at run-time an object which is not an instance of the class corresponding to T. This approach emphasizes the type checking view.

An alternative solution is to regard population constraints as other constraints and thus to check them run-time. This approach does not ensure that a variable of type T, with T corresponding to a derived class, always references a member of the class corresponding to T. Rather a check is performed at run-time to detect whether the variable references an object that meets the population constraint. If not, an error is raised. This approach requires some type checking at run-time and thus it is potentially less efficient.

Note however, that the two above solutions are not mutually exclusive. They can be combined to obtain a good compromise between semantic richness and efficiency. For example, a variable can be allowed to be declared of a type corresponding to a derived class, and updates on the attributes appearing in the population predicate can also be applied to that variable, but run-time checks for that variable (and only for that one) must be performed. More sophisticated solutions, based on flow analysis of application code [13], can also be investigated.

In Cecil, the relationships among predicate classes are specified explicitly by the programmer through inheritance declarations and disjoint and cover declarations. These declarations are used in type checking. In Cecil, if two predicate classes might both be acquired by an object, either one must be known to be more specific than the other, or they must have disjoint method names. In other words, the checker needs to know: when one predicate class *implies* another, when two predicate classes are *mutually exclusive*, and when a group of predicate classes is *exhaustive*. Since in Cecil

---

[6]This is not always true, e.g. if the population predicate makes use of aggregate operators.

population predicates can contain arbitrary user-defined code, the system is not able to infer implication, mutual exclusion and exhaustiveness by examining the population predicates associated with the various predicate classes. Consequently, it must rely on explicit user declarations to determine the relationships among predicate classes. The system dynamically verifies that these declarations are correct. To state that one population predicate implies another, the isa declaration is used. Mutual exclusion among a group of classes can be declared through the disjoint specification. This specification has the effect of stating that the predicate classes will never have simultaneous common members, that is, at most one of their population predicates will evaluate to true at any given time. Finally, the cover declaration asserts that a group of predicate classes exhaustively covers the possible states of some other class.

4 MULTIPLE CLASS DIRECT MEMBERSHIP

As we have seen in the previous section, when state-based dynamic object classification is supported, an object can be classified into different classes, even not related by the inheritance hierarchy. Thus, a modification of an object attribute may result in the dynamic addition of classes to the object, leading to multiple class direct membership. Referring to our *Teams* example, members of class Team can be classified along orthogonal dimensions, such as Non-professional, Professional, First Position Team. According to the intuitive semantics, a team can be both a professional team and a first position team at the same time. Thus, the object representing this team is classified both in class Professional Team and in class First Position Team and it does not have a unique most specific class, rather it has a set of most specific classes.

Although the above situation can be easily represented in a model with multiple inheritance by defining a subclass (say First_Position_Professional_Team) of all the involved classes, this solution may lead to a lot of artificial subclasses, sometimes referred to as *intersection classes* [28]. Referring to the hierarchy above, the meaningful subclasses of the Team class are shown in Figure 2. Thus, this approach can lead to a combinatorial explosion of sparsely populated classes, whose sole purpose is to allow an instance to have multiple most specific classes, without adding new state or behavior. Another problem with the multiple inheritance approach is that it only provides a single behavioral context for an object [25]. Name conflicts among features in the superclasses are solved once for ever in the subclass definition (for example by imposing an order on superclasses, or with an explicit qualification mechanism) and the selected feature is the only one always considered whatever the context of the object reference is. Thus, reducing multiple class direct membership to multiple inheritance, as

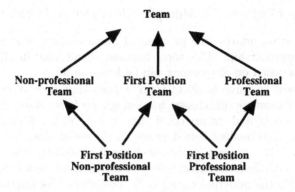

Figure 2. Class hierarchy of our *Teams* example, enriched with some meaningful subclasses

proposed by Stein [31] and Chambers [12], does not account for any context dependence nor for object dependent class ordering.

If multiple class direct membership is supported, two classes C_1 and C_2, with a common superclass C, may have a non-empty intersection even when neither C_1 is a subclass of C_2, nor C_2 is a subclass of C_1. However, when objects belong to several most specific classes, conflicts among different definitions may arise. Indeed, if an object has several most specific classes, the object takes the union of the features of all the classes to which it belongs. Such conflicts resemble conflicts due to multiple inheritance. However, conflicts due to multiple inheritance can be detected at compile time whereas objects may become and cease to be an instance of a class at run time, thus the situation is more complicate for multiple class direct membership.

Referring to our *Teams* database, a team can be at the same time both a professional team and a first position team. The team behaves differently according to the different contexts from which it is accessed, e.g. if the context from which the team object is accessed is Professional Team, the attribute Match_Nbr of the object is not visible.

Some restrictions are imposed on multiple class direct membership in Chimera. An object can belong to several most specific classes only if the classes belong to the same strongly connected component, that is, if they have a common ancestor. The sets of OIDs in different strongly connected components are therefore disjoint. A class in a hierarchy $\mathcal{H}_i$ is therefore *exclusive* with respect to all classes in hierarchy $\mathcal{H}_j$, with $i \neq j$.

In the following subsections we discuss how name conflicts can be solved for models supporting multiple class direct membership, and how semantic constraints can be expressed to impose that two classes have no common instances.

4.1   Name Conflicts for Multiple Class Direct Membership

In this section we address the problem of name conflicts due to multiple class direct membership. This topic has been dealt with in [4], while an extensive discussion on dispatching can be found in [6].

An approach to solve conflicts is to impose that each object, though having several most specific classes, has a single *preferred* class. The binding between an object and its preferred class can be either *fixed* or *context-dependent*. A fixed binding only depends on the set of most specific classes of the object[7]. By contrast, a context-dependent binding also depends on the expression in which the object reference is contained. In a fixed preferred class approach, the preferred class can be determined by imposing a total ordering on classes, or by allowing each object to specify an ordering on the classes to which it belongs[8], or finally by specifying a reference class for each feature in the instance (with an explicit qualification mechanism). Context-dependent preferred class approach leads to a more more flexible language and models both context-dependent access restrictions and context-specific behavior.

In our approach, the context-dependent preferred class is determined by the static type of the object in the expression containing the object reference. Each object reference in each Chimera expression is assigned a single static type. The notion of context of an object reference can be characterized in terms of static types. We analyze conflicts arising in attribute accesses and method invocations. As far as attribute access is concerned, we can disambiguate each access by taking into account only the context of the object reference. By contrast, when considering method dispatching, if we want to ensure a notion of *most specific behavior*, the context alone is not enough to properly dispatch the method. Thus, we propose and compare two different dispatching approaches: the first approach ensures context-dependent behavior, the other one ensures behavior identity.

Consider first the structural component of objects. For an object with multiple most specific classes, the state of the object, that is, the attributes of the object, and the proper domains for these attributes, must be determined. Roughly speaking, the state of an object belonging to several most specific classes is the union of all the attributes defined in these classes. However, the sets of attributes in those classes may not be disjoint. Thus, *name conflicts* may arise. To handle conflicts, we introduce the notion of *source* of an attribute. Intuitively, if an attribute belongs to the intersection of the attribute sets of two classes and it has in both classes the same source, that is, it is inherited by a common superclass, then the attribute

---

[7]A fixed binding does not mean that the binding is immutable for the object lifetime, because an object may acquire and loose classes dynamically.

[8]A reasonable ordering could be the one determined by the acquisition order of classes, in such a way that the most recently acquired behavior prevails (as in Fibonacci [3]).

is semantically unique, and thus the object must have a unique value for this attribute. If, by contrast, the attribute has different sources, the two attributes in the two classes have accidentally the same name, but represent different information, that must be kept separated. Thus, the object may have two different values for the two attributes (a renaming policy is applied).

Consider now the behavioral component of objects, that is, its methods. Each class in a type hierarchy may define a different implementation for the same method. For each method invocation on an object, an implementation must be chosen among the most specific ones. Note that different implementations may return different results or may perform different updates on data. According to one of the basic principles of object-orientation, when, because of subtype polymorphism [10], several method implementations are applicable to a method invocation, the implementation specified in the most specific class of the invocation receiver is executed, as it is the one that *most closely matches* the invocation. Thus, the most specialized behavior prevails, according to the classical late binding mechanism. However, in a model where an object is not characterized by a single most specific class, the choice of the method implementation that "most closely matches" the invocation is not obvious.

There are two different approaches to determine the implementation which most closely matches the invocation, among different implementations in different most specific classes of the object. The first approach, which we call **preferred class** approach, is based on the idea that each object has in each context a *preferred* class, among its most specific ones. Thus, each method invocation is dispatched choosing the implementation in the preferred class in the current context. This approach supports a context-dependent behavior, as the same method invocation may be dispatched differently, and thus may return different results and perform different updates, depending on the context where the method is invoked. The second approach, which we call **argument specificity** approach, does not determine the preferred class of an object to dispatch a method invocation, rather it makes use of the other actual arguments of the method call, thus considering the method as a multi-method [16].

In the following subsections we illustrate and compare these two approaches.

4.1.1 Preferred Class Dispatching Approach

According to this approach, a method invocation is dispatched by taking into account the context-dependent preferred class of the receiver object. As we have seen, in each Chimera expression, each object reference has a single static type. However static typing alone is not enough to select a preferred class for each object in each expression for method dispatching. Indeed, the static type of the object may not belong to the set of most specific classes of the object. Referring to our *Teams* example, consider an expression where an object reference has the static type Team; if at run-time the reference denotes an object belonging to both the class Professional Team and the class First Position Team, the context of the object reference does not help in choosing the preferred class.

In those cases, we must use a total order on classes. This order can be determined by the definition order of classes, eventually overridden by before/after clauses in class definitions. Alternatively, we may consider for each object a total order on its most specific classes, as the one determined by the acquisition order, in such a way that the most recently acquired class precedes the others in the order. We remark that such a total order, that may be considered too arbitrary and unpredictable by the user, is taken into account *only* when the context does not uniquely determine a preferred class for the object. The only alternative in these cases, apart from using that order, would be to simply not dispatch the message, because it is *ambiguous*.

The preferred class approach is based on both static and dynamic information. The static information consists of the static type of the expression, whereas the dynamic information consists of the set of the most specific classes of the object (such classes, in fact, can only be determined at run-time). The total order on classes can be fixed and thus known statically or can, by contrast, be object-dependent and thus known only at run-time.

The preferred class dispatching approach can be stated as follows.

> Let $o_1.m(o_2, \ldots, o_n)$ be a method invocation. The method invocation is dispatched as follows:

> method m in class C is executed if C is the minimum, under the considered total order on classes[9], of the set of classes containing a definition for method m that are subclasses of the static type of object o_1.

The preferred class dispatching approach models context-dependent behavior. In particular, a given method invocation with a fixed set of parameters may produce different results (both in terms of results and data updates), though executed on the same database state, depending on the context of the receiver object reference in the expression containing the invocation.

Under the preferred class approach, any type correct method invocation can be dispatched. Moreover, when the preferred class dispatching strategy

---

[9]Note that the total order must be consistent with the subtype ordering on classes, thus, if C is a minimum with respect to the total order, a most specific behavior for object o_1 is certainly exhibited.

is used with a contravariant redefinition rule for method arguments, type correctness is ensured [6].

4.1.2 Argument Specificity Dispatching Approach

The second approach we consider does not take into account the preferred class of an object, rather it tries to determine the method implementation that most closely matches the invocation by taking into account the types of (all) the actual parameters of the invocation (in addition to the type of the receiver object). This approach is similar to multiple dispatching or multi-method approaches where the selection of the method to execute depends on the types of all the actual arguments of the invocation. In the preferred class approach only the type of the receiver object determines the method to execute and the other arguments only provide the actual values for the method arguments. However, they play no role in method selection. By contrast, in this approach, the method selection is based on the types of *all* arguments, the receiver as well as the other ones.

This approach can be regarded as fully dynamic, as opposed to the other, which is only partially dynamic. Indeed, in this approach dispatching is based only on run-time information, that is, the types of the actual parameters of the invocation. Moreover, whereas the previous approach models context-dependent behavior, the argument specificity approach ensures a notion of behavior identity. In particular, it ensures that a given method invocation, with a fixed set of actual parameters executed on a given database state, returns the same results and produces the same database state, regardless of the expression in which the method invocation is contained. Finally, note that we use multiple dispatching only for choosing an implementation among the ones in sibling classes, and never for choosing an implementation among the ones in a path in a given inheritance hierarchy. Chimera methods, indeed, are not really multi-methods [16] in that they are associated with classes. Thus, the "privileged receiver", though it is not the only one involved in dispatching, has higher priority with respect to other arguments, in that only the implementations in classes that are most specific for the receiver are considered as "candidates" for dispatching. Thus, the dispatching we propose here is not purely multiple in that we maintain a form of "privilege" for the receiver of the method: other arguments are taken into account only to choose among sibling implementations, in the different most specific classes of the receiver object.

To define the argument specificity dispatching rule a notion of *method specificity*, that is, an order on methods must be used. This order is based on the argument specificity (considered in the order from left to right[10]), and, when all the arguments are not comparable under the subtype relationship,

---

[10]Note that this order corresponds to *argument order precedence* proposed in [2].

on the total order of classes where the methods are defined. Such an order is exploited in choosing the method to be executed, among the applicable ones.

The following rule formalizes the argument specificity dispatching method.

Let $o_1.m(o_2, \ldots, o_n)$ be a method invocation, the method invocation is dispatched as follows:

method m in class C is executed if it is the minimum, with respect to the method specificity order, in the set of methods applicable for the invocation.

The argument specificity approach ensures behavioral identity of a method invocation. According to this dispatching rule, the class to which a given message is dispatched does not depend on the context of the message receiver in the expression containing the invocation. Under the argument specificity approach, moreover, any type correct method invocation can be dispatched. The argument specificity approach, however, does not ensure type correctness [6].

4.2 Semantic Constraints for Multiple Class Direct Membership

In our model, an object can belong to several most specific classes. However, there are some classes that should not reasonably have common members, that is, no object must be member of those classes at the same time. For example, it is not reasonable (according to the usual interpretation) that an object be both a person and a car. In Chimera such kinds of constraints are modeled by partitioning the set of objects into different hierarchies, with disjoint extensions. Thus, an object can be a member of two most specific classes only if the classes belong to the same hierarchy, that is, if they have some "similarities". For example, persons and cars should be modeled by classes in different hierarchies.

Thus, the semantic constraint that an object cannot be an instance of two classes that "have nothing in common" can be modeled by hierarchies with disjoint extents. However, this approach is not sufficient to express all semantic constraints on multiple direct membership. Indeed, it might be reasonable that in the same hierarchy two classes exist that have no semantically meaningful common instances. As an example, classes Non-professional Team and Professional Team of our example are both subclasses of Team, and thus belong to the same hierarchy, but they should not have common instances.

These *exclusivity* constraints (e.g., class Non-professional Team is exclusive with respect to class Professional Team) can be expressed in Chimera as untargeted constraints, that is, as constraints that are not associated with any specific class[11]. Suppose that an exclusivity constraint between classes C_1 and C_2 must be expressed. Let C_i be the root of the hierarchy to which both C_1 and C_2 belong (if C_1 and C_2 belong to different hierarchies the extents are automatically disjoint). Then, the exclusivity constraint can be expressed by the following Chimera untargeted constraint (in denial form):

$$not\_excl(X) \leftarrow C_i(X), X \text{ in } C_1, X \text{ in } C_2.$$

Referring to the *Teams* database schema, an exclusivity constraint between classes Non-professional Team and Professional Team is expressed by the following rule:

```
improper_team(X) ← Team(X), X in Non-professional Team,
                   X in Professional Team.
```

Thus, any database state such that the extent of class Non-professional Team and the extent of class Professional Team are not disjoint, would violate the constraint. If the constraint is violated, the violation is reported to the user (together with the OID of the violating object, bound to variable X) and the user can decide how to solve it (e.g., by aborting the transaction, by deleting the object, and so on). These exclusivity constraints, like other Chimera constraints, can also be expressed as triggers [11], containing not only the condition that should not be violated but also the repairing action.

5 ADDITIONAL EXAMPLES

In this section we present few additional examples involving some form of object evolution.

5.1 Polygons, Squares, and Rectangles

Consider the database schema in Figure 3. Class Polygon has as an attribute Vertices, containing the points (pairs of real numbers) representing its vertices. Moreover, it has three methods, one for adding a vertex, one for displaying the polygon, and the last one for computing its area. Subclass Rectangle of Polygon is a derived subclass. Its population predicate requires that the polygon has four vertices and that both the X and Y coordinates of the vertices are pairwise equal. The class has two derived attributes length and width (computed from the coordinates of the vertices) and a method horizontal_scale, which multiplies the width of the

---

[11]Conceptually, they could also been expressed as constraints targeted to the class root of the hierarchy to which the two classes belong. However, the system would not be extensible, in that all the exclusivity constraints on the classes should be known at the time the root is defined.

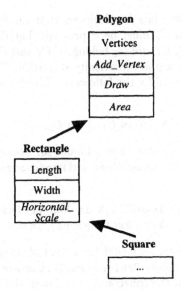

Figure 3. Database schema of our *Polygons* example

rectangle for a given factor (which is a method argument) and appropriately updates the vertices. Moreover, the class redefines methods draw and area of Polygon. Subclass Square of Rectangle is also a derived subclass. Its population predicate requires that the length and the width of the rectangle are equal. No matter which new attributes and methods the class it introduces, it redefines methods draw and area of Rectangle.

When a polygon is inserted in the database, it can be classified as a rectangle or as a square, depending on its geometric properties. If, for example, the polygon is a rectangle, a subsequent execution of method add_vertex causes the generalization of the object to class Polygon, since a polygon with five vertices is no longer a rectangle. Attributes length and width are discarded. By contrast, the execution of method add_vertex on a right-angled triangle may cause the specialization of the triangle to class Rectangle, and the addition of attributes length and width. Similarly, the execution of method horizontal_scale on a rectangle may cause its specialization to class Square, whereas the execution of method horizontal_scale on a Square may cause its generalization to class Rectangle.

5.2 Marital Status

Consider the hierarchy in Figure 4, representing the partitioning of persons with respect to their marital status. Class Person has four different, disjoint, subclasses: Single, Married, Divorced, Widowed. For married

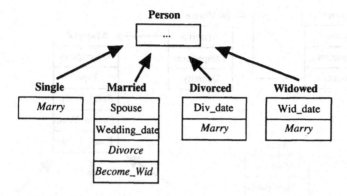

Figure 4. Database schema of our *Marital Status* example

persons the spouse and the wedding date are recorded, while for divorced and widowed persons the date in which they gain that status is kept. Obviously, a person can change its marital status during his/her life, thus object migration from a class to another is possible. Not all the migrations, however, are meaningful. Indeed, once married, a person can never return to the single marital status. Semantically meaningful migrations are those corresponding to methods attached to classes in the schema. Thus, the need of expressing dynamic constraints on object migrations may arise. Note that by using the constraints proposed in [36] we could only state that Person is an essential class, but no other restriction could be imposed. To express these kinds of restrictions, dynamic constraints on object migrations, like those discussed by Su in [32] and by Wieringa et al. in [34], should be employed.

5.3   Pollution Control

Consider the hierarchy in Figure 5, representing information about factories and their wastes, to control the safety with respect to pollution in certain areas. In particular, for each factory its location is recorded, as well as the set of wastes it produces. Wastes are materials, produced in a certain quantity (e.g., per day) and at a certain temperature. Materials are characterized by a number of physical properties and are classified in non-toxic, toxic and highly toxic. For each area the position and the number of inhabitants are recorded. A method to compute the distance of the area from a given location is also provided. Areas are classified as safe, dangerous or critical, depending on the number of inhabitants, and on the distance from factories producing certain quantities of highly toxic or toxic wastes.

Thus, there are several database operations that may cause a re-classification (and thus a class migration) of a certain area: the creation of a new

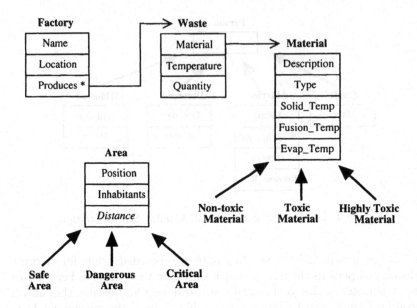

Figure 5. Database schema of our *Pollution Control* example

factory, the change of the factory location, the update of the kind, or of the quantity (or of the temperature, if it influences the toxicity) of the wastes produced by a factory.

6   OBJECT EVOLUTION IN OTHER SYSTEMS AND MODELS

In this section, we first discuss evolution in object systems, other than Chimera, namely in O_2, GemStone and Iris. We then briefly discuss approaches to role modeling. Roles can be used, among other things, to provide alternative and/or additional views of objects and thus can be used to support object evolution.

6.1   *Object Evolution in OODBMSs*

In O_2 [14] instances can be specialized. This enables attributes and methods to be added and redefined for an individual object. In redefining an attribute or a method, the new definition must be compatible with the definition given by the class. In this respect, rules governing subtype definitions are used. For example, the domain of an attribute in an instance can be specialized with respect to the domain specified for the attribute in its class. However, the domain used in the instance must be a subclass of the domain specified in the class.

The only kinds of instance evolution supported in GemStone [8] are state evolution and migration between classes. GemStone allows state evolutions of objects to be controlled, since the state of objects can be "frozen" by using the immediateInvariant message which, when sent to an object, does not allow any further modifications to the state of the object. Note that it can also be specified that all the instances of a class are non-modifiable by using a flag (instanceInvariant) which appears in a class definition. In this case, an instance can only be manipulated during the transaction in which it was created. Once the transaction commits, the instance can no longer be modified. In GemStone, instances can only migrate between two given classes if:

- the new class is a subclass of the old class;

- the new class has no instance attributes in addition to those of the superclass (however, it can have additional instance methods and additional class attributes);

- the new class has the same storage format as the old class;

- the new class has exactly the same attribute domains as the old class.

Therefore, instances can migrate only under very restrictive conditions. The purpose of these restrictions is to allow instance migration only when there are no modifications on the involved instances. The message for requiring the migration of an object is changeClassTo. This message has the class to which the object must migrate as its only argument.

Types in the Iris system [15] can be added to and removed from an object. The object can thus migrate from a type T to a type T'; type T' has just to be added to the object and and type T deleted from the object. A type T' can moreover be added to an object without loosing the previous type to which the object belonged; to do this, the type T' has to be added to the object. Thus, in Iris objects can acquire and loose types dynamically with the instructions ADD TYPE TO and REMOVE TYPE FROM. The ADD TYPE statement also specifies the values to be assigned to the properties of the type which is added. Thus in Iris, arbitrary types can be added to an object. Iris, however, does not support context-dependent behavior since the entire set of types of an object is visible in every context. To avoid conflicts, two different types of an object must not have different methods with the same name.

Table 1 summarizes the various forms of object evolution supported by existing object-oriented database systems. As it can be seen from the table, most systems support very limited forms of evolution. In particular, note that Ode and Orion do not provide any form of object evolution in addition to state modification.

	Chimera	GemStone	Iris	O_2	Ode	Orion
Reference	[11]	[8]	[15]	[14]	[1]	[19]
State modification	YES	YES*	YES	YES	YES	YES
Explicit object migration	YES	Limited	YES	NO	NO	NO
Dynamic state-based classification	YES	NO	NO	NO**	NO	NO
Multiple class direct membership	YES	NO	YES***	NO	NO	NO
Exceptional instances	NO	NO	NO	YES	NO	NO

* As discussed earlier, in GemStone, an object state can be modified provided that the `instanceInvariant` flag has not been set to True in the class of the object.

** A view model has, however, been proposed for O_2 [29].

*** In Iris, arbitrary types can be added to an object. To avoid conflicts, however, two different types of an object cannot have different methods with the same name.

Table 1. Object evolution in existing OO data models

6.2   Role Models

Object models with roles support evolving objects, that is, objects migrating among classes, and objects that cannot be exclusively classified in a single class. In such object models, two different hierarchies are provided: a class (type) hierarchy and a role hierarchy. The role hierarchy is a tree of special types, called *role types*. The root of this tree defines the time-invariant properties of an object. The other nodes represent properties (types) that the object may acquire and loose during its lifetime. At any point in time, an entity is represented by an instance of the root type and an instance of every role type whose role it currently plays. When an entity acquires a new role, a role-specific instance of the appropriate role type is created; when it abandons a role, the role-specific instance is destroyed. Thus, the role concept supports the dynamic nature of entities and their non-exclusive classification. Moreover, entities can exhibit role-specific behavior and roles can be used to restrict access to a particular context. The main drawback of models with roles compared to those allowing an object to be a direct member of multiple classes is that in a model with roles the different hierarchies (role and class ones) highly increases the complexity of the model. Such complexity impacts both the system architecture and the application development. For example, users must choose which features to model as classes and which as roles.

A first approach based on role hierarchies has been proposed by Sciore [28]. In his approach, real-world entities are modeled as object hierarchies where inheritance is determined on a per-object basis, thus merging class-based and prototype-based approaches. When an object receives a message, it either directly replies to the message or delegates the message to its parents. The observed behavior thus depends on the organization of the object hierarchy. A similar approach is proposed in [20]. Richardsons and Schwartz [25] have introduced the concept of *aspect* to model roles in strongly typed object-oriented database systems. More recently, Wieringa et al. in [33] have pointed out that objects may reference a particular role of an object and not only the object itself. The relevance of roles in object-oriented analysis has been stressed by Pernici [24], Papazoglou [23], and Martin and Odell [21]. The Fibonacci object data model [3] and the model proposed in [17] are quite similar. In both a role hierarchy can be associated with a root class; an object in this class can play any role belonging to the hierarchy. In both models, messages are dispatched according to the roles the object plays (though differently).

The emphasis in data models supporting roles is on context-dependent behavior. In Fibonacci [3], the selection of the methods to be executed depends on the role receiving the message. Dispatching is based on the following basic principles: (*i*) the most specific behavior prevails (unless a strict interpretation of messages is explicitly required); (*ii*) the most recently acquired behavior prevails. In Fibonacci, messages are interpreted as follows. When a role receives a message, first it is checked whether a descendant of this role exists having a proper (that is, non-inherited) method to reply to this message. Descendants are considered in inverse temporal order, that is, the more recently acquired descendant is considered first. Subtyping rules ensure that the delegated role can safely replace the receiving role. If no descendant role is able to handle the message, an implementation for the message is then looked for among the methods of the receiver itself. If also this search fails, an implementation for the message is finally looked for in the ancestor role from which the property corresponding to the message has been inherited. If the method invocation is type correct, the last search will certainly succeed. Fibonacci also supports an alternative dispatch mechanism (referred to as *strict binding*) to force an object to exhibit the behavior of a certain role without keeping into account possible specializations of the role. Strict binding must be explicitly required, through a special operator, when a message is sent to a role.

In the role model of Gottlob et al. [17], a message that cannot be handled by any role instance is delegated to the more general instance in the role hierarchy. In that model, however, no priorities are used to select a subrole among a number of candidates; this approach can lead to improper behaviors. Consider, for example, the roles Enterpreneur and Employee of type Person, each defining a method income. The income of a person might not be reduced neither to its income as an employee nor to its income as an entrepreneur, nor to the one of the most recently acquired role. By contrast, the income of a person can be obtained as an aggregate of the incomes of all its roles. Aggregation is one choice, but it is not always the most meaningful one.

7 CONCLUSIONS

In this paper we have discussed the various kinds of object evolution that should be supported in object database systems. The required capabilities include the possibility for an object to change class, either through an explicit migration operation or through state-based dynamic object classification. These kinds of evolution introduce problems both for implementation and consistency. In particular, object evolution introduces problems with respect to type checking, since an object changes its type during its lifetime. Moreover, if multiple class direct membership is allowed, problems concerning name conflicts arise and forms of context-dependence may need to be used. Semantic problems related to object evolution can be handled through appropriate integrity constraints. Those issues have been discussed in the context of the Chimera data model. The forms of object evolution supported by other object-oriented data models have also been surveyed.

Elisa Bertino
Università di Milano

Giovanna Guerrini and Luca Rusca
Università di Genova

REFERENCES

[1] R. Agrawal and N. Gehani. Ode (Object Database and Environment): The Language and the Data Model. In *Proc. of the ACM SIGMOD Int'l Conf. on Management of Data*, pages 36–45, 1989.

[2] R. Agrawal, L. G. De Michiel, and B. C. Lindsay. Static Type Checking of Multi-Methods. In A. Paepcke, editor, *Proc. Sixth Int'l Conf. on Object-Oriented Programming: Systems, Languages, and Applications*, pages 113–128, 1991.

[3] A. Albano, R. Bergamini, G. Ghelli, and R. Orsini. An Object Data Model with Roles. In R. Agrawal, S. Baker, and D. Bell, editors, *Proc. Nineteenth Int'l Conf. on Very Large Data Bases*, pages 39–51, 1993.

[4] E. Bertino and G. Guerrini. Objects with Multiple Most Specific Classes. In W. Olthoff, editor, *Proc. Ninth European Conference on Object-Oriented Programming*, number 952 in Lecture Notes in Computer Science, pages 102–126, 1995.

[5] E. Bertino and G. Guerrini. A Composite Object Model. Technical Report, Dipartimento di Informatica e Scienze dell'Informazione, Università di Genova, 1996. Submitted for publication.

[6] E. Bertino, G. Guerrini, and L. Rusca. Method Dispatching in Object Data Models with Multiple Class Direct Membership. Technical Report DISI-TR-96-17, Dipartimento di Informatica e Scienze dell'Informazione, Università di Genova, 1996. Submitted for publication.

[7] E. Bertino and L. D. Martino. *Object-Oriented Database Systems - Concepts and Architecture*. Addison-Wesley, 1993.

[8] R. Breitl, D. Maier, A. Otis, J. Penney, B. Schuchardt, J. Stein, E. H. Williams, and M. Williams. The GemStone Data Management System. In W. Kim and F. H. Lochovsky, editors, *Object-Oriented Concepts, Databasases, and Applications*, pages 283–308. Addison-Wesley, 1989.

[9] S.J. Cannan and G.A.M. Otten. *SQL - The Standard Handbook*. McGraw-Hill, 1992.

[10] L. Cardelli and P. Wegner. On Understanding Types, Data Abstraction and Polimorphism. *Computing Surveys*, 17:471–522, 1985.

[11] S. Ceri and R. Manthey. Consolidated Specification of Chimera. Technical Report IDEA.DE.2P.006.01, ESPRIT Project 6333, November 1993.

[12] C. Chambers. Predicate Classes. In *Proc. Seventh European Conference on Object-Oriented Programming*, pages 268–296, 1993.

[13] A. Coen Porisini, L. Lavazza, and R. Zicari. Static Type Checking of Object-Oriented Databases. Technical Report 91-60, Dipartimento di Elettronica e Informazione, Politecnico di Milano, 1991.

[14] O. Deux et al. The Story of O_2. *IEEE Transactions on Knowledge and Data Engineering*, 2(1):91–108, 1990.

[15] D. H. Fishman et al. Overview of the Iris DBMS. In W. Kim and F. H. Lochovsky, editors, *Object-Oriented Concepts, Databases, and Applications*, pages 219–250. Addison-Wesley, 1989.

[16] R. Gabriel, J. White, and D. Bobrow. CLOS: Integrating Object-Oriented and Functional Programming. *Communications of the ACM*, 34(9):28–38, September 1991.

[17] G. Gottlob, M. Schrefl, and B. Röck. Extending Object-Oriented Systems with Roles. *ACM Transactions on Information Systems*, 1994.

[18] G. Guerrini, E. Bertino, and R. Bal. A Formal Definition of the Chimera Object-Oriented Data Model. To appear in *Journal of Intelligent Information Systems*, Kluwer Academic Publishers, 1997.

[19] W. Kim et al. Features of the ORION Object-Oriented Database System. In W. Kim and F. H. Lochovsky, editors, *Object-Oriented Concepts, Databasases, and Applications*, pages 251–282. Addison-Wesley, 1989.

[20] G. Kniesel. Implementation of Dynamic Delegation in Srongly Typed Inheritance-Based Systems. Technical Report IAI-TR-94-3, Institut für Informatik, Universität Bonn, 1994.

[21] J. Martin and J. J. Odell. *Object-Oriented Analysis and Design*. Prentice Hall, 1992.

[22] A. Ohori and K. Tajima. A Polimorphic Calculus for Views and Object Sharing. In *Proc. of the Thirteenth ACM SIGACT-SIGMOD-SIGART Symposium on Principles of Database Systems*, pages 255–266, 1994.

[23] M. P. Papazoglou. Roles: A Methodology for Representing Múltifaced Objects. In *Proc. of the International Conference on Database and Expert Systems Applications*, pages 7–12, 1991.

[24] B. Pernici. Objects with Roles. In *Proc. of the ACM Conference on Office Information Systems*, pages 205–215, 1990.

[25] J. Richardson and P. Schwartz. Aspects: Extending Objects to Support Multiple, Indipendent Roles. In J. Clifford and R. King, editors, *Proc. of the ACM SIGMOD Int'l Conf. on Management of Data*, pages 298–307, 1991.

[26] E.A. Rundensteiner. A Methodology for Supporting Multiples Views in Object-Oriented Databases. In *Proc. Eighteenth Int'l Conf. on Very Large Data Bases*, pages 187–198, 1992.

[27] M. Scholl, C. Laasch, and M. Tresch. Views in Object-Oriented Databases. In *Proc. Second International Workshop on Foundations of Models and Languages for Data and Objects*, pages 37–58, 1990.

[28] E. Sciore. Object Specialization. *ACM Transactions on Information Systems*, 7(2):103–122, April 1989.

[29] C. Souza dos Santos, S. Abiteboul, and C. Delobel. Virtual Schemas and Bases. In M. Jarke, J. Bubenko, and K. Jeffery, editors, *Proc. Fourth Int'l Conf. on Extending Database Technology*, number 779 in Lecture Notes in Computer Science, pages 81–94, 1994.

[30] M. Staudt, M. Jarke, M. Jeusfeld, and H. Nissen. Query Classes. In S. Tsur, S. Ceri, and K. Tanaka, editors, *Proc. Third Int'l Conf. on Deductive and Object-Oriented Databases*, number 760 in Lecture Notes in Computer Science, pages 283–295, 1993.

[31] L. A. Stein. A Unified Methodology for Object-Oriented Programming. In M. Lenzerini, D. Nardi, and M. Simi, editors, *Inheritance Hierarchies in Knowledge Representation and Programming Languages*, pages 211–222. John Wiley & Sons, 1991.

[32] J. Su. Dynamic Constraints and Object Migration. In G. M. Lohman, A. Sernadas, and R.Camps, editors, *Proc. Seventeenth Int'l Conf. on Very Large Data Bases*, pages 233–242, 1991.

[33] R. Wieringa, W. de Jonge, and P. Spruit. Roles and Dynamic Subclasses: a Modal Logic Approach. In M. Tokoro and R. Pareschi, editors, *Proc. Eighth European Conference on Object-Oriented Programming*, number 821 in Lecture Notes in Computer Science, 1994.

[34] R. Wieringa, W. de Jonge, and P. Spruit. Using Dynamic Classes and Role Classes to Model Object Migration. *Theory and Practice of Object Systems*, 1(1):61–83, Spring 1995. Special Issue: Selected Papers from ECOOP '94.

[35] P. Yelland. Experimental Classification Facilities for Smalltalk. In A. Paepcke, editor, *Proc. Seventh Int'l Conf. on Object-Oriented Programming: Systems, Languages, and Applications*, pages 235–246, 1992.

[36] S. Zdonik. Object-Oriented Type Evolution. In F. Bancilhon and P. Buneman, editors, *Advances in Database Programming Languages*, pages 277–288. Addison-Wesley, 1990.

ULRICH REIMER, ANDREAS MARGELISCH
AND BERND NOVOTNY

MAKING KNOWLEDGE-BASED SYSTEMS MORE MANAGEABLE: A HYBRID INTEGRATION APPROACH TO KNOWLEDGE ABOUT ACTIONS AND THEIR LEGALITY

1 INTRODUCTION

In more and more companies knowledge-based systems are being considered an adequate means for building systems to support office work in order to increase its quality and efficiency. Such systems need various kinds of knowledge, like knowledge about the terminology underlying the corresponding domain of discourse, and knowledge about what kinds of events and actions can occur in the office work and what changes they cause. As many office tasks underlie organizational regulations as well as federal law, the value of systems for supporting office work is drastically increased if they know about these regulations, thus becoming able to ensure their obedience, or to explain them to the user (this insight already motivated the early LEGOL project [18]). One of the key problems of building such systems is how to properly integrate the various kinds of knowledge: On the one hand, we need a resulting system with adequate efficiency, and on the other hand we want to keep the representation of the various knowledge sources completely independent of each other, mainly due to the following reasons:

- Having one big, monolithic knowledge base would make *construction* and *maintenance* of the knowledge base extremely difficult and error-prone, if not impossible at all.

- The various knowledge sources (esp. knowledge about law and organizational regulations) will typically be employed by more than one application system and should therefore be *reusable*. Thus, it is extremely desirable to represent the knowledge sources only once and just "plug" them in wherever they are needed. As a consequence, they must not be tailored to the needs of the specific application system, but the knowledge represented therein must be kept in a neutral form (without sacrificing efficiency). The issue of knowledge reuse and sharing we are addressing in this paper has been recognized an important topic in the area of knowledge-based systems [12].

R. Pareschi and B. Fronhöfer (eds.), Dynamic Worlds, 247–282.

- Law and regulations should be represented *isomorphically* [1]. This means that there is a one-to-one mapping between the textual structure of the law and the structure of its formal representation. An isomorphic representation is a prerequisite to generate comprehensible explanations for a user and helps to maintain the knowledge base. A representation of the legal knowledge which is adapted to fit into the representation of the other kinds of knowledge clearly cannot be isomorphic.

In this paper we describe an approach to the problem of integrating various knowledge sources that fulfills the requirements stated above. We discuss the proposed approach by showing how we actually employ it for a decision support system for office work. For this purpose, we introduce in Section 2 the decision support system and then describe in Sections 3, 4, and 5 the three knowledge sources used by it. We explain the representation formalism and the reasoning mechanism we have chosen. Section 6 introduces our integration approach and shows how it works for the decision support system introduced in Section 2. Section 7 concludes the paper and identifies still open problems we are currently working on.

2   A KNOWLEDGE-BASED DECISION SUPPORT SYSTEM FOR OFFICE TASKS

In Swiss Life, as in many other companies, office workers for customer support are no longer specialists dealing with certain kinds of office tasks only, but are becoming generalists who must deal with all kinds of tasks. The work of this new generation of office workers is quite demanding and calls for a better support. For this purpose, the Information Systems Research Group of Swiss Life is developing a knowledge-based decision support system, called EULE2[1], that aims at providing a user with a maximal guidance in performing office tasks he or she may not be familiar with.

In EULE2, an office task is divided into several states with predefined actions that lead from one state to another one. Each office task has exactly one initial state and one or more final states. Within a state, the office worker manipulates the knowledge base by creating new concept instances or modifying existing ones. He or she can also perform certain activities external to the system, like sending a letter to a customer or informing a superior. Those results of these external activities that are needed for making decisions later on in the office task (like the endorsement by a superior) must be typed in by the user[2]. Figure 1 gives an example of the

---

[1]EULE2 is the knowledge-based version of a hypertext-based information system called EULE (meaning 'owl').

[2]A later, productive version of EULE2 will be integrated with all the relevant databases so that the user does not need to enter data that already exists.

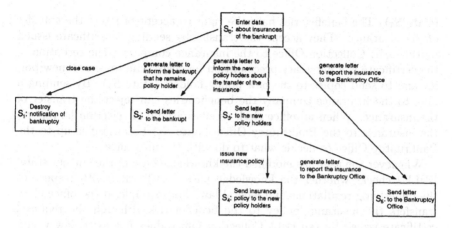

Figure 1. The Office Task *policy-holder-goes-bankrupt*

office task *policy-holder-goes-bankrupt*. Its states are represented by solid boxes (e.g. S_0: *Enter-data-about-insurances-of-the-bankrupt*). A knowledge base manipulation a user typically performs in state S_0 is to create for every insurance where the bankrupt is the policy holder a corresponding instance of the concept *insurance* in the knowledge base. The arrows in Figure 1 stand for the actions that lead from one state to another one and cause certain changes in the knowledge base.

The office task illustrated in Figure 1 describes what an office clerk must do if he gets informed that somebody went bankrupt. The Bankruptcy Office publicly announces all cases of bankruptcy. Everybody who holds properties of the bankrupt is obliged by law to report them to the Bankruptcy Office. The properties will be sold by auction to pay off at least a part of the bankrupt's debts. The property an insurance company may hold of a bankrupt is an insurance where the bankrupt is policy holder. Whenever an office clerk is informed of an opened bankrupt proceeding, he must check if such an insurance exists (state S_0). When the bankrupt is not policy holder of an insurance the office clerk destroys the notification of bankrupt and closes the case (state S_1). Otherwise, the office clerk must report the insurance to the Bankruptcy Office (state S_5), unless an exception is defined by law. One kind of exception states that a provident insurance is exempt from seizure. Thus, provident insurances cannot be sold by auction and it is therefore not necessary to report them to the Bankruptcy Office. Instead, the office clerk informs the bankrupt that he remains policy holder (state S_2). An insurance where the spouse, the children or both are the only beneficiaries is also exempt from seizure. By law such an insurance is transferred to the beneficiaries as soon as the policy holder goes bankrupt. The office clerk informs the beneficiaries that they are the new policy holders (state S_3). The beneficiaries have the right to accept or reject the transfer of the insurance. They accept the transfer by sending a certificate issued by the Debt Collection Office to the insurance company. The reception of the certificate is a necessary precondition for Swiss Life to issue a new policy and to send copies to the new policy holders (state S_4). By sending a note to the insurance company the beneficiaries can reject the transfer of the insurance. When an office clerk receives a note of rejection he reports the insurance to the Bankruptcy Office (state S_5) because it is up to the Bankruptcy Office to decide what to do with the insurance.

Whenever the user has modified the knowledge base in the current state, EULE2 checks whether the knowledge base is still valid with respect to the underlying regulations and federal law. For example, if the office clerk transfers the insurance policy to the beneficiaries although the required certificate issued by the Debt Collection Office does not exist, law would be violated. In this case, EULE2 would reject the transfer and offer an explanation to the office worker about the violation.

Has a knowledge base manipulation proved to be valid, EULE2 checks for each action that leads from the current state to a subsequent state whether it is now executable or not. Certain actions may be illegal, certain others possible, or one of them may be obligatory. The office worker may decide to initiate one of the possible actions, may inquire why an obligatory action must be executed, or may ask why an illegal action is not permitted. Finally, the office worker selects an action for execution. The action causes new instances to be created or existing instances to be modified and leads to a new state.

To achieve the functionality described above EULE2 requires the representation of

- the *office tasks*, mainly consisting of

    - a partially ordered set of actions, leading from a given state into a new state

    - for each of these actions the effects they have on a given state

- the *instances* to be manipulated and the *concepts* they belong to,

- all the *laws and regulations* that must be obeyed by the office tasks.

As we obviously must deal with quite different kinds of knowledge we decided to build a *hybrid knowledge representation system* (cf. Fig.2) which combines

- a *terminological logic* [20, 15] for representing concepts and the instances belonging to them (see Sec.3),

- a first-order language based on the *situation calculus* [9] for representing actions (see Sec.4),

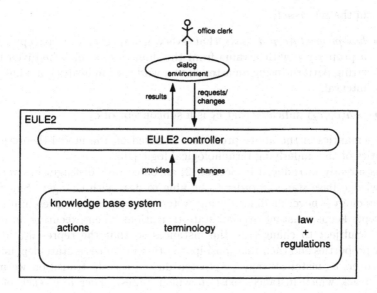

Figure 2. EULE2 System Overview

- a first-order language for representing law and regulations (see Sec.5).

In the following sections we describe each of the representation formalisms used in EULE2 separately. Section 6 will then deal with the integration of these formalisms.

3   KNOWLEDGE ABOUT CONCEPTS AND INSTANCES

The formalism used for representing concepts and their instances is a terminological logic. To facilitate the integration of the terminological knowledge with the other kinds of knowledge it presents itself as a first-order representation to the outside. For the purpose of this paper it suffices to give this first-order representation instead of introducing the terminological logic itself. Furthermore, we omit all representational features not needed in this paper.

In the terminological knowledge, we distinguish between the representation of *concepts* and the representation of their *instances*. A concept can be described through the following predicates (for examples see Fig.3):

- *concept(c)* states that concept c exists;

- *has-relation(c, r, rc-set)* says that every instance of the concept c has a relationship r to at least one instance of one of the concepts given in the set *rc-set*;

- *has-property*(c, p, d) says that every instance of the concept c has a property p with a value from the domain d; d may be given by a string pattern (using an asterisk as a wild card indicator) or a numeric interval;

- *is-a*(c_1, c_2) indicates that c_1 is a subconcept of c_2.

The semantics of the above predicates is based on the model-theoretic semantics of the underlying terminological logic [16].

As already introduced in Section 2, an office task distinguishes various knowledge base states in order to be able to deal with changes. Since the terminology is never modified during system operation, the representation of concepts keeps constant over all state transitions when executing an office task. Subject to change are the instances so that the representation of their properties and their relationships to other instances is state-dependent. Moreover, as instances may be created during a state transition we must keep track which instances exist in which states. Therefore, each of the following predicates for representing instances has an additional argument to indicate the state the description refers to:

- *instance-of*(i, c, s) says that in state s an instance i of the concept c exists;

- *related-to*(i_1, r, i_2, s) says that in state s the instance i_1 is related to the instance i_2 by the relation r;

- *property-of*(i, p, v, s) says that in state s the instance i has a property p with the value v.

There exist instances that must be known to EULE2 independently of any office task currently being performed (like persons and insurance contracts). We thus distinguish a knowledge base which contains all those instances that are persistent with respect to any state transition and call it the *task-independent world description*.

The terminological logic employed provides the common inference services, like classification and instantiation [10].

4   REPRESENTATION OF OFFICE TASKS: KNOWLEDGE ABOUT ACTIONS

An office task has two kinds of appearances. On the one hand, every office task is an instance of the concept *office-task* and thus has properties, like *start-date* and *closing-date*, and relationships to other instances, like the instances being manipulated by it. These aspects are represented as part of

```
concept(office-task)
has-property(office-task, start-date, **.**.****)
has-property(office-task, closing-date, **.**.****)
has-relation(office-task, manipulates, {thing})

concept(policy-holder-goes-bankrupt)
has-relation(policy-holder-goes-bankrupt, manipulates, {person, publication-of-
            bankruptcy, obligation-to-report-property, property})
is-a(policy-holder-goes-bankrupt, office-task)

concept(publication-of-bankruptcy)
has-relation(publication-of-bankruptcy, is-bankrupt, {person})
has-relation(publication-of-bankruptcy, by-bankruptcy-office,
            {bankruptcy-office})

concept(obligation-to-report-property)
has-relation(obligation-to-report-property, is-obliged, {person, corporation})
has-relation(obligation-to-report-property, to-whom, {bankruptcy-office})
has-relation(obligation-to-report-property, reason, {publication-of-bankruptcy})
has-relation(obligation-to-report-property, concerned-property, {property})

concept(property)
has-relation(property, has-owner, {person, corporation})
has-relation(property, hold-by, {person, corporation})

concept(insurance)
has-relation(insurance, is-issued-by, {insurer})
has-relation(insurance, policy-holder, {person, corporation})
has-relation(insurance, beneficiaries, {person})
has-property(insurance, policy-no, ****.***.**)
has-property(insurance, sum-insured, [1, 10'000'000])
is-a(insurance, property)

concept(letter-to-report-property)
has-relation(letter-to-report-property, sender, {person, corporation})
has-relation(letter-to-report-property, recipient, {bankruptcy-office}))
has-relation(letter-to-report-property, for-bankruptcy-case,
            {publication-of-bankruptcy})
has-relation(letter-to-report-property, reported-insurances, {insurance})
```

Figure 3. Fragment of the Terminology for the Office Task *policy-holder-goes-bankrupt* (inherited properties are not shown)

the terminological knowledge (cf. Fig.3). On the other hand, an office task stands for possible sequences of actions. This aspect cannot be represented in the terminological component and thus requires a different representation formalism. Section 4.1 introduces this formalism and describes how knowledge about actions is represented. Section 4.2 outlines the reasoning mechanism used.

4.1 Representing Actions

Central to the representation of office tasks are the notions of a state and a state transition. They are introduced by the following definitions.

DEFINITION 1 (State). A *state* is a collection of concept instances with certain properties and relationships to other instances. It must respect a given terminology (cf. [10], Sec.3.3.2) and satisfy certain integrity constraints (given by the representation of law and regulations). Every instance belonging to the state is identified by the same state descriptor $\langle t, s_j \rangle$ where t is the instance of the office task to which the state belongs, and s_j is a state name unique with respect to the office task concept that t is an instance of. □

The identity of a state is given by its state descriptor, i.e. only when the descriptor changes do we get another state. A modification of the instances associated with a state does not change its identity. As a consequence, a user of EULE2 can modify the knowledge base without causing the system to move into another state.

The state descriptor is a 2-tuple because taking only state names as descriptors (which could be unique over all kinds of office tasks) would not allow us to distinguish the states of two office task instances which belong to the same office task concept. This is, however, necessary because a user may have several instantiations of the same office task at the same time. Therefore, we augment the state name with the corresponding task instance to obtain the state descriptor. For example, the state s_0 in an office task t_1 (which is e.g. instance of the office task *policy-holder-goes-bankrupt*) is denoted by $\langle t_1, s_0 \rangle$.

We can conceive of each state as a knowledge base and have most inferences been drawn on a state only (except, of course, the inferences dealing with state transitions).

DEFINITION 2 (State Transition / Action). A *state transition* is the substitution of a state descriptor by a predefined, new descriptor. It is typically accompanied by a certain modification of the world description as well (but not necessarily). Since state transitions transfer a given world description into another one in a predefined manner we speak of *actions* throughout the remainder of the paper.   □

With the notions of a state and an action (or state transition) we can now explain how knowledge about office tasks is represented in EULE2.

Available actions:

For each office task the possible sequences of actions are defined. To this end, we provide for every action a of an office task ot deduction rules of the following form:

(1) $\forall t : instance\text{-}of(t, ot, \langle t, s_1 \rangle) \Rightarrow available\text{-}action(a, \langle t, s_1 \rangle, \langle t, s_2 \rangle)$

where s_1 and s_2 are arbitrary state names. The rule says that when an office task t of the office task concept ot is in the state $\langle t, s_1 \rangle$ the action a will transfer it into the state $\langle t, s_2 \rangle$. Of course, there may be several rules of the above form leading from the same state s_1 to different new states, i.e., a state may have several possible subsequent states. Every rule of the above form can be graphically visualized as follows:

Combining all the rules for one office task results in a graph like the one depicted in Figure 1.

User-initiated actions:

When a user initiates an action a while dealing with an office task t which is in the state $\langle t, s_1 \rangle$, an atom of the following form will be added to the knowledge base:

(2) $user\text{-}action(a, \langle t, s_1 \rangle, \langle t, s_2 \rangle)$

To be sure that only those user action atoms are added where the action a really leads to the state $\langle t, s_2 \rangle$, the following integrity constraint is provided[3]:

(3) $\forall a, t, s_j, s_k : user\text{-}action(a, \langle t, s_j \rangle, \langle t, s_k \rangle)$
$\Rightarrow$
$available\text{-}action(a, \langle t, s_j \rangle, \langle t, s_k \rangle)$

Valid user-initiated actions:

As an action may be invalid in the current state due to a certain law or regulation (cf. Sec.5) the EULE2 system must check if a user-initiated action

---

[3]Note that formulas (1) and (3) are both implications but (1) is considered a deduction rule which is used to deduce new facts while (3) is an integrity constraint and has the purpose to make sure that the implication stated will never be violated.

is permitted (cf. Sec.6). When this check has been successful an atom of
the following form is added to the knowledge base:

(4) $trigger\text{-}action(a, \langle t, s_1 \rangle, \langle t, s_2 \rangle)$

Modelling the effects caused by an action:
We make use of the situation calculus [9] and represent the effects of an
action by stating what will be true in any state resulting from applying the
action to a given state. As an action can only be executed when it has been
issued by the user *and* when it has been proved valid by the system we get
the following format of an action representation:

(5) $\forall\, t, s_j, s_k :\; user\text{-}action(a, \langle t, s_j \rangle, \langle t, s_k \rangle)\; \wedge$
　　　　　　$trigger\text{-}action(a, \langle t, s_j \rangle, \langle t, s_k \rangle)$
　　　　　$\Rightarrow$
　　　　　　$\langle$description of what will be true in the new state$\rangle$

For example, the following, very simple action definition says that the
action *close-bankruptcy-case* adds the property *closing-date* to the current
task instance (line 3) and that everything else keeps constant, i.e., the new
state consists of the same instances as the old state (line 4) with the same
properties and relationships as formerly (lines 5–9):

(6) $\forall\, t, s_j, s_k :$
　　　$(user\text{-}action(close\text{-}bankruptcy\text{-}case, \langle t, s_j \rangle, \langle t, s_k \rangle)\; \wedge$　　　　1
　　　$trigger\text{-}action(close\text{-}bankruptcy\text{-}case, \langle t, s_j \rangle, \langle t, s_k \rangle)$　　2
　　　$\Rightarrow$
　　　$property\text{-}of(t, closing\text{-}date, today, \langle t, s_k \rangle)\; \wedge$　　　　3
　　　$\forall\, i, c : instance\text{-}of(i, c, \langle t, s_j \rangle)\; \Rightarrow\; instance\text{-}of(i, c, \langle t, s_k \rangle)\; \wedge$　　4
　　　$\forall\, i, c : instance\text{-}of(i, c, \langle t, s_k \rangle)\; \Rightarrow$　　　　5
　　　　$(\forall\, p, v : property\text{-}of(i, p, v, \langle t, s_j \rangle)\; \Rightarrow$　　　　6
　　　　　　　　　　$property\text{-}of(i, p, v, \langle t, s_k \rangle)\; \wedge$　　7
　　　　$\forall\, r, i' : related\text{-}to(i, r, i', \langle t, s_j \rangle)\; \Rightarrow$　　　　8
　　　　　　　　$related\text{-}to(i, r, i', \langle t, s_k \rangle))))$　　　9

The advantage of using the situation calculus for representing actions, instead of, e.g., a production system, is that by sticking to a first-order framework for all representation components their integration becomes much easier.

4.2   Reasoning with the Knowledge

The descriptor of the start state of an office task t_1 is by definition $\langle t_1, S_0 \rangle$.
Thus, a new task t_1 is initiated by copying the task-independent world
description[4], substituting all state descriptors with $\langle t_1, S_0 \rangle$ and adding the

---

[4]Note, that this is a simplified, formal model only. In the implemented system we
actually do not copy all instances because they are by far too many. Instead, we dy-

corresponding office task instance, for example by inserting the following literal:

$$instance\text{-}of(t_1, policy\text{-}holder\text{-}goes\text{-}bankrupt, \langle t_1, S_0 \rangle)$$

This will start an office task t_1 of the office task concept *policy-holder-goes-bankrupt*. Employing the deduction rules of the form shown in (1) the system can then deduce all the actions available in the current state. Subsequently, the user selects an action (due to (3) only available actions can be selected) so that the corresponding *user-action* atom is added to the knowledge base (cf. (2)). If the action is valid (how to determine this is discussed in Sec.6) the corresponding *trigger-action* atom is added (cf. (4)) so that, finally, the action can be executed.

Technically, the action definition, as shown in (5), is considered to be what we call an *auto-corrective integrity constraint*. This means that whenever the integrity constraint is violated a set of corrective updates is triggered so that the knowledge base becomes valid again. The corrective actions are insertions of atoms and are determined automatically according to the algorithm given in Figure 5. Its effect is that an auto-corrective integrity constraint behaves just like an inference rule (with a quite complex right-hand side). In fact, we do not make use of deduction rules in the usual sense but represent all rules to be used for deducing new facts as auto-corrective integrity constraints. Thus, the implication given in (1) is actually an auto-corrective integrity constraint, too. By employing auto-corrective integrity constraints instead of deduction rules we achieve the expressiveness we need for representing actions. Nevertheless, we are still able to specify an algorithm for the reasoning mechanism which is efficient enough for our purposes.

An auto-corrective integrity constraint is a special form of an integrity constraint. We first give the definition of an integrity constraint and then define an auto-corrective integrity constraint.

DEFINITION 3 (Integrity Constraint). An *integrity constraint* (in short: IC) is a function-free, closed, first-order formula with restricted quantification [2]. Such a formula is of one of the following forms:

$$\forall x_1, \ldots, x_n : A_1 \wedge \ldots \wedge A_m \Rightarrow Q \tag{F1}$$

$$\exists x_1, \ldots, x_n : A_1 \wedge \ldots \wedge A_m \ \text{AND} \ Q \tag{F2}$$

where

- $A_1, \ldots, A_m$ are either

    - atoms

---

namically include in the current state only those instances of the task-independent world description that are actually referred to in the state.

— comparisons of the form: $u = v$ and $u \neq v$
(u, v variable or constant)

such that every variable x_i occurs in at least one A_j.

- Q is either true or false or a first-order formula in which some or all x_i are free. If Q contains quantified subformulas, they must be of the form (F1) or (F2).

- the AND operator in (F2) is equivalent to the $\wedge$ operator but is used to separate the formula into a *restriction* on the left-hand side of the AND operator and a *tail* on the right-hand side. In the restriction part all existentially quantified variables must become bound.   □

By restricting the formulas for integrity constraints in the way defined above the efficiency for integrity checking can be remarkably improved. The chosen subset of first-order formulas permits to evaluate only those constraints which are affected by a change in the knowledge base. Furthermore, it is sufficient to evaluate only certain simplified instances of these constraints (for more details cf. [2]).

DEFINITION 4 (Auto-corrective Integrity Constraint). An *auto-corrective integrity constraint* (in short: AIC) is a function-free, closed, first-order formula of the form (F1) or (F2) (see Def.3) where $A_1, \ldots, A_m$ are either

- atoms

- comparisons of the form: $u = v$ and $u \neq v$
(u, v variable or constant)

such that every variable x_i occurs in at least one A_j

and where Q is either:

- *true*   (F3)

- a conjunction of

    — non-negated atoms   (F4)

    — formulas of the form (F1), (F2) where Q is of the form (F1), (F2), (F3) or (F4).

□

It is worth noticing that an AIC contains no negations. However, as we allow equality and inequality as predicates we have with the inequality a specialised negation which does not occur as such on the syntactic level.

$$\forall\, t, s_j, s_k :$$

$$(user\text{-}action(close\text{-}bankruptcy\text{-}case, \langle t, s_j \rangle, \langle t, s_k \rangle) \,\wedge \qquad\qquad 1$$

$$trigger\text{-}action(close\text{-}bankruptcy\text{-}case, \langle t, s_j \rangle, \langle t, s_k \rangle) \qquad\qquad 2$$

$$\Rightarrow$$

$$property\text{-}of(t, closing\text{-}date, today, \langle t, s_k \rangle) \,\wedge \qquad\qquad 3$$

$$property\text{-}of(t, status, case\text{-}closed, \langle t, s_k \rangle) \,\wedge \qquad\qquad 4$$

$$\forall\, i, c : instance\text{-}of(i, c, \langle t, s_j \rangle) \;\Rightarrow\; instance\text{-}of(i, c, \langle t, s_k \rangle) \,\wedge \qquad 5$$

$$\forall\, i, c : instance\text{-}of(i, c, \langle t, s_k \rangle) \;\Rightarrow \qquad\qquad 6$$

$$(\forall\, p, v : property\text{-}of(i, p, v, \langle t, s_j \rangle)) \,\wedge\, (i \neq t) \;\Rightarrow \qquad 7$$

$$property\text{-}of(i, p, v, \langle t, s_k \rangle) \,\wedge \qquad 8$$

$$\forall\, p, v : property\text{-}of(i, p, v, \langle t, s_j \rangle) \,\wedge\, (i = t) \,\wedge \qquad 9$$

$$(p \neq status) \;\Rightarrow\; property\text{-}of(i, p, v, \langle t, s_k \rangle) \,\wedge \qquad 10$$

$$\forall\, r, i' : related\text{-}to(i, r, i', \langle t, s_j \rangle) \;\Rightarrow\; related\text{-}to(i, r, i', \langle t, s_k \rangle)))) \qquad 11$$

Figure 4. Example of an Implicit Deletion

Equality and inequality allow us to implicitly "delete" whole concept instances or property or relation values of an instance by not copying them to the next state. Figure 4 shows an example, where the property *status* for the task instance t is not copied (lines 7 – 10) because *case-closed* is the new value for *status* (line 4) (compare with the action definition (6)).

The algorithm given in Figure 5 evaluates an AIC and computes its corrective actions. For an AIC *aic* the algorithm is initiated by generate-correction(*aic*). If *aic* is satisfied the algorithm will return the empty set as the result. When *aic* is violated the corrective actions (a set of *insert*(⟨*atom*⟩)) are returned. An error message is generated if *aic* is not a syntactically correct integrity constraint. Another error message is returned if more than one variable substitution for an existentially quantified formula exists and if for all of them the restriction is satisfied but not the tail. In this case it is not clear for which variable substitution corrective actions must be computed.

Of course, none of the cases where an error message is produced should occur in EULE2. It is the responsibility of the knowledge engineer to make sure that everything is modelled correctly so that no errors will be encountered. The knowledge engineer will be supported by a modelling tool we are currently developing (cf. Sec.7).

When generate-correction is called for an existentially quantified formula and there exists no variable substitution where the restriction is satisfied new constants are generated for the corresponding variables[5]. The

---

[5]Here, the *AND* operator, which separates the restriction part from the tail, plays a central role because it influences when a new constant is generated and when only a new atom that makes a statement on an existing constant is added. The example given illustrates this aspect.

```
generate-correction(formula);
begin
  if formula = formula1 ∧ formula2 then
    return(generate-correction(formula1) ∪
           generate-correction(formula2));
  elsif formula = ∀x₁,...,xₙ : Restriction ⇒ Q then
    find all substitutions Substᵢ, i = 1,...,m for variables x₁,...,xₙ
    where provable(Restriction(Substᵢ));
    return(  ⋃    generate-correction(Q(Substᵢ)));
           i=1,...,m
  elsif formula = ∃x₁,...,xₙ : Restriction AND Q then
    find all substitutions Substᵢ, i = 1,...,m for variables x₁,...,xₙ
    where provable(Restriction(Substᵢ));
    if m = 0 then
      generate new constants Constₙₑw for variables x₁,...,xₙ;
      return(generate-correction(Restriction(Constₙₑw)) ∪
             generate-correction(Q(Constₙₑw)));
    elsif m = 1 then return(generate-correction(Q(Subst₁)));
    else  /* m > 1 */
      if provable(Q(Substᵢ)) for at least one i, i ∈ {1,...,m} then
        return(∅);
      else return(ERROR: the corrective actions can not
                         definitely be computed);
      end;
    end;
  elsif formula = atom then
    if provable(atom) then return(∅) else return(insert(atom)) end;
  else
    return(ERROR: formula is syntactically not correct);
  end;
end generate-correction;
```

Figure 5. Algorithm for Evaluating AICs and Determining
Possible Corrections

corrective actions are then computed by calling generate-correction for the restriction and for the tail of the formula and by joining the two results. The generation of a new constant only works if the variable stands for an instance (e.g. x in $\exists\, x : instance\text{-}of(x, letter, \langle t, s \rangle)$). It must fail when the variable stands for a property of an instance (e.g. y in $\exists\, y : property\text{-}of(ot_1, closing\text{-}date, y, \langle t, s \rangle)$) because it is very unlikely that an automatically generated, arbitrary constant is a permitted value of the property as required by the terminology. However, this is not a problem in EULE2 because we use existentially quantified variables in AICs only for instances (cf. Fig.6) and not for properties.

The predicate provable(F) is fulfilled iff the current knowledge base is a model of the ground formula F. For that purpose, provable only needs to check the knowledge base for ground atoms which satisfy the formula because every fact that can be inferred is materialized in the knowledge base[6].

$$
\begin{array}{ll}
\forall\, t, s_j, s_k : & 1 \\
(user\text{-}action(report\text{-}property\text{-}to\text{-}bankruptcy\text{-}office, \langle t, s_j \rangle, \langle t, s_k \rangle)\ \wedge & 2 \\
\quad trigger\text{-}action(report\text{-}property\text{-}to\text{-}bankruptcy\text{-}office, \langle t, s_j \rangle, \langle t, s_k \rangle) & 3 \\
\Rightarrow & \\
(\forall\, p, bo, b, i : & 4 \\
\quad instance\text{-}of(p, publication\text{-}of\text{-}bankruptcy, \langle t, s_j \rangle)\ \wedge & 5 \\
\quad instance\text{-}of(i, insurance, \langle t, s_j \rangle)\ \wedge & 6 \\
\quad related\text{-}to(p, is\text{-}bankrupt, b, \langle t, s_j \rangle)\ \wedge & 7 \\
\quad related\text{-}to(p, by\text{-}bankruptcy\text{-}office, bo, \langle t, s_j \rangle)\ \wedge & 8 \\
\quad related\text{-}to(i, policy\text{-}holder, b, \langle t, s_j \rangle) & 9 \\
\Rightarrow & \\
(\exists\, l : & 10 \\
\quad instance\text{-}of(l, letter\text{-}to\text{-}report\text{-}property, \langle t, s_k \rangle)\ \wedge & 11 \\
\quad related\text{-}to(l, sender, Swiss\text{-}Life, \langle t, s_k \rangle)\ \wedge & 12 \\
\quad related\text{-}to(l, recipient, bo, \langle t, s_k \rangle)\ \wedge & 13 \\
\quad related\text{-}to(l, for\text{-}bankruptcy\text{-}case, p, \langle t, s_k \rangle) & 14 \\
\quad AND & \\
\quad related\text{-}to(l, reported\text{-}insurances, i, \langle t, s_k \rangle))))\ \wedge & 15 \\
\forall\, i, c : instance\text{-}of(i, c, \langle t, s_j \rangle)\ \Rightarrow\ instance\text{-}of(i, c, \langle t, s_k \rangle)\ \wedge & 16 \\
\forall\, i, c : instance\text{-}of(i, c, \langle t, s_k \rangle)\ \Rightarrow & 17 \\
(\forall\, p, v : property\text{-}of(i, p, v, \langle t, s_j \rangle)\ \Rightarrow\ property\text{-}of(i, p, v, \langle t, s_k \rangle)\ \wedge & 18 \\
\forall\, r, i' : related\text{-}to(i, r, i', \langle t, s_j \rangle)\ \Rightarrow\ related\text{-}to(i, r, i', \langle t, s_k \rangle)))) & 19 \\
\end{array}
$$

Figure 6. Example of an Action Represented by an AIC

The following example illustrates how the AIC given in Figure 6 is evaluated and how its corrective actions are computed by the algorithm described above. Figure 7 shows a small knowledge base for an office task

---

[6]Inside the terminology componenent not all facts are materialized (e.g. the transitive closure of the is-a and instance-of relations), but to the outside it looks as if this is the case.

$user\text{-}action(report\text{-}property\text{-}to\text{-}bankruptcy\text{-}office, \langle t_1, S_0 \rangle, \langle t_1, S_5 \rangle)$

$trigger\text{-}action(report\text{-}property\text{-}to\text{-}bankruptcy\text{-}office, \langle t_1, S_0 \rangle, \langle t_1, S_5 \rangle)$

$instance\text{-}of(t_1, policy\text{-}holder\text{-}goes\text{-}bankrupt, \langle t_1, S_0 \rangle)$

$instance\text{-}of(Mr\text{-}Smith, person, \langle t_1, S_0 \rangle)$

$instance\text{-}of(Office\text{-}Zurich, bankruptcy\text{-}office, \langle t_1, S_0 \rangle)$

$instance\text{-}of(Pb\#27, publication\text{-}of\text{-}bankruptcy, \langle t_1, S_0 \rangle)$

$instance\text{-}of(Insurance\#70, insurance, \langle t_1, S_0 \rangle)$

$instance\text{-}of(Insurance\#99, insurance, \langle t_1, S_0 \rangle)$

$related\text{-}to(Pb\#27, is\text{-}bankrupt, Mr\text{-}Smith, \langle t_1, S_0 \rangle)$

$related\text{-}to(Pb\#27, by\text{-}bankruptcy\text{-}office, Office\text{-}Zurich, \langle t_1, S_0 \rangle)$

$related\text{-}to(Insurance\#70, policy\text{-}holder, Mr\text{-}Smith, \langle t_1, S_0 \rangle)$

$related\text{-}to(Insurance\#70, hold\text{-}by, Swiss\text{-}Life, \langle t_1, S_0 \rangle)$

$related\text{-}to(Insurance\#70, is\text{-}issued\text{-}by, Swiss\text{-}Life, \langle t_1, S_0 \rangle)$

$related\text{-}to(Insurance\#99, policy\text{-}holder, Mr\text{-}Smith, \langle t_1, S_0 \rangle)$

$related\text{-}to(Insurance\#99, hold\text{-}by, Swiss\text{-}Life, \langle t_1, S_0 \rangle)$

$related\text{-}to(Insurance\#99, is\text{-}issued\text{-}by, Swiss\text{-}Life, \langle t_1, S_0 \rangle)$

Figure 7. Example of a Knowledge Base

t_1 in state S_0. The knowledge base describes the situation that a certain Mr. Smith ($Mr\text{-}Smith$) went bankrupt which was publicly announced by the Bankruptcy Office in Zurich ($Office\text{-}Zurich$) by a publication of bankruptcy ($Pb\#27$). Mr. Smith is the policy holder of two insurances ($Insurance\#70$ and $Insurance\#99$) which are issued and hold by Swiss Life.

To check if the AIC given in Figure 6 is fulfilled, `generate-correction` is called with the AIC as the argument. Since it is an all-quantified formula, all substitutions for the variables t, s_j and s_k are determined for which the left-hand side of the implication (the restriction) is valid. There is one possible substitution:

$\sigma_1 = \{t/t_1, s_j/S_0, s_k/S_5\}$

Next, `generate-correction` is called with the right-hand side of the implication (the tail). In this example we will concentrate on the all-quantified subformula given in lines 4 to 15 in Figure 6 (the effect of the remaining subformulas was already discussed for AIC (6)). We will refer to it by af_1. There are two substitutions which satisfy the restriction part of af_1. As formula af_1 is already restricted by substitution σ_1 this leads to the two substitutions $\sigma_{2.1}$ and $\sigma_{2.2}$ which are extensions of σ_1:

$\sigma_{2.1} = \{p/Pb\#27, bo/Office\text{-}Zurich, b/Mr\text{-}Smith, i/Insurance\#70\} \cup \sigma_1$

$\sigma_{2.2} = \{p/Pb\#27, bo/Office\text{-}Zurich, b/Mr\text{-}Smith, i/Insurance\#99\} \cup \sigma_1$

The right-hand side of af_1 is an existentially quantified formula ef_1 (lines 10 to 15). At first, `generate-correction` is called with $\sigma_{2.1}(ef_1)$. The restriction of $\sigma_{2.1}(ef_1)$ is not provable, because there exists no instance of the concept *letter-to-report-property* in the knowledge base. Therefore, the new constant $L\#87system$ is generated and $\sigma_{3.1}$ is defined as follows:

$$\sigma_{3.1} = \{l/L\#87system\} \cup \sigma_{2.1}$$

With the substitution $\sigma_{3.1}$ the restriction part of ef_1 can be satisfied by performing the following inserts on the knowledge base (the *correction set* for the restriction part):

$Corr\text{-}Set_1 =$
 $\{insert(instance\text{-}of(L\#87system, letter\text{-}to\text{-}report\text{-}property, \langle t_1, S_5 \rangle)),$
  $insert(related\text{-}to(L\#87system, sender, Swiss\text{-}Life, \langle t_1, S_5 \rangle)),$
  $insert(related\text{-}to(L\#87system, recipient, Office\text{-}Zurich, \langle t_1, S_5 \rangle)),$
  $insert(related\text{-}to(L\#87system, for\text{-}bankruptcy\text{-}case, Pb\#27, \langle t_1, S_5 \rangle)))\}$

The correction of the tail of ef_1 with substitution $\sigma_{3.1}$ results in

$Corr\text{-}Set_{2.1} =$
 $\{insert(related\text{-}to(L\#87system, reported\text{-}insurances,$
    $Insurance\#70, \langle t_1, S_5 \rangle)))\}$

After successfully correcting ef_1 under the substitution $\sigma_{2.1}$, the correction of ef_1 under the substitution $\sigma_{2.2}$ has to be made. One expects of the correction algorithm that for all insurances of the bankrupt only one instance of *letter-to-report-property* is generated. In the example this means that the two insurances $Insurance\#70$ and $Insurance\#99$ are related to the same letter (i.e. $L\#87system$). We achieve this effect by formulating in the AIC the condition on the letter instance on the left-hand side of the AND operator (in the restriction part) and listing the atom which relates the insurances to be reported to the letter in the tail (right of the AND – see Fig.6). Thus, for the second insurance $Insurance\#99$ a letter instance already exists which fulfills the restriction, namely $L\#87system$, so that this instance is taken and $Insurance\#99$ is related to it. Would the AND operator be handled like an ordinary $\wedge$ operator, the algorithm would generate a new letter instance because the atom that has formerly been in the tail now becomes part of the conditions stated on the letter instance, causing that no such instance exists so that a new one must be generated. Technically, the correction of $\sigma_{2.2}(ef_1)$ first leads to the following substitution which satisfies its restriction part:

$$\sigma_{3.2} = \{l/L\#87system\} \cup \sigma_{2.2}$$

The correction of the tail of $\sigma_{3.2}(ef_1)$ then results in

$Corr\text{-}Set_{2.2} =$
 $\{insert(related\text{-}to(L\#87system, reported\text{-}insurances,$
    $Insurance\#99, \langle t_1, S_5 \rangle)))\}$

Thus, both insurances, $Insurance\#70$ and $Insurance\#99$, are related to the same instance of the concept *letter-to-report-property*, just as it is expected.

To finish our example, `generate-correction` is called for the all-quanti-fied subformulas in line 16 and lines 17 to 19 and terminates by returning the whole correction set. This set includes the three sets $Corr\text{-}Set_1$, $Corr\text{-}Set_{2.1}$ and $Corr\text{-}Set_{2.2}$.

The correction algorithm for AIC has the worst-case time complexity of $O((m \cdot b)^t)$, where m is the maximal number of conjunctions in the tail of a quantified subformula and b defines the maximal number of substitutions for the restriction of a quantified subformula. An upper bound for b is given by k^n where n denotes the maximal number of quantified variables in a subformula of the AIC and k corresponds to the number of constants in the knowledge base. The factor t denotes the "depth" of an AIC which is defined as follows[7]:

DEFINITION 5 (Depth of an AIC). The tail of an AIC has the form $Q_1 \wedge Q_2 \wedge \ldots \wedge Q_n$.

An AIC has the depth $max(depth(Q_i))$ where the depth of a conjunction Q_i is recursively defined as follows:

1. $depth(Q_i) = 1$ for $Q_i = A$ (atomic formula)

2. $depth(Q_i) = 1$ for $Q_i = true$

3. $depth(Q_i) = 1 + max(depth(Q_j))$ $(j \in \{1, \ldots, k\})$ for
   $Q_i = \exists x_1, \ldots, x_n : R$ AND $Q_1 \wedge \ldots \wedge Q_k$

4. $depth(Q_i) = 1 + max(depth(Q_j))$ $(j \in \{1, \ldots, k\})$ for
   $Q_i = \forall x_1, \ldots, x_n : R \Rightarrow Q_1 \wedge \ldots \wedge Q_k$

□

For the large knowledge base of a real world application[8] an exponential time complexity of an inference service is totally unacceptable. However, the time complexity for correcting AICs as given above is a worst-case one and far from what will actually occur. Only in a few exotic cases the depth will be more than 4, m more than 5 and n more than 5. Moreover, only some subformulas of an AIC will reach these maximal numbers. Thus, in all realistic cases we will be far below the worst case. Nevertheless, there is still the problem that k might be too large. Therefore, we must take measures to remarkably reduce the number of constants in the knowledge base which have to be taken into account when determining the substitutions for the restriction of a quantified subformula. We can achieve this goal by making use of the fact that only a few concept instances and relation instances are relevant for a certain office task. Only these instances are considered, when an AIC is evaluated. Even the case when an AIC refers to a concept with

---

[7] The depth of ICs can be defined in the same way.
[8] To give an example: At Swiss Life we have to deal with aprox. 500000 insurances and about the same number of customers.

many instances is usually not a problem. Typically, not all the instances of the concept but only a few instances with certain properties are meant. To avoid the consideration of all the irrelevant instances, a reordering of the literals of a conjunction in the AIC leads to the appropriate restriction of the number of instances to be handled. For example, by shifting the reference to the concept *insurance* in Fig.6 from line 6 to the position after line 9 only the very few insurances of the policy holder qualify for a substitution and not all the insurances of Swiss Life.

With our first prototype we did not run into any efficiency problems. However, we have to admit that there is a slight chance that the measures sketched above are not sufficient for the productive system and that further measures for improving efficiency must be taken. The same argumentation holds concerning the efficiency of IC evaluation.

5 KNOWLEDGE ABOUT LAW AND REGULATIONS

Law and company regulations have in our view quite a different status. In our understanding, law regulates a domain by giving guidelines (e.g. defining rights, obligations and sanctions if an obligation is not met). It is up to every individual or organisation how to follow these guidelines — a right need not be demanded or an obligation can be ignored at own risk. Company regulations define how the guidelines given by law have to be treated. They specify and interpret law. Moreover, company regulations can introduce rights and obligations additional to those given by law. It can be possible that a company regulation violates law, for example, if an obligation is ignored. This does not entail a contradiction in the knowledge base because law only defines the obligation but does not say that the obligation has been met. Our approach to separate law from its interpretation by regulations is comparable to work done by Johnson and Mead [6].

The representation of law and regulations requires the expressiveness of the formalism we have chosen. A less expressive formalism like (possibly extended) horn logic would not be sufficient (cf. [17]). On the other hand, full first-order logic is undecidable. The classes of formulas introduced by ICs and AICs are a good compromise because they provide the expressiveness needed but still allow decidable and efficient reasoning. Therefore, law and regulations (in the following we will also use the term *legal knowledge*) are represented by AICs and ICs depending on the kind of statements that have to be expressed (cf. Secs.5.1 and 5.2). AICs are used if inferences have to be made, while ICs are used to check if the current knowledge base is valid with respect to certain conditions.

In Section 5.1 we describe the representation of law. Section 5.2 deals with the representation of company regulations and their relationship to law. The reasoning with law and regulations is the topic of Section 5.3.

SchKG 232

1. *The Bankruptcy Office publicly announces the opening of bankruptcy proceedings as soon as it is established that due process of law must occur.*

2. *The announcement contains:*

   ⋮

   4. *the call to those holding property of the bankrupt as pledgees or on other grounds to place this at the disposal of the Bankruptcy Office before the closing date, without any prejudice to their preferential rights, under threat of prosecution in the event of default and with the addition that preferential rights will lapse in the event of unjustified default;*

   ⋮

Figure 8. Fragment of the Original Text of SchKG 232

5.1 Law

An example of the original text[9] of a law is given in Figure 8. The Subsection 232(2)(4) of the Federal Law on Debt Collection and Bankruptcy (SchKG) defines an obligation which states that every person or corporation which holds a property owned by a person who went bankrupt must report this property to the Bankruptcy Office[10]. Thereby an obligation to the Bankruptcy Office is defined. In the concrete situation of a life insurance company this means that the company must issue a report to the Bankruptcy Office if the bankrupt has a policy of that company. The policy owned by the bankrupt is part of his property – the insurance company only holds and administrates that property.

The representation of the law states under what circumstances and for which instances it holds. Company regulations specify how to deal with the situation where a law becomes effective. Thus, in the formal representation of law and regulations there must be some connecting link such that whenever a law applies to a given situation the associated regulations get "informed". We achieve this by representing a law by an AIC which requires the existence of an appropriate instance of the concept *obligation* (or the concept *right*, depending on the law) whenever the law applies. That

---

[9]In fact, the text is a translation of the originally German text.

[10]Obviously, the law contains more detailed information. We extracted this aspect as an example of an obligation. The other aspects would be represented separately but in the same way.

instance represents the obligation (or right) demanded by the law. If the law applies and that instance does not exist it is inferred according to the correction algorithm for AICs (cf. Sec.4.2). Furthermore, the instance is retracted by the reason maintenance component (not described in this paper) if the circumstances no longer hold.

Figure 9 shows the representation of SchKG 232(2)(4). The left-hand sides of the all-quantified implications define the circumstances under which the obligation to report a property holds. The existentially quantified subformula defines the obligation as an instance of the concept *obligation-to-report-property* (with the corresponding relationships to other instances). If this instance does not exist it is introduced by the correction algorithm for AICs. In the case that there are several properties of a bankrupt to be reported, this does not lead to several obligation instances but only to one which is related to all the corresponding property instances via the relationship *concerned-property* (cf. Fig.9). This is technically achieved by placing the corresponding atom $related\text{-}to(o, concerned\text{-}property, p, \langle t, s \rangle)$ in the tail of the AIC formula, i.e. behind the AND operator which separates the restriction part from the tail (see the definition of an AIC in Sec.4). The effect is that whenever a property is not yet covered by the obligation to report to the Bankruptcy Office, i.e., whenever the restriction part is fulfilled but not the tail, the missing tail atom is generated.

An inferred obligation instance only states that an obligation exists. When and how this obligation is to be met is specified by an associated regulation (see Sec.5.2).

Besides rights and obligations a law may also define new concepts. In Section 92 of the SchKG (cf. Fig.10) all things are listed that must be considered as a property exempt from seizure. That section is formally represented by a concept *property-exempt-from-seizure* (see Fig.11) . All things defined in Section 92 to be properties exempt from seizure (e.g. *provident-insurance* which is covered by the claims stated in Subsection 92(13)) are then represented as (direct) subconcepts of the concept *property-exempt-from-seizure*. The atom *legal-source* identifies the law on behalf of which the concept *provident-insurance* is introduced as a subconcept of *property-exempt-from-seizure*. Such an identification is necessary because additional properties may be defined as exempt from seizure at other places in the law and certain sections may refer only to those properties exempt from seizure which are defined in SchKG 92.

5.2   Regulations

As mentioned in the introduction of Section 5, company regulations define how the guidelines given by law must be treated. In the following, we will show how regulations are represented and how the reference to law is established.

$\forall\, t, s, b, bo, pb :$
   $instance\text{-}of(b, person, \langle t, s\rangle)\ \wedge$
   $instance\text{-}of(bo, bankruptcy\text{-}office, \langle t, s\rangle)\ \wedge$
   $instance\text{-}of(pb, publication\text{-}of\text{-}bankruptcy, \langle t, s\rangle)\ \wedge$
   $related\text{-}to(pb, is\text{-}bankrupt, b, \langle t, s\rangle)\ \wedge$
   $related\text{-}to(pb, by\text{-}bankruptcy\text{-}office, bo, \langle t, s\rangle)$
$\Rightarrow$

$\forall\, p, c :$
   $instance\text{-}of(p, property, \langle t, s\rangle)\ \wedge$
   $instance\text{-}of(c, corporation, \langle t, s\rangle)\ \wedge$
   $related\text{-}to(p, has\text{-}owner, b, \langle t, s\rangle)\ \wedge$
   $related\text{-}to(p, hold\text{-}by, c, \langle t, s\rangle)$
   $\Rightarrow$
   $(\ \exists\, o :$
      $instance\text{-}of(o, obligation\text{-}to\text{-}report\text{-}property, \langle t, s\rangle)\ \wedge$
      $related\text{-}to(o, is\text{-}obliged, c, \langle t, s\rangle)\ \wedge$
      $related\text{-}to(o, to\text{-}whom, bo, \langle t, s\rangle)\ \wedge$
      $related\text{-}to(o, reason, pb, \langle t, s\rangle)$
      AND
      $related\text{-}to(o, concerned\text{-}property, p, \langle t, s\rangle)$
   $)$

Figure 9. Auto-Corrective Integrity Constraint Representing
SchKG 232(2)(4)

SchKG 92
The following are exempt from seizure:

   ⋮

10 the pensions and capital sums which are owed or have been paid out
    to the person concerned or, in the event of his death, to his family as
    compensation for physical injury or ill-health;

11 the pensions pursuant to Article 20 of the Federal Law dated Decem-
    ber 20, 1946 on Old Age and Survivors Insurance;

12 the benefits of the Family Allowance Funds;

13 claims on an occupational pension institution for pension benefits
    prior to maturity.

Figure 10. Fragment of the Original Text of SchKG 92

concept(*property-exempt-from-seizure*)
concept(*provident-insurance*)
is-a(*provident-insurance*, *property-exempt-from-seizure*)
legal-source(*provident-insurance*, *property-exempt-from-seizure*, *SchKG*, 92, 13)

Figure 11. Representation of SchKG 92(13) by a Concept and Associated Subconcepts

Regulations can be divided into two categories: *state-independent* regulations and *action-specific* regulations:

1. A *state-independent regulation* is a condition which must hold for all states in all office tasks. A state-independent regulation is represented by an IC.

2. An *action-specific regulation* defines the (necessary or sufficient) preconditions for performing an action in an office task. An action-specific regulation is represented by an IC (necessary precondition) or an AIC (sufficient precondition).

5.2.1 State-Independent Regulations

To discuss the representation of state-independent regulations we first give another short example of a law representation. Figure 12 shows the text of Subsection 81(2) of the Federal Law on Insurance Contracts (VVG). The law regulates the case when an insurance policy owned by a person who went bankrupt is transferred to the beneficiaries of the insurance. The beneficiaries then become the new policy holders. They must inform the insurance company about accepting the transfer by presenting a certificate issued by the Debt Collection Office.

The representation of the law VVG 81(2) as shown in Figure 13 is analogous to the representation of SchKG 232(2)(4) (cf. Fig.9). The corresponding AIC infers an instance of the concept *obligation-to-supply-certificate-of-debt-collection-office* when the conditions of the law are fulfilled. If there are several beneficiaries they are all related to the same *obligation* instance *o* via the relationship *is-obliged*.

The law VVG 81(2) is taken into account by the Company Regulation No. EV/29 given in Figure 14. The regulation states that Swiss Life always demands the certificate from the beneficiaries as specified in VVG 81(2). If the conditions of the law apply but the certificate does not exist then the state-independent regulation is violated. The regulation is represented by an IC (cf. Fig.15). Reference to the law represented in Figure 13 is made

---

VVG 81

Right of pre-emption of the spouse and the descendants

⋮

2 *The beneficiaries are obliged to notify the insurer of the transfer of the insurance by presenting a certificate issued by the Debt Collection Office or the Official Receiver. If there are several beneficiaries, they must appoint a representative to accept the notifications incumbent upon the insurer.*

Figure 12. Original Text of VVG 81(2)

$\forall\, t, s, b, pb, i, v :$
    $\textit{instance-of}(b, person, \langle t, s \rangle) \land$
    $\textit{instance-of}(pb, publication\text{-}of\text{-}bankruptcy, \langle t, s \rangle) \land$
    $\textit{related-to}(pb, is\text{-}bankrupt, b, \langle t, s \rangle) \land$
    $\textit{instance-of}(i, insurance, \langle t, s \rangle) \land$
    $\textit{instance-of}(v, insurer, \langle t, s \rangle) \land$
    $\textit{related-to}(i, is\text{-}issued\text{-}by, v, \langle t, s \rangle) \land$
    $\textit{related-to}(i, policy\text{-}holder, b, \langle t, s \rangle)$
    $\Rightarrow$
$\forall\, p :$
        $\textit{instance-of}(p, person, \langle t, s \rangle) \land$
        $\textit{related-to}(i, beneficiaries, p, \langle t, s \rangle) \land$
        $\Rightarrow$
    $(\, \exists\, o :$
            $\textit{instance-of}(o, obligation\text{-}to\text{-}supply\text{-}certificate\text{-}of\text{-}debt\text{-}$
                        $collection\text{-}office, \langle t, s \rangle) \land$
            $\textit{related-to}(o, is\text{-}bankrupt, b, \langle t, s \rangle) \land$
            $\textit{related-to}(o, for\text{-}insurance, i, \langle t, s \rangle) \land$
            $\textit{related-to}(o, to\text{-}whom, v, \langle t, s \rangle)$
            AND
            $\textit{related-to}(o, is\text{-}obliged, p, \langle t, s \rangle)$
    $)$

Figure 13. Auto-Corrective Integrity Constraint RepresentingVVG 81(2)

Company Regulation No. EV/29:

If in case of a bankruptcy a transfer of a policy to the beneficiaries of the insurance has to take place a certificate of the Debt Collection Office has to be presented by the new policy holders. Swiss Life will not accept any other certificates. Without a certificate Swiss Life considers the transfer to have not taken place. The original policy holder is then considered to be still policy holder.

(Reference: VVG 81(2))

Figure 14. Company Regulation No. EV/29

by the instance o of the concept *obligation-to-supply-certificate-of-debt-collection-office*. Whenever such an instance exists and a transfer of the insurance to the beneficiaries as the new policy holders has taken place, the existence of an instance of the concept *certificate-of-debt-collection-office-for-change-of-policy-holders* is required by the IC. Nothing has to be inferred so that an IC is sufficient. If the formula given in Figure 15 is interpreted as an AIC an instance of the concept *certificate-of-debt-collection-office-for-change-of-policy-holders* would be created by the correction mechanism for AICs. However, to supply the certificate of the Debt Collection Office is an external activity so that the system must not create this instance itself. The system is only informed about the existence of this instance by the user.

5.2.2 Action-Specific Regulations

Action-specific regulations can define necessary or sufficient preconditions for an action.

Necessary preconditions are represented as ICs and conform to the following schema:

$$\forall\, t, s_j, s_k:\; user\text{-}action(a, \langle t, s_j \rangle, \langle t, s_k \rangle) \;\Rightarrow\; <necessary\ precondition>$$

where $<necessary\ precondition>$ is a formula with restricted quantification as described in Section 4.2. It represents the necessary precondition for action a, leading from state $\langle t, s_j \rangle$ to state $\langle t, s_k \rangle$. An example of a regulation that states a necessary precondition is given in Figure 16. In a more formalized way the regulation states: A notification of the Bankruptcy Office must only exist if the insurance company holds at least one property of the bankrupt (according to SchKG 232(2)(4)). The IC for the regulation is shown in Figure 17. It is related to the law SchKG 232(2)(4) by the instance o of the concept *obligation-to-report-property* (cf. Fig.9).

$\forall\, t, s, o, i, i', p, ti :$
   $instance\text{-}of(o, obligation\text{-}to\text{-}supply\text{-}certificate\text{-}of\text{-}debt\text{-}$
                  $collection\text{-}office, \langle t, s \rangle) \wedge$
   $instance\text{-}of(i, insurance, \langle t, s \rangle) \wedge$
   $related\text{-}to(o, for\text{-}insurance, i, \langle t, s \rangle) \wedge$
   $related\text{-}to(o, to\text{-}whom, Swiss\text{-}Life, \langle t, s \rangle) \wedge$
   $instance\text{-}of(ti, transfer\text{-}of\text{-}insurance, \langle t, s \rangle) \wedge$
   $related\text{-}to(ti, from\text{-}insurance, i, \langle t, s \rangle) \wedge$
   $related\text{-}to(ti, to\text{-}insurance, i', \langle t, s \rangle) \wedge$
   $related\text{-}to(o, is\text{-}obliged, p, \langle t, s \rangle) \wedge$
   $related\text{-}to(i', policy\text{-}holder, p, \langle t, s \rangle)$
   $\Rightarrow$
   $\exists\, c :$
        $instance\text{-}of(c, certificate\text{-}of\text{-}debt\text{-}collection\text{-}office\text{-}for\text{-}change\text{-}of\text{-}$
                 $policy\text{-}holders, \langle t, s \rangle) \wedge$
        $related\text{-}to(c, for\text{-}insurance, i', \langle t, s \rangle)$

Figure 15. Representation of the State-Independent Regulation of Figure 14 by an IC

Company Regulation No. EV/31:

In case of a bankruptcy announced by the Bankruptcy Office, Swiss Life will only inform the Bankruptcy Office if the bankrupt is insured at Swiss Life. Swiss Life will never inform the Bankruptcy Office about the fact that the bankrupt is not policy holder at Swiss Life. In that case nothing will be done.

(Reference: SchKG 232(2)(4))

Figure 16. Company Regulation No. EV/31

$\forall\, t, s_j, s_k :$
   $user\text{-}action(report\text{-}property\text{-}to\text{-}bankruptcy\text{-}office, \langle t, s_j \rangle, \langle t, s_k \rangle)$
   $\Rightarrow$
   $\exists\, o :$
        $instance\text{-}of(o, obligation\text{-}to\text{-}report\text{-}property, \langle t, s_j \rangle) \wedge$
        $related\text{-}to(o, is\text{-}obliged, Swiss\text{-}Life, \langle t, s_j \rangle)$

Figure 17. Representation of the Necessary Precondition of an Action-Specific Regulation by an IC

A sufficient precondition is represented as an AIC of the form:

$$\forall\, t, s : \, <sufficient\ precondition> \, \Rightarrow \, obligatory\text{-}action(a, \langle t, s \rangle)$$

Thus, whenever the precondition $<sufficient\ precondition>$ is fulfilled for an action a the corresponding *obligatory-action* atom is inferred (if it does not already exist). The atom represents the fact that the corresponding action must be executed in the current state $\langle t, s \rangle$.

For example, consider Company Regulation No. EV/40 shown in Figure 18 which says that Swiss Life always fulfills its obligation of notification of the Bankruptcy Office (see Fig.8) unless one of the exceptions holds (e.g. Fig.10). The regulation defines a sufficient precondition for the action *report-property-to-bankruptcy-office*. The corresponding AIC is given in Figure 19.

Company Regulation No. EV/40:
Swiss Life always informs the Bankruptcy Office when a bankrupt announced by the Bankruptcy Office is policy holder at Swiss Life, unless an exception holds.
(Reference: SchKG 232(2)(4))

Figure 18. Company Regulation No. EV/40

$\forall\, t, s, o :$
    $instance\text{-}of(o, obligation\text{-}to\text{-}report\text{-}property, \langle t, s \rangle) \,\wedge$
    $related\text{-}to(o, is\text{-}obliged, Swiss\text{-}Life, \langle t, s \rangle) \wedge$
    $\neg\ obligatory\text{-}action(inform\text{-}new\text{-}policy\text{-}holders\text{-}about\text{-}transfer, \langle t, s \rangle) \,\wedge$
    $\neg\ obligatory\text{-}action(inform\text{-}bankrupt, \langle t, s \rangle)$
    $\Rightarrow$
    $obligatory\text{-}action(report\text{-}property\text{-}to\text{-}bankruptcy\text{-}office, \langle t, s \rangle)$

Figure 19. Representation of the Company Regulation No. EV/40 by an AIC as an Action-Specific Regulation with a Sufficient Precondition

5.3 Reasoning with Law and Regulations

As law and regulations are represented by ICs and AICs reasoning with them amounts to integrity checking in the case of an IC (using the algorithm described in [2]) and to inferring corrective actions in the case of an AIC (according to the algorithm given in Fig.5). Thus, there is no reasoning mechanism that is specific to law and regulations. An elaborate example of reasoning with an AIC was given in Section 4.2.

6 INTEGRATING KNOWLEDGE ABOUT LAW AND REGULATIONS WITH KNOWLEDGE ABOUT ACTIONS

So far we have discussed how to represent knowledge about office tasks (Sec.4) and how to represent knowledge about law and regulations (Sec.5). It is still open how to integrate both kinds of knowledge so that only those actions of an office task which are valid with respect to the law and regulations are executable. A straightforward way to achieve this would be to integrate the representation of law and regulations directly into the preconditions of the actions they must block in case they are not fulfilled, and to integrate them into the new state description of an action to make sure that the action only leads to valid states. However, such an approach is not a good idea because it brings along severe disadvantages:

- The knowledge about law and regulations would be intricately interwoven with the knowledge about office tasks and thus difficult to be reused. This is a considerable drawback since the legal knowledge would also be needed in other knowledge-based applications.

- The knowledge representation of law and regulations could no longer be isomorphic [1] so that maintenance becomes more difficult and it is not possible to generate appropriate explanations.

- Construction and maintenance of the knowledge base would become extremely difficult as we would have one big, monolithic knowledge base.

In order to avoid these disadvantages, we suggest to employ ideas underlying *hybrid knowledge representation systems* (see [11] for an overview) and to separate the knowledge about law and regulations into a representation component of its own. Although the idea to adopt a hybrid approach is not new in the area of legal reasoning, it has so far been confined to integrating a terminological representation with the law representation proper [4, 5]. An elaborate but pure theoretical discussion of how to organize various kinds of legal knowledge (like legislation, case law, meta-knowledge, etc.) into different subcomponents can be found in [13]. [14] describes a hybrid, legal reasoning system that integrates rule-based and case-based reasoning.

Much closer to our approach is the work described in [7]. Their system for supporting office task processing separates different kinds of knowledge. A frame language is used to represent the terminology, while production rules represent regulations (called "guidelines") which restrict the order of activities in an office task. This distinction resembles ours except that the formalism of production rules is much weaker than our first-order approach. A great difference to EULE2 is the representation of office tasks. They are represented in the frame language, too (like the terminology), and make use of special kinds of slots which specify (sub-)goals to be achieved by a task and activities that can be used. Executing an office task means to initiate it properly and then to start a planning process which builds a plan from the goals and activities given. This is in contrast to EULE2 where the (partial) order of actions that make out an office task is predefined and not generated during system execution. This results in less overhead but also causes less flexibility (which is not needed in EULE2). Another difference is that in EULE2 the actions take place completely outside of the system while their required effect is modelled in the action component. In [7] the actions – which are given by programs and human activities – directly take effect in the knowledge base so that the required (sub-)goals are reached as a side-effect. It is not necessary to infer the new state from the fact that a certain kind of action has been performed, as in EULE2. This fundamental difference between both systems results from their different requirements. While EULE2 is meant as a decision support system only, the system in [7] additionally automates parts of the office tasks and integrates workflow aspects.

In the following, we motivate and present our hybrid integration approach (Sec.6.1) and discuss the associated hybrid reasoner (Sec.6.2).

6.1 Hybrid Integration

Due to the arguments given above, the knowledge about law and regulations should be represented completely independent from the knowledge about office tasks. Thus, any coupling between the legal representation component and the action component that introduces a dependency on the side of the law component must be avoided. A dependency of the action component on the law component should also be kept small but is of minor relevance as the interest to reuse the knowledge about office tasks is much smaller.

6.1.1 State-Independent Regulations

State-independent regulations need not only to be checked after the user has modified the current state of the office task but also after an action has been performed to see if it has led into a new state that is valid. The obvious way to make state-independent regulations effective for those actions for which they are relevant is to augment the corresponding action definitions so that the conditions the new state must fulfill additionally include those regulations. Obviously, no regulation can be violated in this way. To avoid that the legal knowledge depends on the action knowledge one would not put the regulation itself in all action definitions but include a predicate (defined in the law component) which is true if and only if the regulation is fulfilled. The legal knowledge keeps independent from the action knowledge, as required. However, the main drawback of this approach is still its mixing up of two completely different kinds of knowledge, thus making knowledge base maintenance unnecessarily difficult.

Our approach does not show the drawback of the approach above and avoids the dependency of the action component on the law component. The basic idea is that no explicit coupling is needed because the components can be coupled implicitly via their common terminology. As we have seen in Section 4 the action component accesses concept and instance descriptions in the terminology component. To represent law and regulations we also need a terminology (i.e., we provide a deep model as discussed in [3, 8]). As the domains of discourse of both representation components overlap it is an obviously good idea to provide a common terminology which is shared between both components. It is through this sharing of terminology that we get a coupling between action and law component. Consequently, we do not need to modify the representation of law and regulations as given in Section 5 in order to achieve a coupling.

A possible argument against coupling two representation components via a common terminology is that we only have shifted the problem, because now we cannot change the terminology for the purposes of one component without re-checking with the other one. Of course, it is not possible to make arbitrary changes in the terminology without considering the effects in both, the action and the law component; however, we still gained a considerable improvement with this approach because

- as the expressiveness of the terminology component is rather restricted, the effects of terminology changes are of much less far-reaching consequences and thus can more easily be controlled,

- most of the changes would be extensions that do not cause any problems at all,

- those changes which amount to restructuring concept definitions are often relevant to both components anyway.

6.1.2 Action-Specific Regulations

Action-specific regulations are integrated with knowledge in the action component via the common terminology, too. However, as these regulations state when a certain action is permitted or required (cf. Sec.5.2) an explicit reference to the corresponding action is necessary. Here, we get an unavoidable dependency of the law component on the action component insofar as the law component knows what kind of actions exist. However, the law component still does not need to know *how* these actions are defined. The representation of action-specific regulations as described in Section 5.2.2 already conforms to the format needed for the coupling.

6.2   Hybrid Reasoning

Besides the inferences drawn inside the action and the law component there are inferences needed which can only be drawn by using knowledge from both components. Such inferences are called *hybrid* [11]. To find out which actions being available in the current state are permitted or prohibited requires a hybrid inference which combines inferences in the action and in the law component. In the following, we describe the reasoner needed to perform this applicability check.

The basic idea underlying the hybrid reasoner we developed is to perform the action to be checked, to look if any violations occur, and then to reset the knowledge base to its original state. A pseudo code description of the reasoner is given in Figure 20. Some comments on that algorithm seem appropriate: After having made a checkpoint of the current knowledge base to where it will be reset later on (line 1) it adds the appropriate *user-action* atom to the knowledge base (line 2) which pretends that the user wishes to execute the corresponding action (cf. Sec.4.1). Then, control is given to the integrity checker of the law component (line 3) which looks if there are any action-specific regulations violated that state necessary preconditions of the action. If this is the case the action is prohibited. Otherwise, the appropriate *trigger-action* atom is added to the knowledge base (line 4) so that the action can actually be executed. This is done by calling the action component (line 5). It evaluates the auto-corrective integrity constraint defining the action to be executed and performs the corrective operations on the knowledge base[11]. Subsequently, the law component is called again (line 7), this time to evaluate all auto-corrective integrity constraints and to do all necessary corrective knowledge base modifications (e.g. to infer obligations should they exist – cf. Sec.5.1). Next, all state-independent regulations are checked (line 9). If this last check yields a positive result the action being considered is executable, otherwise not. Finally, the knowledge base is reset to its original state (line 10).

EULE2 uses the result of the applicability check to indicate the user which actions she or he may perform in the current state and which not. If an obligatory action is permitted, all other actions are not allowed. This is automatically ensured by the modelling tool we provide for the knowledge engineer (cf. Sec.7). The case that there is more than one permitted obligatory action cannot occur. This is also ruled out by the modelling tool for

---

[11] As the action and the law component are hybridly integrated with the terminology, determining corrective actions for an AIC may trigger terminological inferences in the terminological component. In this paper, we do not pursue this aspect further.

```
check-applicability-of-action(action,current-state,new-state,result);
begin
  make-knowledge-base-checkpoint;                                              1
  add-to-knowledge-base(user-action(action,current-state,new-state));         2
  call(law-component,check-integrity,result);                                 3
  if result = ok then
      add-to-knowledge-base(trigger-action(action,current-state,new-state));  4
      call(action-component,eval-auto-corrective-ICs,result);                 5
      if result ≠ ok then modelling-error; end;                               6
      call(law-component,eval-auto-corrective-ICs,result);                    7
      if result ≠ ok then modelling-error; end;                               8
      call(law-component,check-integrity,result);                            9
  end;
  reset-knowledge-base-to-checkpoint;                                        10
end check-applicability-of-action;
```

Figure 20. Pseudo Code Description of the Hybrid Reasoner

EULE2.

It is currently not totally clear if a look-ahead of one state is sufficient for determining the applicability of an action. It might be the case that the precondition of an action must take additional criteria into account in order to guarantee that later on in the office task execution no dead end situation occurs because earlier in the office task a certain action should not have been performed. So far we have not encountered any such situation, but we are looking deeper into this matter.

The efficiency of the applicability checker shown in Figure 20 is sufficient as the integrity checking is done on the quite small sub-knowledge-bases which correspond to the states of an office task. We further increase efficiency by allowing as integrity constraints only formulas with restricted quantification (cf. Definition 3 in Sec.4.2) and by using the efficient algorithm described in [2] for integrity checking. The correction algorithm for AICs is fast enough for our purposes, too, as no deduction is done. Therefore, we think that our approach will scale up with the size of the knowledge base because the size of the office task states will keep small as in a state only a limited number of concept instances are relevant. This amount is rather independent from the total number of concepts and concept instances in the task-independent world description. However, this estimate still has to be confirmed by deploying EULE2 in a productive environment.

The system architecture of EULE2 as given in Figure 21 reflects the hybrid approach discussed above. Its heart is the EULE2 controller on top of the knowledge base system which comprises the three representation components (action, terminology, law and regulations) and the hybrid reasoner

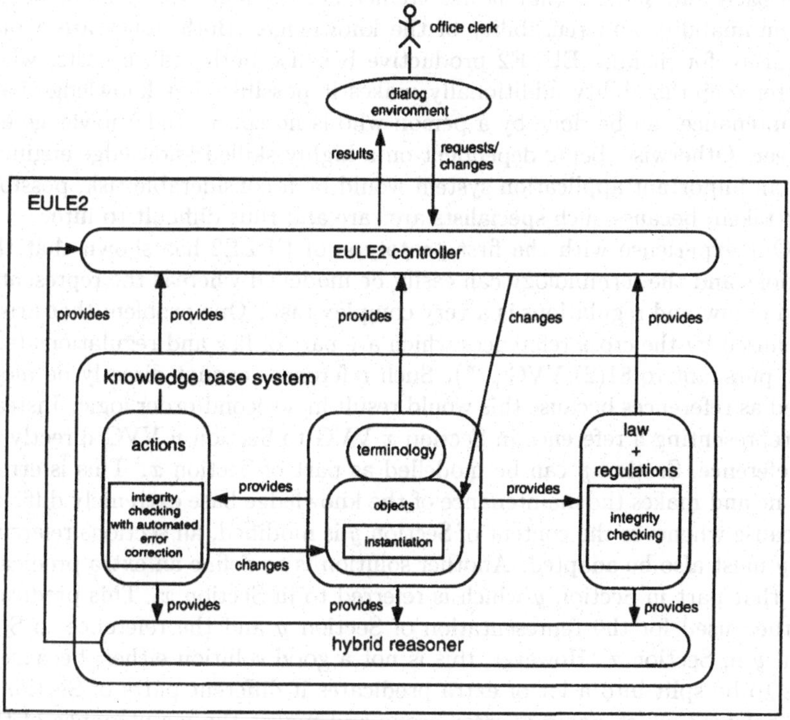

Figure 21. Detailed Overview of the EULE2 System

described in Figure 20. Figure 21 also shows quite clearly the central role played by the terminology component which provides its knowledge to all other components.

7 CONCLUSIONS

We started from the requirement to build a decision support system for office work that knows due to which laws and regulations certain actions in an office task are not allowed and which actions are obligatory. We made clear what kinds of knowledge are needed by such a system and described in detail how we represent that knowledge in the prototype system we have built (called EULE2). The main emphasis of this paper has been on the representation of knowledge about office tasks and the actions they are composed of, and on how to integrate knowledge about law and regulations with the knowledge about actions. We argued in favor of a hybrid integration approach and showed that it has tremendous benefits in terms of better maintainability and reusability of the knowledge. Both issues are a prerequisite for making EULE2 productive because both reduce costs, while better maintainability additionally makes it possible that knowledge base maintenance can be done by a person who is no specialised knowledge engineer. Otherwise, being dependent on a highly-skilled knowledge engineer for an important application system would be a considerable risk, possibly not taken, because such specialists are rare and thus difficult to hire.

Our experience with the first prototype of EULE2 has shown that the actions and the terminology can easily be modelled whereas the representation of law and regulations is a very complex task. One problem that arises is caused by the cross-references which are part of law and regulations (e.g. "... pursuant to 81(2) VVG ..."). Such references cannot directly be modelled as references because this would result in a second-order logic. Instead of representing a reference in Section x VVG to Section y VVG directly as a reference, Section y can be modelled as part of Section x. This is error-prone and makes the maintenance of the knowledge base extremely difficult because whenever the content of Section y is modified, all sections referring to y must also be adapted. Another solution is to define an extra predicate for that part in Section y which is referred to in Section x. This predicate is then used for the representation of Section y and the reference to Section y in Section x. However, this is not a good solution either, because y has to be split into a lot of extra predicates if different parts of Section y are referred which again is error-prone and makes the maintenance of the knowledge base extremely difficult.

Since we are interested in increasing the maintainability of the knowledge in EULE2 one of our current research activities aims at developing a very high-level language for modelling the knowledge needed by EULE2 (or similar kinds of systems). The design of the high-level language is based on a functional model of a legal system and the role played by law and regulations. By this model the legal knowledge can be divided into different categories leading to a small set of templates (e.g. concept, obligation, right). The templates allow to structure the knowledge to be represented and therefore are useful guidelines for the modelling process (in a sense they can be compared with an ontology – see [19]).

We mimic the natural language representation of law and regulations and provide the high-level language with formal constructs that are motivated by the natural language constructs, like constructs for cross-references, exceptions, analogies. Using the high-level language results in a representation that reflects the organisational structure of the natural language representation so that the legal knowledge can be maintained and verified with much less effort because it can more easily be compared to the original text.

The knowledge represented in the high-level language is automatically compiled into the formalisms of EULE2 described in this paper. Therefore, the knowledge engineer is relieved of keeping track of all the myriads of tiny details as it is necessary when he or she models directly in the EULE2 formalisms. For example, the construct for cross-references allows to represent references to other sections of law directly as references. The knowledge engineer does not have to copy all the referenced sections into the places where they are referenced. Moreover, the risk of inconsistent changes simply vanishes when references are maintained by the system only. Thus, when Section y is modified only the representation of Section y must be adapted by the knowledge engineer – the sections referring to y remain unchanged in the high-level representation.

The high-level language can be compiled into quite different low-level representation formalisms, thus allowing to reuse that knowledge with a small expense.

Rentenanstalt / Swiss Life, Zürich

ACKNOWLEDGEMENTS

We are very grateful for the reviewers' comments on an earlier version of this paper and for the critical questions and comments by Wolfgang Reif. They all helped to considerably improve our paper.

REFERENCES

[1] T.J.M. Bench–Capon and F. Coenen. Exploiting Isomorphism: Development of a KBS to Support British Coal Insurance Claims. In M. Sergot, editor, *Proceedings of the Third International Conference on Artificial Intelligence and Law*, pages 62–69. ACM Press, 1991.

[2] F. Bry, H. Decker, and R. Manthey. A Uniform Approach to Constraint Satisfaction and Constraint Satisfiability in Deductive Databases. In J.W. Schmidt, S. Ceri, and M. Missikof, editors, *Advances in Database Technology – EDBT'88*, pages 488–505. Springer, 1988.

[3] T.J.M. Bench–Capon. Deep Models, Normative Reasoning and Legal Expert Systems. In *Proceedings of the Second International Conference on Artificial Intelligence and Law*, pages 37–45. ACM Press, 1989.

[4] T.J.M. Bench–Capon and J. Forder. Knowledge-Based Systems and Legal Applications. In T.J.M. Bench–Capon, editor, *Knowledge-Based System and Legal Applications*, chapter 12, pages 245–263. Academic Press, 1991.

[5] J. Breuker. Modelling Artificial Legal Reasoning. In N. Aussenac, G. Boy, B. Gaines, J.-G. Ganascia, and Y. Kodratoff, editors, *Knowledge Acquisition for Knowledge-Based Systems (EKAW'93)*, pages 66–78, 1993.

[6] P. Johnson and D. Mead. Legislative Knowledge Base Systems for Public Administration - Some Practical Issues. In *Proceedings of the Third International Conference on Artificial Intelligence and Law*, pages 108–117. ACM Press, 1991.

[7] D. Karagiannis and K. Hinkelmann. Context-Sensitive Office Tasks: A Generative Approach. *Decision Support Systems*, 8:255–267, 1992.

[8] L.T. McCarty. Intelligent Legal Information Systems: Problems and Prospects. In C. Campbell, editor, *Data Processing and Law*, pages 125–151. Sweet and Maxwell, 1984.

[9] J. McCarthy and P.J. Hayes. Some Philosophical Problems from the Standpoint of Artificial Intelligence. In B. Meltzer and D. Michie, editors, *Machine Intelligence*, volume 4, pages 463–502, 1969.

[10] B. Nebel. *Reasoning and Revision in Hybrid Representation Systems*. Springer, Berlin, 1990.

[11] B. Nebel. What is Hybrid in Hybrid Representation and Reasoning Systems? In F. Gardin and G. Mauri, editors, *Computational Intelligence, II*, pages 217–228. North Holland, 1990.

[12] B. Neches, R. Fikes, T. Finin, T. Gruber, R. Patil, T. Senator, and W.R. Swartout. Enabling Technology for Knowledge Sharing. *AI Magazine*, 12(3):36–56, 1991.

[13] A. Oskamp. Model for Knowledge and Legal Expert Systems. *Artificial Intelligence and Law*, 1(4):245–274, 1993.

[14] K. Pal and J.A. Campbell. A Hybrid System for Decision-making about Assets in English Divorce Cases. In *Proceedings of the First United Kingdom Workshop on Progress in Case-Based Reasoning*, pages 152–165, 1995.

[15] U. Reimer. A Representation Construct for Roles. *Data & Knowledge Engineering*, 1(3):233–251, 1985.

[16] U. Reimer, P. Lippuner, M. Norrie, and M. Rys. Terminological Reasoning by Query Evaluation: A Formal Mapping of a Terminological Logic to an Object Data Model. In G. Ellis, R.A. Levinson, A. Fall, and V. Dahl, editors, *Proc. Int. KRUSE Symposium: Knowledge Retrieval, Use, and Storage for Efficiency*, pages 49–53, USA, 1995. University of California at Santa Cruz.

[17] M.J. Sergot. The Representation of Law in Computer Programs. In J.E. Hayes, D. Michie, and J. Richards, editors, *Machine Intelligence 11*, pages 209–260, 1988.

[18] R. Stamper. LEGOL: Modelling Legal Rules by Computer. In B. Niblett, editor, *Computer Science and Law*, pages 45–71. Cambridge University Press, 1980.

[19] A. Valente. *Legal Knowledge Engineering*. IOS Press, 1995.

[20] W.A. Woods and J.G. Schmolze. The KL-ONE Family. *Computers and Mathematics with Applications*, 23(2–5):133–177, 1992.

APPLIED LOGIC SERIES

1. D. Walton: *Fallacies Arising from Ambiguity.* 1996   ISBN 0-7923-4100-7
2. H. Wansing (ed.): *Proof Theory of Modal Logic.* 1996   ISBN 0-7923-4120-1
3. F. Baader and K.U. Schulz (eds.): *Frontiers of Combining Systems.* First International Workshop, Munich, March 1996. 1996   ISBN 0-7923-4271-2
4. M. Marx and Y. Venema: *Multi-Dimensional Modal Logic.* 1996
    ISBN 0-7923-4345-X
5. S. Akama (ed.): *Logic, Language and Computation.* 1997   ISBN 0-7923-4376-X
6. J. Goubault-Larrecq and I. Mackie: *Proof Theory and Automated Deduction.* 1997
    ISBN 0-7923-4593-2
7. M. de Rijke (ed.): *Advances in Intensional Logic.* 1997   ISBN 0-7923-4711-0
8. W. Bibel and P.H. Schmitt (eds.): *Automated Deduction - A Basis for Applications.* Volume I. Foundations - Calculi and Methods. 1998   ISBN 0-7923-5129-0
9. W. Bibel and P.H. Schmitt (eds.): *Automated Deduction - A Basis for Applications.* Volume II. Systems and Implementation Techniques. 1998   ISBN 0-7923-5130-4
10. W. Bibel and P.H. Schmitt (eds.): *Automated Deduction - A Basis for Applications.* Volume III. Applications. 1998   ISBN 0-7923-5131-2
    (Set vols. I-III: ISBN 0-7923-5132-0)
11. S.O. Hansson: *A Textbook of Belief Dynamics.* Theory Change and Database Updating. 1999 including *Solutions to exercises.* 1999.   Hb: ISBN 0-7923-5324-2;   Set: (Pb): ISBN 0-7923-5329-3
12. R. Pareschi and B. Fronhöfer (eds.): *Dynamic Worlds.* From the Frame Problem to Knowledge Management. 1999   ISBN 07923-5535-0
13. D.M. Gabbay and H. Wansing (eds.): *What is Negation?.* 1999
    ISBN 0-7923-5569-5
14. M. Wooldridge and A. Rao (eds.): *Foundations of Rational Agency.* 1999
    ISBN 0-7923-5601-2

KLUWER ACADEMIC PUBLISHERS – DORDRECHT / BOSTON / LONDON